Contents

Preface

"A Second Complete AutoCAD Databook" describes all the major features of AutoCAD Release 11, the latest version of the industry standard draughting and design package. It is an integrated text that will appeal both to the absolute beginner with no computer experience and to the experienced AutoCAD user.

The scope of the book covers all aspects of AutoCAD usage, from the initial set-up, through the creation and editing of simple two-dimensional line drawings to the most complex 3D and solid modelling, (AME), aspects of the package. This includes the complexities of the paper space environment, which are explained in depth. The reader is lead through this progression in an ordered step-by-step manner.

The readable style and no-nonsense approach differentiates this book from all other publications in this field.

We have had many years of experience with AutoCAD from its earliest release and have set up one of the first AutoCAD Authorised Training Centres in the UK within the University of Salford's Centre for Computers in Education and Training (CCET). This Centre was subsequently chosen by the Department of Trade and Industry as one of only six in the country to be responsible for the training of Further Education lecturers, themselves responsible for setting up CAD training centres nationwide.

We have designed and taught AutoCAD courses within the CCET, orientated to individual industrial and academic requirements and to specific groups from overseas under the auspices of the United Nations.

The many industrialists and educationalists attending our courses have commented on the clear and easy-to-use learning guide provided by our previous book, which has now been adopted as a course book by many Universities and Technical Colleges. This has encouraged us to offer a second book covering AutoCAD Release 11.

Features

A speciality of this text is that descriptions of related commands are grouped together, and cross-referenced to other groups of commands where appropriate. This permits the reader to master all aspects of a particular area of AutoCAD with ease.

The format of commands and responses is presented on the page to resemble, as closely as possible, the appearance of the text as presented on the screen. This prepares the reader for the range of responses that may be expected when issuing a command.

Over 300 original imaginative drawings, sketches and designs in 2D, 3D and solid modelling, (AME), enhance and illustrate the use of the vast range of AutoCAD commands and features described within the text. All the drawings in the book were produced and printed using AutoCAD Release 11, running on an IBM compatible '386 PC interfaced with a Brother HL-8PS laser printer.

Fully worked examples covering simple and advanced drawing techniques are distributed throughout the text. In addition, the Appendices contain tried and tested worked tutorials, plus valuable additional information on the operation of the Disk Operating System (DOS), the AutoCAD environment and the database package dBASE III+.

The use of the Paper Space environment is covered in detail, helping the reader to unravel the complexities of this new world. Paper Space allows the user to enhance the presentation of the drawing prior to plotting, by setting up a number of independent viewports, each free to contain a selected view of a single construction at a suitable scaling factor.

The construction of complex 3D designs using the advanced features of the package is covered in depth. A clear and concise explanation of the User Co-ordinate System (UCS) and the surface mesh commands, fundamental to successful 3D and solid constructions, is given and drawing tips are supplied. The structured series of worked examples in the Appendices is designed to help the reader to "think in 3D". Without such assistance the transition between 2D and 3D thinking can prove to be a major barrier.

AutoCAD's solid modeller, the Advanced Modelling Extension (AME), allows the creation of solid three dimensional entities which can have a number of physical properties, (e.g. density, Young's modulus, thermal conductivity, etc.,) attributed to them for a variety of construction materials. The many new and complex commands are covered in detail in the main text, with a step-by-step tutorial in the Appendices to demonstrate their application.

The important subject of data transfer between AutoCAD and dBASE III+, which allows the extraction of selected data directly from the drawing to be analyzed by the powerful facilities of this industry standard data base package, is fully explained. Again, a fully worked tutorial example incorporating proven dBASE programs, which may be typed in and tried, is detailed in the Appendices.

Other advanced features covered include reference drawings (Xrefs), the generation of user specified shapes, line types and hatch patterns, writing screen and tablet menus tailored to the reader's own requirements and the use of script files to generate free running presentation programmes.

This second book also lends itself to being used for the preparation of student-centred work sheets - as most further education courses are now being structured - with the hard-pressed lecturers being able to incorporate the clear explanations and the worked tutorials within their own material.

Acknowledgements

We are very grateful to our friend and colleague, Dr R D Tomlinson, for his help in the preparation of the explanatory section on dBASE III and for writing the dBASE III programs in Appendix 11. We also wish to thank Professor D G Armour, Chairman of the Department of Electronic and Electrical Engineering at the University of Salford, for his support and encouragement.

The support of Brother Industries Ltd for their donation of a laser printer for the preparation of camera-ready copy is gratefully acknowledged.

Finally, thanks are due to the numerous participants on our courses who have provided comments and feedback which has been invaluable in the preparation of this book.

The future at your fingertips

This book has been produced from camera-ready copy, prepared using AutoCAD and Word Perfect software, and printed on a Brother HL-8PS laser printer, donated by courtesy of Brother Industries Ltd.

1. Hardware requirements: specifying an AutoCAD PC installation

Choosing the component bits of an AutoCAD system involves making decisions on a number of different units:

- *Computer and keyboard*
- *VDU/Monitor and graphics board*
- *Mouse/digitiser*
- *Printer*
- *Plotter*

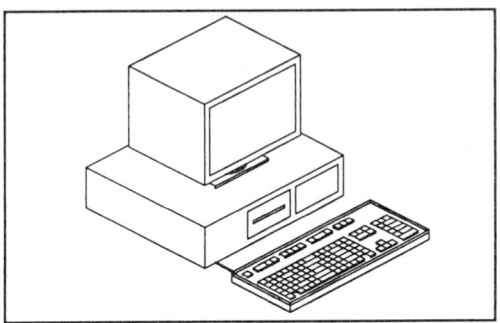

Figure 1.1   A basic computer system

1.1 THE COMPUTER

This will probably be an IBM or IBM-compatible personal computer (PC) (see Figure 1.1). A typical hardware configuration could be as follows:

- *RAM:* The Random Access Memory (RAM) figure gives the size of the working memory of the computer. AutoCAD *requires* a minimum of 640 kbytes of conventional RAM plus a further 1 Mbyte of extended memory, but it is recommended that a minimum of 4 Mbytes of RAM is installed. The larger the memory, the fewer the references that must be made to the hard disk and therefore the faster the system.
- *Hard disk, 20 Mbytes or larger:* The hard disk stores not only the CAD software but in most cases also holds the completed drawings. A full installation including sample drawings and the Advanced Modelling Extension (AME) requires approximately 9 Mbytes of disk space. A simple diagram may take up a few thousand bytes but a complicated drawing could be well over a megabyte in size, so a large-capacity hard disk is always an advantage.
- *Maths co-processor:* This is an extra "chip" which fits into the computer to speed up the calculations which are performed every time a new entity is drawn or a drawing is expanded, contracted, viewed from a different angle, etc. The addition of such a chip will increase the computer's operating speed, typically by a factor of 3.
  AutoCAD *requires* the co-processor to be fitted before it will operate. The new generation of '486 machines have the co-processor incorporated into the main 80486 microprocessor chip.

The overall operating speed of AutoCAD is limited by the rate at which the computer can operate. This depends in part upon the type of microprocessor chip at the heart of the machine. As time goes by, microprocessors become faster and faster. The original IBM-type machines used a processor called the 8086 but this has been overtaken by the 80286, the 80386 and the 80486. Still-faster processors will soon be available. A '386 machine will run CAD at least 5 times faster than the old machines so, as usual, "you pay your money and you take your choice!" If you have a '386 or '486 machine then you can use a version of AutoCAD especially written to maximise the benefits offered by these fast machines. Alternatively you may use a basic version of AutoCAD which will run on a '286 or '386 machine. If you intend to use AutoCAD's Advanced Modelling Extension (AME) then you *must* have a '386 or '486 machine and also the faster software.

1.2 THE VISUAL DISPLAY UNIT (VDU) OR MONITOR

The choice of a VDU is almost as important as the choice of a computer. The VDU's performance has a dramatic effect on the presentation of a drawing and on the ease with which that drawing can be produced.

VDUs come in a variety of sizes but the largest is not necessarily the best for your particular usage. Very broadly the choice of size can be summed up as follows:

14 inch	minimum	for general desk-top use
20 inch	professional	for the drawing office
26 inch	demonstration	for teaching or board-room

A less obvious choice is between mono and colour. The VDU may operate in mono, colour or either. Mono systems may well be of a higher resolution than colour for a given price but a colour system will usually be preferred.

The VDU must be driven by a Graphics Board which is an electronic circuit board mounted inside the computer. The board and the VDU *must* be compatible both with each other *and* with AutoCAD. It is the combination of VDU and graphics board which determines the colours and resolution of the system.

There are very many manufacturers of graphics boards and VDUs, but most units conform to one of the following standards:

	Colour	*Resolution*
Hercules	Mono only	720 x 348
IBM Colour Graphics Adaptor (CGA)	Colour/mono	640 x 200
IBM Enhanced Graphics Adaptor (EGA)	Colour/mono	640 x 350
IBM Video Graphics Adaptor (VGA)	Colour/mono	680 x 480

The cost of high resolution colour apparatus increases rapidly with the size of the VDU.

1.3 MICE AND DIGITISERS

Although AutoCAD will allow you to input all your drawing data from the keyboard, this is a very unsatisfactory process. It is far better to be able to move the cross wires on the VDU screen by making corresponding movements with a mouse rather than by tapping the relevant keys on the keyboard.

A mouse is simply a small hand-held device which, when moved around on a suitable flat surface, sends signals to the computer which are used to position the screen cross wires (see Figure 1.2). Some mice require a special optical surface to move on, others will work on any desk top. In addition, every mouse will carry at least one push button. This is used to "pick" objects on the screen after the cross wires are in position. More versatile mice may have several additional buttons, the exact function of which can be controlled by AutoCAD's software. AutoCAD also allows you to set the function of these extra buttons to your own requirements. Mice are generally inexpensive and reliable.

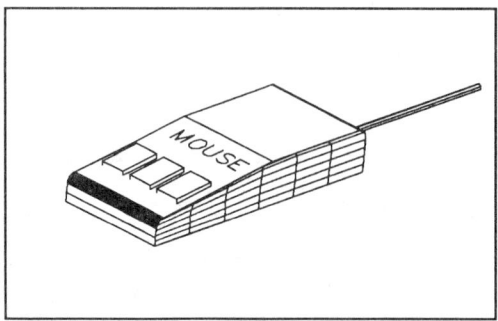

Figure 1.2   A mouse

At first sight a digitiser seems to do the same job as a mouse but at many times the cost. It consists of a flat base-plate and a mouse-type pointer, called a puck, which may be single- or multi-button. It may be used for pointing and picking exactly as a mouse (see Figure 1.3). In place of the puck some digitisers offer an alternative pen-type pointing device.

Figure 1.3   A digitiser

The important "extra" that you get with a digitiser is that you can use it to give commands. A special overlay or template may be placed on the digitiser tablet which can be divided up into over a hundred small printed areas, each one representing a command or a special shape to be used in the drawing (see Figure 1.4). You can then pick a command or a shape by pointing to the relevant area and pressing the pick button.

AutoCAD allows you to design your own template and to tailor the corresponding software to accommodate the shapes and commands most useful to you. Even unique shapes which you have devised yourself can be handled in this way.

A digitiser is also essential if you wish to trace an irregular sketch for insertion into an AutoCAD drawing. The digitiser tablet can be calibrated so that the scale and orientation of the sketch are automatically accommodated.

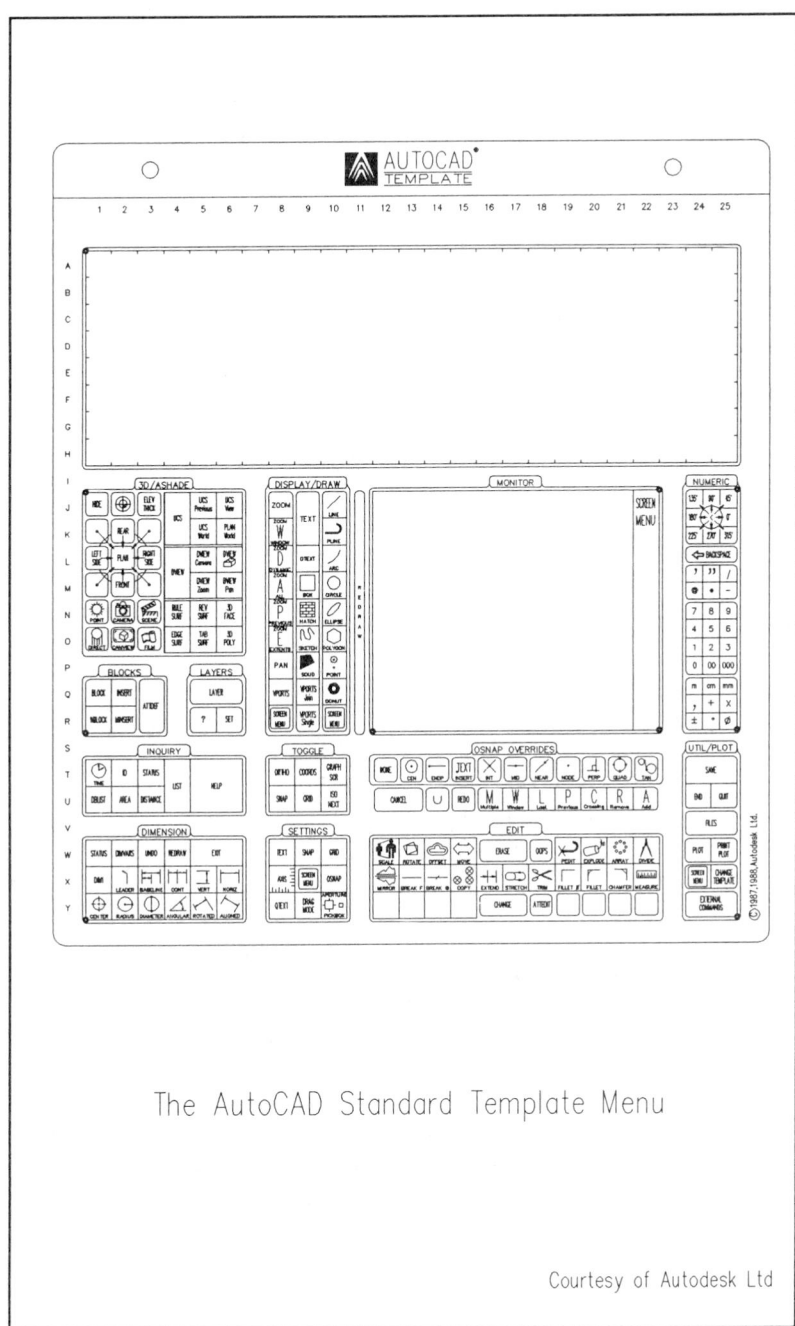

Figure 1.4 The AutoCAD standard template menu (Courtesy of Autodesk Ltd)

1.4 PRINTERS AND PLOTTERS

While digitisers and mice are input devices, printers and plotters handle output. Although both can be used to record text or drawings on paper (hard copy devices), they operate quite differently from each other.

The simplest type of printer is a dot matrix printer (see Figure 1.5). It forms its image by passing a head across the paper a line at a time (raster scanning). The head carries a matrix of 9 or more steel pins which can be moved in and out very rapidly under control of the computer to print a dot pattern on the paper through a typewriter-style ribbon. The process is relatively fast and the resultant quality can be quite good, particularly if several head passes are made for each line. Most results are in monochrome, although expensive models using multi-stripe coloured ribbons are available.

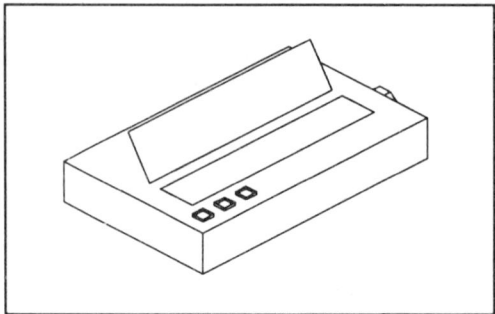

Figure 1.5   A dot matrix printer

The benefits of such a printer are:

- Relatively cheap
- Rapid printing of drawings irrespective of complexity
- The same printer can be used for printing documents (for instance, from your word processor package)

Laser and ink-jet printers are now available which give a much higher quality of output than dot matrix printers and which are faster in operation, although they can be considerably more expensive. Colour ink jet printers can faithfully reproduce a coloured drawing quickly and accurately.

The disadvantage of these printers is that they are nearly always limited to relatively small paper sizes - A4 (10.5" x 8") to A3 (16" x 10.5").

A plotter works on a principle which is entirely different from that of a printer. It consists of a pen which can be driven in both X- and Y- directions by stepping motors to trace out each element of the drawing (see Figure 1.6). The computer sends data to the plotter, telling it about start- and end-points of lines and whether the pen should be raised or lowered. It can also request a pen change to give a line a different colour or width. The drawing is built up by each object being drawn sequentially rather than by the raster-scan principle used by the printers.

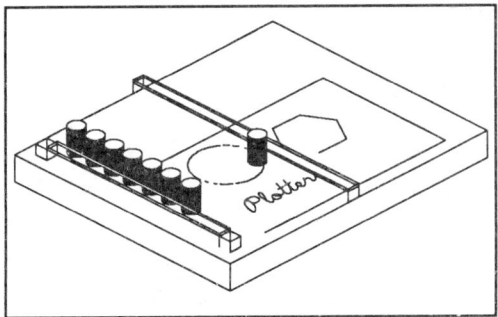

Figure 1.6 A multi pen plotter

Alternatively, the pen can be driven in the X-direction only and the paper can be moved in the Y-direction. The latter set-up is more usual for large plotters. A stepping motor is able to move the pen or paper or both in precise steps or increments. The size of one step determines the accuracy of the plotter and is typically a small fraction of a millimetre.

In operation the plotter must first decide, or be told, where the origin or reference point of the drawing is. From then on, it "knows" where the pen is by simply counting the number of steps taken in both the X- and Y- directions. (If you nudge it and spoil its count it can become totally confused!)

Although a plotter can be expensive it has the following powerful advantages:

● It produces professional quality drawings on a range of paper sizes, typically A4 (10.5" x 8") to A0 (43" x 33")
● Multiple pen operation is available on most plotters (typically 4 - 12 pens) to produce coloured drawings
● Special-ink pens can be used e.g. for transparent foils, printed circuit board production, etc.

Many installations will use both a printer and a plotter - the printer to produce rapid working sketches etc. and the plotter to produce the final drawing.

2. Running AutoCAD for the first time

2.1 INSTALLATION

AutoCAD is delivered to you on a number of 3.5" or 5.25" floppy disks and the first task, after making a backup set of these disks (see Appendix 1) for security, is to *install* the files onto your hard disk.

The organisation of the files and directories on the hard disk is now largely determined by the INSTALL.EXE program which *must be used*. However, you will be given the opportunity to specify the names of some of the directories. Most systems will be set up something like that shown in Figure 2.1, with a System Directory, called ACAD, and a number of subsidiary directories for holding the resultant drawing files and various other files which AutoCAD requires.

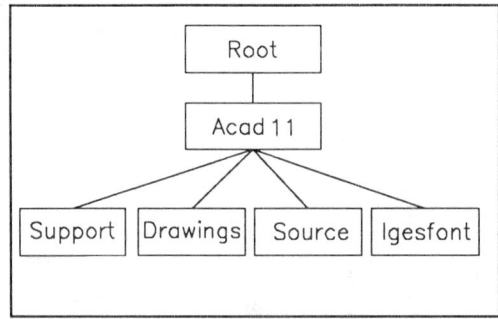

Figure 2.1   A typical directory structure

Place the Executables 1 floppy disk in its drive and type:

A> INSTALL

Follow the instructions presented on the screen to install the required files on to your hard disk.

A feature now incorporated is that personalisation of your AutoCAD package is now compulsory and you will be prompted for your name and address and for your Dealer's name and telephone number. These details will be incorporated permanently into the software and will subsequently be displayed each time the package is used.

If you have purchased the Advanced Modelling Extension (AME) with your AutoCAD software you must respond "yes" when prompted. Although this will load the AME files on to the hard disk you will not be allowed to use them without supplying the special authorisation code, prompted for when you first request the use of the AME facility from within AutoCAD) which should be supplied with the package.

The INSTALL program will now proceed automatically. After installation of the AutoCAD files is complete, the INSTALL program checks your CONFIG.SYS file for the line FILES=40 and will offer to make any necessary changes. It will also suggest writing a start up batch file called ACAD386.BAT. You should allow this file to be written but you will probably wish to modify it to suit your own requirements, (see Section 2.2.1).

2.1.1 Don't Forget the Dongle

Depending on your country of operation, Autodesk may supply a hardware lock device, often called a dongle, which must be installed before you try to run the package. Failure to do this, or removal of the dongle while AutoCAD is running, will prevent the package from working. The dongle is plugged into the parallel printer port at the back of the computer (prior to Release 10, the dongle plugged into the serial port). If you wish to use the printer as well then this can be plugged into the back of the dongle but you may find that the printer must be switched on before AutoCAD accepts the dongle.

2.2 GETTING STARTED

Assuming that you are in the System Directory, where all the AutoCAD files are kept, or that you are in a suitable sub-directory, then to start AutoCAD running simply type ACAD at the DOS prompt

C> ACAD

The machine will then look for the file ACAD.EXE, and this and other system files will be loaded automatically.

If the system has previously been configured then, after a short delay, the AutoCAD main menu will be displayed. If the package has not been run previously then you will automatically be switched to the configuration routine.

2.2.1 Automatic Start-up from a Batch File

Although the simple command ACAD described above may always be used to start up AutoCAD, it is more convenient to issue this command from within a batch file (see Appendix 1 for information on DOS batch files). The advantage of a batch file is that a number of commands may be issued automatically whenever the file is run. Thus, in addition to issuing the ACAD start-up command you can also include commands to SET (see Appendix 1) a number of environment variables which allow AutoCAD to operate more efficiently. (See Appendix 2 for a fuller explanation of AutoCAD's environment variables.)

The batch file ACAD386.BAT supplied with the package may resemble:

```
SET ACAD=C:\ACAD\SUPPORT;C:\ACAD\SAMPLES;C:\ACAD\ADS
SET ACADCFG=C:\ACAD
C:
CD\ACAD
ACAD %1 %2
```

However, it is advisable to modify this file to take account of the need to set an appropriate path, to set the environment variables to suitable values and to return the user to the root directory after leaving AutoCAD.

EXAMPLE

A typical batch file which will specify a working directory called MYFILES, a SUPPORT directory containing text fonts, menus etc., and which will set various environment variables (see Appendix 2) to suitable values before running AutoCAD is given below:

PATH=C:\ACAD\MYFILES	Opens a path from ACAD to MYFILES
CD\ACAD\MYFILES	Changes directory to MYFILES
SET ACADCFG=C:\ACAD\MYCONF	Sets the configuration directory
SET LISPHEAP=42000	Reserves 42k of RAM for AutoLISP
SET LISPSTACK=2500	Reserves 2.5k of RAM for AutoLISP

SET ACAD=C:\ACAD\SUPPORT	Informs AutoCAD of SUPPORT directory
ACAD	Runs AutoCAD
CD\	Returns user to root directory

2.2.2 Hardware Configuration

AutoCAD is a large software package which may be run on a wide variety of machines with a choice of plotters, printers and digitisers. Before you can use the package it must be set up or *configured* to work with your particular set of hardware.

In this case the package will request information on the type of VDU and graphics system in the computer, the type of plotter and printer and whether a digitiser or mouse is to be used.

In some cases the configuration program will ask other related questions, such as which screen colours you require, how sensitive the mouse is to movement etc. If in doubt about the answers to these particular questions it is probably best to accept the "default" response which is always shown in brackets < >.

When configuration is complete a new file called ACAD.CFG will be written to the disk and this file will carry all the configuration data which you have just supplied. Next time you start up AutoCAD, this file will be read and AutoCAD will assume that the configuration requirements are unchanged. You will thus be allowed to proceed to the main menu without being asked to configure the system. Multiple configuration is covered in Section 18.4.

2.2.3 The Main Menu

This is the starting point for most AutoCAD operations:

0. Exit AutoCAD
1. Begin a NEW drawing
2. Edit an EXISTING drawing
3. Plot a drawing
4. Printer plot a drawing
5. Configure AutoCAD
6. File utilities
7. Compile shape/font description file
8. Convert old drawing file
9. Recover damaged drawing

Enter Selection:

The **Enter Selection:** prompt is asking you to choose one of the tasks by number.

Tasks 1 - 4 are the most commonly used, being concerned with all aspects of drawing and plotting. *Task 1* is for starting a brand new drawing. *Task 2* is used to load an existing drawing from disk and to display it on screen where it may be viewed, and additions or deletions made where necessary. *Tasks 3* and *4* cover the output of a permanent paper record of the drawing on a plotter or on a printer.

Task 5 allows you to re-configure AutoCAD (for example, if you wished to use a different plotter or digitiser). *Task 6* is a file-handling utility allowing you to list, delete, re-name, copy or unlock files on the disk. *Task 7* is used when designing special symbols or lettering fonts, while *Task 8* allows you to work with old AutoCAD drawings produced under earlier versions of the package. *Task 9* allows you to recover a drawing which contains corrupted data (assuming that the drawing was originally generated using an AutoCAD package not earlier than Release 11).

2.3 STARTING A NEW DRAWING

To start a completely new drawing from the main menu simply type 1, followed by the "return" or "enter" key.

> **Enter Selection:** 1   Press the return key

All drawings must have a title, and AutoCAD will respond with a prompt for the name of the drawing. Supply a suitable name:

> **Enter NAME of drawing:** TEST   (Press the return key)

The screen will clear while the Drawing Editor, the piece of software which controls all drawing operations, is loaded. After a few moments the screen will be set up ready for drawing, (see Figure 2.2), with a screen menu down the right hand side of the display, a command line at the bottom and the UCS icon in the bottom left hand corner, (see Section 2.3.4). The last items to appear are the cross wires which are controlled either by the digitiser, or mouse, or alternatively by the arrow keys on the number pad on the right of the keyboard.

2.3.1 Coordinates

At the top of the screen you will see a pair of coordinates. These represent the position of the cross wires. As you move the cross wires these coordinates should change. If they do not, try pressing function key F6. This should toggle the coordinates On/Off. If they still do not work, check your configuration and consult your mouse or digitiser manual.

Some people find the continually changing coordinate display to be distracting. In this case the display may be disabled by pressing function key F6, after which the coordinates will only change when a point is selected.

```
┌─────────────────────────────────────────────────────────────────────┐
│  ┌────────────────────────────────────────────────────┬──────────┐   │
│  │ Layer 0 Snap          230.233, 160.435             │ AutoCAD  │   │
│  │                                                     │ * * *    │   │
│  │                          │                          │ BLOCKS   │   │
│  │                          │                          │ DIM:     │   │
│  │                          │                          │ DISPLAY  │   │
│  │                          │                          │ DRAW     │   │
│  │                          │                          │ EDIT     │   │
│  │                          │                          │ INQUIRY  │   │
│  │                          │                          │ LAYER:   │   │
│  │                          │                          │ MVIEW    │   │
│  │──────────────────────────┼────────────────────────│ PLOT     │   │
│  │                          │                          │ SETTINGS │   │
│  │                          │                          │ SOLIDS   │   │
│  │                          │                          │ SURFACES │   │
│  │                          │                          │ UCS:     │   │
│  │                          │                          │ UTILITY  │   │
│  │                          │                          │ ASHADE   │   │
│  │                          │                          │ RMAN     │   │
│  │                          │                          │ BONUS    │   │
│  │                          │                          │ SAVE:    │   │
│  │─────────────────────────────────────────────────────          │   │
│  │ Command:                                            │          │   │
│  └────────────────────────────────────────────────────┴──────────┘   │
└─────────────────────────────────────────────────────────────────────┘
```

Figure 2.2 The graphics screen

2.3.2 Drawing Units

The coordinates at the top of the screen will show you which system of drawing units is specified in your prototype drawing, (see Section 2.3.6). These can easily be changed to one of the alternative systems.

There are 5 different systems of drawing units. If you call up UNITS from one of the menus, or if you simply type the command UNITS, the following menu is displayed:

Command: UNITS

Systems of units:	(Examples)

1.	Scientific	1.55E+01
2.	Decimal	15.50
3.	Engineering	1'-3.50"
4.	Architectural	1'-3 1/2"
5.	Fractional	15 1/2

Enter choice, 1 to 5 <default>:

You have a totally free choice. Just because you are an engineer does not mean that you have to choose option 3! The alternative units are there for your convenience. When in doubt, option 2, the simple decimal system, is probably the best.

After choosing the required system of units and setting the precision (e.g. the number of decimal places), AutoCAD proceeds to the Angle menu:

Systems of angle measure: **(Examples)**

1.   **Decimal degrees**   **45.0000**
2.   **Degrees/minutes/seconds**   **45d0'0"**
3.   **Grads**   **50.0000g**
4.   **Radians**   **0.7854r**
5.   **Surveyor's units**   **N 45d0'0" E**

Enter choice, 1 to 5 <default>:

AutoCAD normally measures angles in degrees, taking positive angles to be measured counter-clockwise from a horizontal reference, (see Figure 2.3). As with most of AutoCAD's units, you can change this if you wish, but it is probably better to stick with the usual notation.

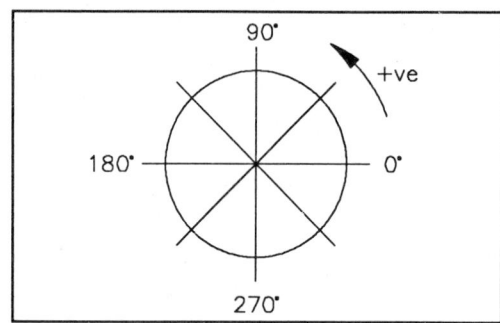

Figure 2.3   Angle convention

The whole subject of drawing units causes unnecessary concern. The coordinates of the drawing are simply *arbitrary units* and it is up to the user to decide on their meaning. The decimal units of System 2, for instance, can be thought of as millimetres or miles.

When you come to plot out your finished drawing, you will have the chance to tell the plotter either to plot it to an exact scale, say 1 millimetre on the paper = 5 drawing units, or simply to plot the complete drawing to some convenient size which will fit comfortably on the page.

2.3.3 Drawing Limits

People get the wrong idea about drawing limits. The name rather implies that these are limits to a drawing which can never be crossed. In fact, the idea of drawing limits is to *aid* you in laying out a drawing if it must conform to a particular size.

AutoCAD assumes that all drawings will be constructed full size . It is therefore useful to set the limits of the drawing to a value slightly larger than the outside dimensions of the object(s) to be drawn.

EXAMPLE

If your drawing extremities are 200mm by 100mm then you may find it helpful to set the system of units to decimal, the bottom left hand limits to 0,0 and the top right limits to 240,180.

> **Command:** LIMITS
> **ON/OFF/<Lower left corner><0.00,0.00>:**
> **Upper right corner <400,300>:** 240,180

An On response will set the system variable LIMCHECK, (see Section 2.3.7) to On, and this will warn you if you subsequently transgress the limits.

After changing the limits it should be noted that the screen will still be set to the original limits (see the coordinates - top right); to change the screen to the new limits use the ZOOM All command.

> *Note:*   If you wish to observe the area bounded by the current limits, you should turn on the grid, (see Section 4.1.2), which will be displayed only within this area.

   With the introduction of the concept of Paper Space, (see Chapter 13), it is now necessary to use the LIMITS command initially to set the size of the paper space area to match the actual paper size of the final plot.

2.3.4 The UCS Icon

At the bottom left corner of the screen you will see a crossed arrows symbol, (see Figure 2.4). This is called the UCS (User Coordinate System) Icon and is used primarily when constructing 3D drawings. (See Chapter 16.)

   Users may at first find this to be distracting, in which case the icon may be removed from the screen by the command UCSICON, followed by OFF.

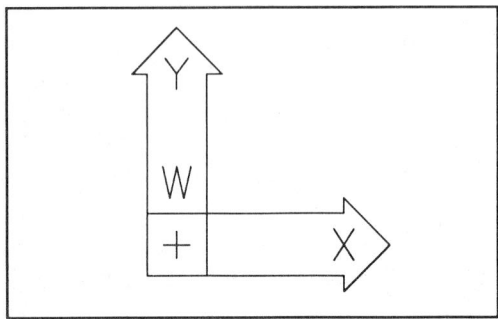

Figure 2.4   The UCS icon

2.3.5 Function and Control Keys

Many of the function keys act as toggle switches (On/Off) for some of AutoCAD's most useful functions. These include:

F6	Coordinates On/Off
F7	Grid On/Off
F8	Ortho On/Off
F9	Snap On/Off
F10	Tablet On/Off

In addition, if your system is configured for a single VDU performing both text and graphics functions, then function key F1 acts as a toggle between the two modes.

Some of the function key commands are duplicated by control (Ctrl) keys. These are activated by holding down the Ctrl key together with the corresponding letter key.

Ctrl B Snap On/Off	(see Section 4.1.1)
Ctrl C Cancel	(see Section 2.4.1)
Ctrl D Coordinate control	(see Section 2.3.1)
Ctrl E Isoplane left/top/right	(see Section 15.1)
Ctrl G Grid On/Off	(see Section 4.1.2)
Ctrl O Ortho On/Off	(see Section 4.1.3)
Ctrl Q Print echo	
Ctrl T Tablet On/Off	(see Section 3.3.1)
Ctrl X Delete keyboard errors	

2.3.6 The Prototype Drawing

When you start a new drawing using *Task 1*, the drawing area will be clear, but you are in fact already using an existing drawing called ACAD.DWG. This is the *prototype drawing* supplied with the package. Although it looks blank, the prototype drawing contains all the preset values and parameters which AutoCAD needs in order to operate. It can be thought of as a framework upon which your new drawing will be built.

If the prototype drawing is absent then the package will complain and return you to the main menu. You can get round the problem by responding with an = sign after your drawing name:

Enter Selection: 1
Enter NAME of drawing: TEST=   (return)

This will get you started by setting all the parameters to their default value. These values are stored as *system variables*, (see Section 2.3.7). However, the problem will recur and you should at some stage recover ACAD.DWG via main menu *Task 1*, simply by entering:

Enter Selection: 1
Enter NAME of drawing: ACAD=

Press the return key to start a new drawing called ACAD

Command: END

This saves the new drawing called ACAD with the default parameter settings and returns you to the main menu.

You can use any drawing as the prototype, simply by citing it as the prototype when you start a new drawing:

Enter Selection: 1
Enter NAME of drawing: TEST=MYPROTO   (return)

This will cite the existing drawing called, say, MYPROTO, as the prototype for the new drawing TEST, so that TEST is built on top of MYPROTO. If MYPROTO incorporates a feature such as a company logo or a draughtsman's name, then this will be incorporated into the new drawing automatically.

If you wish to make MYPROTO the default prototype drawing, this may be achieved from the configuration menu by selecting :

   8.   **Configure operating parameters**

and then selecting from the operating parameters menu:

2.   Initial drawing setup

2.3.7 System Variables and the SETVAR Command

The drawing parameters which are contained in the prototype drawing are known collectively as *System Variables*. (Appendix 4 gives a full list of all AutoCAD's system variable for reference.) They control just about everything within the drawing from its overall size down to the way the smallest point is represented. There are over 150 of these system variables - which is why the prototype drawing system is so useful. Without this you would have to set all these variables manually. As it is, you can be happily unaware of the existence of the vast majority of these parameters and their function. However, as you become more adept at using AutoCAD you will need to be able to access and change the system variables within a drawing. This may be done simply by entering the name of the system variable at the command prompt. For example, if you wish to be warned when you transgress the limits of the drawing you will need to change the system variable LIMCHECK to 1.

> **Command:** LIMCHECK
> **New value for LIMCHECK <0>:** 1

A possible problem may occur when a system variable carries the same name as a command. In this case the command will be executed preferentially and if you wish to have access to the system variable you must use the SETVAR command.

> **Command:** SETVAR
> **Variable name or ?:**

If you respond with a ?, you will be presented with the full list of all the system variables and their current values (but no explanation of what each one does - see Appendix 4). Locate the one you want, repeat the SETVAR command and supply the system variable name. AutoCAD will then respond with the current value of this variable and allow you to change it.

When you save the drawing the new values of all the system variables will be recorded so that, when the drawing is later retrieved, the variables will remain set to their new values.

2.4 GIVING COMMANDS

You may give an AutoCAD command in any one of the following ways:

- *From the keyboard:* the command will be echoed below the drawing area on the *command line*. The command is executed by pressing the return key or the space bar - either immediately or after some secondary information has been typed in.

> *Note:* AutoCAD is unusual in that the space bar acts as a return key, except when inputting text.
>
> The last command issued may be repeated simply by pressing the return key or the space bar.

- *Through the screen menu:* If the digitiser or mouse is moved beyond the extreme right of the drawing it can be used to highlight items on the screen menu. Pressing the "pick" button causes the highlighted command to be executed. Alternatively, the screen menu area may be accessed from the keyboard by first pressing the 0/Ins key on the numeric keypad and using the arrow keys to select the required menu item.

  Because there is room only for a few commands to appear on the screen at any given time they are arranged into a "tree" structure as shown in Figure 2.5. Similar types of command are grouped together on one branch of the tree. Thus, all drawing commands are grouped together, as are edit commands, display commands, utility commands etc. All menus have the word AUTOCAD as the first item and *selecting this will always return you to the root or outermost menu of the tree.*

- *Through a pull down menu:* If the digitiser/mouse pointer is moved to the top of the screen then a menu bar appears - picking one of these menu items reveals a pull down menu on screen from which the desired command can be selected.

> *Note:* There is no way to access the pull down menus other than by a mouse or digitiser.

The standard pull down menu structure can be seen in Figure 2.6. It is possible to mix command entries from the keyboard and from the menus, i.e. you could pick the main command from one of the menus and enter secondary information from the keyboard. It is useful to have some familiarity with the menu tree, even if you normally enter commands from the keyboard because it gives a useful insight into the way the package is structured.

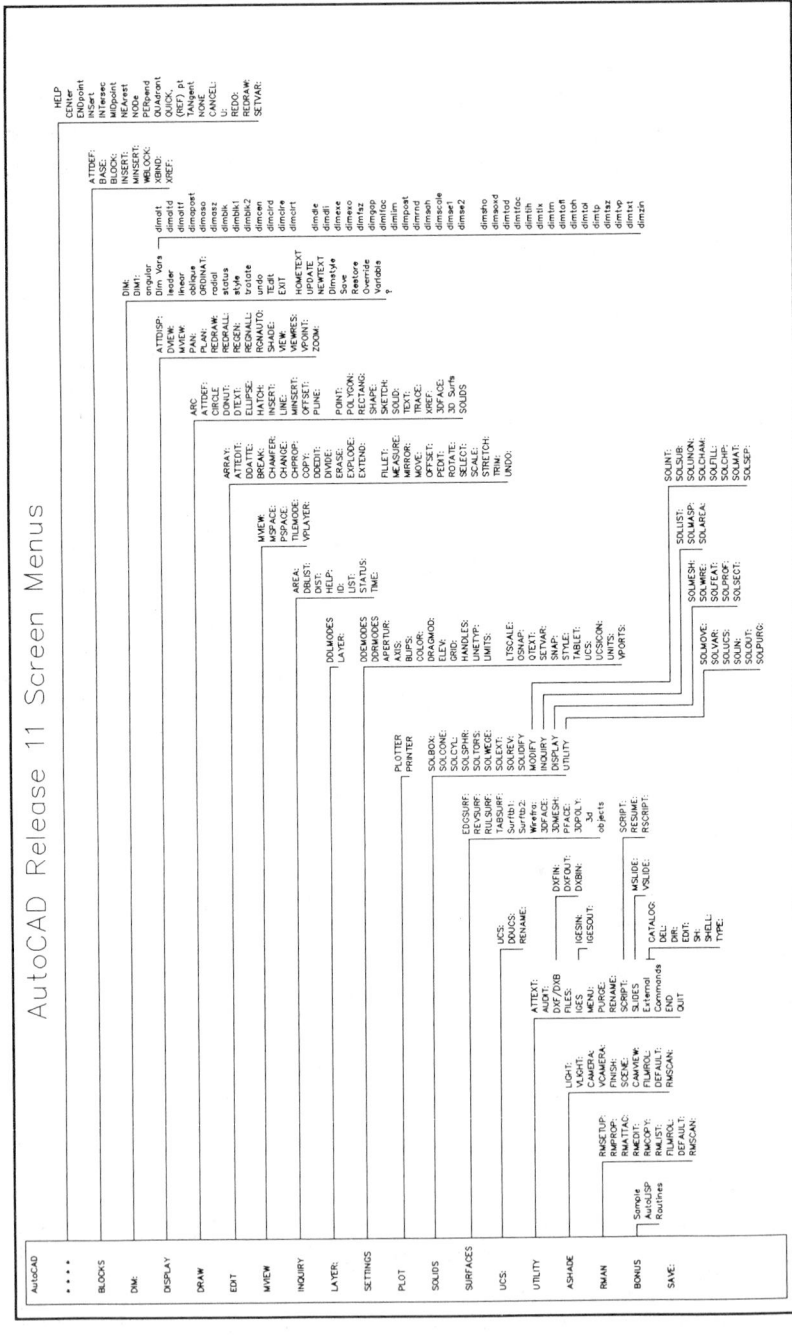

Figure 2.5   Screen menu tree (courtesy of Autodesk Ltd)

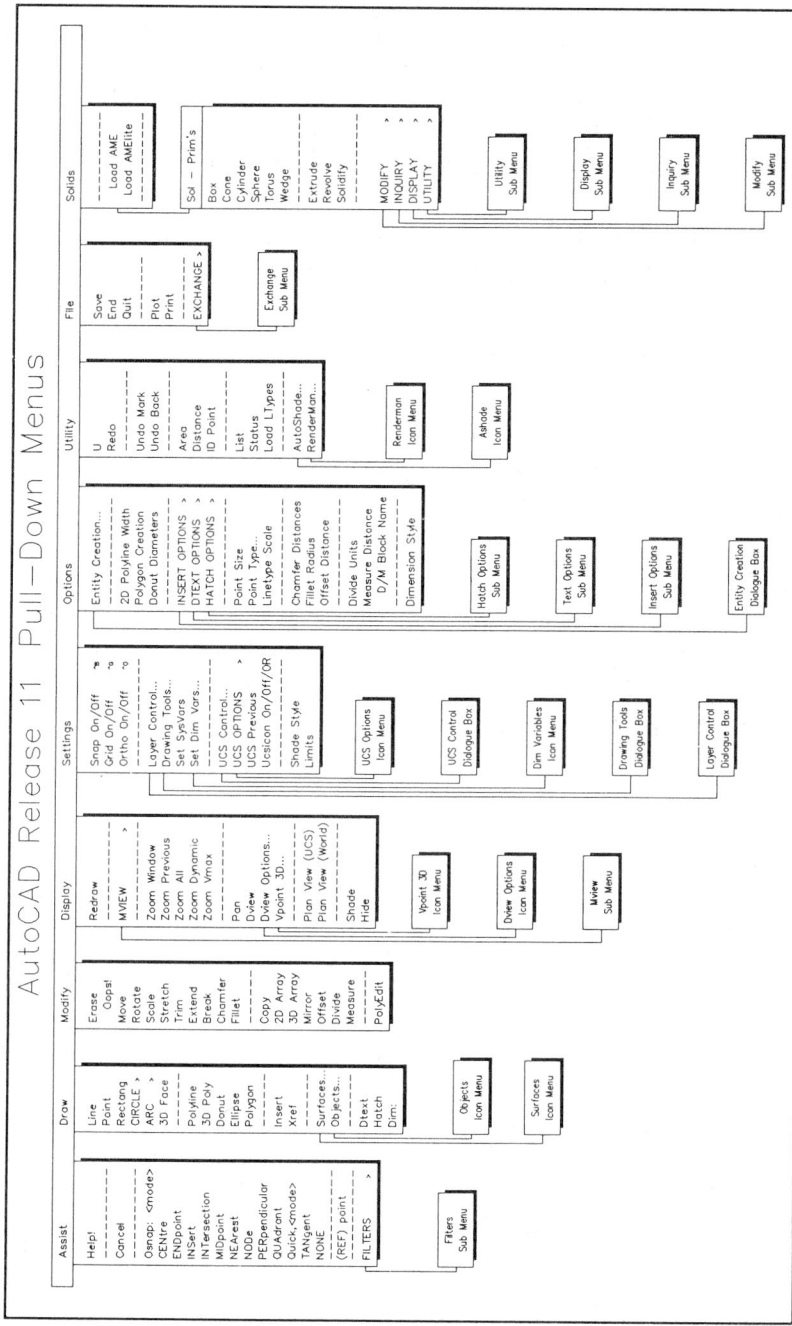

Figure 2.6 Menu bar and pull down menus (courtesy of Autodesk Ltd)

- *Through a tablet menu:* If a digitiser is used instead of a mouse, it is possible to assign areas on the digitiser surface to act as input pads for selected commands. An overlay/template placed on the digitiser tablet can then be used and the various commands picked as required. This is particularly useful when specialised symbols are to be used, a custom-designed overlay can give quick access to these non-standard shapes, (see Chapter 18).

Screen, pull down and tablet menus can be purpose-designed to suit the individual user, (see Chapter 20).

2.4.1 Getting Out of a Command

If you give a wrong command, or if you find that AutoCAD has assumed that you wish to stay with an old command, then you will need some way of getting out of it. The universal cancel command is Ctrl C - hold down the control key and at the same time press the letter C. You will find that AutoCAD releases you and returns you to the **Command:** prompt awaiting the next instruction. You will find that this cancel routine is *built in* to most of the menu commands, so that picking a menu item will release you from an existing command - but be careful, this is not so in every case and you may have to use the manual cancel described above. Commands can also be cancelled by picking the word **AutoCAD** from the top of the screen menu, or by picking Cancel from the **Assist** pull down menu. It can be helpful if one of the mouse or digitiser buttons is programmed to give this cancel command. (See Section 20.1.)

2.5 HELP

AutoCAD is a large package with over 250 major commands and variables. These are all described in some detail in the AutoCAD reference manual but this is not always conveniently to hand. There is a very useful help facility built in to the package; just type HELP or ?, or pick HELP off one of the menus. If you now enter the name of the command or variable name for which help is needed the screen will display some notes that should be useful. If further help is available then the relevant chapter of the manual will usually be given.

If you give a return after HELP or ?, instead of the name of a command, the screen will show a complete list of all the AutoCAD commands and system variables. If you are already *within* a command and require help, then type an apostrophe before the command e.g. 'HELP or '?. The relevant section of the HELP file will then be displayed.

The apostrophe (') makes the command "transparent" which allows the command to be used while another command is in operation. (See Section 5.2.1.)

2.6 SAVING AND QUITTING

There are two methods of leaving a drawing and returning to the main menu - the method you choose will depend on whether you require the drawing to be saved or not. Alternatively, you may save the drawing and remain in the drawing editor.

2.6.1 END

The END command automatically saves the current drawing before returning to the main menu. The filename used will be the current drawing name. If your drawing is a new drawing, the current drawing name will be that which you supplied under main menu *Task 1*. If the current drawing is not a brand new drawing and was retrieved from disk, under main menu *Task 2*, then the current drawing name will be the name under which the drawing was originally filed. You are not allowed to have two drawings on disk with the same name so, in this case, when the drawing is saved again using END, the original version of the drawing will be converted to a backup file (extension .BAK), while the new updated drawing will be saved in a drawing file (extension .DWG) with the original filename, see (Figure 2.7).

Command: END

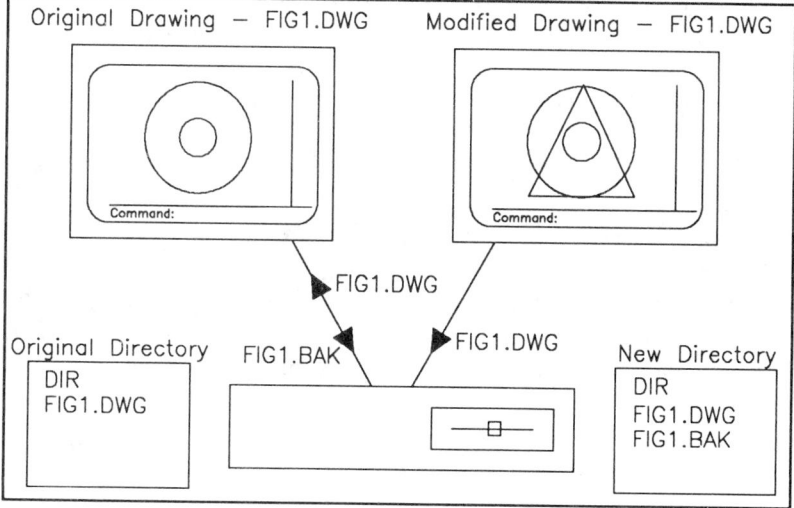

Figure 2.7   Saving an updated drawing

2.6.2 QUIT

The QUIT command returns the user to the main menu without saving the current drawing. If an old drawing has been recalled for editing and it is decided that the changes made should not be saved, then QUIT will keep the original drawing file intact and discard any alterations. When using QUIT, Autocad will respond with the question **Really want to discard all changes to drawing?**. This is a safety feature and if the answer is "yes" then the user must respond by typing Y from the keyboard.

> **Command:** QUIT
> **Really want to discard all changes to drawing?:** Y

2.6.3 SAVE

It is normal to save a drawing periodically to disk without leaving the drawing editor. This protects the work from accidental loss during its construction but avoids the bother of having to return to the main menu using END and then having to re-load the drawing.

> **Command:** SAVE

The file dialogue box, (see Section 2.7.3), will automatically appear, (see Figure 2.8). This will allow you to specify the filename (and directory) under which the drawing will be saved. The filename may be chosen from the list of existing files - *Caution: this will overwrite the chosen file* - or it may be typed in from the keyboard by selecting the **Type it** box.

The current drawing name comes up as the default and may be selected by choosing the **OK** box.

2.7 FILE HANDLING AND FILE TYPES

There are two ways in which AutoCAD allows the user to manipulate files; one leaves the operator in the drawing editor, while the other is a task on the AutoCAD main menu - *Task 6*. Both methods take the user to the file utility menu.

2.7.1 File Handling from the Main Menu

To access the file utilities menu from the main menu, select **6. File utilities**. The file utility menu will appear (as shown below). Files can be listed, deleted, renamed, copied or unlocked.

2.7.2 File Handling from within the Drawing Editor

While remaining in the drawing editor, the command FILES can be used to access the file utilities menu.

Command: FILES

> **File Utility Menu**
>
> | 0 | Exit file utility menu |
> |---|---|
> | 1 | List drawing files |
> | 2 | List user specified files |
> | 3 | Delete files |
> | 4 | Rename files |
> | 5 | Copy file |
> | 6 | Unlock file |
>
> **Enter selection (0 to 6) <0>:**

Note: For all options other than *Task 1*, the full file name and extension must be given.

---

1. List drawing files

Jf the user requires to see the drawing files, then selection 1 will give a list of all the files with the extension .DWG. AutoCAD needs to know which disk drive and directory to search and will therefore respond:

> **Enter drive or directory:**

Press return for the default directory.

2. List user specified files

This option allows the user to specify an exact file or group of files; AutoCAD will then search the specified drive for files which match the input criteria. The user can again specify the path to a sub-directory on a given drive. Wild cards such as ? and * can be used as with standard DOS commands.

There are various file types associated with AutoCAD; each has its own special extension which is automatically added by the AutoCAD package:

.ADT	Audit report file
.BAK	Drawing file backup
.BK(N)	Emergency backup files (created on system "crash")

.CFG	Configuration file
.DWG	Drawing file
.DXB	Binary drawing interchange file
.DXF	Drawing interchange file
.DXX	Attribute extract file (dxf format)
.HLP	Main help file
.HDX	Help index file
.IGS	IGES interchange file
.LIN	Linetype library file
.LSP	AutoLISP programme library file
.LST	Printer plot output file
.MAT	Materials files (for AME mass property calculations)
.MNU	Menu source file
.MNX	Compiled menu file
.MSG	Startup message file
.OLD	Original version of converted drawing file
.PAT	Hatch pattern library file
.PGP	ProGram Parameters file
.PLT	Plot output file
.PRP	ADI printer plotter output file
.PWD	Login file
.SCR	Command script file
.SHP	Shape/font definition source file
.SHX	Shape/font definition compiled file
.SLD	Slide file
.SLB	Slide library
.TXT	Attribute extract or template file (cdf/sdf format)
.UNT	Units file
.XLG	External references log file

3. Delete files

Delete files is used primarily if there is lack of space on a drive to save the current drawing. Files such as backup files can then be deleted to make room. AutoCAD will ask if the file specified should really be deleted from the disk - if you are sure, then respond with a Y.

4. Renaming files

This option allows the changing of an existing file name to a new name specified by the operator. *Remember to include the file extension.*

Enter current filename: FILE1.DWG
Enter new filename: FILE2.DWG

It also allows files to be transferred between directories, but not between disks.

Enter current filename: /DIR1/FILE1.DWG
Enter new filename: /DIR2/FILE2.DWG

5. Copy file

This allows the copying of files from one disk drive to another.

Enter name of source file: A:FILENAME.DWG
Enter name of destination file: C:FILENAME.DWG

6. Unlock file

This allows the user to unlock any drawing file which has been locked against simultaneous entry by a second user when operating on a networked system.

Enter file(s) specification:

AutoCAD will then report on the named file and ask if you wish to unlock it.

2.7.3 File Handling with the File Dialogue Box

Many commands which require an input of a filename cause the file dialogue box to be displayed (as shown in Figure 2.8). This can be a convenient method of viewing and selecting existing files. The files are listed according to the search pattern (file extension) and directory specified in the relevant boxes. There is only one file dialogue box but, depending on which command calls the box, the dialogue box title, the default directory and the default search pattern, will be changed. The directory and search pattern may be altered manually if you wish by selecting these boxes.

To use this dialogue box, use the mouse to pick the required file from the list. This filename will be echoed in the **File** box. If you now pick **OK** this file will be used in the current command. Alternatively you may **Cancel**, or you may use **Type it** to enter a filename from the keyboard.

The scroll bar, which appears to the right of the file list, is useful only when the list of files is too long to fit the screen display. Picking one of the arrow heads at the top or bottom of the scroll bar will cause the list to scroll up or down by *one* position. Picking the button of the scroll bar and moving it to some other position on the bar and pressing pick again, gives you access to any position in the list - i.e. moving the button to the bottom of the scroll bar takes you to the bottom of the file list, halfway down the scroll bar takes you to halfway down the file list, etc.

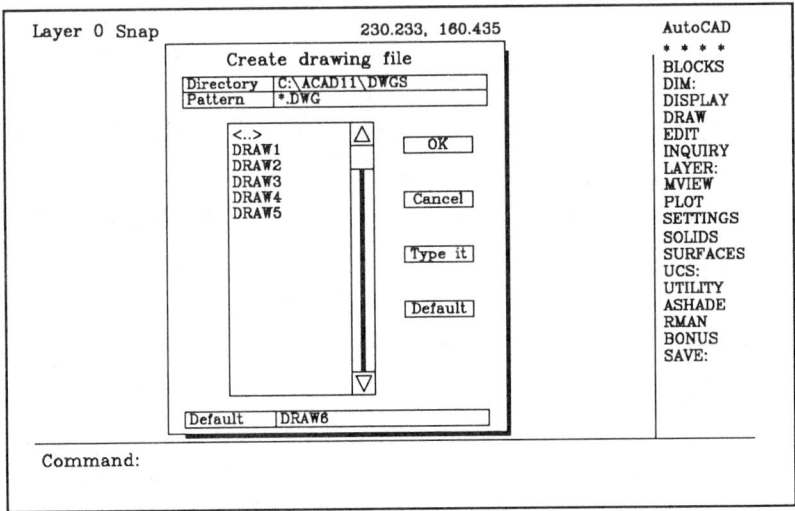

Figure 2.8   File dialogue box

Commands which invoke the file dialogue box are:

ATTEXT	DXBIN	DXFIN	DXFOUT
FILMROLL	IGESIN	IGESOUT	LINETYPE
LOAD	MENU	MSLIDE	SAVE
SCRIPT	STYLE	VSLIDE	WBLOCK

Note: The visibility of the file dialogue box is controlled by the FILEDIA system variable. If FILEDIA=0 then the File dialogue box will not appear and a prompt for the relevant filename will appear on the command line. You can force the dialogue box to appear even when FILEDIA=0 by responding to this prompt with a tilde ~.

3. Simple 2D construction

As described in the previous chapter, commands can be issued from the screen menus, from the digitiser tablet or from the keyboard. You should practice with each method and find the one which suits you best.

> *Note:* You should always keep an eye on the command line at the bottom of the screen where useful prompts and messages are displayed.

You will find that AutoCAD will sometimes respond slightly differently, depending on which method you choose. Don't worry, this is simply because the keyboard command is the basic AutoCAD command but the version from the pull down may have been slightly modified by the person who wrote the menu. When you become more skilled with AutoCAD you will be able to use other menus created for specific purposes, write your own menus - or modify other people's, (see Chapter 20).

3.1 BASIC ENTITIES

3.1.1 LINE

One of the simplest drawing entities is the line. Select LINE from the **Draw** pull down menu, (see Figure 3.1).

Command: LINE

The command line will prompt for a starting point with:

From point:

To indicate the starting point you may move the cross wires to the required position with the digitiser/mouse and press the "pick" button. You will then see that the start point has been fixed, and an "elastic band" cursor joins this point to the current position of the cross wires. The command line prompts for the next point with the words:

To point:

This process can be continued indefinitely. When the last point has been specified the command can be terminated by pressing either the return key or the space bar, after which the elastic band cursor disappears and you are returned to the command prompt.

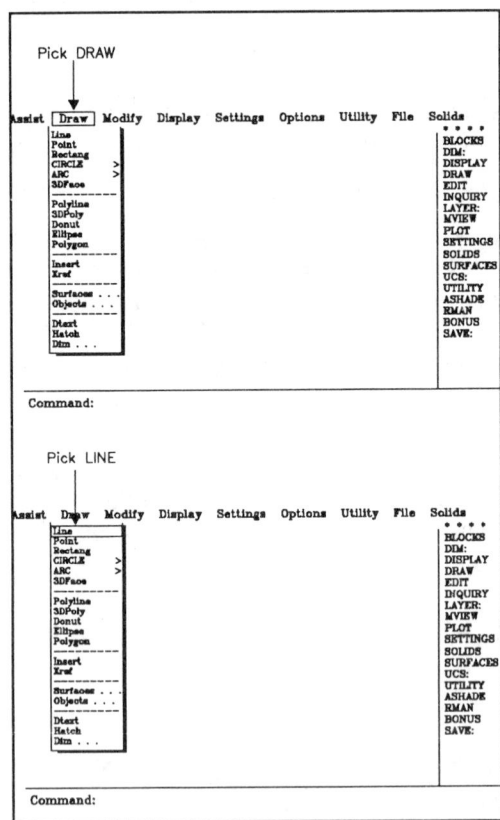

Figure 3.1   Selecting LINE from the **Draw** pull down menu

An alternative to "pointing" with the digitiser/mouse is to specify the *absolute coordinates* of the various points from the keyboard; these are always with reference to the current coordinate system origin. The absolute coordinates may be specified in Cartesian or polar form.

EXAMPLE
Using Cartesian coordinates:

> **Command:** LINE
> **From point** 100,100
> **To point:** 200,200

The values of the X- Y- coordinates of each point on the line are specified individually.

Using polar coordinates, the same line would be specified in terms of the distance from the current origin together with the angle subtended:

> **Command:** LINE
> **From point** 141.4<45
> **To point:** 200<45

Remember AutoCAD normally measures angles in degrees, taking positive angles to be measured counter-clockwise.

Alternatively, you may use *relative coordinates*, which means that you specify the X and Y *distances* from the last point on the line to the next point. The @ symbol indicates that the coordinates are relative.

EXAMPLE

> **To point:** @200,30

This will result in the next point on the line being located 200 drawing units horizontally and 30 drawing units vertically beyond the previous point.

Finally, you may use *relative polar coordinates*. These specify the length and the angle of the new line segment relative to the last point on the line.

EXAMPLE

To point: @50<45

results in a new line segment of length 50 drawing units drawn at an angle of 45 degrees to the horizontal.

The various coordinate types are illustrated in Figure 3.2.

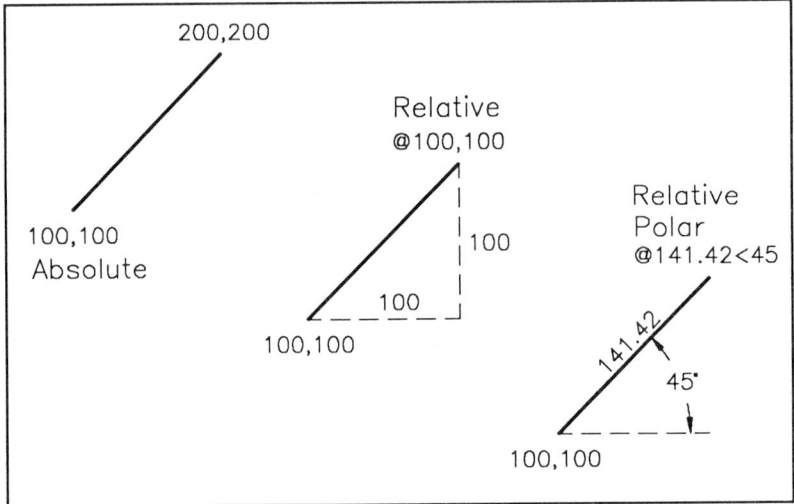

Figure 3.2 2D coordinate types

If you make a mistake and wish to remove the last segment of a line, it is possible to do this without exiting the LINE command. If you respond to the **To point:** prompt with U (for UNDO):

To point: U

this erases the last segment. Multiple U's backtrack through the line segments, erasing the most recent one each time.

If the last segment of your line is intended to *close* the figure, i.e. to return to the starting point, this can be done automatically by responding with C, (see Figure 3.3):

To point: C

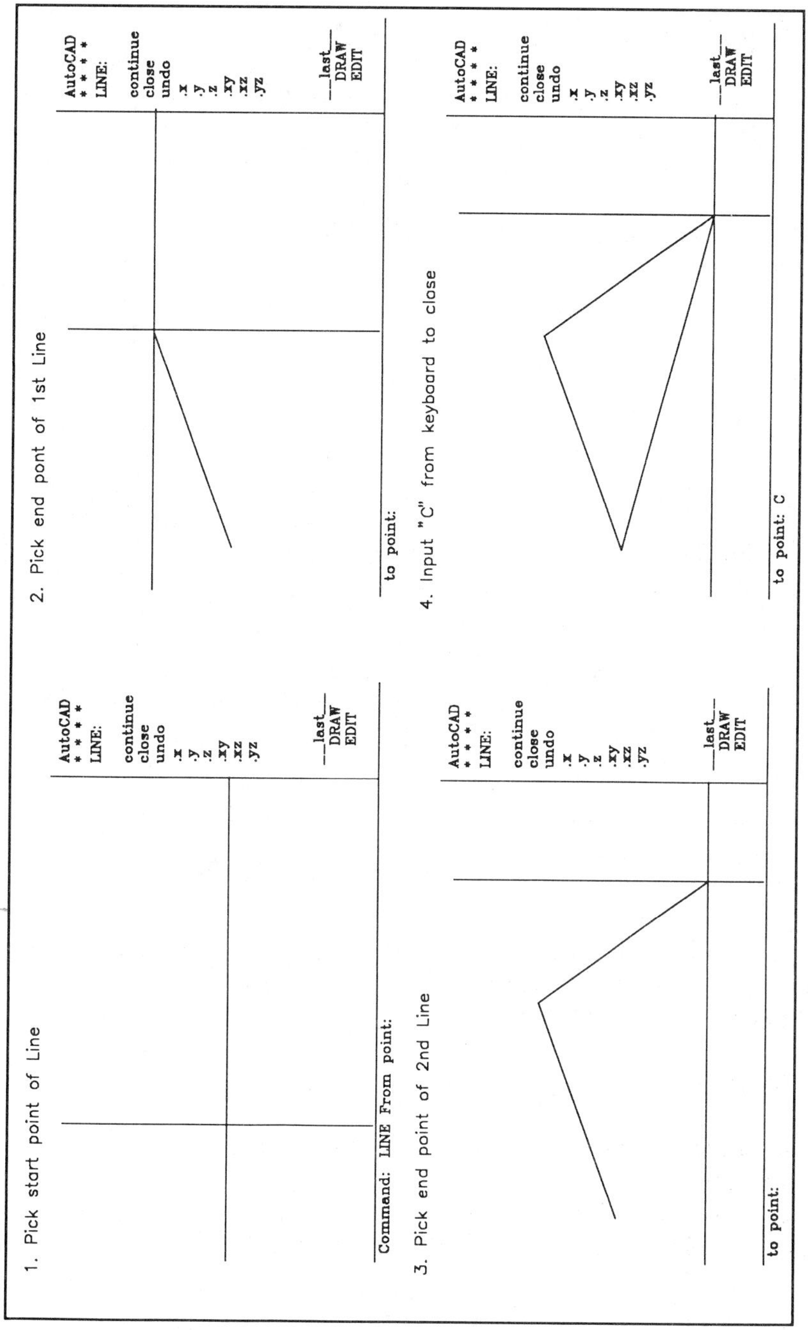

1. Pick start point of Line

AutoCAD
* * * *
LINE:

continue
close
undo

.x
.y
.z
.xy
.xz
.yz

___last___
DRAW
EDIT

2. Pick end pont of 1st Line

AutoCAD
* * * *
LINE:

continue
close
undo

.x
.y
.z
.xy
.xz
.yz

___last___
DRAW
EDIT

Command: LINE From point:

3. Pick end point of 2nd Line

AutoCAD
* * * *
LINE:

continue
close
undo

.x
.y
.z
.xy
.xz
.yz

___last___
DRAW
EDIT

to point:

4. Input "C" from keyboard to close

AutoCAD
* * * *
LINE:

continue
close
undo

.x
.y
.z
.xy
.xz
.yz

___last___
DRAW
EDIT

to point:

to point: C

Figure 3.3 Drawing LINEs

If in response to the **From point:** prompt you answer with a return or pick **continue** from the screen menu, this will take the initial point of the new line to be the final point of the line or arc drawn previously. This is called *continuation mode*.

The start and end coordinates of a line may also be specified in three dimensions by including a Z coordinate. (See Section 16.4.1.)

3.1.2 POINT

The POINT command allows the positioning of a point on the drawing.

> **Command:** POINT
> **Point:**

The POINT can be positioned using a mouse, a digitiser or by entering the X- Y- coordinates.

Two system variables control POINT mode; PDMODE controls the style of the point, whilst PDSIZE controls its size. PDSIZE can be set both positive and negative; a positive value causes all points to be an absolute size, a negative value gives the point a relative size so that it always appears the same size on the screen (after a REGENeration).

Note: When changing PDMODE it is possible to have a number of different POINT styles on the screen at one time. This is an illusion - after REGENeration *all* the points will assume the current PDMODE style.

The first variable, PDMODE, represents point entities as follows:

PDMODE	*Point representation*
0	A dot (default value)
1	Invisible
2	A cross (like a + sign)
3	A cross (like an X)
4	A short vertical line extending upwards

These choices may be further extended by plotting any of the above inside a circle (add 32 to the above numbers, e.g. 32, 33, 34 etc.), a square (add 64), or both (add 96).

Note: A slide illustrating these options may be temporarily displayed on screen by picking Examples from the POINT menu accessed from the **Draw** screen menu. This slide may be removed and your drawing restored by the REDRAW command. (See Figure 3.4.)

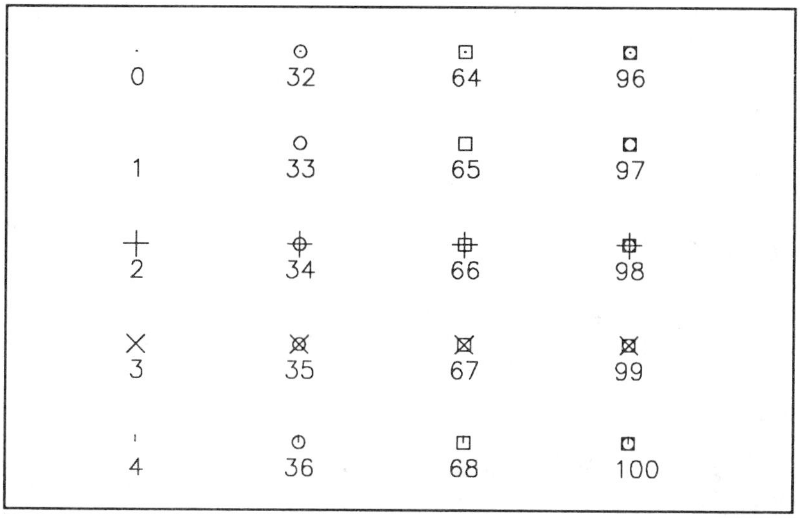

Figure 3.4   POINT modes set with system variable PDMODE

PDSIZE controls the point size for all settings of PDMODE, except 0 or 1. These system variables can now be set from the POINT SIZE and POINT TYPE options on **Options** pull down. The POINT TYPE option calls up a slide showing the different point modes for easy selection.

Remember, the size and the appearance of existing points remain unchanged until the next REGENeration.

3.1.3 Rectangle

This is not a true AutoCAD command but is a good example of how a LISP program can be incorporated into a menu to create a command whenever it is required. As such, it cannot initially be called from the keyboard *before* having been selected from the pull down menu.

> *Note:* The command from the keyboard is that which is defined in the LISP program, which may not necessarily be the same as the name on the pull down. In the case of this command, the keyboard command is RECT and not RECTANG.

The effect of the command is to draw rectangles of any shape or size by prompting for the coordinates of opposing corners.

3.1.4 CIRCLE

Call up CIRCLE from the pull down menu:

Command: CIRCLE

A screen menu will now appear asking you to choose a method for specifying the circle. This is echoed on the command line:

3P/2P/TTR/<Center point>:Diameter/<Radius>:

This response is rather confusing. AutoCAD is offering alternative ways of drawing circles (see Figure 3.5).

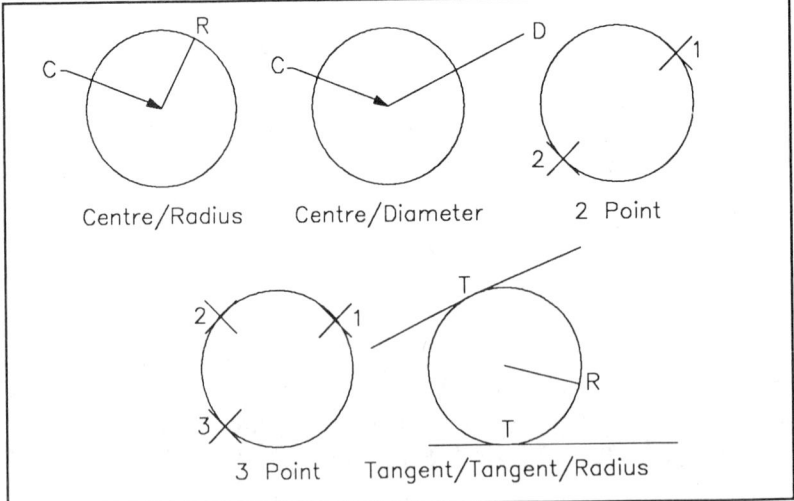

Figure 3.5 CIRCLE definition options

Thus **2P** will draw a circle through two specified points on a diameter, **3P** will draw the unique circle passing through any three specified points, and **TTR** will draw a circle of specified radius which is tangential to two other objects.

However, you will probably not use these more complicated circle routines very often and the remaining methods, **Center,Rad** and **Center,Dia** are the simplest.

To draw a circle using **Center,Rad**, simply select a centre point with the mouse/digitiser. The command line will now prompt for a radius. An elastic band cursor will indicate the appearance of circles with this centre and with a radius as specified by the cross wires. When you are satisfied with the size of the circle, press the pick button and the circle will be drawn.

Alternatively, the centre point and/or the radius may be specified numerically from the keyboard.

Use of **Center,Dia** is similar except that, after setting the centre point, the cross wires are used to indicate the diameter rather than the radius.

3.1.5 ARC

Arcs are called up by the ARC command and the drawing technique is similar to that for circles. However, AutoCAD allows the arc to be specified in 10 different ways and this again can lead to confusion. The simplest technique is to use the **3-point** method. (If you are giving commands from the keyboard, this is the default route as indicated by the angled brackets < >. This defines the unique arc which passes through 3 specified points.

    Command: ARC
    Center/<Start point>:   Supply start point
    Center/End/<Second point>:   Supply second point
    End point: Supply end point

The other routes for specifying an arc are shown in Figure 3.6. The default routes are shown as dotted paths at each decision point. Some duplication occurs in the process - for example, there are three possible routes for drawing an arc with specified Centre, Second point and End point - but other routes are unique and offer useful alternatives for arc specification.

Arcs may also be called up from the screen menu but here the different routes are identified by initials. Thus, SCE refers to definition by Start point, Centre and End point; CSA by Centre, Start point and the included Angle, etc.

The final route is called Continuation mode. This may be initiated by picking from the last item on the screen menu or by responding with a return at the first ARC prompt from the keyboard. The effect is to make the end point of the previously drawn line or arc be the start point of the new arc. Because the angle of this previously drawn entity also defines the initial direction, it is only necessary to supply the End point before the arc can be drawn.

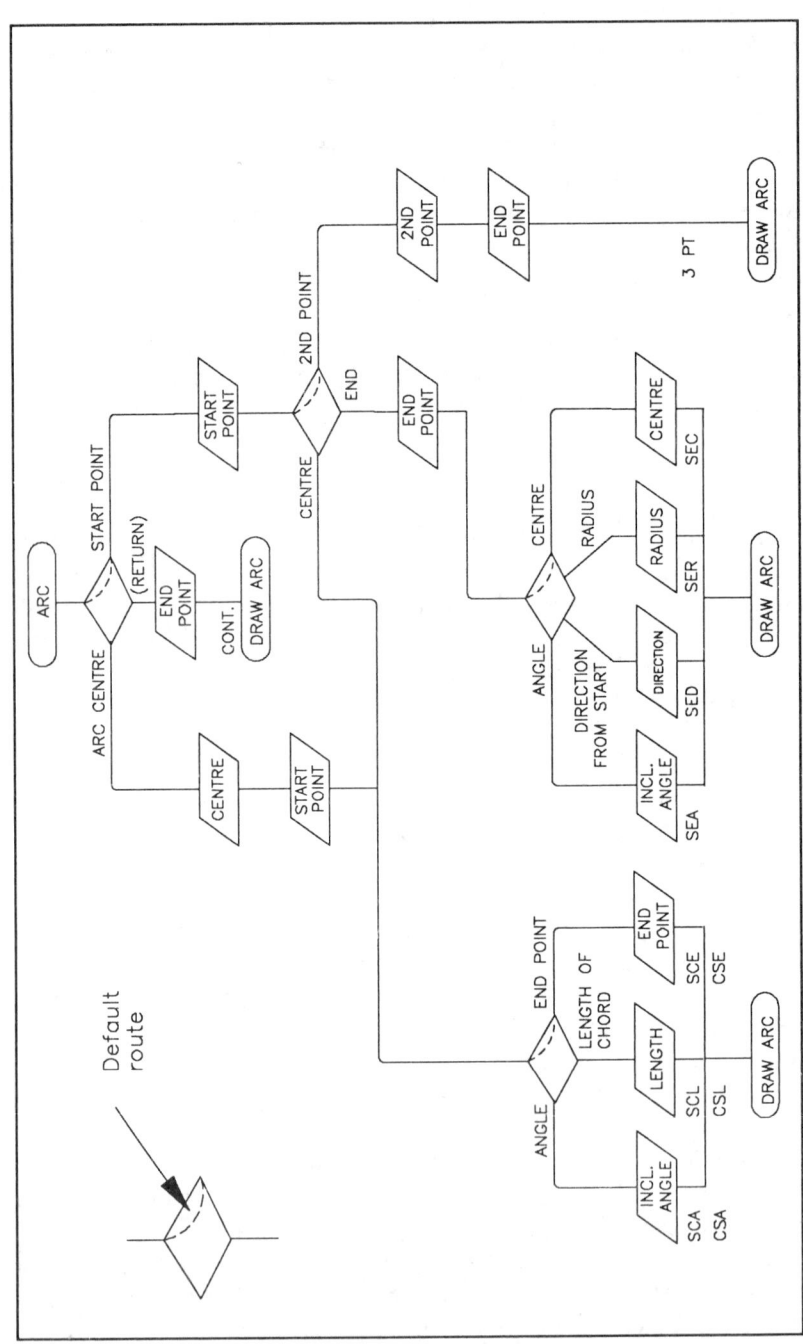

Figure 3.6 Specifying ARCs

Note: AutoCAD draws circles and arcs counter-clockwise by default. Therefore if the arc you specify goes the wrong way then reverse your start and end points.

A common use of arcs is shown in Figure 3.7, where a triangle may be constructed from a knowledge of the lengths of each of the sides.

3.1.6 DOUGHNUT or DONUT

This command will draw filled circles or rings. If the command is selected from the screen menu or the keyboard then the response is as follows:

Command: DOUGHNUT (or DONUT)
Inside diameter: 25
Outside diameter: 80
Center of doughnut: Supply a centre point

This last prompt is repeated indefinitely (until terminated with a return), allowing the figure to be replicated at will.

When picking the command from the **Draw** pull down menu, AutoCAD will not allow you to set the inside or outside diameters but instead will automatically take the last used values by default. To change these default settings, either proceed with the DONUT command from the keyboard as described above or select Donut Diameters from the **Options** pull down menu.

If a solid doughnut (without the hole in the middle) is required, the internal diameter may be set to zero.

The doughnut is normally drawn as a "solid" figure i.e. FILLed in. This can be changed to an unfilled figure if the FILL command is used to switch the fill function off, (see Figure 3.8).

Command: FILL
ON/OFF <default>

Note: The effect of changing the FILL setting will not be seen until a REGENeration has been performed.

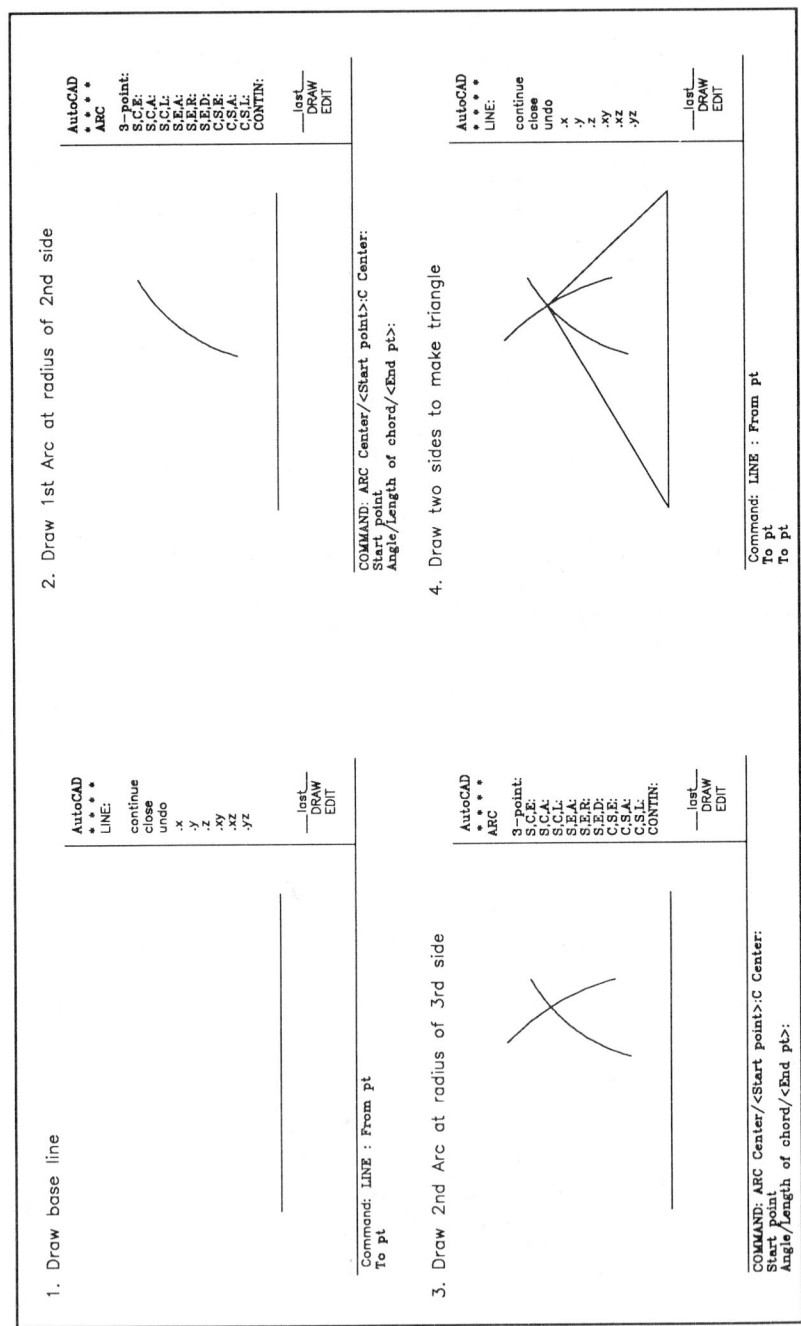

1. Draw base line

```
AutoCAD
* * * *
LINE:

continue
close
undo

.x
.y
.z
.xy
.xz
.yz

——last——
DRAW
EDIT
```

Command: LINE : From pt
To pt

2. Draw 1st Arc at radius of 2nd side

```
AutoCAD
* * * *
ARC

3-point:
S.C.E:
S.C.A:
S.C.L:
S.E.A:
S.E.R:
S.E.D:
C.S.E:
C.S.A:
C.S.L:
CONTIN:

——last——
DRAW
EDIT
```

COMMAND: ARC Center/<Start point>:C Center:
Start point
Angle/Length of chord/<End pt>:

3. Draw 2nd Arc at radius of 3rd side

```
AutoCAD
* * * *
ARC

3-point:
S.C.E:
S.C.A:
S.C.L:
S.E.A:
S.E.R:
S.E.D:
C.S.E:
C.S.A:
C.S.L:
CONTIN:

——last——
DRAW
EDIT
```

COMMAND: ARC Center/<Start point>:C Center:
Start point
Angle/Length of chord/<End pt>:

4. Draw two sides to make triangle

```
AutoCAD
* * * *
LINE:

continue
close
undo

.x
.y
.z
.xy
.xz
.yz

——last——
DRAW
EDIT
```

Command: LINE : From pt
To pt
To pt

Figure 3.7   Construction of ARCs

Figure 3.8   DOUGHNUT - Fill On/Off

3.1.6 TRACE

A LINE is considered to have zero width. The TRACE command permits the construction of lines which have a finite width. (See Figure 3.9.)

> **Command:** TRACE
> **Trace width <10>:**
> **From point:**
> **To point:**
> etc.

The command prompts repeat as with the LINE commands until terminated by a return.

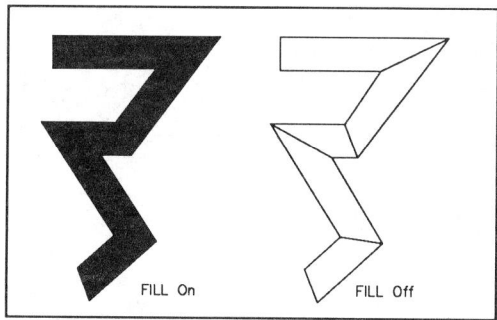

Figure 3.9   TRACE - Fill On/Off

You will notice that the first TRACE section does not appear on screen after entering the second point, as would be the case with a LINE, but will be shown after the entry of the third point. This is to allow the correct mitre angle between the first two TRACE sections to be drawn. This is repeated for all subsequent sections. You are not allowed to use a C to close the figure.

As with DOUGHNUTs, FILL may be invoked to give either a "solid" or outline TRACE.

3.1.7 SOLID

SOLID is used to create solid filled areas composed of either 3- or 4-sided elements.

> **Command:** SOLID
> **First point:**
> **Second point:**
> **Third point:**
> **Fourth point:**

> If the fourth point is coincident with the third point, a triangle results; if it is a separate point, an automatic close will be executed to produce a closed four-sided solid.

> **Third point:**

> This prompts for the third point of the next solid element, and assumes that the first two points have already been specified as points 3 and 4 of the previous solid. (See Figure 3.10.)

> **Fourth point:**   (see above)
> **Third point:**   "
> **Fourth point:**   "
>   .
>   .
>   .

A return terminates the command.

As with DOUGHNUTs, FILL may be invoked to give either a solid or outline figure.

> *Note:* When attempting to produce a rectangular solid area, it is important to specify the corner points in the correct order, otherwise a "bow tie" effect will result. (See Figure 3.11.)

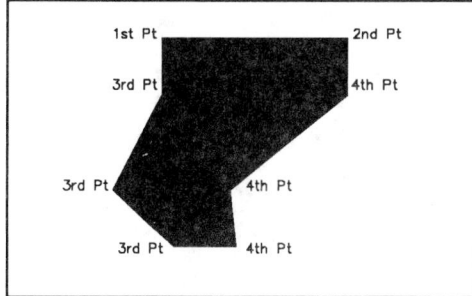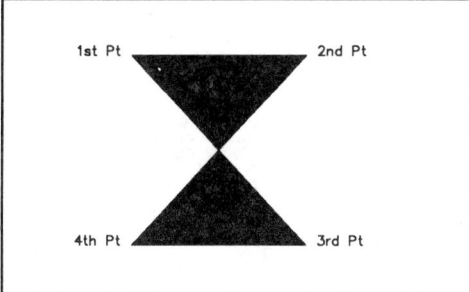

Figure 3.10   SOLID definition   **Figure 3.11**   Bow tie effect using SOLID

3.1.8 ELLIPSE

The ELLIPSE command can specify an ellipse in a number of ways, as shown in Figure 3.12. The default route is to specify one axis of the ellipse by defining its two endpoints, P1 and P2. The second axis is then defined as a distance from the centre point of this axis to P3. Alternatively, the first axis may be defined from a centre point and P2.

> **Command: ELLIPSE**
> **<Axis endpoint 1>/Center:**
> **Axis endpoint 2:**
> **<Other axis distance>/Rotation:**
>
> Instead of specifying the point P3, the "roundness" of the ellipse may be set by an angle of rotation. If this route is taken, the points P1 and P2 are considered as points on the diameter of a circle. If the angle of rotation is set at 0° then the ellipse is drawn circular, i.e. as a circle viewed from above. As the rotation angle increases towards 90°, the circle is assumed to be rotated, presenting an increasingly elliptical view and tending to a straight line at an angle of 90°. (The package will only accept angles up to 89.4°.)

An ellipse, even when circular in shape, is constructed from a closed polyline. This is clearly shown when an ellipse is interrogated by the LIST command.

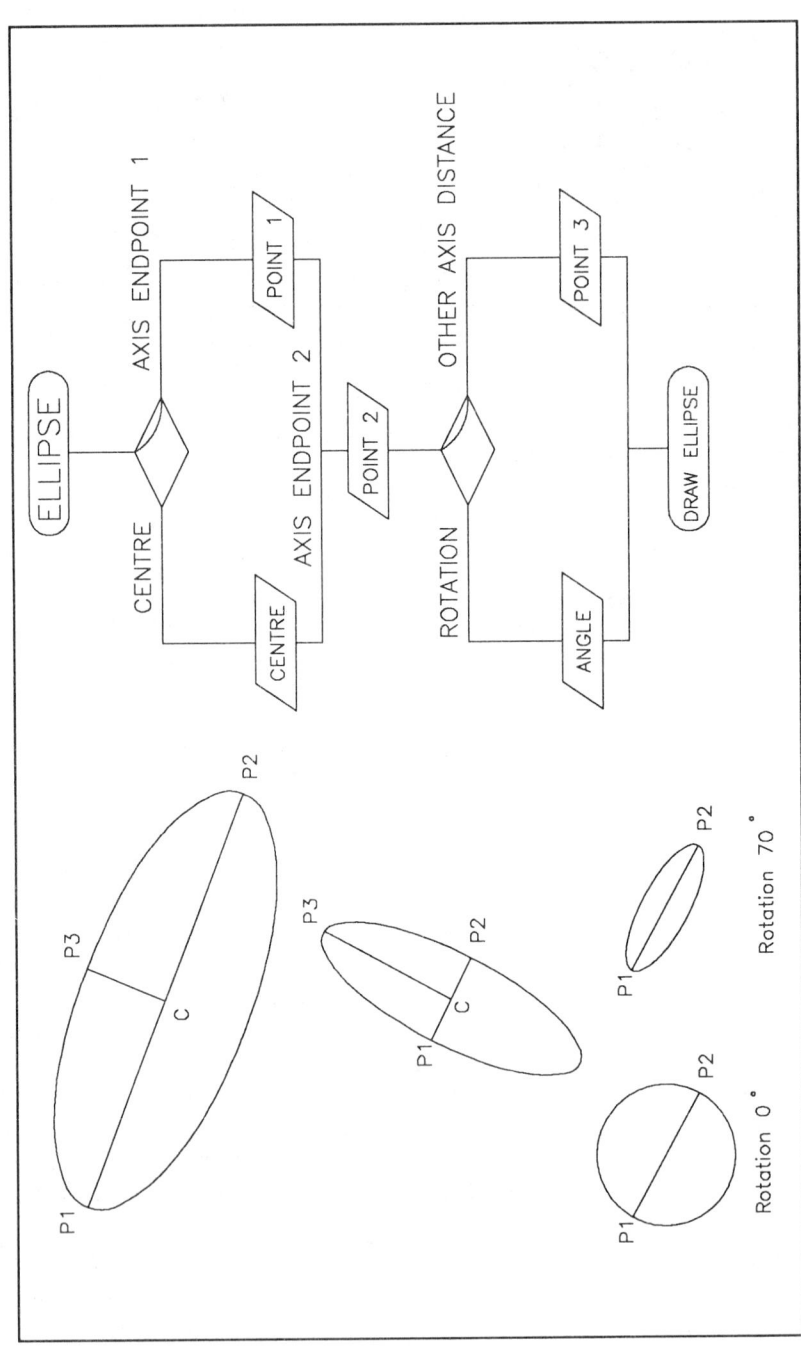

Figure 3.12 Specifying ELLIPSEs

3.1.9 POLYGON

This is a useful command for drawing regular shapes with between 3 and 1024 sides.

> **Command:** POLYGON
> **Number of sides:** 7
> **Edge/<Center of polygon>:**   Supply a centre point
> **Inscribed in circle/Circumscribed about a circle (I/C):**

If you reply with an I, you will be prompted for the radius of the circle within which the polygon will just fit. If you reply with a C, you will be prompted for the radius of the circle which the polygon will just fit around, (see Figure 3.13).

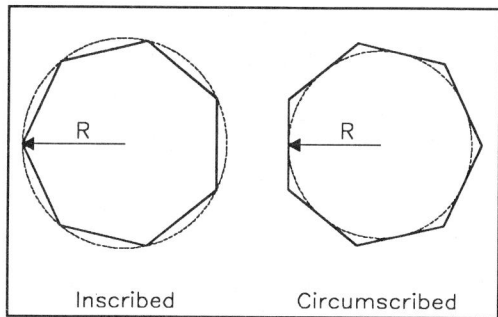

Figure 3.13   POLYGON definition

If you reply with E at the earlier prompt:

> **Edge/<Center of polygon>:** E

you can specify the size and position of the polygon by giving the two endpoints of one of the sides or edges. As in the case of an ellipse, a polygon is also constructed from a closed polyline.

If you wish to preset the number of sides and the method by which you specify the polygon (Edge/Center, Inscribed/Circumscribed), then select Polygon Creation from the **Options** pull down menu. Once this data has been set, the POLYGON command, as selected from the **Draw** pull down, will *always* respond using these preset values. If, on the other hand, you prefer to be prompted for the number of sides etc., each time you use POLYGON from the pull down, then the preset values may be erased by responding with a . during Polygon Creation.

Although it may seem complicated at first sight, POLYGON is a really useful command - try using it for drawing squares or equilateral triangles for instance.

3.2 POLYLINES

Polylines incorporate the properties of both lines and arcs. They also have a number of additional properties which include variable line width (parallel or tapered), curve fitting and the construction of complex *single entities* composed of both lines and arcs, (see Figure 3.14).

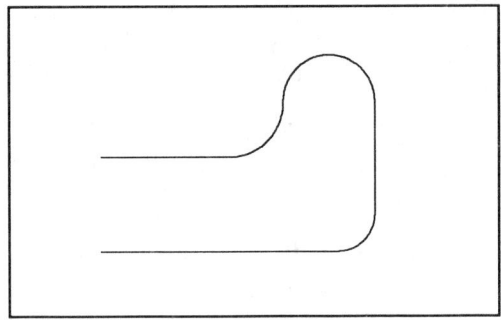

Figure 3.14   Single polyline made up of arcs and lines

A major feature is that an existing polyline may be extensively modified by comprehensive special editing facilities using the PEDIT command, (see Section 4.3).

Command: PLINE
From point:

When the starting point of the polyline is given, the currently set line width will be displayed. This can be changed at any time during the use of PLINE.

3.2.1 Straight lines

Initially PLINE will assume that a straight line is to be drawn. The following prompt will be displayed:

Arc/Close/Halfwidth/Length/Undo/Width/<Endpoint of line>:

Arc   Switches to arc mode (new prompt). (See Section 3.2.2.)

Close   Allows the closing of a group of lines/arcs, with a line or arc connecting the last point to the original starting point.

Length   Produces a line connected to the last segment (at the same angle as that segment), of the length specified.

Undo   Removes the last segment drawn, whether it was a line or an arc.

Width   Allows the setting of the line width, this can be set to produce a parallel or tapered line/arc, (see Figure 3.15).

Halfwidth   Same as width but half the total width is specified.

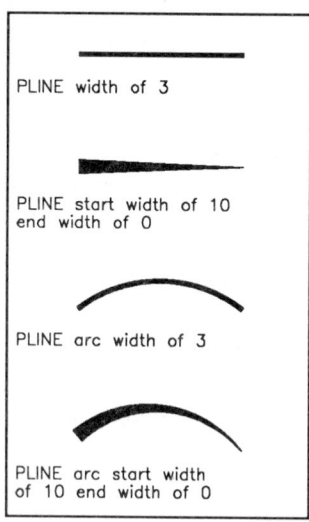

Figure 3.15   Variation of width

3.2.2 Arcs

Arcs are drawn by convention in the *counter-clockwise* direction. If Arc is selected from the above prompt, then a new prompt will be displayed:

Angle/CEnter/CLose/Direction/Halfwidth/Line/Radius/Second pt/Undo/ Width/<Endpoint of arc>:

Angle   Allows the setting of the included angle - the angle the arc will span, (see Figure 3.16). For an arc to be drawn clockwise, input a negative angle.

CEnter   Normally an arc will be drawn at a tangent to the previous segment: Center allows a specific centre point to be set (Figure 3.17).

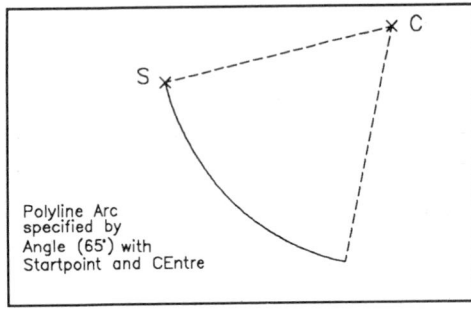

Figure 3.16 Polyline arc: angle specification

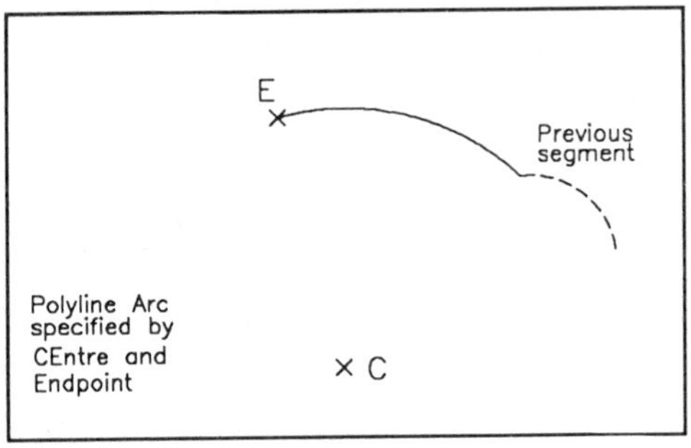

Figure 3.17 Polyline arc: centre, endpoint specification

CLose   Same as Close for the line option but closes with an arc.

Direction   Allows the setting of an explicit starting direction, (see Figure 3.18).

Line   Switches back to line mode.

Radius   Allows the setting of a specific radius.

Second pt   Allows the input of a second point through which the arc must pass, (see Figure 3.19).

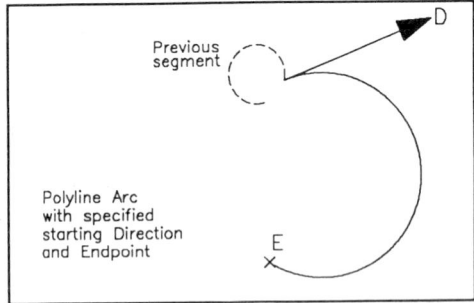

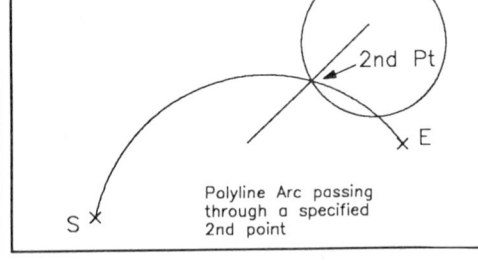

Figure 3.18 Polyline arc: direction specification

Figure 3.19 Polyline arc: second point specification

3.3 SKETCH MODE

Most people who are unfamiliar with the way a CAD system operates assume that drawings are produced by using the mouse or digitiser as a sort of magic pen to draw directly on to the screen. In fact, as we have seen already, this is not how drawings are usually constructed. However, there are occasions when it is useful to be able to sketch irregular shapes and SKETCH mode allows you to do this. A simple example is shown in Figure 3.20.

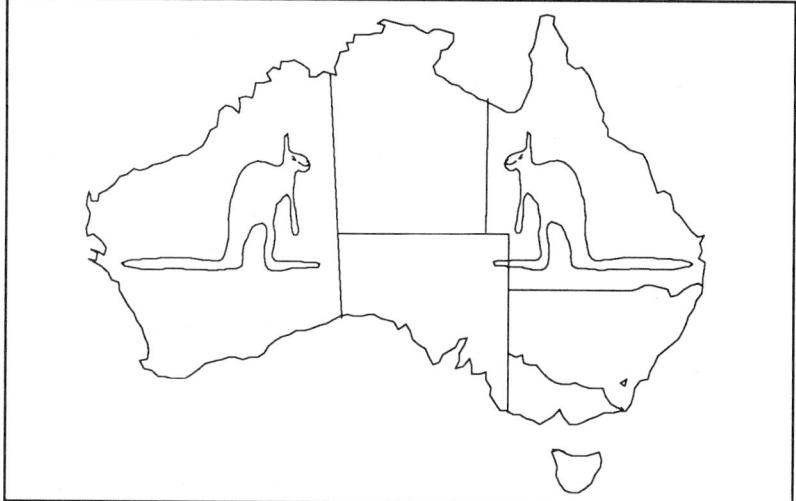

Figure 3.20   Use of SKETCH

Although it is possible to use a mouse in sketch mode, in practice you will obtain better results when using a digitiser. This is because the digitiser puck or pen is designed to allow you to follow outlines accurately using its cross wires or pen-like tip. The mouse has no such corresponding feature.

When in sketch mode, it is almost as if you have temporarily left AutoCAD and entered a separate, simple package which has only *seven* commands.

Sketch mode is initiated by the SKETCH command:

Command: SKETCH
Record increment:

This prompt requests an incremental length which will set the coarseness of the sketch. The sketch is divided up into sequential elements and the length of each element is equal to the record increment. Clearly, you will obtain much smoother sketches if the increment is small, but remember that a large sketch will contain an enormous number of elements which will take up a significant amount of computer storage space and time to process.

Sketch. Pen eXit Quit Record Erase Connect .

P	Raise/lower "pen"
X (or space or return)	Record lines and exit to AutoCAD
Q (or Ctrl C)	Discard lines and exit to AutoCAD
R	Record lines
E	Erase
C	Connect
.	Line to point

P   The puck is considered to be a pen in sketch mode. A P command from the keyboard (or pressing the pick button on the puck) acts as a toggle and controls whether this "pen" is down - and hence makes a line - or up, when no line is made. The pen up/down mode has no *physical* significance.

R   This records the sketch, i.e. any sketched lines drawn to date are imported into the AutoCAD drawing. After this, they are outside the control of the SKETCH commands but they can, of course, be manipulated by the normal AutoCAD commands and are treated as a series of separate elements. Whether these elements are treated by AutoCAD as lines or polylines depends on the value of the system variable SKPOLY (0=LINE , 1=POLYLINE). Use of the R command leaves you still in sketch mode.

X or space or return   These commands all have the effect of recording the sketch but they also return you from sketch mode to normal AutoCAD mode.

Q or Ctrl C   These commands discard all sketch lines not previously recorded and return you to AutoCAD.

E   The Erase sub-command produces the prompt:

Erase:Select end of delete

Point to that element of the sketch preceding the error(s) to be erased. The sketch will then be blanked out on the screen *from this element to the last-drawn element of the sketch*. Depending on your computer and the complexity of the sketch, the speed with which this occurs may range from instantaneous to very slow. Pressing P or the pick button then permanently erases the blanked-out section and returns you to the SKETCH menu.

Elements of a sketch which have previously been recorded cannot be erased by this method. Pressing E a second time will abort the erase.

C   The Connect command allows you to continue with the sketch from the previous endpoint. Assuming that the "pen" is up, approach the endpoint. When you are *within one elemental length,* the "pen" is automatically lowered and sketching continues. Again, this will only work for elements of a sketch which have not yet been recorded. If your record increment is very small, you will find it difficult to make this connection.

. (period)   This will draw a straight line from the end of the previously-drawn sketch line to the current position of the "pen", which must initially be up.

Snap and Ortho settings will still apply in sketch mode. Ortho is very limiting when sketching and should not normally be used. The Snap setting will dominate the record increment so that the "coarseness" of the sketch will be controlled by the Snap setting. There is thus no point in setting the record increment on the sketch to be smaller than the Snap interval if Snap is on.

3.3.1 Calibrating the Digitiser for SKETCH

When using a digitiser in SKETCH mode, the length of line (in drawing units) on the screen is proportional to the distance travelled by the puck on the tablet but this will *not* be an exact 1:1 relationship. It will depend primarily on the size of the screen pointing area as defined on the tablet, (see Section 20.5). Thus, if you wish to use the puck to trace the outline of an object placed on the tablet, the shape will be transferred into your drawing but the size and position on the screen will be arbitrary.

Calibration of the tablet allows you to map the tablet area onto the screen at any suitable scale and position.

Suppose that you have an accurate outline of an irregular object and you wish to transfer this to a *particular position and scale* in an existing drawing.

First, attach the outline to the digitiser tablet, then use the CALibrate option of the TABLET command:

Command: TABLET
ON/OFF/CAL/CFG: CAL

You are then prompted to digitise one point on the outline and type in the coordinates of this point in your drawing. This is repeated for a second point. The tablet is now calibrated. You may notice, depending on the scales involved, that the movement of the cross-wires on the screen is now much reduced - even for full movement of the puck across the tablet surface.

EXAMPLE

If one point of the outline is to be positioned at point 100,150 in the drawing and a second point at 300,350 then:

> **Command:** TABLET
> **ON/OFF/CAL/CFG:** CAL
> **Calibrate tablet for use...**
> **Digitise first known point:**
> **Enter coordinates for first point:** 100,150
> **Digitise second known point:**
> **Enter coordinates for second point:** 300,350

You can now use the SKETCH command in the normal way and the outline will be introduced into the drawing at the correct scale and position. Even if the outline has been attached to the tablet "on the skew", AutoCAD will compensate for this and reproduce the shape squarely into the drawing.

If you wish to return the digitiser to its normal un-calibrated mode, you simply have to switch it Off with the TABLET command. Alternatively, the tablet may be toggled On and Off at any time using the F10 key.

> *Note:* If the digitiser has been configured to allow the use of template menus, (see Section 20.5), only the designated screen pointing area on the digitiser may be used for sketching whether or not you are in calibrated mode. You may digitise points outside this area when setting up the calibration but you will not be able to access them for sketching - they remain reserved for issuing commands from the template menus irrespective of whether TABLET is in the On or the Off state.

4. Aids to construction and simple editing

4.1 AIDS TO CONSTRUCTION

The drawing modes Snap, Grid, Ortho, Axis and Blip etc., are provided as drawing aids to assist you in the construction of drawings. Correct and frequent use of these aids is one of the secrets of getting the most out of AutoCAD. These modes can be toggled On/Off as many times as you like during the drawing but this does *not* affect the default setting. If you wish to change the On/Off defaults you must set the relevant system variables - SNAPMODE, GRIDMODE, ORTHOMODE, AXISMODE and BLIPMODE to 1 or 0.

The drawing modes can all be set by selecting the DRAWING TOOLS option on the **Settings** pull down. This invokes a dialogue box, (see Section 4.1.6).

4.1.1 SNAP

The Snap mode causes an imaginary rectangular grid to be set up, all input coordinates are then locked onto the intersections of this grid. When Snap is in operation you will see that the cross wires "snap" from one intersection point to the next - it is impossible to force them to take up an intermediate position.

Snap allows the input of accurately placed points and the perfect alignment of lines, circle centres and other entities. The size of the imaginary grid (grid spacing) is referred to as the Snap resolution and can be altered at any time. (To make this grid visible, see the GRID command)

The Snap mode may be invoked by typing SNAP:

> **Command:** SNAP
> **Snap spacing or ON/OFF/Aspect/Rotate/Style<10>**

The Snap options are:

ON   The On option invokes the previous Snap grid resolution.

OFF   The Off option deactivates Snap but remembers the settings so that they can be reactivated.

Spacing   If you respond to the Snap option prompt with a numeric input, Snap will be activated using the input as the Snap resolution, e.g. if the value is 10 then the Snap grid will be set up with a resolution of 10 drawing units.

Aspect   The spacings along the x-axis and y-axis are normally equal but they can be independently set using this option. If the aspect option is not invoked the x and y spacings will default to the same value.

Rotate   The Snap grid can be rotated about a designated point between -90 and 90 degrees. A positive angle rotates the grid counter-clockwise whereas a negative angle rotates the grid clockwise.

Style   There are two *Styles* available, Standard and Isometric. Standard refers to the standard rectangular grid. Isometric refers to a grid designed for isometric drawing with grid points aligned at 30, 90, 150, 210 and 330 degrees. (See Chapter 15).

It is not necessary to use the SNAP command simply to switch Snap On and Off - this can be done at any time, even from within another command such as LINE, by toggling either Ctrl B or Function Key F9 or by picking Snap On/Off from the **Settings** pull down. You can easily keep track of the current state of SNAP because, when Snap is On, the word **Snap** is displayed on the status line in the top left-hand corner of the drawing.

4.1.2 GRID

The GRID command displays a reference grid of dots with any desired spacing and is *displayed over the area specified by the limits*. It is usually set up so that the grid dots occur at the Snap intersection points, thus making them visible. The grid is *not* part of the drawing and will not be reproduced when the drawing is plotted or printed out. It is used purely as a drawing aid to give a "feel" for the size of drawing entities.

> **Command:** GRID
> **Grid spacing(X) or ON/OFF/Snap/Aspect<20>**

The main options **Spacing**, **ON**, **OFF** and **Aspect** have the same functions as the Snap options of the same name.

Snap   The Snap option provides a method of locking the grid to the set Snap resolution. If the value of the Snap resolution is altered the grid is automatically changed to the new Snap value. A numerical spacing of 0.000 has the same effect.

It is not necessary to use the GRID command simply to switch Grid On and Off - this can be done at any time, even from within another command, by toggling either Ctrl G or function key F7 or by picking Grid On/Off from the **Settings** pull down.

4.1.3 ORTHO

Ortho mode is used primarily with the LINE, TRACE and PLINE commands. It ensures that all lines are drawn orthogonal with respect to the current Snap grid. Assuming that the Snap style is standard, i.e. the grid has not been rotated, then all lines or traces will be either vertical or horizontal, (see Figure 4.1).

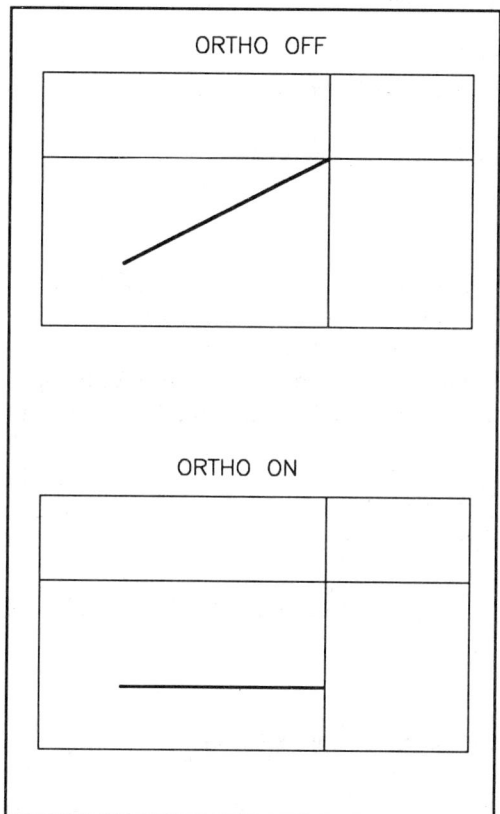

Figure 4.1   ORTHO

If the Snap grid has been rotated then ortho rotates accordingly; the same applies to the "isometric" Snap style mentioned above.

> **Command:** ORTHO
> **ON/OFF:**

Alternatively, Ortho can be toggled using either Ctrl O, function key F8 or by picking Ortho On/Off from the **Settings** pull down. Like Snap, the current state of Ortho is displayed in the top left-hand corner of the drawing.

Ortho is certainly a useful aid but the beginner may well find the behaviour of the elastic band cursor very confusing when Ortho is operative. It is not recommended that Ortho be switched On all the time.

4.1.4 AXIS

The AXIS command can be used to place graduation marks on the drawing axes which, like grid, are helpful in maintaining a feeling for the scale of a drawing. However, again like grid, they are *not* part of the drawing and will not be reproduced on a plot.

> **Command:** AXIS
> **Tick spacing (X) or ON/OFF/Snap/Aspect<0.0000>**

The main options have the same functions as for SNAP.

4.1.5 Blips

The blip mode provides a temporary mark, +, on the screen whenever you pick an object or place a point within the drawing. For example, when drawing a circle, the first requirement is to position the centre point. A blip mark will be placed at this point. It is only temporary and will be erased on REDRAW, REGEN, ZOOM and PAN. Blips are used primarily as construction marks. If you wish you can disable the Blips:

> **Command:** BLIPMODE
> **ON/OFF<current>:**

Alternatively, Blips can be disabled from the DRAWING TOOLS option on the **Settings** pull down.

4.1.6 Setting the Mode using Dialogue boxes

There are six dialogue boxes which may be accessed directly from the keyboard. These fall into two groups, four that give an "at a glance" display of some of the current drawing parameters and provide a very convenient means of changing them within the drawing, and two that are used for editing text and attributes.

The four drawing parameters dialogue boxes may be accessed from the pull down menu, (under **Settings** and **Options**) while the two editing dialogue boxes may be accessed from the screen menu (under **Edit**). All dialogue boxes may be accessed from the keyboard.

Menu Item		*Keyboard Command*	*Options*
Drawing Tools (Figure 4.2)		DDRMODES	Grid Snap Ortho Axis Blip
Entity Creation (Figure 4.3)		DDEMODES	Colour Layer name Linetype Text style Elevation Thickness
Layer Control (Figure 4.4)		DDLMODES	On/Off Freeze/Thaw New Set Colour . Linetype
UCS Control (Figure 4.5)		DDUCS	User Coordinate System Data
DDATTE	(Figure 4.6)	DDATTE	Attribute editing
DDEDIT	(Figure 4.7)	DDEDIT	Text and attribute definition editing

The Drawing Tools dialogue box (DDRMODES) gives immediate access to the Snap, Grid, Ortho, Axis and Blip modes and is probably the most convenient way to modify their values. If you wish to toggle one of the mode settings, move the screen arrow to the relevant section of the dialogue box and press the pick button to set the tick symbol. When you are satisfied with all the mode settings you must tick the OK box to return to the drawing.

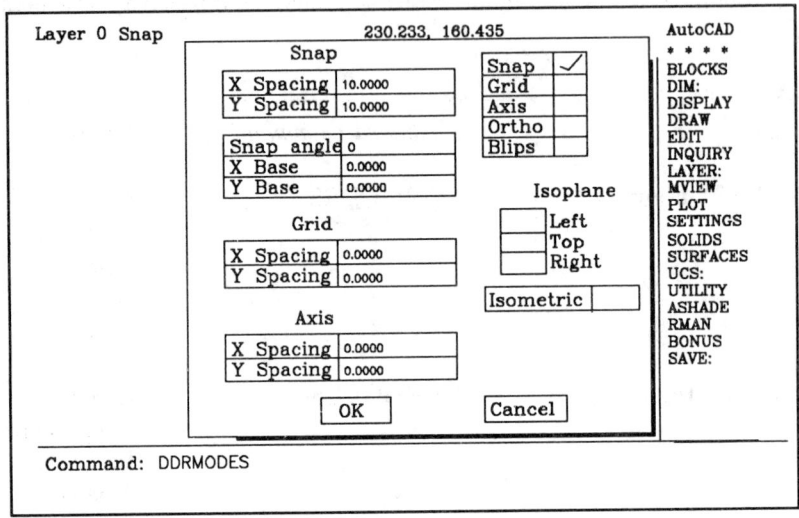

Figure 4.2 Drawing Tools dialogue box

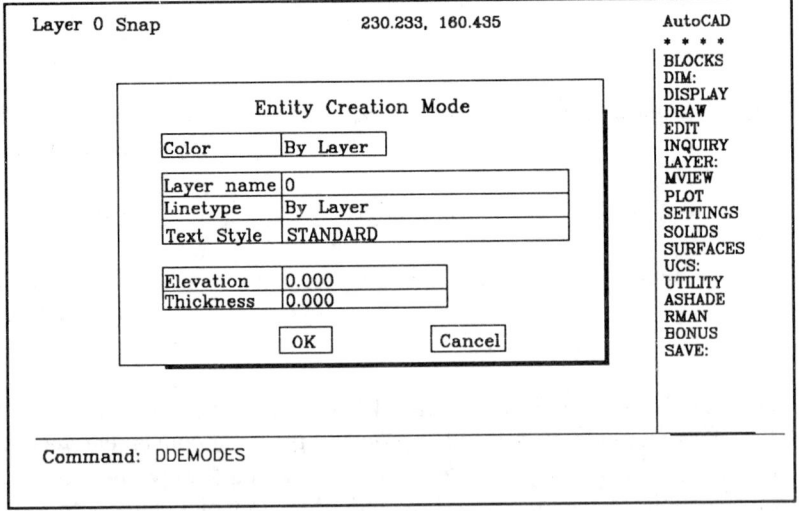

Figure 4.3 Entity Creation dialogue box

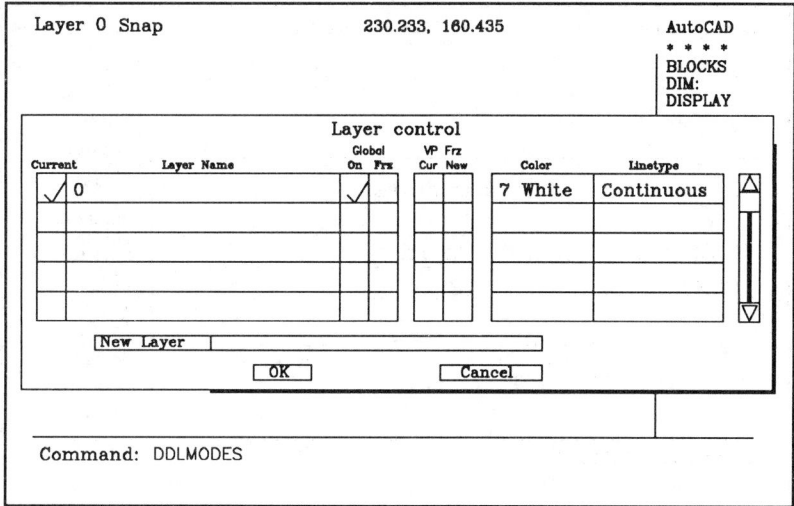

Figure 4.4 Layer Control dialogue box

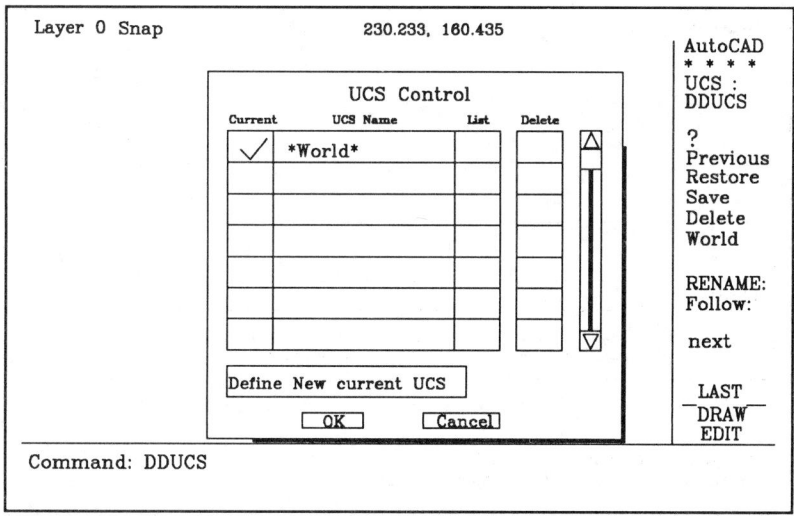

Figure 4.5 UCS dialogue box

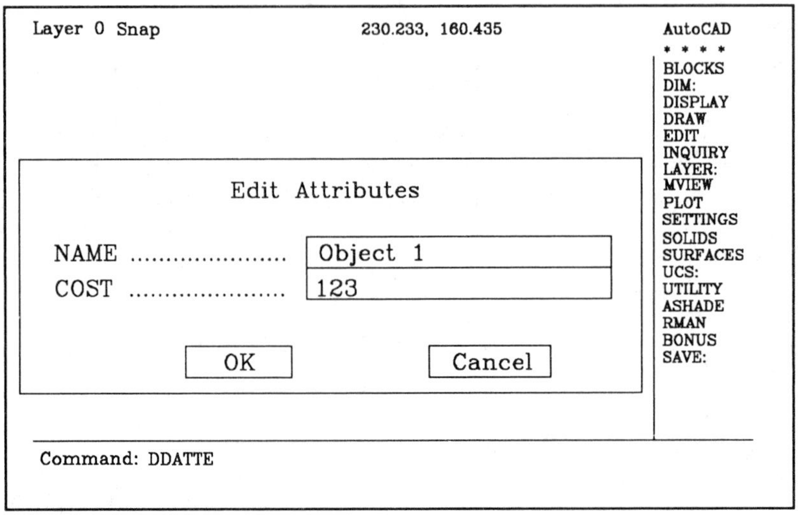

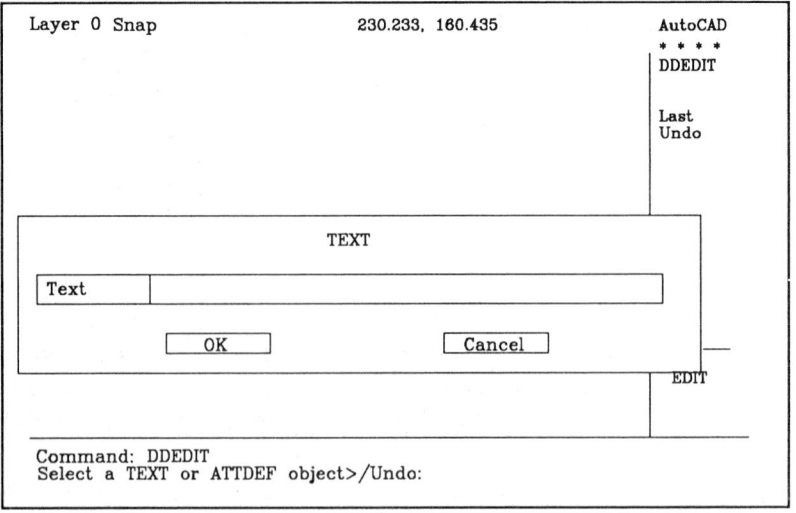

Figure 4.6   Attribute Edit dialogue box

Figure 4.7   Text Editing dialogue box

The drawing parameters dialogue boxes (with the exception of DDUCS) when selected from the pull downs can be accessed at any time, even when using another command. They are *transparent* commands, (see section 3.4.4).

4.1.7 Setting and Saving a Mode

If you wish to make a more permanent change to Snap, Grid, Ortho, Axis and Blip, then type the corresponding system variables SNAPMODE, GRIDMODE, ORTHOMODE, AXISMODE and BLIPMODE and make the desired changes. These changes will then be saved with the drawing, whereas changes made via the commands SNAP, GRID, ORTHO etc., or via a dialogue box, are only temporary.

4.2 SIMPLE EDITING

4.2.1 Selecting Objects

When editing a drawing it is necessary first to select the objects which are to be edited. AutoCAD has a number of different selection modes including:

- Pointing to a specific object
- Using one of the window commands (window or crossing; see Figure 4.8)
- Selecting the last object drawn
- Selecting a set of previously selected objects.

When any of the editing commands is invoked AutoCAD automatically drops into its SELECT routine to allow you to build up a *selection set*. The cross wires are temporarily replaced by a small square called the Pickbox. The size of this box may be adjusted by altering the value of the system variable PICKBOX.

When assembling a selection set, the command line gives the prompt:

Select objects:

picking   Whenever the select objects routine is invoked, a small square box appears instead of the cross wires; this can be moved around the screen with the mouse, "picking" the objects to be selected. As always, keep an eye on the command line - this will tell you when an object has been selected, when it is a duplicate selection and so on. The select routine will allow you to continue indefinitely until you turn it Off with a return. This signifies that the selection set is complete.

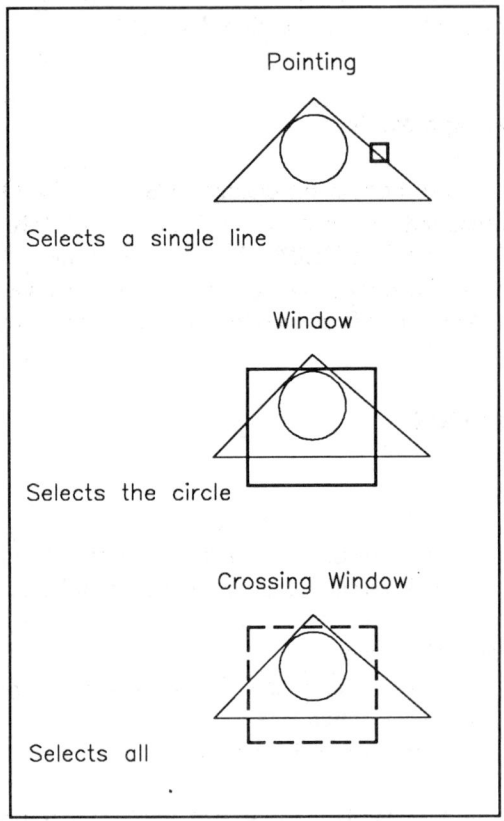

Figure 4.8 Selecting entities

Remove	An R at the **Select objects:** prompt changes the prompt to **Remove objects:** and allows you to remove subsequently-selected objects from the selection set. This is useful if you have included some objects by mistake.
Add	After removing objects from a selection set you can return to the default **Select objects:** prompt, Addition mode, by entering an A.
Undo	If an object(s) is selected by mistake its selection can be cancelled by using Undo. This may be applied repeatedly to step back and undo previous selections.
Window	Entering a W at the **Select objects:** prompt allows the user to use the mouse to specify two opposite corners of a window. Any objects *totally*

enclosed by this window will be selected and you will then be returned to point selection mode so that further selection can continue.

Crossing Entering a C at the **Select objects:** prompt again allows the user to specify two corners of a window. Any objects *enclosed or touched* by the crossing window will be selected, after which you will be returned to point mode. The Crossing window is displayed as a dashed box to differentiate it from the standard window.

Last Entering an L at the **Select objects:** prompt automatically selects the last object drawn.

Previous Entering a P at the **Select objects:** prompt selects the previous selection set.

BOX Inputting BOX at the **Select objects:** prompt lets the user specify two corners of a window (as for Window and Crossing). If the second point is to the right of the first then a standard window is invoked, if it is to the left then a crossing window is invoked.

AUto Inputting AU at the **Select objects:** prompt puts the select mode into automatic selection mode. A point is first requested for a single object selection. If no object is found when the pick button is pressed then the point selected will become the first corner of the BOX sub-command, (see Figure 4.9).

Note: If the select routine is invoked within a command called from a Pull Down menu you may find that a full selection set is not built up before the main command is executed. Selection and execution are repeated as often as required. As explained earlier, this is because the command from this menu is operated as a mini programme and uses more than the "raw" AutoCAD commands.

4.2.2 ERASE

The ERASE command allows specific entities to be removed from the drawing.

Command: ERASE
Select objects: Assemble the desired selection set

Erase is a clear example of a command which behaves differently when invoked from a pull down, compared with simply typing the command from the command line. When

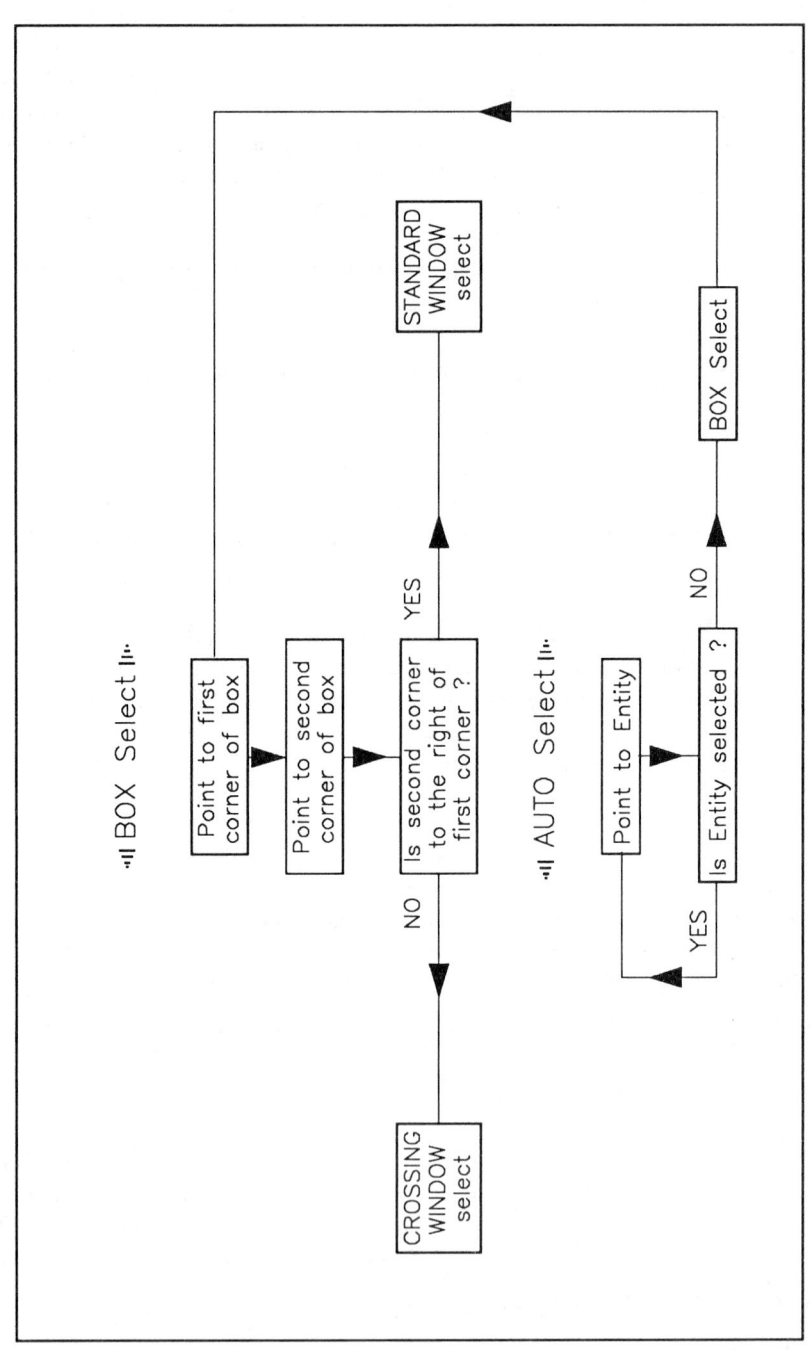

Figure 4.9 Box and Auto selection

called from the pull down, each selected sub-set is erased as soon as it is chosen (by pointing or windowing etc.) and then the **Select objects:** prompt returns to allow further selection. Auto mode is the normal mode in this case. Last can be used to erase the last entity to be drawn; if it is repeated then you can step back through the drawing, erasing entities in the reverse order to that in which they were drawn.

If ERASE is invoked from the keyboard, objects selected for erasure are assembled into a selection set and are only erased following a return.

4.2.3 OOPS

The OOPS command restores entities which have been inadvertently ERASED. OOPS will only be effective if invoked *immediately* after an ERASE command.

4.2.4 U and UNDO

The simplest way to undo an error is to use the command U. This simply undoes the previously executed command.

Command: U

AutoCAD responds with the name of the previously executed command.

The UNDO command, which can be selected from the **Utilities** pull down menu or from the **Edit** screen menu, is more comprehensive than the U command and in some ways is over complicated.

Command: UNDO
Auto/Back/Control/End/Group/Mark/<Number>:

If you wish step backwards through the drawing undoing one command at a time then it is sufficient to respond repeatedly with returns (this is the same as repeated use of the U command).

Alternatively, you may undo a specified number of previous commands at a single stroke by responding to the above prompt with the required number.

All previous commands may be undone in a single operation by responding with Back. This in effect completely erases any new drawing produced under *Task 1* of the main menu or any new modifications to an existing drawing introduced under *Task 2*. As such, this is an extremely powerful aspect of the UNDO command and should be used with care. If you wish to limit the scope of the Back option, then you may insert a Mark at any point during the construction of a drawing and this will act as a stop beyond which UNDO Back is inoperative.

Control may be used to limit the scope of the UNDO command so that it may either be totally disabled or limited to a single operation. End and Group are little used except in customized menu writing.

4.2.5 REDO

REDO is only active after an UNDO or U has been performed. It may be used to recover those commands which were removed by the *single preceding* UNDO or U command.

4.2.6 MOVE

The MOVE command allows the movement of entities from one position on the drawing to another. Once the objects to be moved have been selected Autocad will ask for two points of displacement, these are the **Base point** (move from) and the **Second point** (move to).

> **Command:** MOVE
> **Select objects:**   Assemble the desired selection set
> **Base point or displacement:**
> **Second point of displacement:**

If you respond to **Base point** with DRAG this allows you to drag the selected objects around the drawing to the correct position if the DRAGMODE system variable is set to ON. If the DRAGMODE system variable is set to AUTO, drag will be invoked automatically. (See Section 4.3.2.) If a null response is given at the second prompt and the **Base point or displacement** is given as an XYZ coordinate, then this will be interpreted as an XYZ displacement.

4.2.7 COPY

The COPY command is similar to the MOVE command but instead of moving the selected objects around the drawing it places copies of the selected object(s) at the specified point(s), leaving the original(s) intact.

> **Command:** COPY
> **Select objects:**   Assemble the desired selection set
> **Base point or displacement>/Multiple:**
> **Second point of displacement:**

Each copy is totally independent of the original and can be edited etc., as if drawn as a separate entity, (see Figure 4.10).

Multiple copies of the selected objects can be made by answering Multiple after the objects have been chosen. Repeated copies of the selected items can then be positioned throughout the drawing. As with the MOVE command, if a null response is given at the second prompt and the **Base point or displacement** is given as an XYZ coordinate, then this will be interpreted as an XYZ displacement.

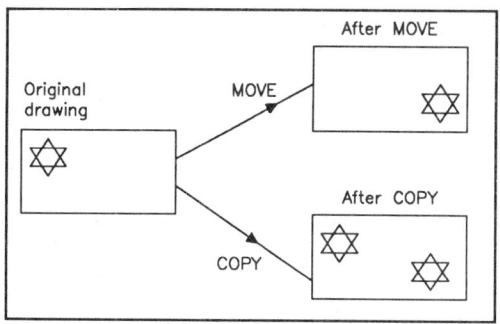

Figure 4.10 COPY and MOVE commands

4.2.8 ROTATE

Entities can be rotated about a specified point by a specified number of degrees.

> **Command:** ROTATE
> **Select objects:** Assemble the desired selection set
> **Base point:** This is the point about which rotation will occur
> **<Rotation angle>/Reference:**

A positive angle will rotate the selected objects counter-clockwise. Responding with an R invokes reference mode which allows the specification of a reference or base angle. The new value of this angle is then supplied and AutoCAD calculates the degree of rotation necessary to achieve this.

4.2.9 MIRROR

The MIRROR command allows mirror images of selected objects to be made, while allowing the original objects to remain or be erased as required.

> **Command:** MIRROR
> **Select objects:** Assemble the desired selection set
> **First point of mirror line:**
> **Second point:**
> **Delete old objects?<N>**

The mirror line represents the axis about which the objects are mirrored and can be at any orientation. The selected object(s) may be deleted or left in its original position as required.

If an object and its connected text are mirrored then the text will also be a mirror image of the original and so will not be much use. To mirror objects and their connected text but keeping the text readable, set the MIRRTEXT system variable to 0 (default value = 1), see Figure 4.11.

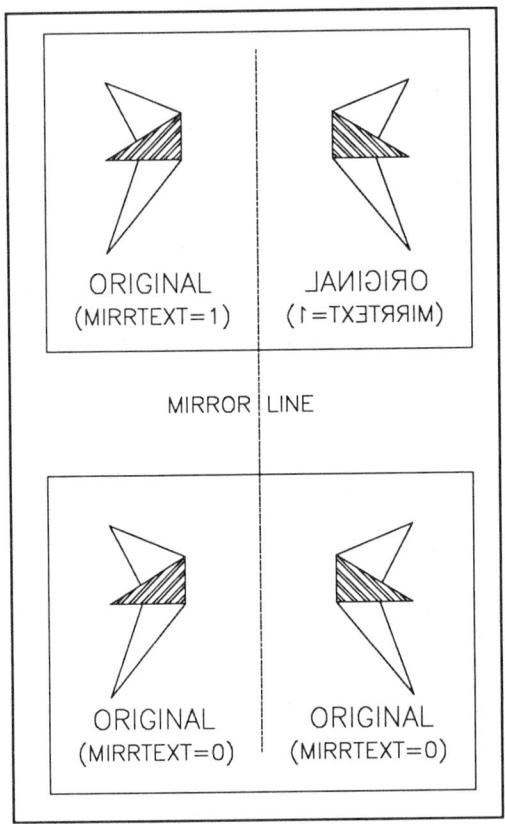

Figure 4.11 The effect of the MIRRTEXT system variable

4.3 PEDIT - THE SPECIAL POLYLINE EDIT COMMAND

The special command PEDIT is used to edit polylines in the following way:

- Change the width of the entire polyline.
- Change the width or taper of individual segments of a polyline.
- Open a closed polyline, or close an open polyline.
- Straighten lines and arcs between two specified points.
- Break the polyline into two or more segments.
- Join individual polylines to make one single polyline.
- Move a selected vertex or add a new one.
- Curve fit.
- Convert a non-polyline into a polyline.

Polyline editing is accessed by the PEDIT command:

Command: PEDIT
Select Polyline:

The chosen line will be checked to see whether it is a polyline; if it is not you will be asked if you wish to change it into a polyline. Once a polyline has been selected the following prompt will be displayed:

Close/Join/Width/Edit vertex/Fit curve/Spline curve/Decurve/Undo/eXit <X>:

Close   If the chosen polyline is "open" then the Close sub-command effects the true closing of the polyline. Even a polyline which has been drawn to start and finish at the same point is considered "open". In this case applying Close will have no *visible* effect but the polyline will now be treated as a closed figure. When a polyline is closed the Open sub-command will be displayed at the prompt in place of Close, (see Figure 4.12).

Join   Allows the joining of arcs, lines and other polylines to the selected polyline, (see Figure 4.13). The selected objects to be joined must be positioned *exactly* at one endpoint of the selected polyline. Lines meeting a polyline to form a T will not be joined. Join will not work with closed polylines.

Width   Allows the polyline to be given a new overall width, (see Figure 4.14).

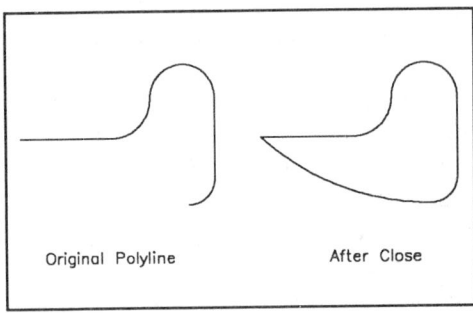

Figure 4.12 Closing a polyline

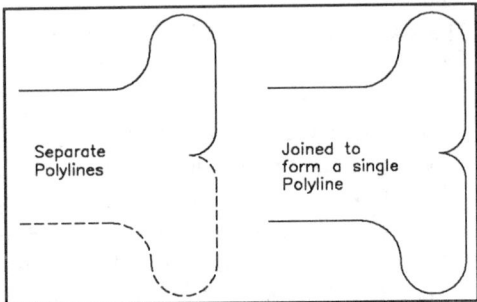

Figure 4.13 Joining polylines

Fit curve   A smooth curve is fitted to the polyline vertices, (see Figure 4.15). This can be edited using the Edit vertex sub-command.

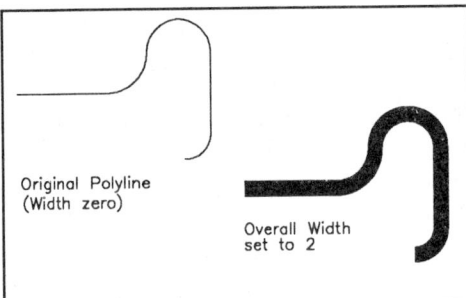

Figure 4.14 Width adjustment

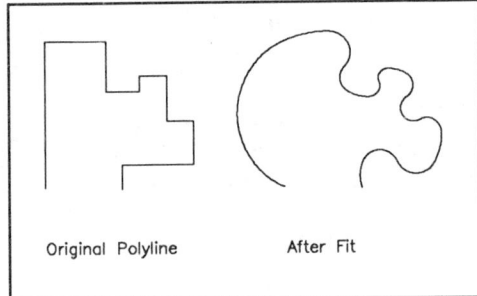

Figure 4.15 Smoothing

Spline curve There are two spline curve options available, quadratic and cubic, controlled by the system variable SPLINETYPE (5=quadratic and 6=cubic). Each produces a far more accurate curve than the one produced by the Fit curve command, (see Figure 4.16). The vertices are used as control points, the curve passing through the first and last points. It is pulled towards the other points but not necessarily through them. The more points the more accurate the curve. The system variable SPLINESEGS controls the number of line segments generated to produce the curve (default=6). Setting the system variable SPLFRAME to 1 allows the original polyline to be displayed in addition to the spline curve. The above system variables may be accessed from an icon menu by picking Polyvars from the PEDIT screen menu. (See Figure 16.48).

Decurve   Reverses the Fit curve and Spline curve sub-commands.

Undo Undoes the last PEDIT sub-command. By repeating this sub-command you are allowed to step back through the PEDIT sub-commands.

eXit Exit from the PEDIT command.

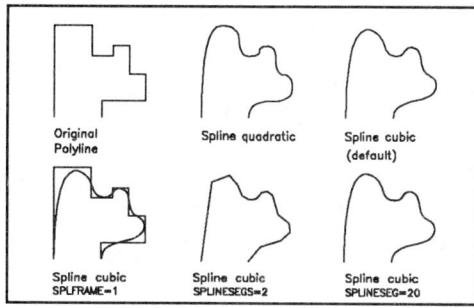

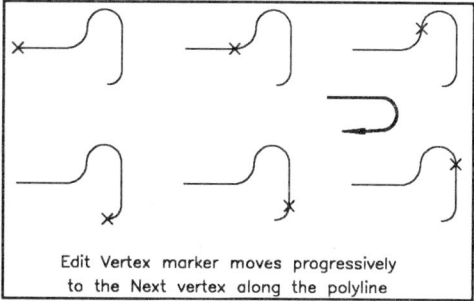

Figure 4.16 Spline curve options   **Figure 4.17** Edit vertex marker

Edit vertex When using this option a cross will be drawn on the first vertex of the selected polyline, (see Figure 4.17) and the following prompt will be displayed:

Next/Previous/Break/Insert/Move/Regen/Straighten/Tangent/Width/eXit <N>:

Next Moves the cross to the next vertex.

Previous Moves the cross to the previous vertex.

Break Splits the polyline into two at the selected vertex. A new sub-menu is now displayed:

Next/Previous/Go/eXit <N>:

The **eXit** sub-command effectively cancels Break. The **Go** sub-command results in an invisible break at the selected vertex. **Next/Previous** will move the cross to an adjacent vertex; a **Go** will now result in the section of the polyline between the initial and the current cross positions being deleted, (see Figure 4.18).

Insert Allows the insertion of a new vertex into the selected polyline, (see Figure 4.19).

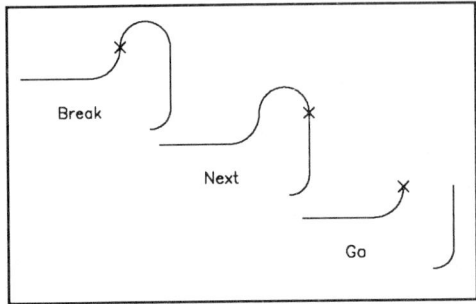

Figure 4.18 Stages in breaking a polyline

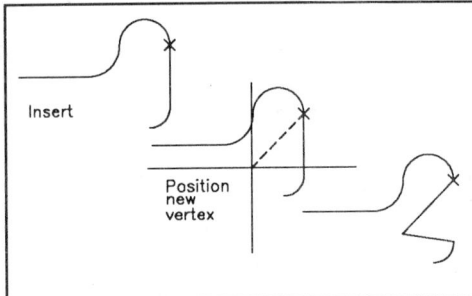

Figure 4.19 Inserting an extra vertex

Move   Allows the movement of the currently selected vertex to a new position, (see Figure 4.20).

Regen   Regenerates the polyline, removing construction lines etc.

Straighten   Allows the straightening of the section of a polyline between selected vertices, (see Figure 4.21). As with the Break sub-command, a new sub-menu is displayed to allow selection of the relevant vertices.

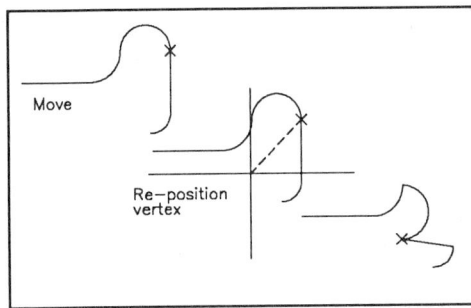

Figure 4.20 Moving an existing vertex

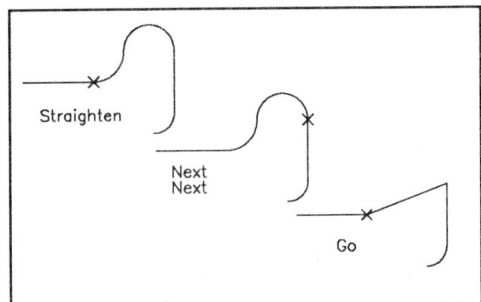

Figure 4.21 Stages in straightening a polylines

Tangent   Allows the input of a tangent direction to use with the curve fitting option.

Width   Allows the changing of width for the segment *following* the marked vertex. To see the result of this command the **Regen** command must be given, (see Figure 4.22).

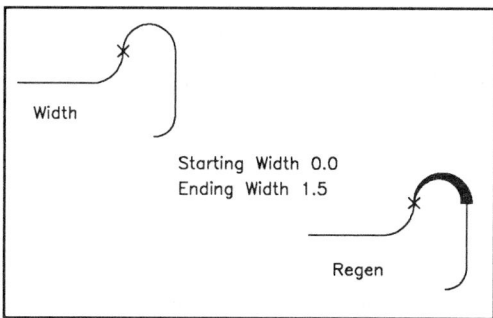

Figure 4.22 Altering the width of a segment

4.3.1 EXPLODE

EXPLODE is a special command used with blocks, dimensions, meshes and polylines. After EXPLODE has been executed the constituents will no longer be a single entity but will now be treated as individual entities. For example, when a polyline is exploded, it will be reduced to its basic line and arc entities and all information about the original polyline, such as its width, will be discarded - the resulting lines and arcs will follow the old centre line.

Command: EXPLODE
Select block reference, polyline, dimension or mesh:

4.3.2 DRAGMODE

DRAGMODE is used in conjunction with editing commands such as COPY, MOVE, SCALE, ROTATE etc., and also with some of the drawing commands e.g. CIRCLE, ARC or PLINE. It allows *dynamic dragging* of the chosen object about the drawing area to the required position.

Command: DRAGMODE
ON/OFF/Auto<Auto>:

If DRAGMODE is set to Auto it will automatically be invoked when a command is used which supports drag. In some instances, depending on the speed of your computer, the process of dragging can be time-consuming. Under these circumstances DRAGMODE can be set to On; it will only then be activated if the sub-command Drag is executed within a command which supports it.
The initial setting of the DRAGMODE system variable is governed by the default value, which is set by the prototype drawing.

5. Display controls

As their name implies, the display controls allow you to alter the way a drawing is displayed on the screen. They *do not* alter the drawing itself - in particular, the size of the drawing in terms of drawing units will be unchanged.

5.1 REDRAWING AND REGENERATION

5.1.1 REDRAW

This causes the redrawing of the *current* screen display, deleting any blips present and redrawing objects which have been partially erased from the screen (but not from the drawing) due to editing of other objects.

5.1.2 REGEN

This completely regenerates the entire drawing by recalculating the positions of all the component entities and adjusts the resolution to suit the current screen "magnification". Regeneration will in some cases be performed automatically as a consequence of using other display commands such as ZOOM. (This feature may be disabled by use of the REGENAUTO command)

> **Command:** REGENAUTO
> **ON/OFF <On>:** OFF

5.1.3 REDRAWALL AND REGENALL

The normal REDRAW and REGEN commands will only work on the *active viewport*, (see Section 5.5). If you require all the current viewports to be redrawn then use the REDRAWALL command. To regenerate all the current viewports use REGENALL.

5.2 ZOOM

The ZOOM command allows areas of the current drawing to be either increased or decreased in size on the screen while maintaining the original dimensions. By increasing the apparent size of an object you view a smaller area of the drawing; decreasing the apparent size allows you to view a larger area of the drawing.

ZOOM may be called up from the keyboard by typing ZOOM:

> **Command:** ZOOM
> **All/Center/Dynamic/Extents/Left/Previous/Vmax/Window/<Scale(X/XP)>:**

Alternatively, ZOOM may be called from the screen or pull down menus, in which case the number of options offered will be slightly different but the basic ZOOM functions will be the same.

The various ZOOM options are:

All   Changes the display so that the complete drawing as defined by the current drawing LIMITS is shown on the screen.

Center   Allows the entry of the centre point of the region to be displayed. The height of the new display can be entered which in effect magnifies the display about the specified centre point, (see Figure 5.1).

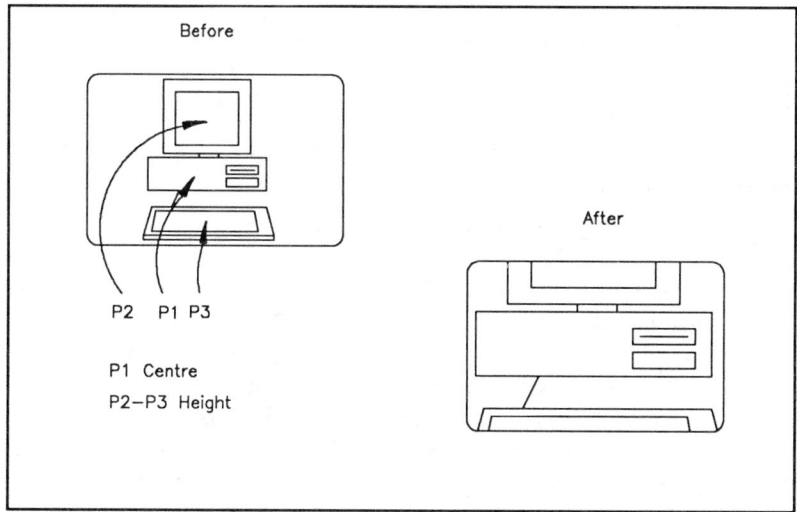

Figure 5.1   ZOOM centre

Command: ZOOM
All/Center/Dynamic/.........Nmax/Window/<Scale(X)>: C
Center point:
Magnification or Height <default>:

Dynamic　When ZOOM Dynamic is used various boxes are drawn on the screen. The drawing extents will be surrounded by a box made up of a continuous line, whereas the generated area (area which may be viewed at high speed) is surrounded by four corners. If a zoom of the original drawing was previously in operation then a box made up of dotted lines will also appear on the screen indicating the area previously zoomed. If not, then the four corners will be joined by dotted lines showing that the generated area was the previous view, (see Figure 5.2).

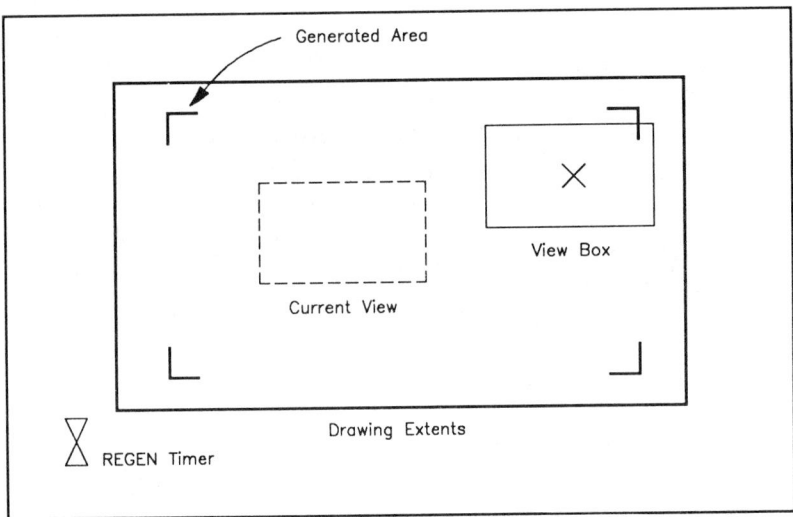

Figure 5.2　ZOOM dynamic

A view box (containing a cross) the same size as the current screen will initially be displayed, and can be moved to any part of the drawing. To adjust the size of the view box press the pick button on the mouse and an arrow will appear against the right hand side of the box. Moving the mouse now sets the size of this box; pressing the pick button a second time fixes the size and allows the movement of the view box to the part of the drawing to be zoomed. To zoom to the chosen area, press the return key on the keyboard. If the viewbox is positioned outside the generated area then an hourglass symbol will appear in the bottom left hand corner indicating that a regeneration of the display will occur.

Note: One of the main benefits of using ZOOM Dynamic is that the width/height ratio of the box sides exactly corresponds to that of the screen with the result that the appearance of the display after zoom can be accurately predicted.

Extents　　The ZOOM Extents mode zooms the complete current drawing to the *largest possible size* to fill the screen.

Left　　ZOOM Left is the same as ZOOM Center but instead of specifying the centre point of the zoomed window the lower left corner is specified, (see Figure 5.3).

> **Command: ZOOM**
> **All/........./Left/..../Window/<Scale(X)>: L**
> **Lower left corner point:**
> **Magnification or Height <default>:**

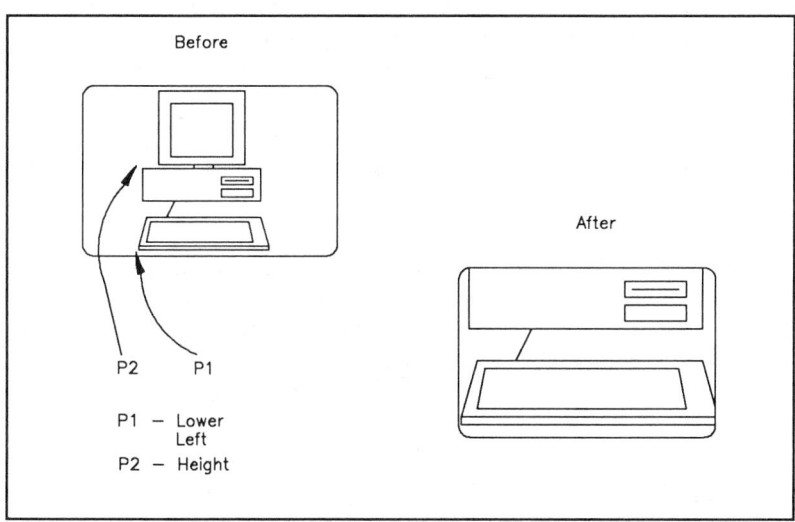

Figure 5.3　ZOOM left

Previous　　ZOOM Previous is useful as it allows the operator to return to previous views of the drawing. ZOOM Previous can be used sequentially to return through the previously executed ZOOM and PAN commands, up to a maximum of ten.

Vmax   ZOOM Vmax allows you to zoom out as far as possible without forcing
                  a regeneration.

Window   The window command is probably the most frequently used of all the
                  ZOOM commands. It prompts for input of two corners of the ZOOM
                  Window, either by coordinate entry from the keyboard or, more usually,
                  from the mouse. The window can be any size and in any position on the
                  drawing.

> **Command: ZOOM**
> **All/Center/........./Window/<Scale(X/XP)>: W**
> **First corner:**
> **Other corner:**

Note: Because the shape of the window can be varied at will and may
not correspond to the shape of the screen, the display following ZOOM
Window may contain some entities in addition to those selected.

Scale   The scale command allows the input of a single value which is the
                  magnification factor *relative to the complete drawing*, i.e. if a factor of
                  1 is used then the complete drawing will be displayed on the screen, a
                  factor of 2 will double the size of the drawing whereas a factor of 0.5
                  will halve the size of the drawing.
                       If the magnification value is followed by an X, the scaling will be
                  computed for the *current view on screen* and not the complete drawing.
                  It follows that repeated use of Scale(X) will continuously reduce or
                  increase the size of the current view.
                       When the scale option is chosen, AutoCAD will re-display the
                  zoomed view relative to the centre point of the previous view and
                  therefore objects at the edge of the drawing could well be forced out of
                  view, off the edge of the screen.
                       The use of scale as described above applies only to model space.
                  When working in Paper Space the X is replaced by XP, (see Chapter
                  13).

5.2.1 Transparent ZOOM

A transparent command is one which can be used while another command is in
operation. For instance, transparent ZOOM could be used within the LINE command
to enable the second point of a line to be positioned with greater accuracy. This is *very*
useful. To make ZOOM transparent the command should be prefixed by an apostrophe:

Command: LINE
From point: Point to start position
To point: 'ZOOM   The apostrophe denotes transparent mode
>>Center/Dynamic/Left/Previous/Vmax/Window/<Scale(X/XP)>: W
>>First corner: >>Other corner:
Resuming LINE command.
To point: Point to next line point

Transparent commands cannot always be used. If the command requires a regeneration of the drawing then the transparent command will be ignored. ZOOM Dynamic is useful in this respect because there is a visual warning given when a regeneration will be required.

5.3 PAN

The PAN command allows you to move about a drawing without changing the magnification, i.e. objects that are not visible (off the screen) can be panned into view or, conversely, a clear area of screen can be obtained. The direction and distance which the drawing moves is called the displacement and is entered, either as a relative displacement by typing in the corresponding X and Y displacement values followed by a return, or as two separate coordinate points; the drawing is panned from the first point to the second, (see Figure 5.4).

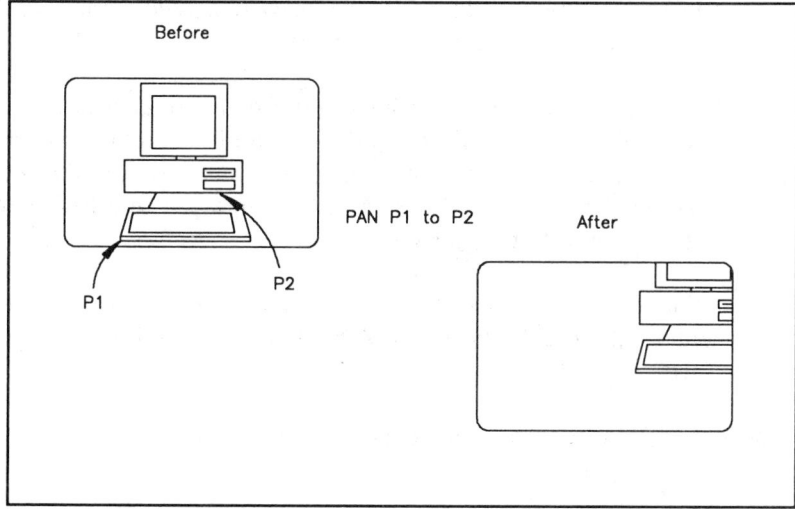

Figure 5.4   PAN

Command: PAN
Displacement: Enter first coordinates
Second point: A return indicates a relative displacement

or

Command: PAN
Displacement: Enter first coordinates
Second point: Enter second coordinates

Input of the coordinates can be made through the keyboard or via the mouse. PAN can be made transparent by using an apostrophe prefix, i.e. 'PAN.

5.4 VIEW

When a large drawing is being undertaken it is often very useful to be able to call up specific views of the drawing. VIEW permits a specified area of the drawing on the screen to be nominated and this view can then be recalled at any time.

Command: VIEW
?/Delete/Restore/Save/Window:
View name:

?   Lists the names of all the saved views relating to the current drawing.

Delete   Deletes a currently saved view.

Restore   Changes the current display to the view requested, assuming that the view requested has previously been saved.

Save   The area of the drawing which you require to save has first to be displayed on the screen as it is the screen display which will be saved for later retrieval. If the name you give to this view already exists then the new view replaces it. Once saved the view can be called at any time - it is saved with the drawing file.

Window   Window allows a specified area of the screen display to be saved without the need to invoke a ZOOM command followed by a VIEW Save.

Like ZOOM and PAN, VIEW can also be used transparently.

5.5 VIEWPORTS

The VPORTS command allows you to split the viewing screen into a number of separate areas, each of which can contain a different view of the current drawing. The maximum number of viewing areas is 16. When the VPORTS command is invoked one of the viewports created will be the "active" viewport, identified by the presence of the cross wires. Moving the cursor into one of the other viewports produces the arrow symbol instead of the cross wires. It is possible to modify any view of the current drawing in any of the defined viewports by taking the cursor into the required viewport and pressing the pick button - the cross wires appear in this viewport indicating that it is now active.

A major feature of viewports is that any modifications made to the drawing are automatically reflected in all viewports. In addition it is possible to work in more than one viewport, e.g. a line may be started in one viewport and terminated in another.

There are two ways of accessing the VPORTS command; from the command line, and from the screen menu under Settings. From the command line:

Command: VPORTS
Save/Restore/Delete/Join/SIngle/?/2/<3>/4:

Save   Saves the current viewport configuration under a user-defined name.

Restore   Restores a previously saved viewport configuration.

Delete   Deletes a previously saved viewport configuration.

Join   Converts two adjacent viewports into a single larger viewport. The drawing resident in the active (dominant) viewport will be drawn in the single viewport. AutoCAD prompts:

        Select dominant viewport <current>:
        Select viewport to join: select an adjacent viewport

SIngle   Returns to the standard single viewport mode.

?   Returns a list of the current and saved viewports. This list is made up of the name of the saved viewports together with the special coordinates used to define each individual viewport. These special coordinates use the convention 0,0 for the bottom left hand corner of the screen and 1,1 for top right corner. Thus 0,0 .5,1 and .5,0 1,1 describes the two viewports obtained by equally dividing the screen vertically, (see Figure 5.5).

2   Splits the active viewport into half - either vertically or horizontally.

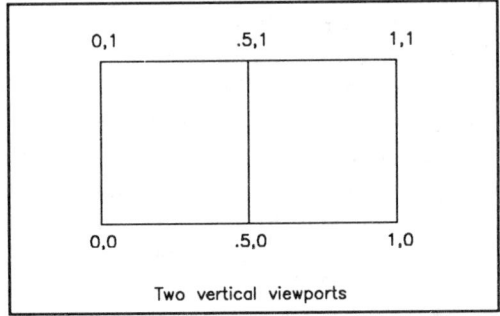

Two vertical viewports

Figure 5.5   Viewport coordinate notation

3   Divides the active viewport into three areas. AutoCAD prompts:

Horizontal/Vertical/Above/Below/Left/<Right>:

Horizontal and Vertical divide the area into three equal viewports. Above and Below divide the area horizontally into three - one large and two small. Left and Right divide the area vertically into three - again one large and two small. (See Figure 5.6.)

4   Divides the screen into four equal viewports.

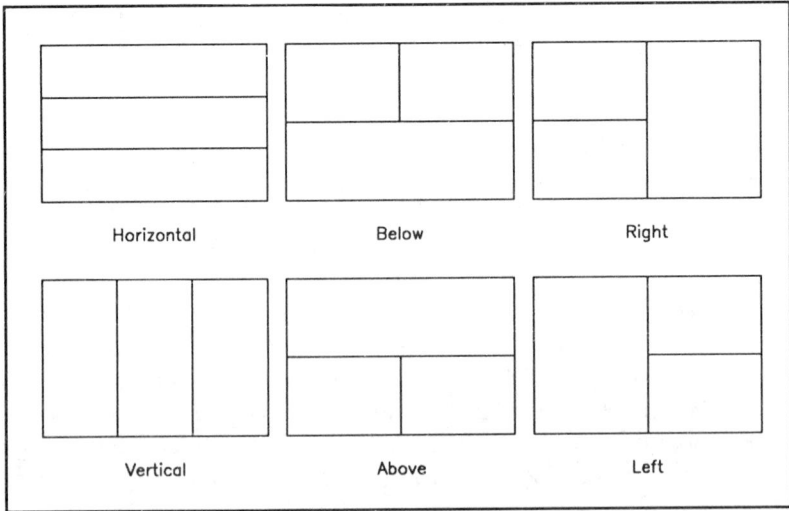

Figure 5.6   Triple viewport definition

6. Additional editing and inquiry commands

6.1 ADVANCED EDITING

6.1.1 SCALE

This command enables you to change the *size* of existing entities by evenly scaling in both X- and Y- directions.

> **Command:** SCALE
> **Select objects:**   Assemble the desired selection set
> **Base point:**   Give base point
> **<Scale factor>/Reference:**   Input numerical scale or pick a second point

The default response must be a numerical scale factor. To reduce the object in size the scale factor must lie between 0 and 1; to enlarge it the scale factor must be greater than 1, (see Figure 6.1). The mouse may also be used to give the scale. Pick a point - the number of drawing units between that point and the Base point defines the scale factor.

The same result may be achieved with less accuracy by dragging using the mouse. Remember that scaling is applied equally in the X- and the Y- directions, so it is not possible to change an object's shape - such as changing an ellipse into a circle - using SCALE.

The alternative response to **Scale factor** is **Reference**. This simply performs the scale factor calculation for you. If you enter an existing length (either numerically or by pointing) followed by the desired new length (again you may point or "drag" if you prefer) then the correct scaling is performed automatically, (see Figure 6.2). This is very useful for scaling an entire drawing to a desired final size.

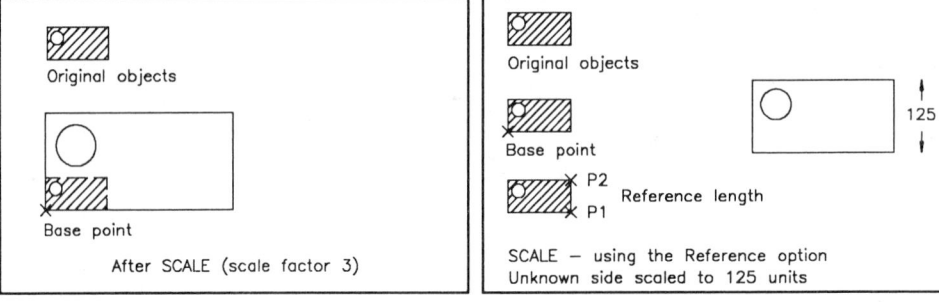

Figure 6.1   Scaling   Figure 6.2   SCALE: reference point

EXAMPLE

<Scale factor>/Reference: R
Reference length: 525
New length: 125

This will apply the correct reduction factor of 0.2381 to the selected objects.

6.1.2 STRETCH

This very useful command allows you to move a group of objects around within a drawing while at the same time stretching or compressing any lines, arcs, traces, solids or polylines which connect the group to the rest of the drawing. Such connecting lines behave as if they were elastic bands while the objects of the group remain unaltered. (See Figure 6.3.)

The command is simple in operation but the syntax used can be confusing.

Command: STRETCH
Select objects to stretch by window... C

This is the confusing bit. The selected objects form the group to be *moved* - these objects are not in fact "stretched". Also, you *must* use a window to select the group but do not respond with the standard W for Window. This would not select the entities joining the group to the rest of the drawing and STRETCH would not work. Instead you should *always* type C for Crossing window.

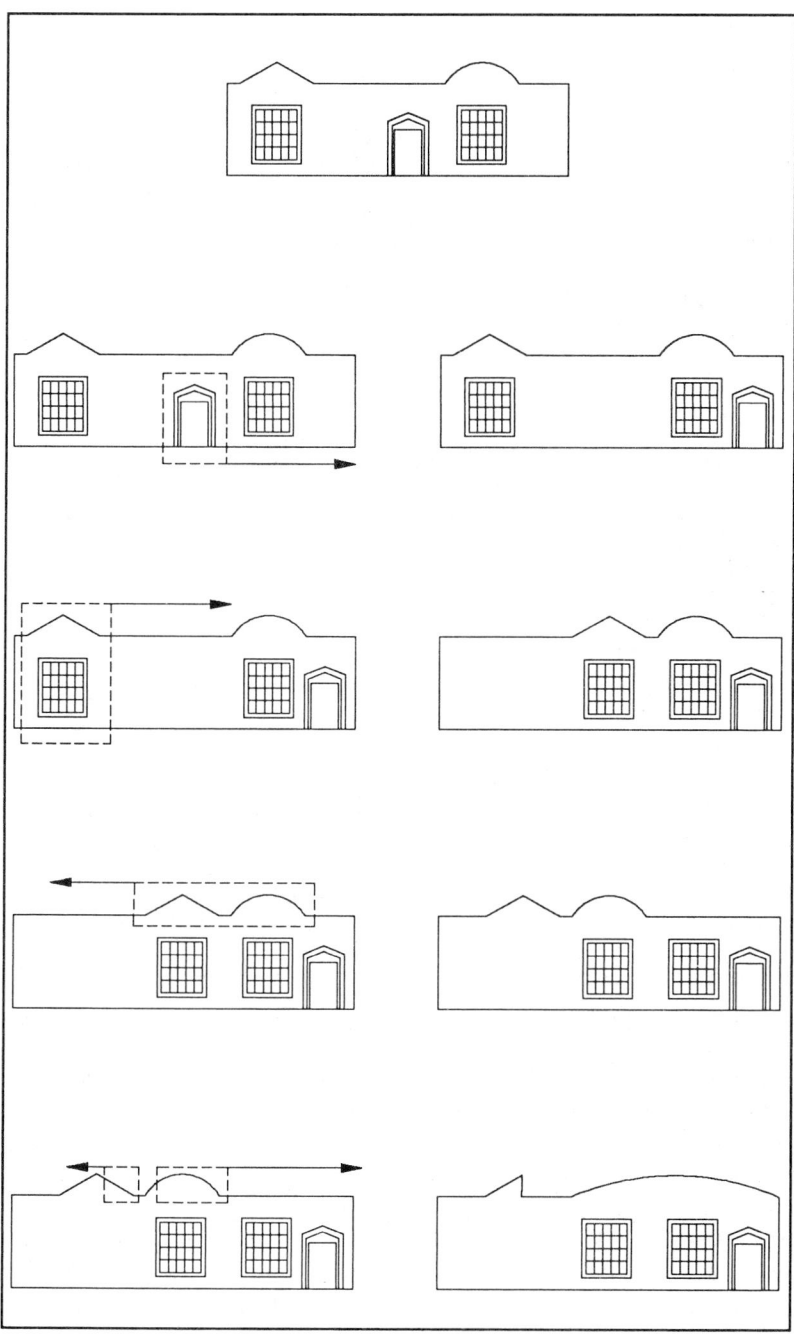

Figure 6.3   Using STRETCH to transform a drawing

Select objects:

This is the standard object selection prompt which will be repeated until you press return.

It is not normally needed unless you have used the standard Window selection mode in which case you must now point to every line crossing the Window boundary.

Base point:

Select a convenient base point relevant to the group to be moved

New point:

Specify final position of the group. You may use "drag" to observe the effect.

Entities other than lines, arcs, traces, solids or polylines are not affected by STRETCH - they are either moved, if their *definition point* lies within the specified window, or they are left alone. The definition point is the centre of a circle, the location point of a point, the insertion point of a block or shape and the left-hand end of the base line of any text or attribute definition.

6.1.3 TRIM

It is often difficult to ensure that two objects meet each other exactly without any overshoot. With TRIM this is made easy. One of the objects must be considered as a cutting edge acting on the other.

```
Command: TRIM
Select cutting edge(s)...    Point to the cutting object.
Select objects:
```

Be careful. This is *still* asking you to select cutting edges: you may select more than one cutting edge which may be a line, arc, circle or polyline.

<Select objects to trim>/Undo:

Select object(s) by pointing, not by windowing. Make sure you *point to the part of the object to be trimmed away* or you may trim the wrong bit. In this case select Undo (or type U from the keyboard) and the error will be rectified.

An example of the use of TRIM is shown in Figure 6.4.

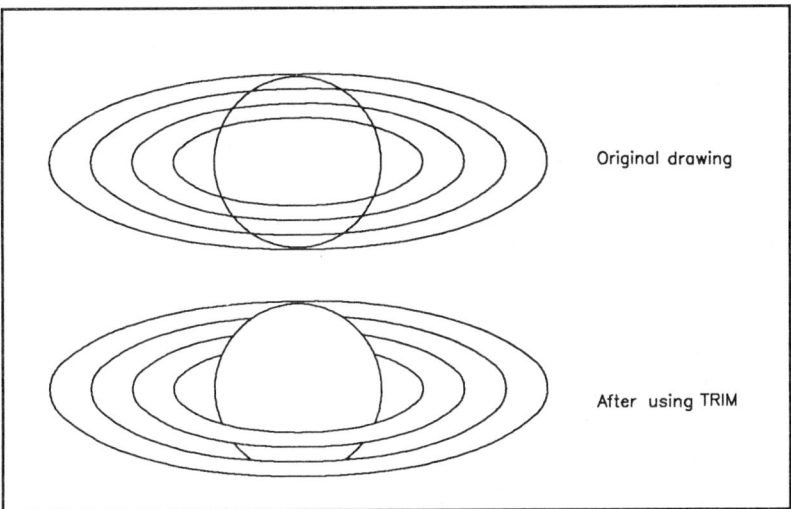

Figure 6.4 Use of TRIM

The following error messages are sometimes encountered:

No edges selected.
None of the selected cutting edges is suitable.

Entity does not intersect an edge.
There is no selected entity intersecting a cutting edge.

Cannot TRIM this entity.
Invalid entity for trimming, e.g. a block or text.

Circle must intersect twice.
You can only trim a chord off a circle if it intersects the cutting edge twice - obvious when you think about it.

6.1.4 EXTEND

EXTEND can be thought of as the reverse of TRIM. A selected object will be extended until it meets a specified boundary such as a line, arc, circle or 2D polyline. Thus lines will be extended indefinitely in their original direction, (see Figure 6.5), and arcs will be extended with their original radius of curvature, (see Figure 6.6). If the extensions cannot reach the required boundary the command is aborted.

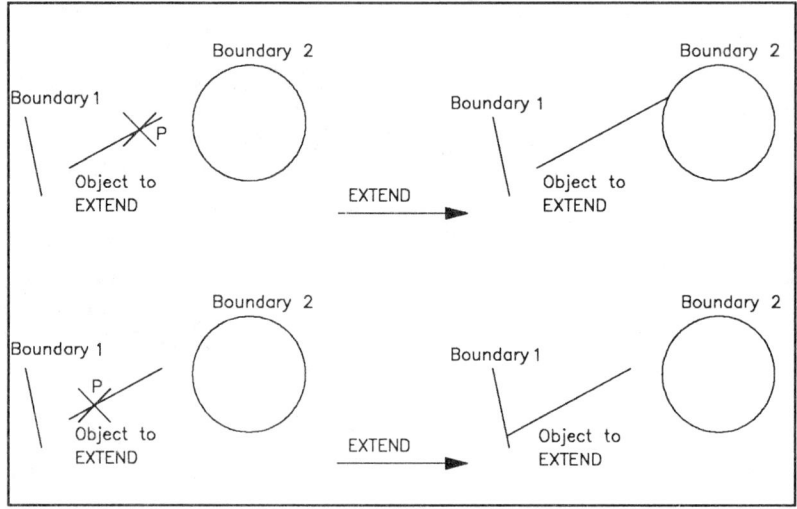

Figure 6.5   EXTENDing lines

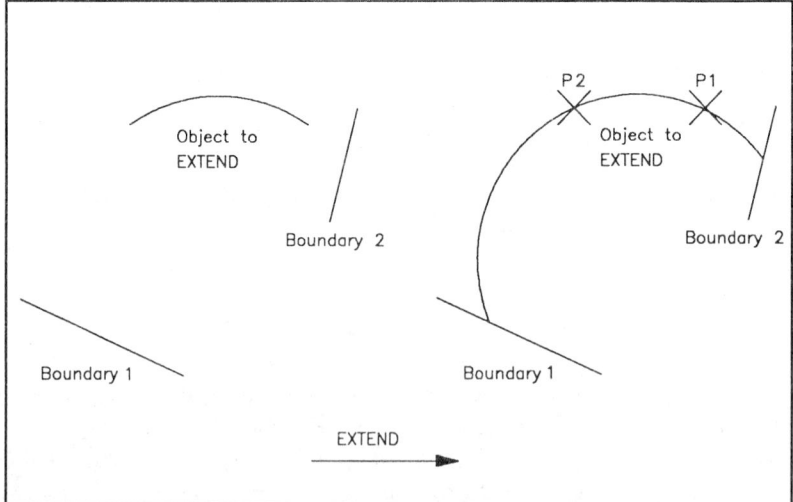

Figure 6.6   EXTENDing arcs

Command: EXTEND
Select boundary edge(s)   Point to final boundary of extended line.

Select objects:

This enables further boundaries to be specified (you may select lines, arcs, circles or 2D polylines). Press return to end boundary edge selection.

<Select object to extend>/Undo:

Point to (do not window) the object to be extended.

Objects are extended from the end closest to the point by which the object was selected. If multiple boundary edges are specified the selected object will be extended to the nearest boundary. The object may be extended to successive boundaries by picking it repeatedly. If you make a mistake and EXTEND to the wrong boundary, select Undo to remove the unwanted extension. *Remember that arcs will be extended in their positive direction, i.e. counter-clockwise.*

6.1.5 BREAK

The BREAK command can be used to erase parts of entities such as lines, circles, arcs or 2D polylines.

Command: BREAK
Select object: Use Last, Window, Pointing etc.
Enter first point: Point to one end of deletion
Enter second point: Point to other end of deletion

The selected section will then be removed.

If you use pointing to select the object then the **Enter first point:** prompt is omitted and the second prompt is modified to:

Enter second point (or F for first point):

This is because AutoCAD assumes that the point used to select the entity is actually the point specifying one end of the deletion. If this is not the case then type F to invoke a prompt for the first point.

The second point need not actually lie on the entity to be erased; AutoCAD will find the nearest point on the entity. If the second point lies within the entity then the region between the points will be removed. If it lies beyond the end of an open entity such as a line or an arc then the region between the first point and the end will be erased. This is useful because it avoids the danger of leaving a minute piece of the entity behind when you erase.

If you wish simply to break the entity into two without erasing an appreciable part of it then you should enter the same point at both the first and second prompts. This can be done by entering an @ symbol at the second prompt - this will be interpreted as "repeat of last coordinate". (See Figure 6.7.)

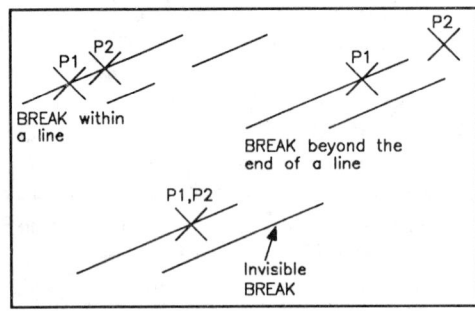

Figure 6.7 BREAKing lines   **Figure 6.8** BREAKing a circle

When breaking a circle, care must be taken when choosing the first and second break points. Remember that AutoCAD always works counter-clockwise, so the relative positions of the two break points will affect which section of the circle is removed, (see Figure 6.8).

6.1.6 FILLET

Adjacent lines which may or may not be touching can be filleted to a desired radius using the FILLET command.

Command: FILLET
Polyline/Radius/<Select first objects>:

It is first necessary to specify the desired radius by responding with an R. This radius will become the default value within the present drawing.

Enter fillet radius <0.00>:

Then re-invoke FILLET and select two lines.

Command: FILLET
Polyline/Radius/<Select first objects>:
Select second object:

If at the **Polyline/Radius...**prompt you respond with a P you may select a single polyline instead of two separate lines.

Select polyline:

See Figure 6.9.

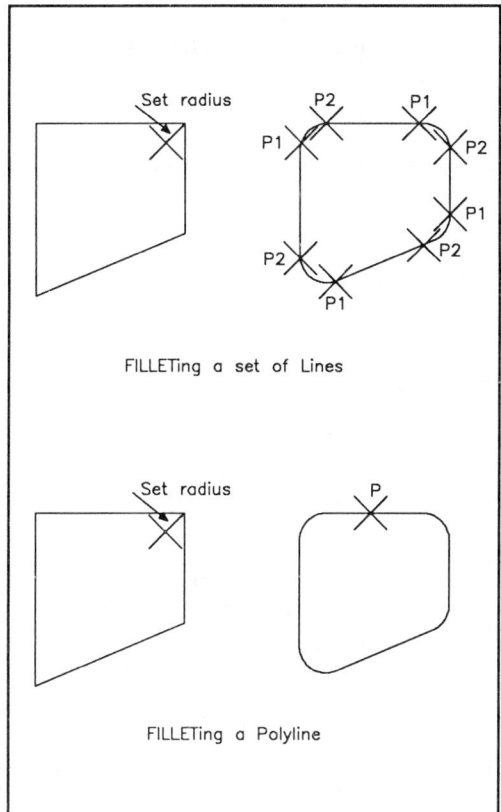

Figure 6.9   FILLETing

An alternative method of setting the radius default value is to select Fillet radius on the **Options** pull down.

6.1.7 CHAMFER

CHAMFER follows the same rules as FILLET but instead of supplying a radius AutoCAD will ask for two distances. These represent the distance along each line to which the chamfer will be taken, (see Figure 6.10).

Command: CHAMFER
Polyline/Distance/<Select first line>: D
Enter first chamfer distance <0.00>:
Enter second chamfer distance <0.00>:

Again, the **Polyline...**option works as for FILLET.

An alternative method of setting the default chamfer distances is to select Chamfer Distances on the **Options** pull down.

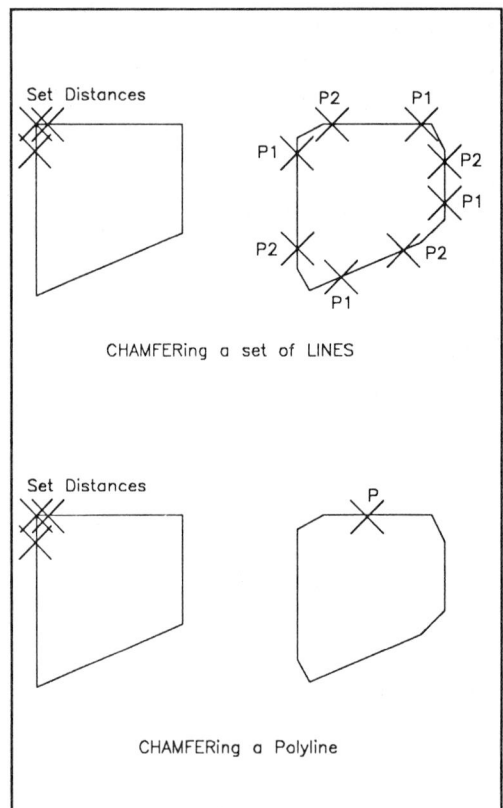

Figure 6.10 CHAMFERing

6.1.8 2D ARRAY

The ARRAY command allows the user to take an entity, group of entities or a block(s) and replicate it to form either a rectangular or a polar array.

The array element must be on the screen before ARRAY is called up. This is true even if the element is a named block.

> **Command:** ARRAY
> **Select objects:**   Assemble the desired selection set
> **Rectangular/Polar array (R/P):** R
> **Number of rows (---)<1>:**
> **Number of columns (||||)<1>:**
> **Unit cell or distance between rows (---):**
> **Distance between columns (||||):**

Instead of supplying the distances between rows and columns from the keyboard you can respond to the **...distance between rows...** prompt by picking a point with the mouse. You will be then be prompted for the **Second point** of a window which defines both the row and column separation of the array. The rectangular array is now drawn, (see Figure 6.11).

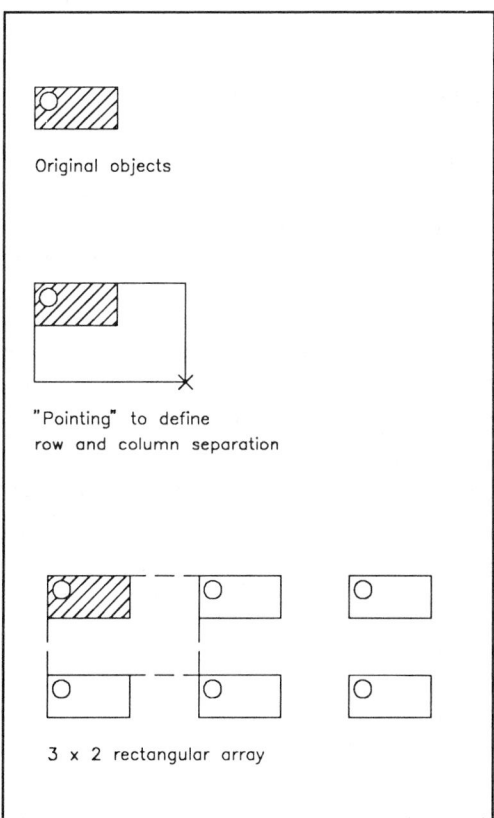

Original objects

"Pointing" to define
row and column separation

3 x 2 rectangular array

Figure 6.11   A rectangular ARRAY

A polar array is produced in a similar manner:

> **Command:** ARRAY
> **Select objects:**   Assemble the desired selection set
> **Rectangular/Polar array (R/P):** P
> **Center point of array:**   Point to centre or give coordinates
> **Number of items:** 7 (say)
> **Angle to fill (+=ccw, -=cw) <360>:**

This is requesting the angular rotation, clockwise or counter-clockwise, through which the whole array is to be rotated. A return selects the default value of 360°.

> **Rotate objects as they are copied?:** Y

The whole circular array is now drawn, (see Figure 6.12).

> *Note:*   If you are using a version of AutoCAD prior to Release 10 be careful when you request the objects not to be rotated. On earlier versions, if the selection set is composed of a number of separate entities rather than a single entity or a block, then you will find that the objects seem to "explode" as they are arrayed. This is because, without rotation, the distance from each entity in the set to the centre of the array is variable and, while this looks alright in the original position, it will cause the elements apparently to fly apart as they are arrayed. The best way round this problem is to make the offending elements into a block.

6.1.9 OFFSET

The OFFSET command can be used with all the standard AutoCAD entities, i.e lines, circles, arcs etc., and produces a parallel entity separated from the original by a *constant* distance.

In the simplest case the offset of a straight line will be an identical line parallel to the first. However, in most other cases the offset entity will differ in length and shape from the original as shown in Figure 6.13.

> **Command:** OFFSET
> **Offset distance or Through <Through>:** T
> **Select object to offset:**
> **Through point:**

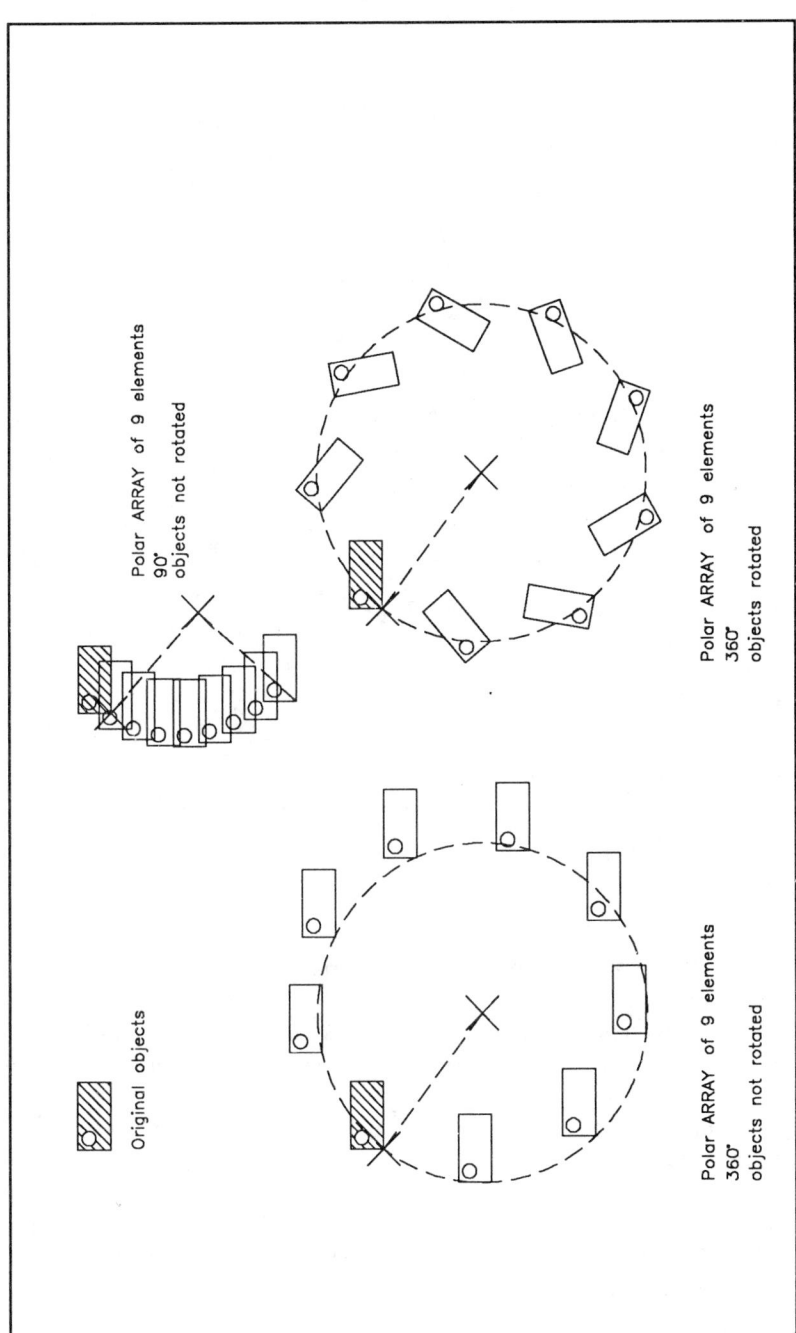

Figure 6.12 A polar ARRAY

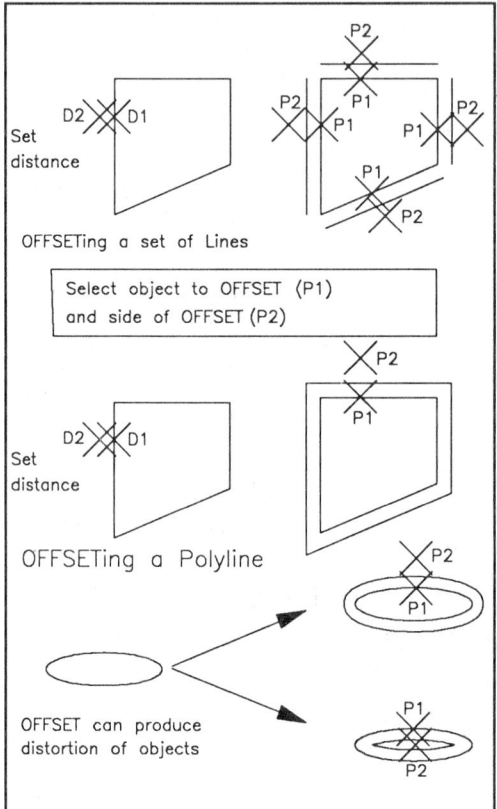

Figure 6.13 OFFSETing

If you take the default **Through** option you will be prompted for the position of a point through which the offset will pass.

Alternatively, if you input an **Offset distance** instead of the default a further prompt will ask which side of the original object the offset should be drawn.

> **Select object to offset:**
> **Side to offset?**

The **Select object to offset:** prompt is repeated indefinitely until the command is terminated. The Offset Distance or the choice of the Through option may be preset from the **Options** pull down.

6.1.10 DIVIDE and MEASURE

DIVIDE allows you to divide up an entity such as a line, arc, circle etc., into a specified number of parts, (see Figure 6.14). The entity *is not broken*; the division is achieved by placing point entities, (see Section 3.1.2), as markers along its length.

MEASURE operates in a very similar manner but in this case the spacing between the markers, rather than their number, is specified, (see Figure 6.15).

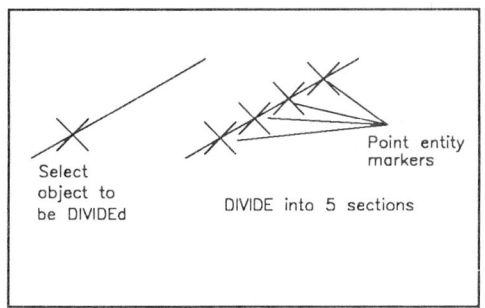

Figure 6.14   Dividing a line

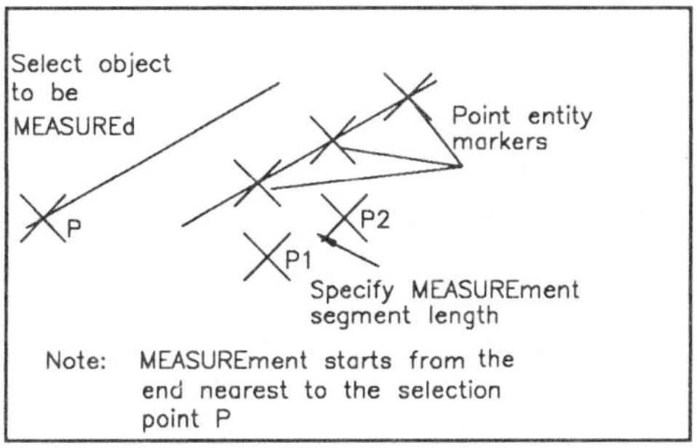

Figure 6.15   Measuring a line

Command: DIVIDE
Select object to divide: Point to object
<Number of segments>/Block: Enter a number between 2 and
                                    32767 !!
Command: MEASURE
Select object to measure: Point to object
<Segment length>/Block:

Reply with a numerical distance or use the mouse to indicate the segment length.

The object will then be divided as requested with point entity markers inserted at each division. *These may well be invisible.* A point entity with PDMODE set to 0 or 1 can only be seen when it is separate from any other object. However, the invisible points can still be used, for instance with Node object snap to attach new entities at each division. (See Chapter 7.) Alternatively, use PDMODE and PDSIZE to make the point entities visible.

You can replace the point entity division markers with a previously defined block. If you respond to the second prompt with Block or just B then AutoCAD will prompt for the name of a block. This must be a block *currently defined within the drawing*. A block stored on disk using WBLOCK *cannot* be used here. (See Chapter 7.)

AutoCAD will then ask if the block is to be aligned with the object and after this the division or measurement will be performed and the marker blocks inserted instead of the point entities. This can be very useful - for instance if you needed to insert a block representing an electrical outlet at regular intervals along a wall in a room plan then DIVIDE could handle this in one operation, (see Figure 6.16).

The Divide Units, the Measure distance and the default block name may all be preset using the **Options** pull down.

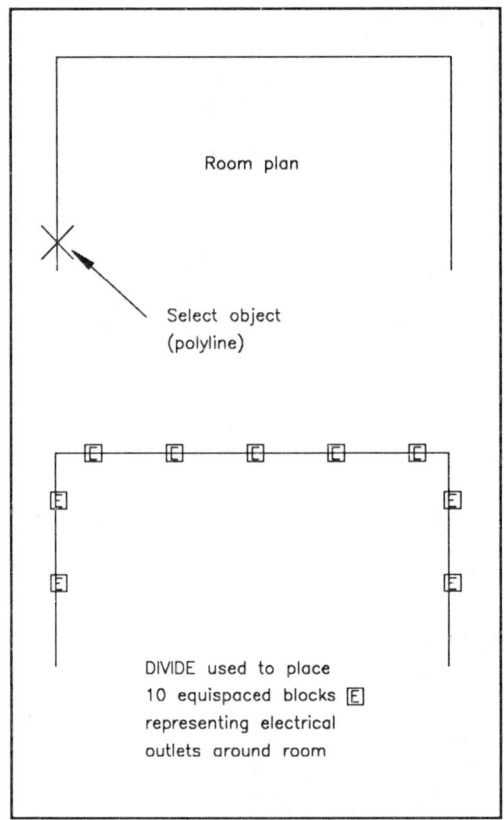

Room plan

Select object
(polyline)

DIVIDE used to place
10 equispaced blocks [E]
representing electrical
outlets around room

Figure 6.16 Dividing using block markers

6.1.11 CHANGE

CHANGE is a very powerful editing command in that it can be used to alter both the size and position of an entity and also various other properties such as layer, colour etc.

Command: CHANGE
Select objects: Select entity(s)
Properties/<Change point>:

The default response requests a Change Point (CP). This may be supplied from either the mouse or the keyboard. Depending on the entity selected, CHANGE will modify the entity relative to the CP. (See Figure 6.17.)

* *Line:* The end point closest to the CP will be moved to the CP.
* *Circle:* The radius will be adjusted so that the circle passes through the CP while the centre point remains fixed.
* *Block:* The CP becomes the new insertion point and you will be prompted for a new rotation angle.
* *Text:* May be moved to the specified CP and in addition the height, rotation angle, style and content may be altered.
* *Multiple lines:* Will *all* be modified to meet at the CP. When a number of different entities are selected the lines will all be treated as above but circles will trigger a prompt for a new radius and blocks a prompt for a new insertion point.

If you require to change a property of the selected entity(s) then respond with a P at the **Properties/<Change point>** prompt.

Properties/<Change point>: P
Change what property(Color/LAyer/LType/Thickness) ?

Each time you select a change in a property you will be returned to the above menu allowing further changes to be made. Only when you respond with a return will the changes be executed.

6.1.12 CHPROP

If you wish only to change the properties of an entity then the CHPROP command may be used instead of CHANGE.

Command: CHPROP
Select objects:
Change what property (Color/LAyer/LType/Thickness) ?

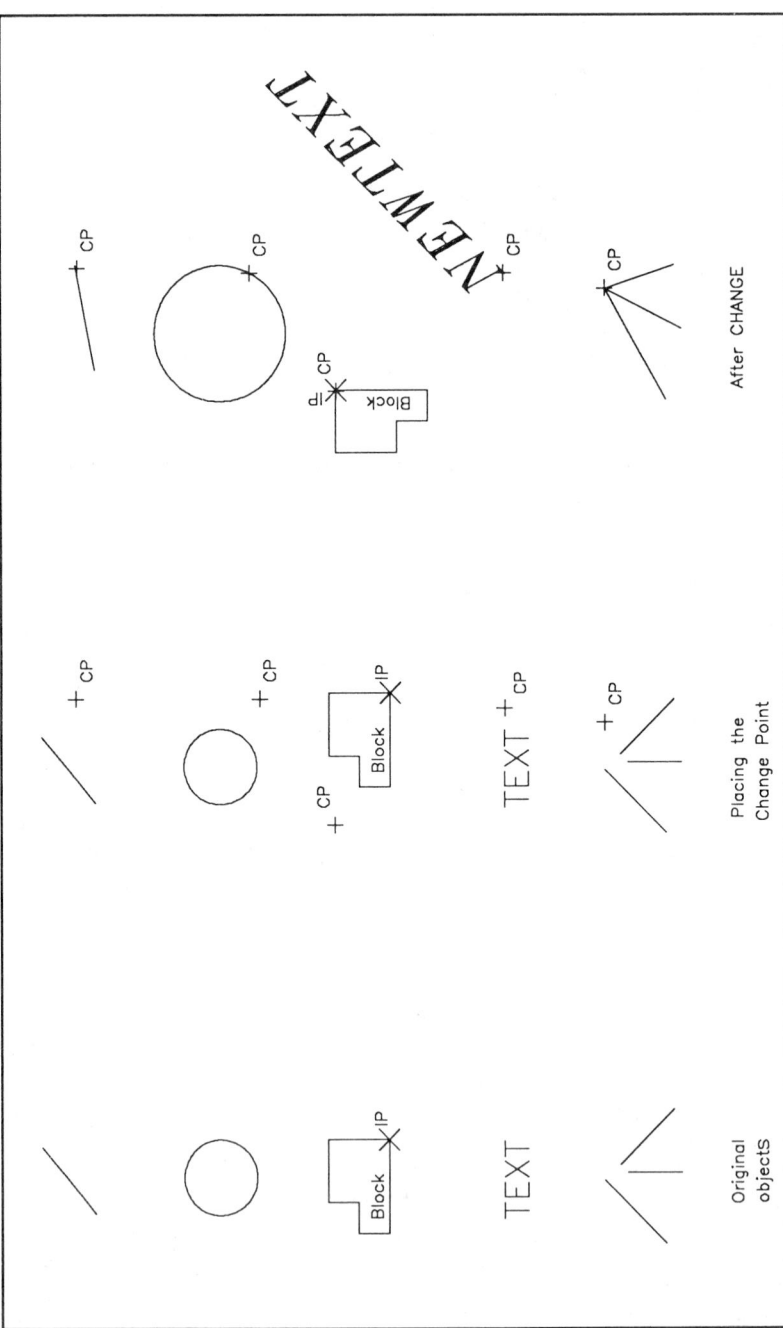

Figure 6.17 The versatile CHANGE command

6.1.13 RENAME

Several AutoCAD features require a user-defined name, e.g. blocks, views, text styles etc. RENAME allows these names to be changed at any time.

> **Command:** RENAME
> **Block/Dimstyle/LAyer/LType/Style/Ucs/VIew/Vport:**
> **Old** (feature) **name:**
> **New** (feature) **name:**

6.1.14 PURGE

This is the only command which allows existing user-defined features to be deleted from a drawing. In practice PURGE may *only* be used *immediately* after loading a previously saved drawing and before any new entities have been added or any existing entities have been modified.

> **Command:** PURGE
> **Purge unused Blocks/Dimstyle/LAyers/LTypes/SHapes/STyles/All:**

AutoCAD responds by offering the selected items one at a time for deletion.

6.2 INQUIRY COMMANDS

6.2.1 LIST

LIST, which can found on the **Utility** pull down or on the **Inquiry** screen menu, is a generally useful command which gives full details of any selected entity and is particularly useful when editing.

> **Command:** LIST
> **Select objects:**

AutoCAD responds with a list of the coordinates and tangent direction of selected lines, the centre and radius of circles and arcs, together with information about layer, colour, linetype, Mspace or Pspace etc. The area and perimeter of a closed polyline, circle, polygon and ellipse is also given.

6.2.2 DBLIST

This is the same as List, but the data for the *complete* drawing is displayed. DBLIST can take a very long time if the drawing is large and it is difficult to read as there is no way of stopping scrolling; use Ctrl Q to echo the output to the printer.

6.2.3 ID

The ID command displays the X-, Y- and Z- coordinates of a chosen point in the drawing.

> **Command: ID**
> **Select point:**

> *Note:* Picking ID Point from the **Utility** pull down does *not* issue the true ID command. Instead an AutoLISP routine is activated which is transparent and can therefore be used to report coordinate points from inside some other command.

The true ID command, as picked from the screen menu or issued from the keyboard, can be very useful when positioning an entity at an exact distance from an unknown point in a drawing.

EXAMPLE
If a line is to be drawn 50 units away from an unknown point in 0° direction, first use the ID command to select and identify the point then enter the line command. At the prompt **From point:** enter the relative coordinate @50<0. AutoCAD uses the ID point as a point to which the relative coordinate is referenced.

The same result can be produced by picking (REF)point from the **Assist** pull down menu.

6.2.4 DISTANCE

The DISTANCE command responds with the distance and angle between any two specified points whether 2D or 3D.

> **Command: DIST**
> **First point:**
> **Second point:**

6.2.5 AREA

The AREA command allows the specification of an entity or any number of points enclosing a 2D area, the last point specified is assumed to be connected to the first point specified. The area command calculates both the area and the perimeter of the specified region.

Command: AREA
<First point>/Entity/Add/Subtract:
Next point:

.

.

Next point:<return>
Area=<calculated area>, **Perimeter=**<calculated perimeter>

If the **Entity** option is selected, AutoCAD responds with:

Select circle or polyline:

This obviates the need to specify multiple points to define these shapes. Polylines do not need to be closed.

The **Add** option allows you to sum a number of specified areas while the **Subtract** options allow you to subtract one area from another.

6.2.6 STATUS

The STATUS command lists certain properties associated with the drawing and its environment. The following is a typical example:

25 Entities in Test

Model space limits are	X:	0.00	Y:	0.00	(off)	
	X:	420.00	Y:	27.00		
Model space uses	X:	10.00	Y:	0.00		
	X:	420.00	Y:	285.00		
Display shows	X:	0.00	Y:	0.00		
	X:	420.00	Y:	304.19		
Insertion base is	X:	0.00	Y:	0.00	Z:	0.00
Snap resolution is	X:	10.00	Y:	10.00		
Grid spacing is	X:	0.00	Y:	0.00		

Current space: Model space
Current layer: 0
Current colour: BYLAYER -- 0(White)
Current linetype: BYLAYER -- CONTINUOUS
Current elevation: 0.00   thickness: 0.00
Axis off   Fill on   Grid off   Ortho off   Qtext off   Snap on   Tablet off
Object snap modes: None

Free disc: 12439280 bytes
Virtual memory allocated to program: 2224K
Amount of program in physical memory/Total (virtual) program size: 78%
Total conventional memory: 388K   Total extended memory: 3408K
Swap file size: 388K bytes
Page faults: 16   Swap writes: 0   Swap reclaims: 0

7. Layers, colours and linetypes

7.1 LAYERS

An AutoCAD drawing usually incorporates a number of *layers*. The layers themselves are invisible and it is probably helpful to think of them as a group of transparent sheets of film on which the different parts of the drawing are placed. By looking down through the sheets a complete picture is obtained, (see Figure 7.1). By removing or colouring certain sheets, selected parts of the picture can be hidden or emphasized. Correct handling of layers is essential in order to make the best use of AutoCAD.

Layers are most easily demonstrated when using a colour monitor but their use is by no means limited to a colour installation. There is no limit to the number of layers you may have in a drawing, nor to the number of entities that can be held on a single layer.

A typical use of a layer would be to group together related objects such as electric wiring, pipework etc. Similarly, text and dimensions may be more easily handled if grouped together onto their own layers; this is especially true when using Paper Space, (see Chapter 13).

When starting a new drawing you will only have one layer, Layer 0. This special layer *cannot be deleted or re-named* and has special properties relating to blocks.

Extra layers can be created at any time. One of the layers of a drawing may be nominated as the *current layer* - any new entity drawn will be placed on this layer by default.

The current layer name is displayed in the top left hand corner of the screen on the status line.

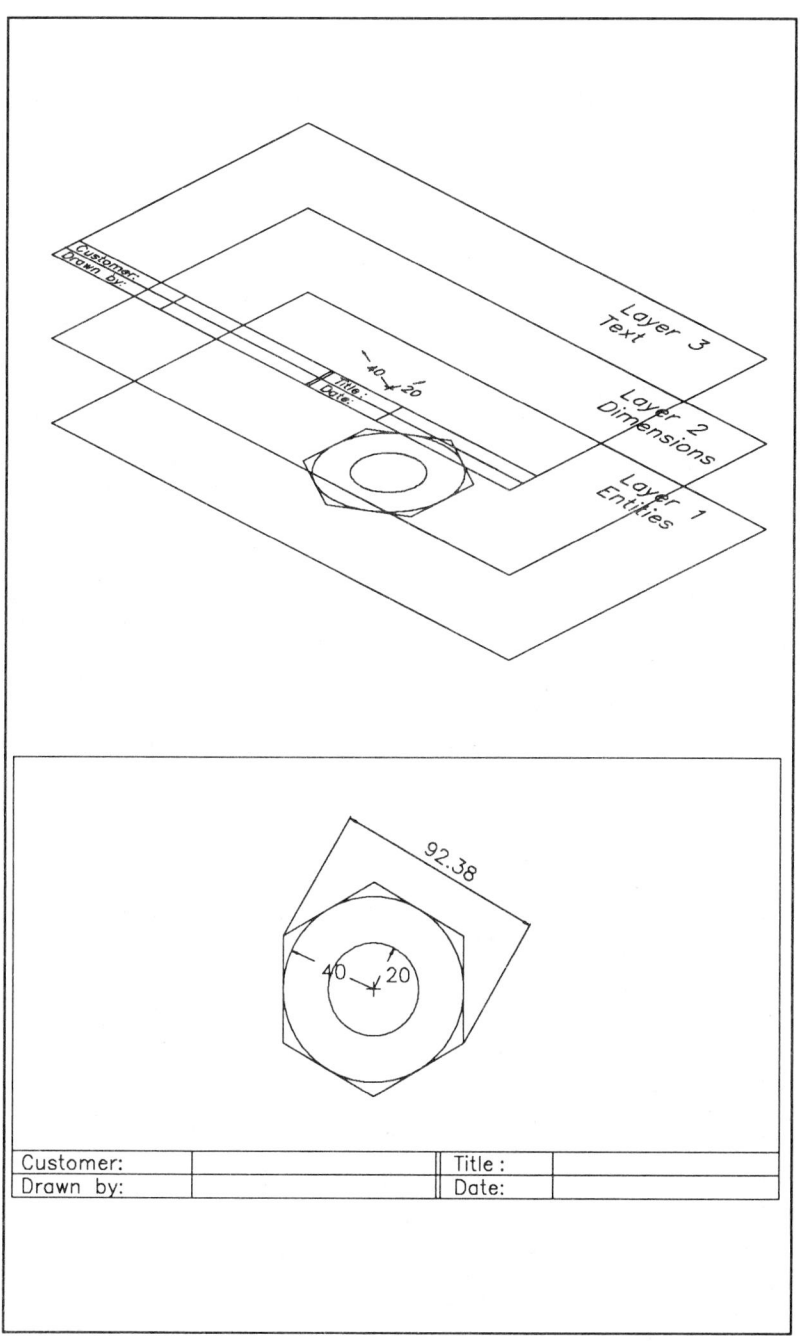

Figure 7.1 Use of layers

7.1.1 Properties of Layers

- *Name:* A layer must be given a unique name to distinguish it from all other layers. The name may simply be a number: 1, 5, 65...., or it may be a word (up to 31 characters long) which is in some way descriptive of the contents of the layer, e.g. ELECTRICWIRING or SECOND_FLOOR. The first 8 characters of the name of the current layer are *always* displayed in the top left hand corner of the drawing.

> *Note:* Spaces in names are not allowed; a hyphen or an underscore may be used instead.

- *On/Off:* A layer, together with all its contents, can be switched On or Off at any time. When Off, the contents of the layer become invisible although they are still handled for certain functions such as ZOOM, PAN and REGENeration. Layers that are Off are not plotted but they are still included in a drawing when it is saved.
- *Colour:* A layer normally has a colour assigned to it so that all entities drawn on the layer will automatically take the same colour. This is a default situation which can be over-ridden when required so that individual entities on the layer can be forced to take any desired colour, (see Section 7.2).

    The colours are referred to by number from 1 to 255. Unfortunately, there is little standardization between different hardware systems as to the interpretation of colours by number. However, the first 7 numbers can usually be considered as standard:

    1 - Red
    2 - Yellow
    3 - Green
    4 - Cyan
    5 - Blue
    6 - Magenta
    7 - White   (default)

Any new layer and any layer which does not have a user-specified colour will default to colour 7 (white). Nearly all colours systems (colour board and VDU) will support these seven colours but beyond colour 7 different systems vary tremendously. You certainly can *not* assume that all 255 colours will be represented. Try loading one of the AutoCAD-supplied colour drawings such as CHROMA or COLORWH to see how your system performs. You may get a shock.

   If you are using a monochrome system the colours will all be represented identically on screen. The colours are still useful because each colour can be assigned to a different pen on a pen plotter.

- *Linetype:* The treatment of linetypes within a layer closely follows that of the treatment of colours. All lines within a layer normally take up the linetype previously assigned to that layer, e.g. dashed or dotted. Individual entities can be forced to take up a linetype which is different from that of the layer, (see section 7.3). The default linetype for new layers is CONTINUOUS.
- *Freeze/Thaw:* The Freeze/Thaw state of a layer is superficially similar to its Off/On state. A frozen layer is invisible both on screen and on the plotter but a frozen layer is completely ignored by the package for virtually all commands other than Save. This means that a complicated frozen layer will not slow down the ZOOM, PAN and REGENeration processes - so it is good practice to freeze any layers that are not currently being used. They can easily be thawed out later.

7.1.2 Changing and Creating Layers

By far the easiest way to control layers is through the layers dialogue box accessed via Layer Control under the **Settings** pull down. This may also be accessed by selecting **Layer** from the screen menu and then selecting DDLMODES or alternatively by typing DDLMODES from the keyboard.

The dialogue box clearly shows the layers which have already been created for use with the current drawing, (see Figure 7.2). It also shows for each layer its name, On/Off state, Global Freeze/Thaw state, ViewPort Freeze state, (see Section 13.2.3), Colour and Linetype. A tick in the Current box shows which layer is current, i.e. the layer onto which any new entities will be drawn. Finally, there is a box for creating new layers to be added to the set.

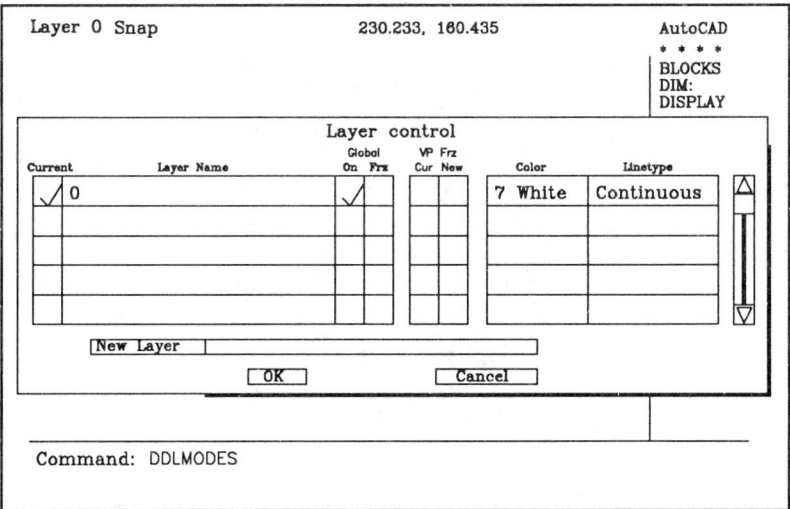

Figure 7.2   Layer editing

It is very easy to change any of these settings; simply use the mouse to move the arrow to the relevant box and press the pick button. In the case of colours (Figure 7.3) and linetypes (Figure 7.4), subsidiary dialogue boxes will appear.

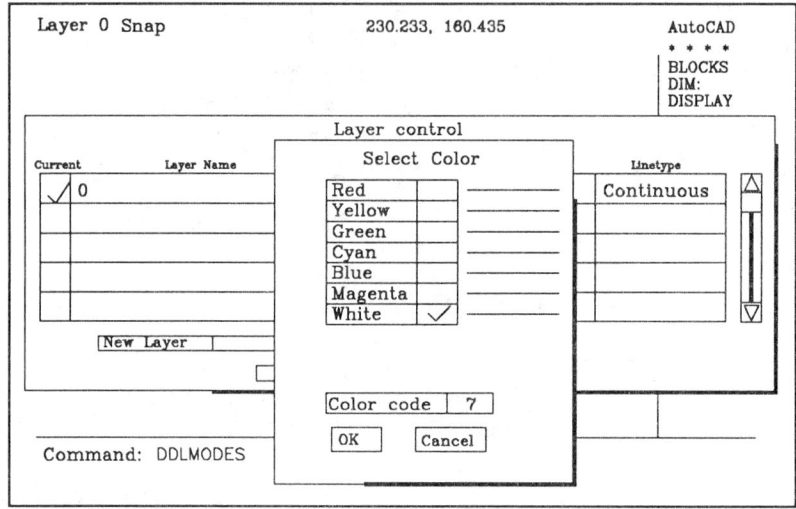

Figure 7.3   Layer colour editing

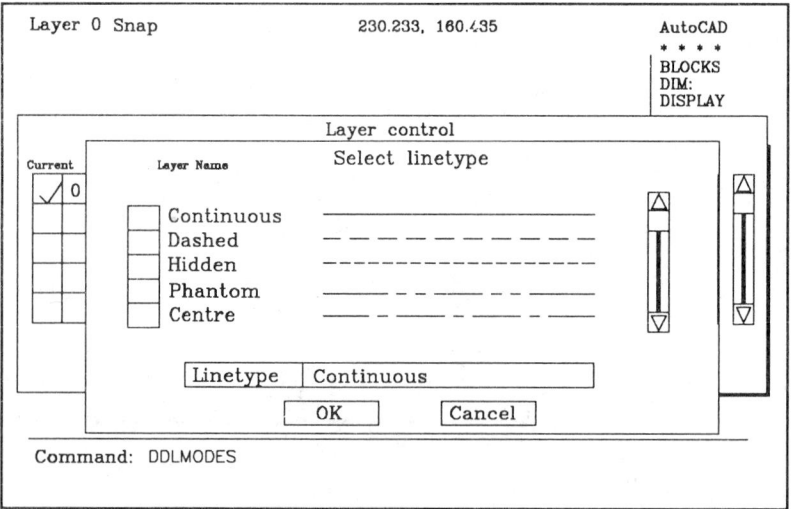

Figure 7.4   Layer linetype editing

When you have made your selection, pick the **OK** box and you will be returned to the main dialogue box. When you have finished making all the required changes, again tick the **OK** box and you will be returned to the drawing.

The LAYER command from the keyboard gives access to all the properties in the dialogue box but it is rather more cumbersome to use.

Command: LAYER
?/Make/Set/New/ON/OFF/Color/Ltype/Freeze/Thaw

Because you will often need to specify more than one property of a layer at a time, the AutoCAD response to a request for, say, a change in layer colour is not immediate but instead you are returned to the above menu. This can be confusing because the requested change will not have occurred. The rule is that, after you have made all the required changes to the layer and you have been returned to the layer menu yet again - *give a final return*. This "fixes" all your requests which will at last be obeyed and the **Command:** prompt will re-appear.

Some of the items on the layer menu are obvious, some less so.

?   The question mark response gives a display of the names of all the layers incorporated in your drawing, together with their On/Off state, colour and linetype. To return to the drawing simply press the F1 function key.

Make   When you start a new drawing only one layer exists. This is always called layer 0, it always has a default colour of white (or black if your system is configured to use dark vectors on a light background) and a continuous linetype (which cannot be changed). Make allows you to define a new layer and in addition *sets that layer to be the current layer*. Other features of the new layer such as colour, linetype etc., can be set before exiting the layer menu.

Set   This sets the new current layer but the layer must already be in existence and it must not be frozen.

New   This creates a new layer but it does not set it to be the current layer.

ON/OFF   Controls the visibility of a layer or layers. Several layers can be specified by single On or Off statement provided that the layer names are separated by commas. ALL layers may be switched On or Off by using the * wild card.

Color   The colour of specified layers can be set by responding with a valid colour number between 1 and 255 or by the name of one of the seven standard colours, e.g. RED. When prompted for the layer name to which the new colour applies you can again reply with multiple layer names. A null response will be taken to indicate the current layer only.

Ltype   The response to this request is:

Linetype (or ?) <CONTINUOUS>

The ? will result in a list of linetypes *in current use in the drawing*. Other linetypes are available but they must be loaded from the file ACAD.LIN. Don't worry, this is done automatically for you when you request the new linetype.

Freeze   Freezes a given layer or layers. You cannot freeze the current layer.

Thaw   Thaws a given layer or layers.

7.1.3 The VPLAYER Command

The VPLAYER command is used only for freezing layers in specific viewports when working in a Paper Space environment. This command is discussed fully in Section 13.2.3.

7.2 THE COLOUR OR COLOR COMMAND

There is a separate COLOUR command which allows you to force the colour of an individual entity, no matter what colour is set for the layer on which it is drawn.

    Command: COLOUR
    New entity color: RED

This sequence will over-ride the layer colour for all subsequently-drawn entities. To return to the colouring-by-layer system the COLOUR command is repeated but the response is BYLAYER.

    The entity colour can also be set by entering the Entity Creation dialogue box (DDEMODES) under the **Options** pull down, or under the **Settings** screen menu, picking Color, entering a subsidiary dialogue box, (see Figure 7.5), and selecting the required colour with your mouse or digitiser.

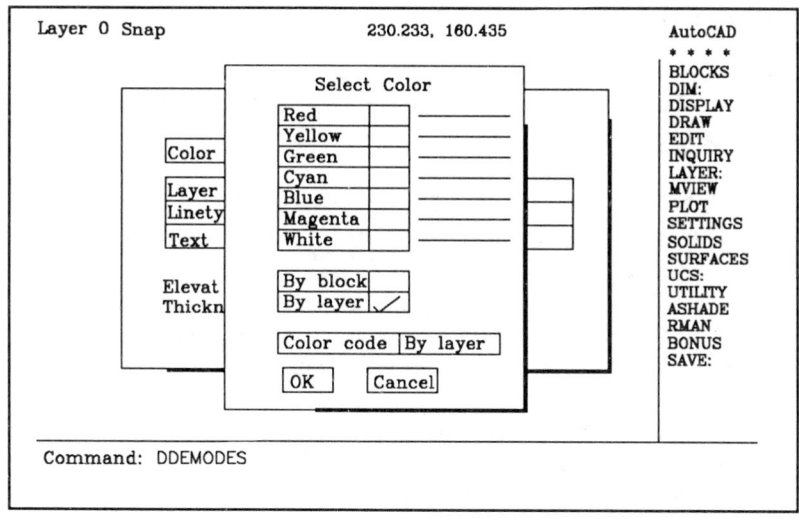

Figure 7.5   Setting entity colours

7.3 LINETYPES

The LINETYPE command acts in a similar fashion to the COLOUR command and allows entities to be drawn using a number of different line types. AutoCAD contains a library of various linetypes which can be called at any time during the drawing execution. The standard AutoCAD linetypes are kept in a library file called ACAD.LIN. A selection of these is shown in Figure 7.6.

——————————	Continuous
— — — — — — —	Dashed
------------------	Hidden
— · — · — · — · —	Center
——— — — ——— — — ———	Phantom
· · · · · · · · · · ·	Dot
— · — · — · — · — · —	Dashdot
— —· — · — ·— — · —	Border
— ·· — ·· — ·· — ·· —	Divide

Figure 7.6   Linetypes

It is possible to create your own linetypes (containing only dots and dashes) and library file. (See Section 18.5.)

> *Note:* There are certain rules which must be observed when using the linetype command:
>
> 1. Only lines, arcs, circles, ellipses, polygons and polylines can have their linetype changed. All other entities are drawn with the "continuous" linetype.
>
> 2. A linetype definition must exist in a linetype library before it can be loaded into a drawing or assigned to a layer.
>
> 3. When the linetype has been loaded into the drawing its definition is read into the drawing file; it is therefore not necessary to reload the linetype from the library file for subsequent use.

It is possible to change the linetype for entities drawn on a specific layer by using the Ltype sub-command (displayed when the LAYER command is invoked). AutoCAD will perform an automatic REGEN using the new linetype definition and all entities previously drawn to take up the default layer linetype (BYLAYER) will take up the new linetype.

All commands associated with LINETYPE can be executed either from the screen menu or directly from the keyboard but the Entity Creation dialogue box, (see Figure 7.7), (found under the **Options** pull down menu) can only be used to Set the current Linetype.

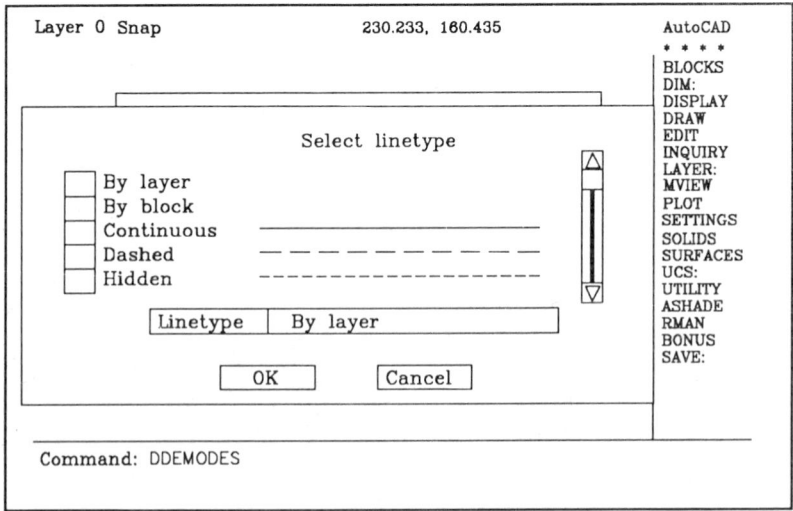

Figure 7.7 Linetype dialogue box

Command: LINETYPE
?/Create/Load/Set:

? The ? will show the linetypes which are available for loading into your drawing file from the requested library file. If the only library file which exists is the AutoCAD standard linetype library file ACAD.LIN then this will be the default. If you have created your own library file then this can be called and will then become the default.

AutoCAD prompts:

File to list <default>:

Load Before a linetype can be loaded into a drawing file it must exist in a library file. When load is called then the linetype name has to be entered followed by the library file name. AutoCAD will search this file for the requested linetype.

Name of linetype to load: * will load all linetypes
File to search <default>:

Note: Linetypes may not be loaded using either the DDEMODES or DDLMODES dialogue box.

Set When the linetype has been loaded into the drawing file it can then be made the current linetype by using the Set option. All new drawing entities will then take the new linetype.

New entity linetype (or ?) <current>:

There are also a number of other responses which are allowed at this point: If you respond with BYLAYER then the linetype will be that which has previously been set for the layer on which the entities are being drawn. The special instruction BYBLOCK causes all entities to be drawn with a "continuous" linetype until they are grouped together into a block. Whenever the block is inserted it will then inherit the current entity linetype. The final special instruction is the ? which lists the *currently loaded* linetypes.

Create Allows you to create your own simple linetypes, (see Section 18.5).

The Linetype of an entity may be altered by using either the CHANGE or CHPROP command, (see Section 6.1.11).

If the requested linetype is not resident in the drawing file AutoCAD will search the standard library file (ACAD.LIN) automatically. If the linetype cannot be found AutoCAD will then check to see whether it is in another library file - if so *you* must load the linetype using the LINETYPE command.

7.3.1 LTSCALE

The linetype dash specification, (see Section 18.5), is defined in terms of drawing units. It is useful to be able to scale the linetype. LTSCALE allows this.

A linetype scale of 1.0000 is the usual default value. When the scale is changed then the drawing is automatically regenerated.

Command: LTSCALE
New scale factor <default>:

Note: If LTSCALE is set too large or too small then the effect is to make most linetypes appear to be continuous, (see Figure 7.8).

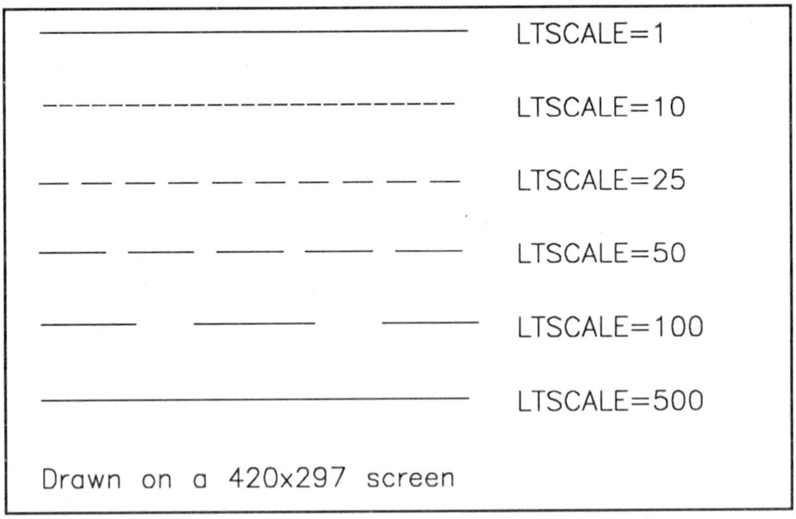

LTSCALE=1

LTSCALE=10

LTSCALE=25

LTSCALE=50

LTSCALE=100

LTSCALE=500

Drawn on a 420x297 screen

Figure 7.8 The effect of LTSCALE

8. Object snap

8.1 PRINCIPLES OF OBJECT SNAP

Object snap allows you to snap the cross wires of the cursor on to a variety of key points related to existing objects in the drawing. This complements the basic snap facility which locks on to the coordinate system and greatly enhances the accuracy with which drawings may be constructed.

For instance, it can be very difficult to draw a line to meet the centre point of an existing circle if the centre point is not marked and the circle was not drawn with basic snap in operation. Object snap allows this hidden point to be accessed immediately.

Object snap may be operated either continuously by default (background mode) or it may be called up for a *single* drawing operation (override mode) - such as drawing a single line originating from the exact mid-point of another.

The precise feature of an object onto which the cursor snaps is determined by the *object snap mode(s)* which are currently invoked. There are several of these modes to choose from and it is possible to use a combination of several modes at one time. They are listed either on the **Assist** pull down menu or on the corresponding screen menu (which is called up by picking the ******** symbol near the top of the screen menu under the word AutoCAD).

When object snap is operating, there is no visible effect until AutoCAD requests a point, e.g. the **From point:** prompt encountered within the LINE command. The normal cross wires of the cursor are then supplemented with a square target box at their intersection, (see Figure 8.1).

The size of the target box may be adjusted through the APERTURE command.

Command: APERTURE
Object snap target height (1-50 pixels)<10>:

This indicates the search area within which AutoCAD will look for entities which are able to satisfy the current object snap mode.

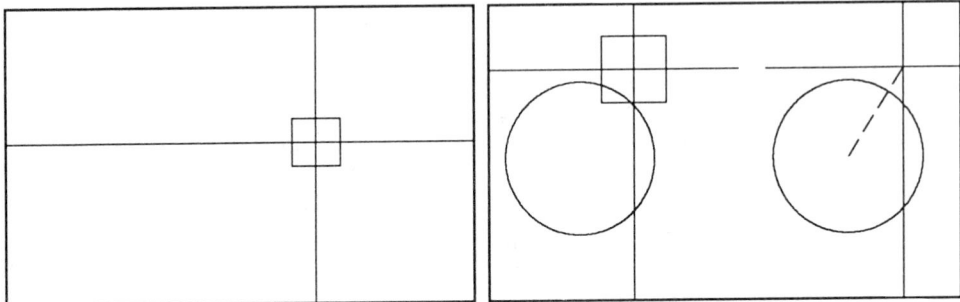

Figure 8.1   The object snap target box   **Figure 8.2**   Drawing a line from an unknown centre point

EXAMPLE

For example, if within the LINE command the object snap mode is set to look for the centres of circles (CENtre mode), then if the target box overlaps part of a circle and the pick button is pressed, AutoCAD will place the start point of the line at the centre of the circle, (see Figure 8.2).

8.1.1 Object Snap Modes

The following available object snap modes are illustrated in Figures 8.3 and 8.4.

- *NEArest:**   snaps to the *nearest position* on any line, polyline, circle or arc
- *ENDpoint:*   snaps to the nearest *endpoint* of a line, polyline or arc
- *MIDpoint:*   snaps to the *midpoint* of a line, polyline or arc
- *CENter:*   snaps to the *centre* of an arc or circle
- *NODe:*   snaps to a *point* entity
- *QUAdrant:*   snaps to the nearest *quadrant* point of an arc or circle, i.e. 12 o'clock, 3 o'clock, 6 o'clock or 9 o'clock. If the circle or arc has been rotated these quadrant points will be rotated also.
- *INTersection:**   snaps to the *intersection* of any lines, polylines, circles or arcs which lie nearest to the centre of the target box.
- *INSert:*   snaps to the *insertion point* of a block, shape or text entity.
- *PERpendicular:**   allows a line to be drawn perpendicular to the object specified.
- *TANgent:**   snaps to that point on a circle or arc which, when connected to the last point specified, forms a *tangent* to the circle or arc.

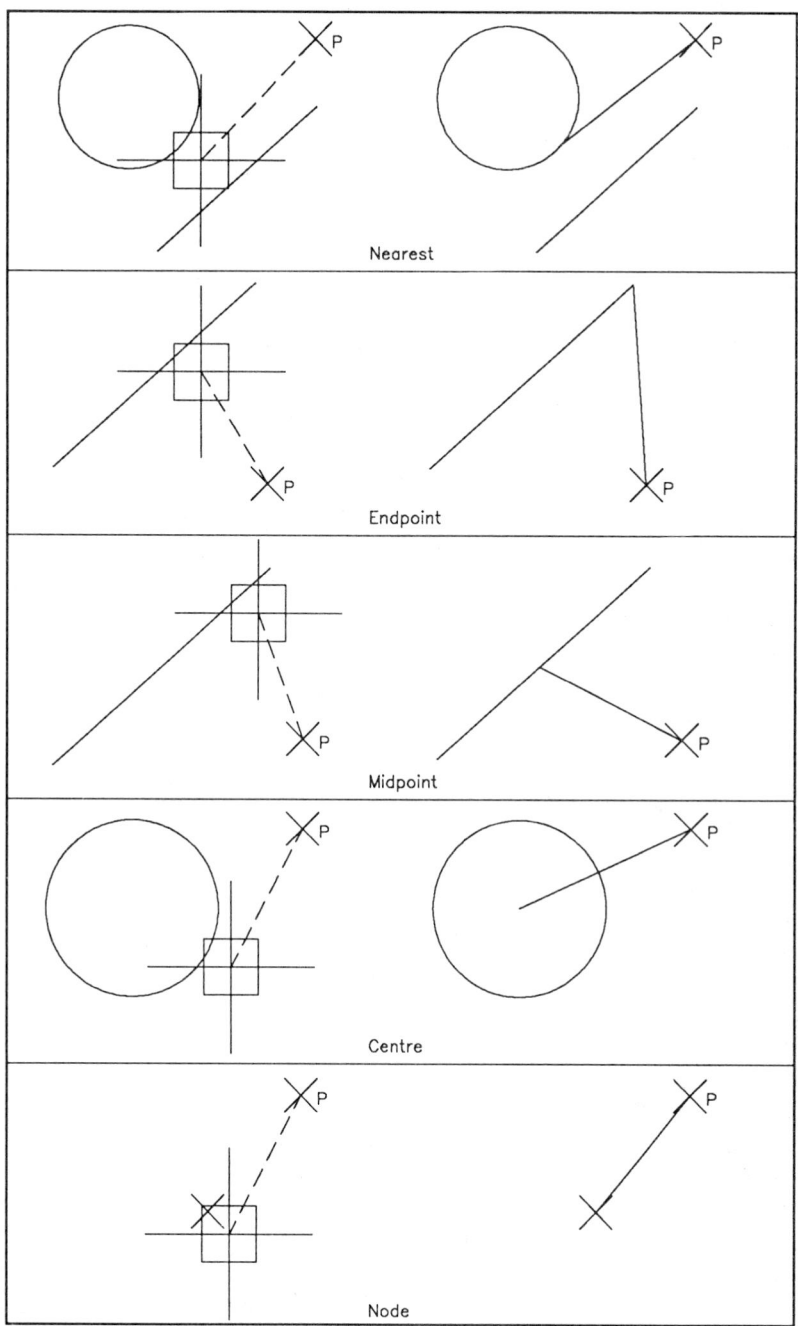

Figure 8.3 Use of various object snap modes

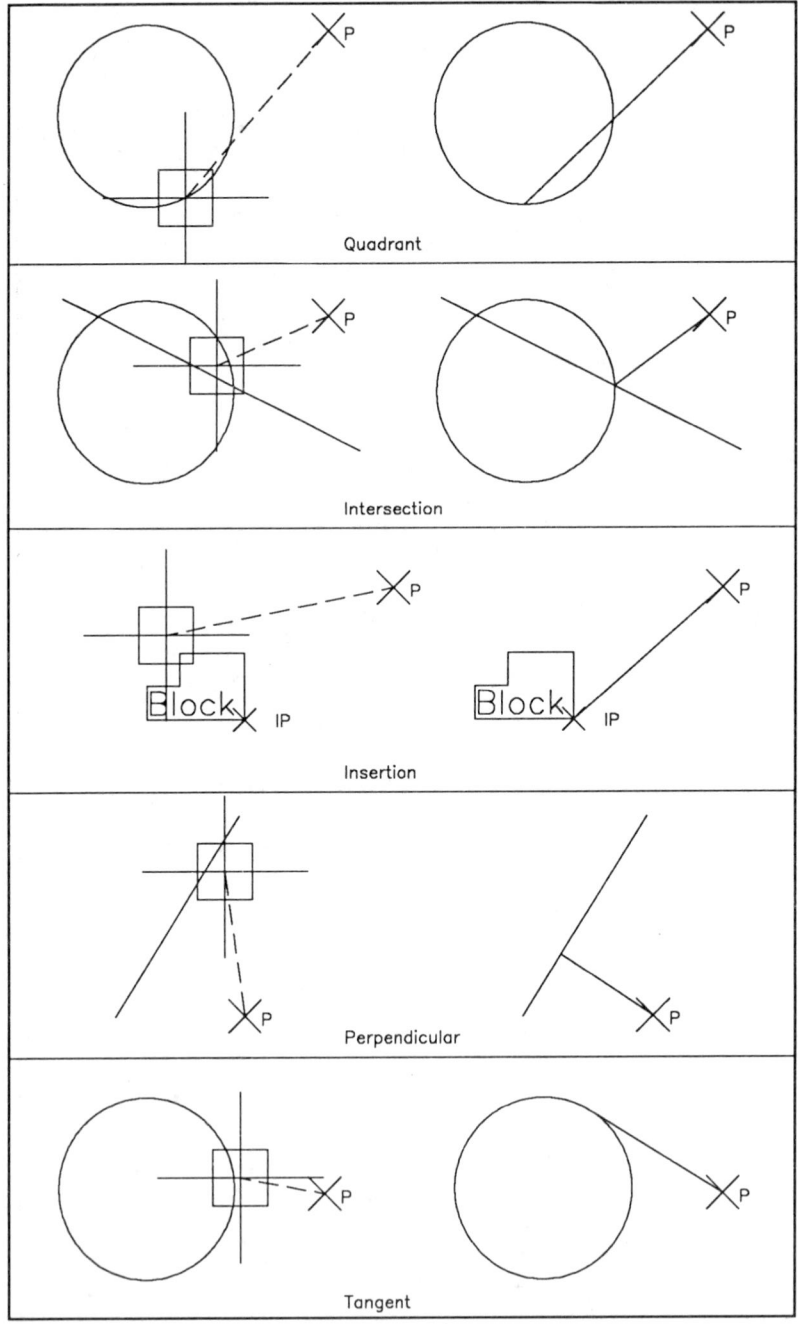

Figure 8.4 Use of various object snap modes

● *QUIck:* this mode is *only* used in conjunction with other object snap modes. It ensures that the snap point selected is the *first one* which satisfies the mode criteria. Without Quick all possible candidate points are examined to see which is nearest to the centre of the target box.

● *NONe:* *Disables* object snap

Note:

1) Some object snap modes will not operate or are restricted when used with objects which are contained in blocks. These modes are indicated with a *.

2) Each section of a polyline is treated as a separate line or arc entity.

3) Object snap considers only the centre line of wide polylines, (see Figure 8.5).

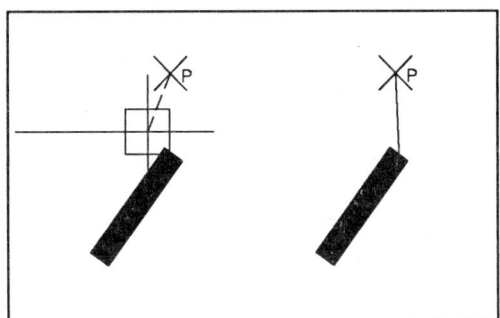

Figure 8.5 Object snap finds the centre of a wide polyline

8.2 INVOKING OBJECT SNAP

8.2.1 Background or OSNAP mode

Object snap may be set up in its background mode by giving the command OSNAP

Command: OSNAP
Object snap modes: END,MID,QUA

This has the effect of setting the running object snap modes to ENDpoint, MIDpoint and QUAdrant.

> *Note:*   Only the first 3 letters of any mode name are needed.

The snap point chosen will be the one which satisfies at least one of these modes and which is nearest to the centre of the target box. These background modes, unless changed, will remain in operation throughout the drawing and will be saved as part of the drawing.

8.2.2   Single Point Override Mode

This is often more useful than the background mode. It allows you to select the mode(s) you want but it will only remain in force for just one point selection. As the name implies, it can be used to override the background mode for the current point, after which the background mode will take over again. Single point override can be used even when there is no background mode set, i.e. it can be used when object snap background mode is NONe.

To invoke this single point object snap, you can simply respond to *any* AutoCAD point prompt with the required mode name. This may be picked up from the pull down or screen menus or typed in directly (first three letters). AutoCAD then responds appropriately, supplying helpful prompt words such as **of** or **to** on the command line.

EXAMPLE

Suppose that your drawing includes a circle and an arc, and that you wish to construct a line from the centre of the circle to the midpoint of the arc. Using object snap the task is very simple:

> **Command:** LINE
> **From point:** CEN **of**   Point to the circle
> **To point:** MID **of**   Point to the arc

See Figure 8.6.

If you don't think that was clever, try doing it without object snap !!

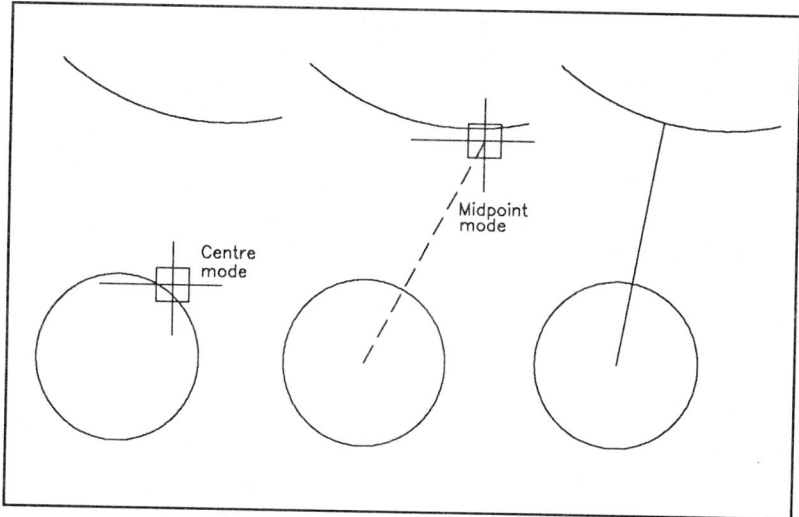

Figure 8.6 Constructing a line from the centre of a circle to the mid-point of an arc

9. Introducing text

9.1 JUSTIFIED TEXT

Text can be incorporated into an AutoCAD drawing using the TEXT or DTEXT commands. The text positioning, justification and height can be altered as required, as can the text style and font.

> **Command:** TEXT
> **Justify/Style/<Start point>:** Pick a text start point
> **Height:** Type in a height or point using the mouse
> **Rotation angle:** 0 for horizontal text
> **Text:** Enter text

This will result in the required text being printed in the default style, (probably called STANDARD, incorporating the Simplex font) and left justified from the selected point. The indicated point sets the left-hand extremity of the baseline of the text.

If you select **Justify** by typing J, the following prompt will appear:

Align/Fit/Center/Middle/Right/TL/TC/TR/ML/MC/MR/BL/BC/BR:

Align   This prompts for two points which set the extremities of the text *baseline*. The overall character size and orientation of the text is adjusted to fit these limits. Consequently there will be no prompts for Height or Angle.

Fit   Similar to Align. The two points requested set the limits of the text but the height is separately specified. The character width is then stretched or compressed to fit.

Center   This prompts for a point which sets the centre point of the *baseline* of the text.

Middle   Similar to Center. The specified point sets the mid-point of the *body* of the text.

Right   The text *baseline* is right justified from the specified point.

TL   The specified point defines the Top Left corner point.

TC   The specified point defines the Top Center point.

TR   The specified point defines the Top Right corner point.

ML   The specified point defines the Middle Left point.

MC   The specified point defines the Middle Center point.

MR   The specified point defines the Middle Right point.

BL   The specified point defines the Bottom Left corner point.

BC   The specified point defines the Bottom Center point.

BR   The specified point defines the Bottom Right corner point.

See Figure 9.1

> *Note:*   If you have previously used the TEXT command in your drawing, then if you respond to the Start point prompt with a return, the height and the angle of the last text entry will be assumed. In addition, the new text will adopt the previous alignment mode and will automatically be positioned immediately below the previous text.

9.2 TEXT STYLES

The remaining option on the TEXT sub-menu is **Style**. This determines the appearance of the text rather than its position. It selects a text style which has previously been defined using the STYLE command. The default style supplied is called STANDARD and uses the Simplex text font.

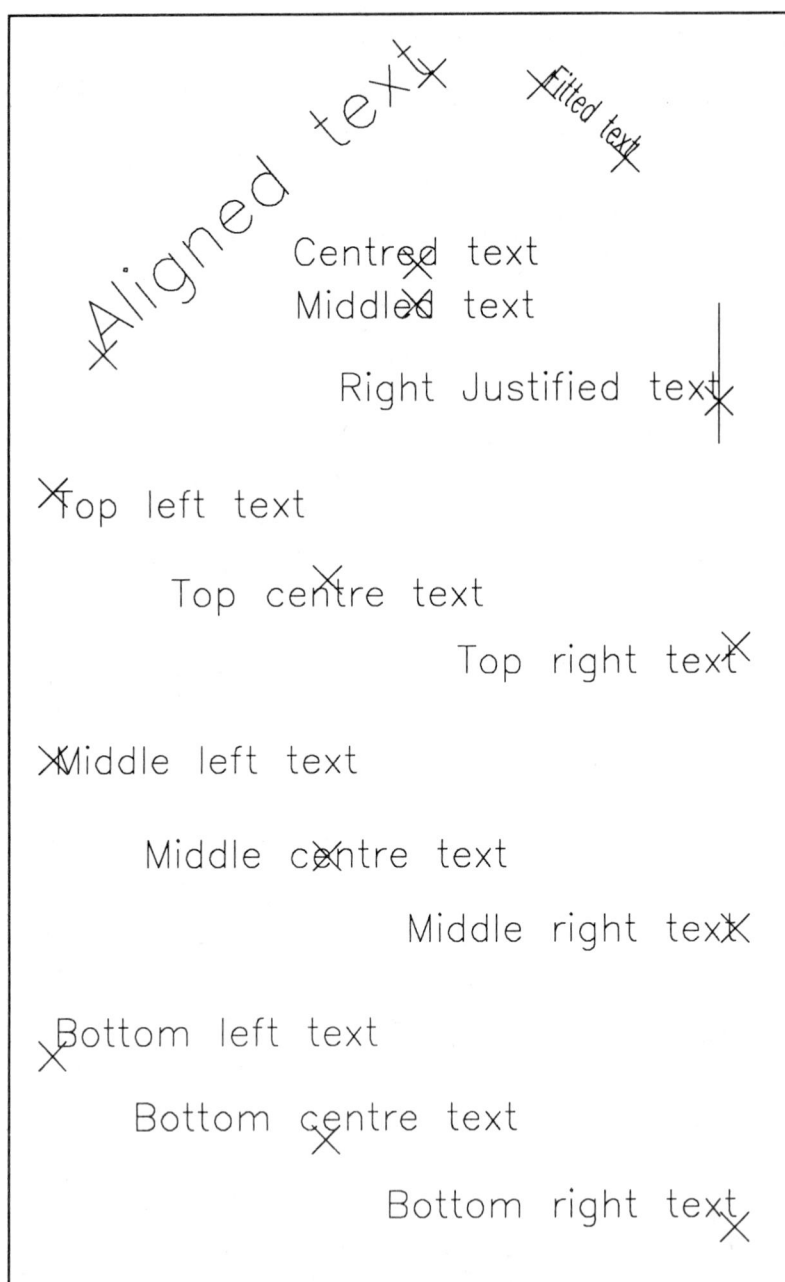

Figure 9.1 Justification modes

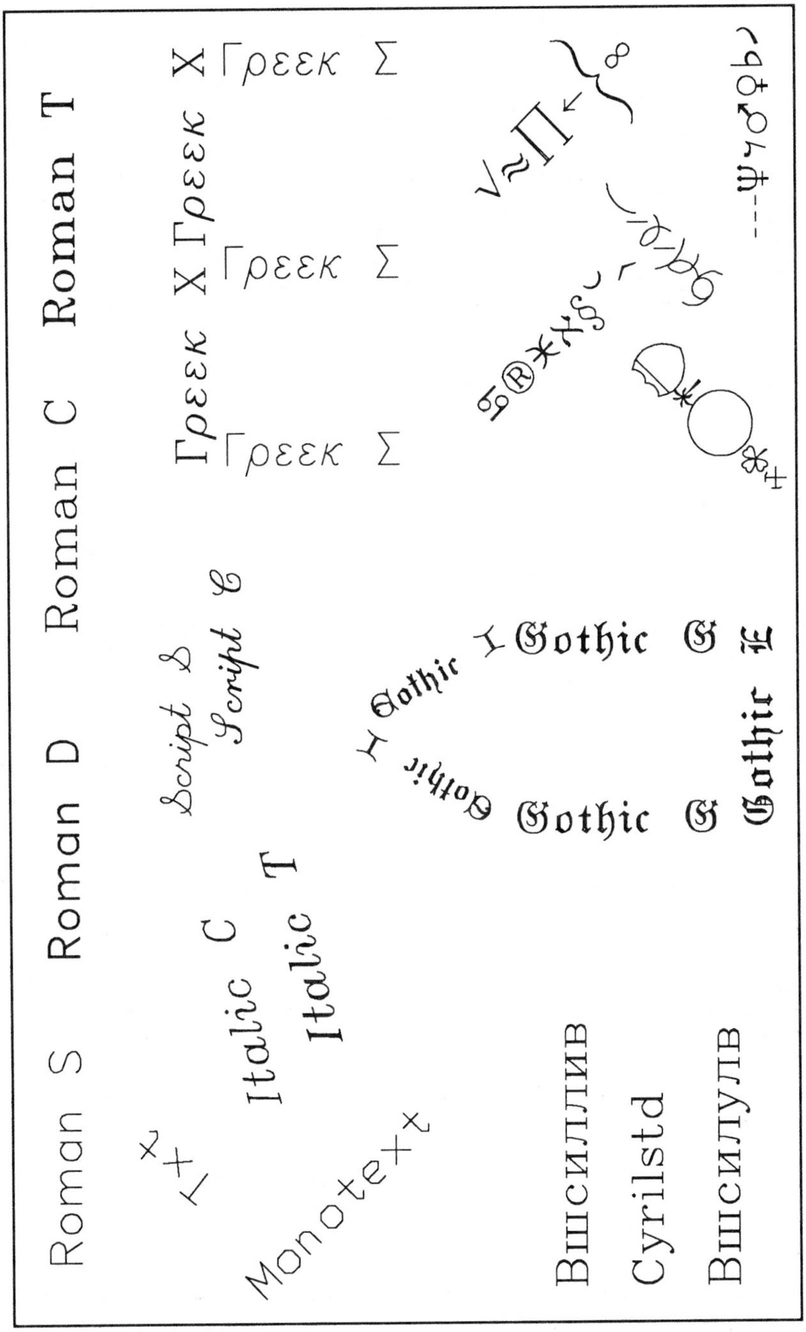

Roman S Roman D Roman C Roman T

Script S

Script C

Italic C

Italic T

Monotext

Γρεεκ Σ Γρεεκ Χ ΧΓρεεκ Σ ΧΓρεεκ Σ

Gothic G Gothic F

Gothic G Gothic G Gothic E

Вп силлив

Cyrilstd

Вп силул в

Figure 9.2 Text fonts

9.2.1 The STYLE command

If you do not wish to use the STANDARD style, then you can define your own using the STYLE command.

A user defined text style determines the text *font* to be used, e.g. Monotext, Romanc, Gothice etc. There are over twenty font styles available, ranging from Italic to music symbols, (see Figure 9.2). If you select the Text font... option under the DTEXT OPTIONS item on the **Options** pull down menu, an Icon Menu is displayed giving a visual representation of the fonts available.

The style also determines the height, width factor, and obliquing angle of the text together with options for backwards, upside-down and vertical orientation, (Figure 9.3).

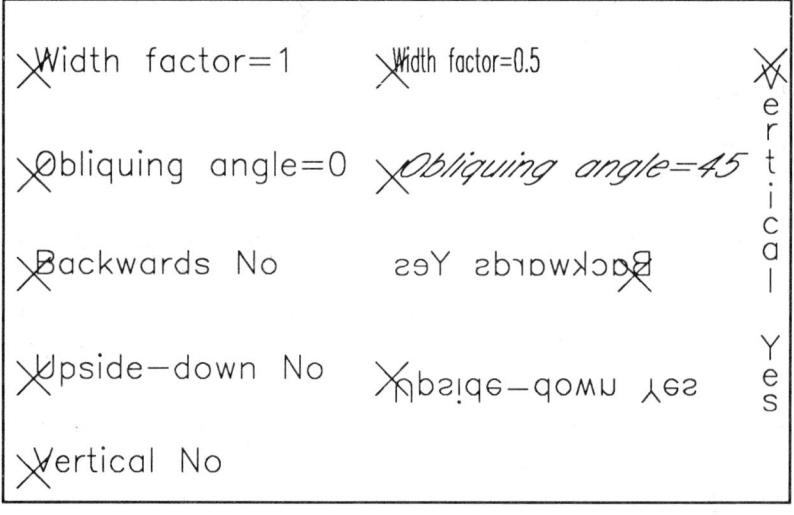

Figure 9.3   Aspects of text style

Command: STYLE
Text style name (or ?) <STANDARD>: MYSTYLE
New style.
Font file <txt>: GOTHICE
Height <0.00>:
Width factor <1.00>:
Obliquing angle <0.0000>:
Backwards? <N>
Upside-down? <N>
Vertical? <N>
MYSTYLE is now the current style

The default style, STANDARD, has a height of 0 (which allows you to adjust the height each time the style is used), a width factor of 1, an obliquing angle of 0 and it has the backward, upside-down and vertical options all normal.

> *Note:* If you re-define an existing style (using the original style name but changing the font), then any text previously written in this style will be changed to the new font.

A useful quick way to set a new text style is again to use the Text font... icon menu. If you now pick a text font from the icon menu, AutoCAD will proceed to set up a new text style using this font. The only difference from using the STYLE command from the keyboard is that you will not be allowed to give your own choice of name to the new style; the style name will default to the name of the font chosen.

9.3 SPECIAL CHARACTERS

AutoCAD supports a limited number of special characters in addition to the standard characters found in the text fonts, (see Figure 9.4). These are identified by the %% sign which must be inserted within the text string to warn AutoCAD that a special character is about to be used:

%%u - Toggle underline mode on/off
%%o - Toggle overline mode on/off
%%d - Draw "degrees" symbol °
%%p - Draw "plus/minus" symbol +-
%%c - Draw "circle diameter" symbol O/

What you type	What you get
%%uUNDERLINED%%u NORMAL	UNDERLINED NORMAL
%%oOVERLINED%%o NORMAL	OVERLINED NORMAL
25%%dC	25°C
%%p0.1mm	±0.1mm
%%c50mm	⌀50mm

Figure 9.4 Special character definitions

In addition to the above, it is possible to specify *any* of the characters in a font file by way of their ASCII code numbers. The ASCII (American Standard Code for Information Interchange) code numbers used in an AutoCAD font range from 1 to 126, (although codes 1-31 are control characters which are not normally used). The remaining characters may be specified using

%%nnn

where nnn represents the three digits of the ASCII code. This allows you to have access to all the characters of the font *even if they do not appear on your keyboard.*

It is also possible to add non-standard symbols to the character set and assign them code numbers between 130 and 255. In this case, the %%nnn method is the *only* way that you will be able to access them. (See Section 18.7.7.)

9.4 DYNAMIC TEXT (DTEXT)

DTEXT is an improvement on TEXT in that it allows you to see the text appearing on the screen as you type it on the keyboard. You can also edit each line with the backspace key and enter multiple lines of text within one command.

The command sequence is initially identical to TEXT.

Command: DTEXT
Justify/Style/<Start point>:   Pick a text start point
Height: Type in a height or point using the mouse
Rotation angle: 0 for horizontal text
Text: Enter text

When the **Text:** prompt appears, a box is drawn on the screen indicating the position, height and angle of the first character. As the text is entered it is echoed on the screen as well as on the command line. As each line of text is returned, the box cursor drops to a position one line below the starting point and the **Text:** prompt is repeated. A final return terminates DTEXT by re-writing all the text on the screen in its final form, obeying any Fit, Middle or other justification criteria.

Successive characters or lines of text within the same DTEXT command can be placed at different points on the screen, with the same justification mode, by using the mouse to point to the new start position.

The special %% characters may be used within DTEXT but they will be printed on the screen *verbatim*, e.g. as **%%p**, until the DTEXT command is terminated, at which time they will be translated into the relevant special symbol.

9.4.1 DTEXT option from the pull down menu

The DTEXT command may be accessed from the **Draw** pull down menu, but you will find that the response is different from the raw command entered from the keyboard. You will not see the **Justify/Style/<Start point>:** prompt but instead will be prompted:

Align/Fit/Center/Middle/Right/TL/TC/TR/ML/MC/MR/BL/BC/BR:

Unfortunately, the effect is to bar you from using the simple left justification mode which is normally initiated by picking **<Start point>:**. The remaining height and rotation angle options may be specified as before.

It is now possible to pre-set *any* of the above justification modes, and also the height and rotation angle of the text, by selecting DTEXT OPTIONS from the **Options** pull down *before* entering the DTEXT command. In this case, the corresponding prompts will not be given.

The text height and rotation may be pre-set simply by selecting the Text Height or Text Rotation option. You will be prompted:

Enter default text height or . to prompt each time <.>:

or

Enter default text rotation or . to prompt each time <.>:

A . response effectively cancels the preset.

The justification mode may be pre-set by selecting the Text alignment... option. This causes an icon menu to be displayed (see Figure 9.5). Selection of the relevant icon pre-sets any of the above justification modes *except* for simple left justification.

> *Note:* It should be possible to set this simple mode by choosing the third icon in the first column but in practice this gives you BL mode, as does the fourth icon in this column!

9.5 QUICK TEXT (QTEXT)

QTEXT acts as a toggle that can be switched On or Off at any time.

Command: QTEXT
ON/OFF: ON

When QTEXT is On, any existing text will be replaced at the next regeneration by a simple rectangular box outline which *approximately* covers the position previously occupied by the text, (see Figure 9.6). This greatly speeds up the regeneration process

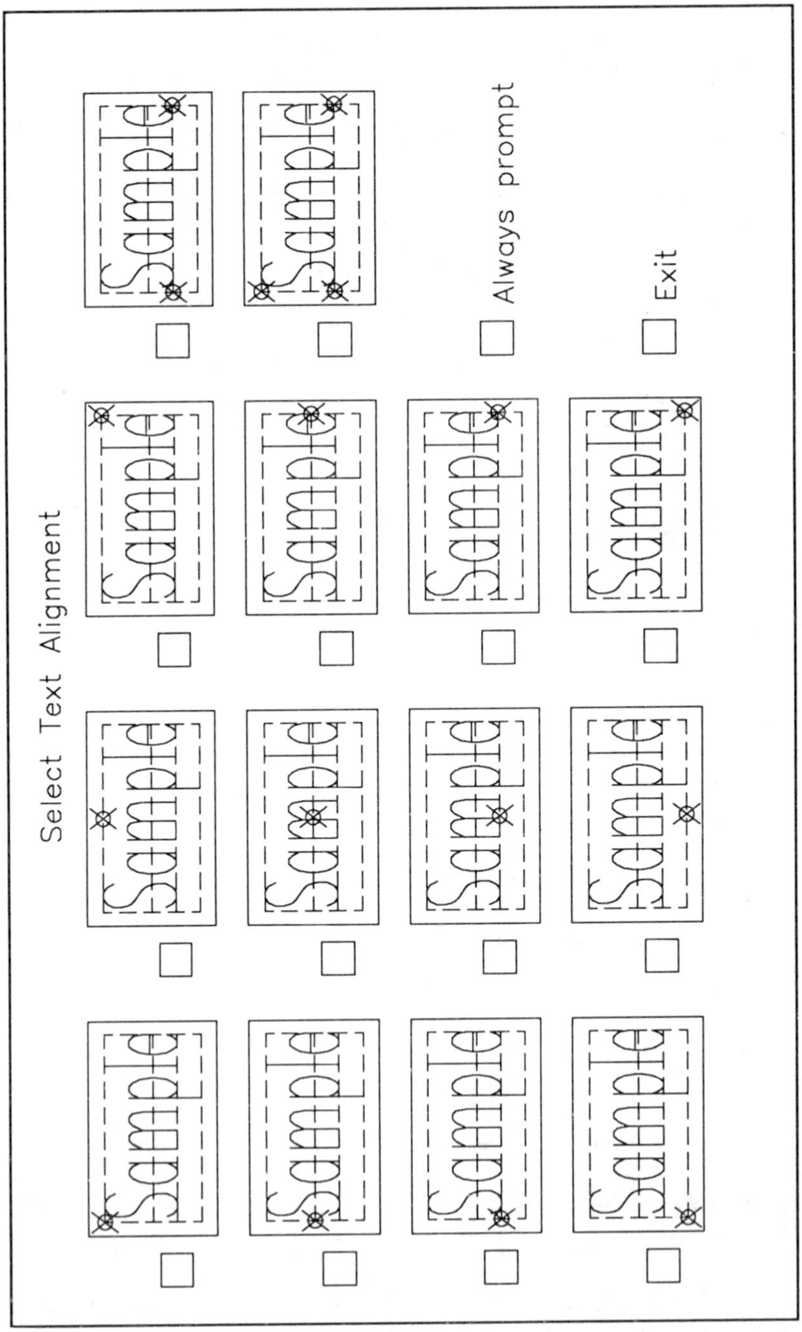

Figure 9.5 Text alignment icon menu

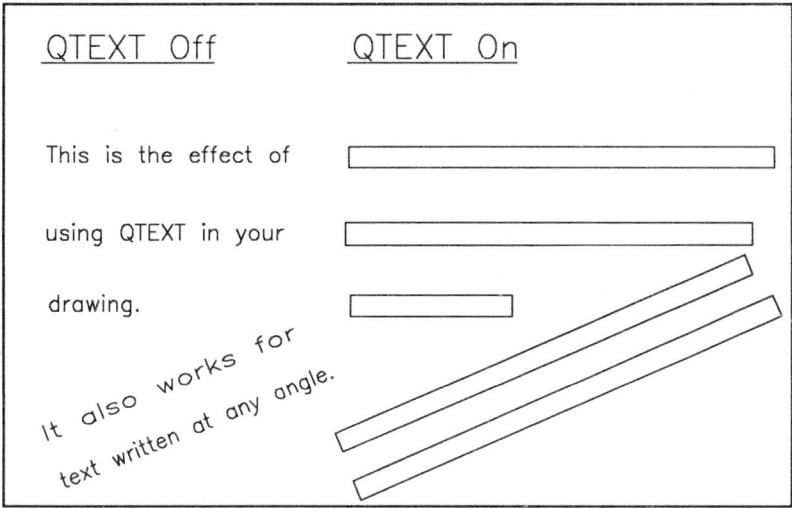

Figure 9.6   The effect of QTEXT

because the box is much quicker to draw than the text, particular if a complex text font is employed. At the same time, the position of the text is clearly shown to facilitate the layout of the drawing.

Text entered after Qtext mode has been turned On will initially be displayed normally, but after the next regeneration it also will be displayed in rectangular box form.

The current Qtext mode prevailing when the drawing is saved will be preserved and re-instated when the drawing is retrieved. When you wish to plot the full drawing, switch QTEXT off followed by REGEN.

9.6 TEXT EDITING USING DDEDIT

Existing text on screen may be edited using the text editor. This may be accessed the keyboard or from the **Edit** screen menu by selecting DDEDIT.

Command: DDEDIT
<Select a TEXT or ATTDEF object>/Undo

Select the text to be edited. A dialogue box containing the selected text will appear, (see Figure 9.7). If the text string is longer than the space in the dialogue box, an arrow at the end of the text box indicates that the text has overrun. picking this arrow gives access to the remainder of the text. To edit the text, point to the text box with

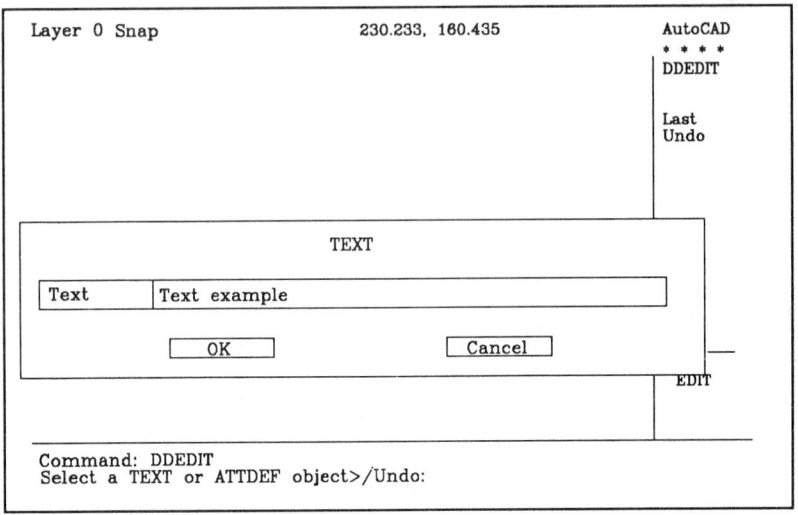

Figure 9.7 Text Editing dialogue box

the cursor arrow. If you now start to type new text from the keyboard, the old text will be totally erased and replaced by the new text. However, if you point to the text box and *then press the pick button* a box cursor will placed in the existing text at that point. Any editing (insertions or erasures) can now be effected from the keyboard at that point. The position of the box cursor may be moved, as often as required, by picking a different position within the text string. When editing is complete, pick the OK boxes to return to the drawing when the text will automatically be updated. Selecting Undo at this point will reverse the effect of the editing.

> *Note:*   The text style, height, rotation angle and justification mode of the text will remain unchanged after editing.

9.7 IMPORTING TEXT INTO AUTOCAD

ASCII (DOS text format) text may be imported into an AutoCAD drawing by selecting the Import text option under EXCHANGE on the **File** pull down menu. This causes a LISP routine (called ASCTEXT.LSP) to be executed which creates a new command, AT or ASCTEXT.

File to read (including extension):
Start point or Center/Middle/Right/?:

All the standard text justification modes are available as described in Section 9.1.

Height <3.00>:
Rotation angle <0.0000>:
Change text options? <N>:

If the default N is accepted then the specified text will be placed in the drawing. If you respond with a Y:

Distance between lines/<Auto>:
First line to read/<1>:
Number of lines to read/<All>:
Underscore each line? <N>:
Overscore each line? <N>:
Change text case? Upper/Lower/<N>:

The default N leaves the text in its original form; a U converts all the text to upper case and an L converts it all to lower case.

Set up columns? <N>:
Distance between columns:
Number of lines per column:

This set of prompts allows you to split up the text into any number of columns, each column containing the specified number of text lines. Take care to allow sufficient space between the columns to accommodate the longest line of text.

10. Blocks, attributes and Xrefs

10.1 INTRODUCING BLOCKS

A block is a series of objects grouped together to form a single entity. Once the user-specified block name has been given, the objects comprising the block are chosen,and the block is saved. It can then be recalled at any time and inserted in the drawing at any point and at anv scale and orientation, (see Figure 10.1).

After insertion blocks are treated as *single entities* and as such can be selected for scaling, rotating, moving, erasing etc., by simply pointing to any part of that block.

Blocks normally reside within the original drawing, but they can also be saved separately on to disk to be available for use in other drawings. This makes it possible to build up libraries of commonly used parts/objects which can be inserted as needed, thus simplifying the drawing procedure.

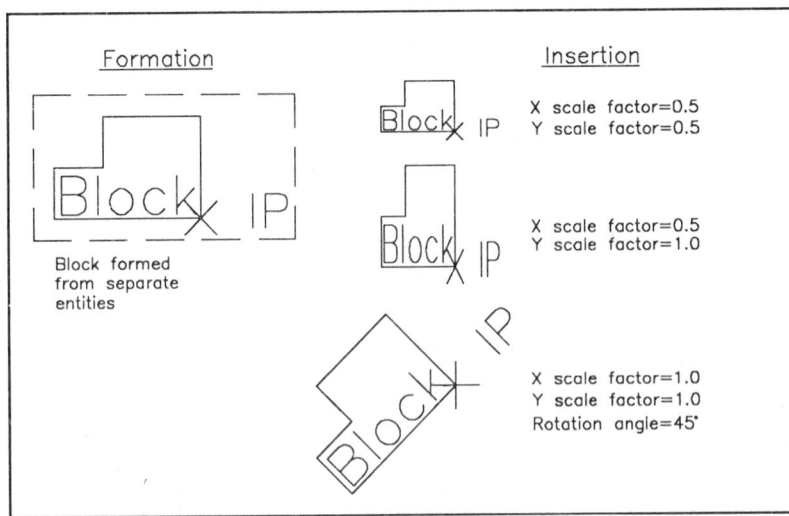

Figure 10.1   Use of blocks

It is possible for blocks to be made up of entities taken from any number of layers, and of any number of colours and linetypes. When the block is inserted into a drawing, these layers, colours and linetypes will be recreated.

There are a few exceptions to this:

● Any block made from objects drawn on layer 0 will be inserted into the current drawing layer and not onto layer 0.
● Objects drawn with the colour BYBLOCK or BYLAYER will take the current entity or layer colour when inserted.
● Objects drawn with the linetype BYBLOCK or BYLAYER will take the current entity or layer linetype when inserted.

It is easy to produce nested blocks, i.e. blocks within blocks, but the rules regarding colour, linetype etc., become more complicated.

10.2 BLOCK

The BLOCK command is used to define the block - to name it, choose an appropriate insertion point and select the objects which will become part of the final block.

Command: BLOCK
Block name (or ?):

Enter the block name, or the ? to see a list of the block names already in use in the current drawing.

Insertion base point:

This prompt is requesting a reference point to assign to the block. When the block is recalled it will be positioned with respect to this reference point, i.e. the insertion point of the block will be "tied" to the cross wires.

Select objects:

Use the standard **Select objects** methods to choose the objects/entities which are to become part of the block; these can also include other blocks. After all the objects have been chosen, press return to create the block.

> *Note:* When the block has been created the objects chosen will *always* be erased from the drawing. If you wish to retrieve then *immediately* use the OOPS command.

Blocks can also include text information as *attributes*, covered in detail in Section 10.5.

10.3 INSERT

The command INSERT is used to retrieve a previously saved block and add it to the current drawing. The inserted block can be scaled in the X-, Y- and Z- directions and rotated about the reference (insertion) point. This can be achieved before (Preset insertion) or after the block has been dragged to its final position.

> **Command:** INSERT
> **Block name (or ?):**
> **Insertion point:**
> **X scale factor <1> / Corner / XYZ:**
> **Y scale factor (default=X):**
> **Rotation angle:**

Some of these prompts need a bit of explanation:

- **Block name (or ?):** Respond with the name of any block defined in the current drawing *or* with the name of a previously saved drawing, (see Section 10.4). If you respond to this prompt with a ?, you will be given a list of blocks defined in the current drawing but if you respond with a ~ a file dialogue box will appear listing drawings within the current directory, (see Section 2.7.3).
- **Insertion point:** The position within the drawing where the block is to be placed. When the block was originally saved an insertion base point was specified; this will be located at the insertion point.
- **X scale factor <1> / Corner / XYZ:** The **X scale factor** can be set to whatever value is required. If the return key is the response to this prompt, the block will be inserted with its original scale. A negative scale factor can also be used; this has the effect of "mirroring" the block. **Corner** is used to specify both the X- and Y- scales at the same time, using the insertion point and another user-specified point as the corners of a box. **XYZ** relates to 3D visualization.
- **Y scale factor (default=X):** The **Y scale factor** will default to the X scale if the return key is the response, otherwise a separate Y- scale can be entered.
- **Rotation angle:** The angle by which the block is rotated about its insertion point can be specified here.

See Figure 10.1.

10.3.1 Preset Insertion

As described above, when the **insertion point:** prompt is displayed the block is normally dragged to the required position in the drawing and then scaled and rotated. However, there are a number of very useful alternative inputs which can be used at the **insertion point:** prompt *before* fixing the position of the block:

Scale	Allows the overall scale to be preset.
Xscale	Presets the X- scale factor.
Yscale	Presets the Y- scale factor.
Zscale	Presets the Z- scale factor.
Rotate	Presets the rotation angle.
PScale	Same as **Scale** but after the object has been positioned a scale factor is requested again.
PXscale	Same as **PScale** but only affects the X- scale.
PYscale	Same as **PScale** but only affects the Y- scale.
PZscale	Same as **PScale** but only affects the Z- scale.
PRotate	Same as **Rotate** but after the block is in its final position the rotation angle is requested again.

See Figures 10.2 and 10.3.

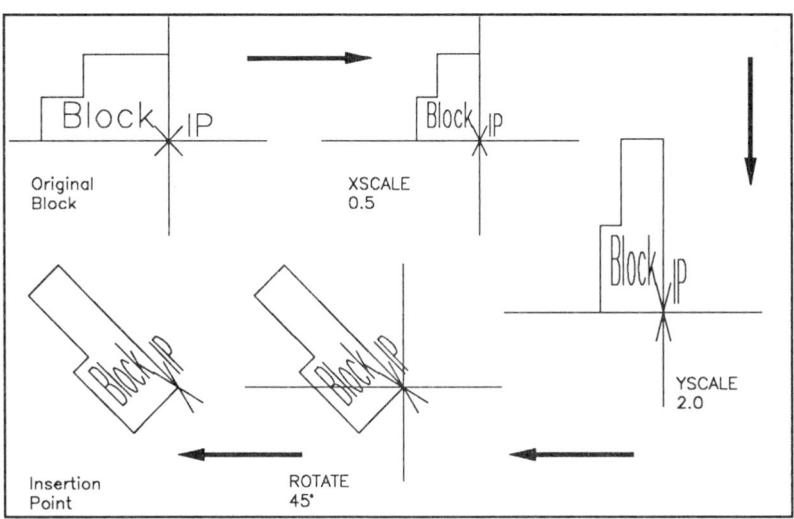

Figure 10.2   Scale and rotate before insertion

10.3.2 Exploding a block

When a block has been inserted it is treated as a single entity and can therefore be erased, moved, copied etc., by selecting a single point of that block. EXPLODE is used to change the block from its single entity form to its component parts. This makes it is possible to edit individual parts of the block.

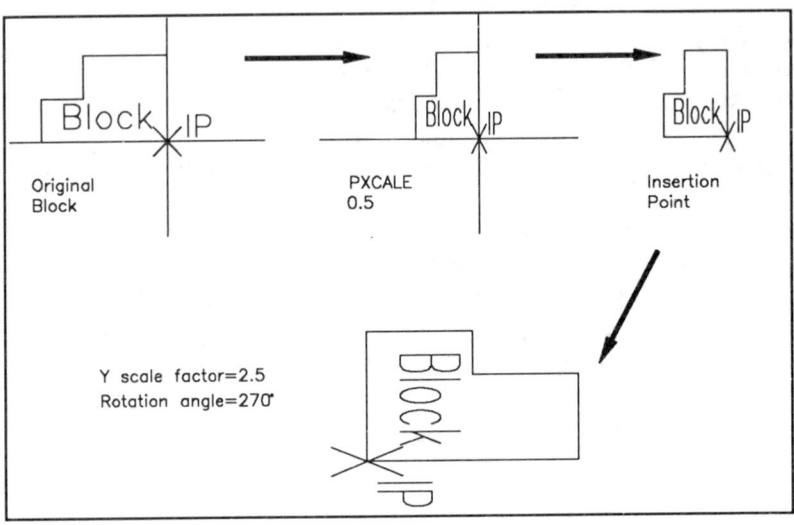

Figure 10.3   Preset insertion using PXscale

Command: EXPLODE
Select block reference, polyline, dimension or mesh

If a block has been inserted with the X-, Y- and Z-scale values not equal, then it cannot be exploded and the following error message is displayed:

X, Y, and Z scale factors must be equal.

10.3.3 Insert*

If the INSERT command is used and a * is entered *before* the block name, the block will in effect be pre-exploded on insertion into the drawing.

Command: INSERT Block name (or ?): *<Block name>
Insertion point:
Scale factor <1>:
Rotation angle <0>:

Only one scale factor is requested and this is then applied to both X- and Y- scales; negative scale factors cannot be used.

10.3.4 MINSERT

The MINSERT command allows a rectangular array of the chosen block to be inserted into the drawing. When MINSERT is called up, the standard INSERT command prompts appear, followed by the rectangular ARRAY command prompts.

```
Command: MINSERT
Block name (or ?):
Insertion point:
X scale factor <1> / corner / XYZ:
Y scale factor (default=X):
Rotation angle:
Number of rows (---) <1>:
Number of columns (|||) <1>:
Unit cell or distance between cells (---):
Distance between columns (|||):
```

After the standard INSERT prompts, AutoCAD will ask for the number of rows and columns, followed by a request for the distances between them (Figure 10.4). See Section 6.1.8 for a fuller treatment of arrays.

> *Note:* As with the INSERT command, responding to the block name prompt with a ~ displays a dialogue box of available drawings in the current directory.
>
> A MINSERTed block cannot be exploded.

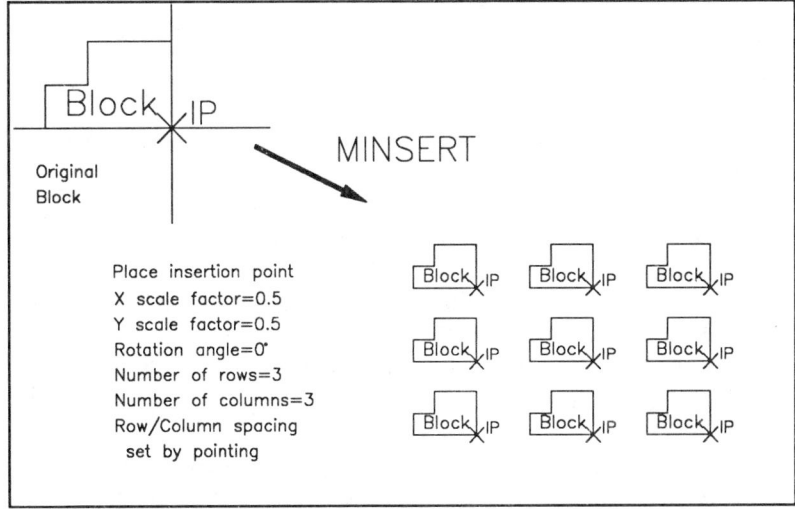

Figure 10.4 Multiple inserts

10.4 WBLOCK

Ordinary blocks may only be used within the drawing in which they were created. WBLOCK, which stands for Write BLOCK, is used to write a block out to disk so that it can be inserted into other drawings. A block saved to disk by WBLOCK carries a .DWG extension and is therefore indistinguishable from an ordinary drawing file. Conversely, a previously saved drawing may be treated as a block and inserted into the current drawing, (see Figure 10.5).

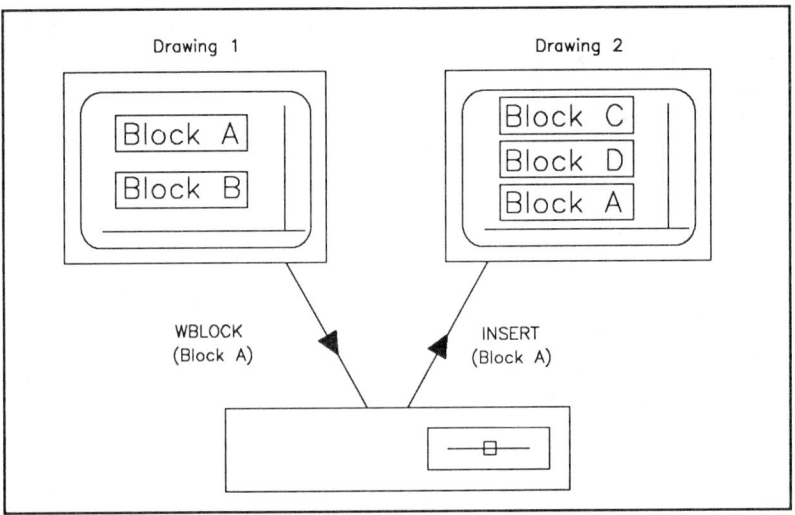

Figure 10.5   Block transfer between drawings

Command: WBLOCK
File name:

This is the name under which the block will be *filed on the disk* - it is your choice.

Block name:

There are 4 allowed responses to **Block name**. This can be rather confusing. If the entities which are to comprise the Wblock have already been defined in an ordinary block, then it would be a waste of time to re-define them. The first two of the following responses are alternative ways of referencing this block:

● **name** Input the name of the previously-defined block; this will be copied to the disk as the Wblock under the file name.

- **=** This is used when you have arranged that the Wblock file name is the same as that of an existing block name.
- ***** The entire drawing is made the Wblock; this has the same effect as the SAVE command.
- (blank) i.e. give a return.   Autocad will ask for the user to select objects and an insertion point as with the ordinary BLOCK command.

10.5 BLOCK ATTRIBUTES

It is possible to include in a block information other than just the geometric shapes which make up its visible structure. Such data are called *attributes*. An attribute is treated as text and may consist of letters, numbers or symbols. When a block is defined, any attribute text strings are included in the block definition. Subsequent insertions of the block will include the attribute data.

The simplest attribute is a *constant*. A constant attribute has the same value for every occurrence of the block and it cannot easily be changed. A typical example would be a part code number associated with a component in an engineering drawing. Every insertion of that particular component would thus carry the identifying code.

Conversely, the attribute may be made *variable* so that the text may be changed at every insertion. In this case, a prompt for the text is given as part of the block insertion sequence. The wording of the prompt is your choice and is saved with the block. Variable attributes are invaluable for grouping otherwise identical blocks under suitable headings, for example Room Number, Owner, Process Type or Component Value.

Finally, there are *preset* attributes. These are attributes which are variable, but normally take up their default value on insertion, i.e. there is normally no prompt. In this respect they behave as constant attributes. Where preset attributes differ from both constant and variable attributes is in the method of insertion of the block. If the block is inserted via keyboard or screen menu commands, then the preset attribute is automatically set to its default value (assuming the ATTDIA system variable is set to 0). If however the block is inserted using the dialogue box, (accessed via the INSERT command if ATTDIA is set to 1), then the preset attribute is treated as a variable and the dialogue box will offer you the default value which may be either accepted or changed. (See Section 10.5.3.)

Attributes, either constant, variable or preset, are stored in the block definition together with an identifying text label called an *attribute tag*. The tag has a similar function to a field name in a database and allows you to access the attributes separately. Multiple attribute tags may be appended to a single block, provided that tag names are not duplicated, (see Figure 10.6).

After a block has been inserted into a drawing the associated attribute values are added, (see Figure 10.7), and may be made *visible* or *invisible* as required. Any change made to the overall visibility will force a regeneration of the drawing. If all the attributes are visible, the process of regeneration can be slowed down significantly while the attribute data are printed on the screen.

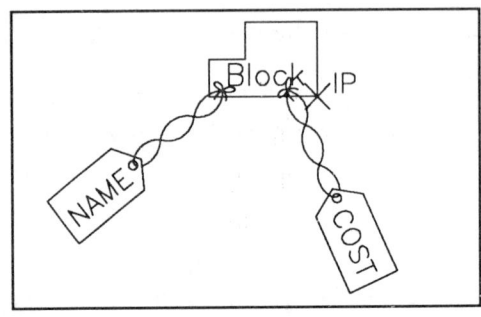

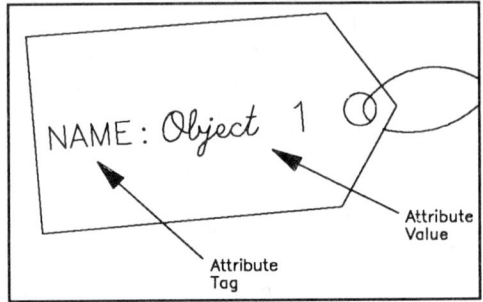

Figure 10.6   Attribute tags   **Figure 10.7**   Adding attribute values

10.5.1 Defining Block Attributes

Attributes must be defined *before* the block definition process.

Command: ATTDEF
Attribute modes - Invisible:N Constant:N Verify:N Preset:N

This prompt allows you to set three features of the attribute:

- The visibility of the attribute, (although this can be overridden after insertion using the ATTDISP command).
- Whether the attribute is to be treated as a constant, a variable or a preset.
- Whether you wish to have a chance, during the insertion process, to verify that the attribute's value is correct.

The initial response to all four alternatives is **N**, as shown. To alter any response to **Y** you must return an I, C, V or P as required. The prompt will then re-appear with the relevant N changed to a Y. I,C,V and P may be toggled N/Y indefinitely. When all four responses are satisfactory, press return to accept. AutoCAD then prompts:

Attribute tag:

Define the attribute tag using any characters except blanks.

Attribute prompt:

Enter text to be used to prompt for the attribute value upon insertion of the block. *This is not applicable if the attribute is to be a constant; in this case the prompt is omitted.*

Attribute value:

If the attribute is to be a constant, this prompts for the constant value. If the attribute is to be a variable or preset this prompt is used to offer a default value on insertion of the block. This may be a null if desired.

AutoCAD now proceeds to prompt for the positioning, height and angle of the text of the attribute, exactly as for a DTEXT or TEXT command, i.e. BL, TR, centred, right-justified, etc. The attribute tags will then be displayed on the drawing as specified. You can automatically align a series of attributes as with a series of text strings - simply enter a space or return when prompted for the text starting point - AutoCAD will align each new attribute tag below the previous one.

EXAMPLE

To define a variable attribute with a tag NAME and a default value of OBJECT 1:

Command: ATTDEF
Attribute modes - Invisible:N Constant:N Verify:N Preset:N

Note that the **N** against **Constant** indicates a variable attribute.

Attribute tag: NAME
Attribute prompt: Please name this item
Default attribute value: OBJECT 1
Justify/Style/<Start point>:
Height:
Rotation angle:

Attributes may be edited at this stage if necessary using the DDEDIT command. (See Section 9.6.)

When all the required attribute definitions have been entered the block can be defined. Proceed as normal with the block definition. When prompted to select the objects of the block, simply include the attribute tags as displayed - using a window to include all the tags is probably the easiest method. When selection is complete, the block will be defined and, as usual, will disappear from the screen. The attribute tags will also disappear and will not normally be seen again.

10.5.2 Inserting a Block with Attributes

It is important when inserting a block with preset attributes into a drawing to remember the following points:

- If the preset attributes are to be considered constant, then the commands can be entered from the keyboard or from any of the screen, pull down or tablet menus
- If the preset attributes are to be treated as variable, then the dialogue box *must* be used.

When the block is to be inserted into a drawing, the usual prompts about position, scale and orientation are given. If the attributes of the block are all constants, then block insertion occurs immediately. If the attributes are set to "visible", then the *attribute values* (not the *attribute tags*) are displayed with the same text style, position and justification etc., as was specified for the tags at the definition stage.

If any of the attributes are variable then the prompt for their value is issued, together with the specified default. This is repeated for all the variable attributes, after which the block is inserted as before.

10.5.3 Insertion using the Dialogue Box

To insert a block with attributes using the dialogue box, the system variable ATTDIA must be set to 1. The dialogue box displays all the variable and preset attribute names, along with their default values. The desired values can then be modified and, once all are correctly set, the block is inserted by picking the **OK** square in the dialogue box. (See Figure 10.8.)

Note: If you call INSERT from the draw pull down menu then ATTDIA is temporarily set to 1.

10.5.4 Suppression of Attribute Request

The system variable ATTREQ controls the suppression of the attribute request prompts. The default setting for this variable is 1 and normal attribute request prompts appear. If ATTREQ is set to zero then, on block insertion, *no* attribute prompts appear, and all attributes take up their default values.

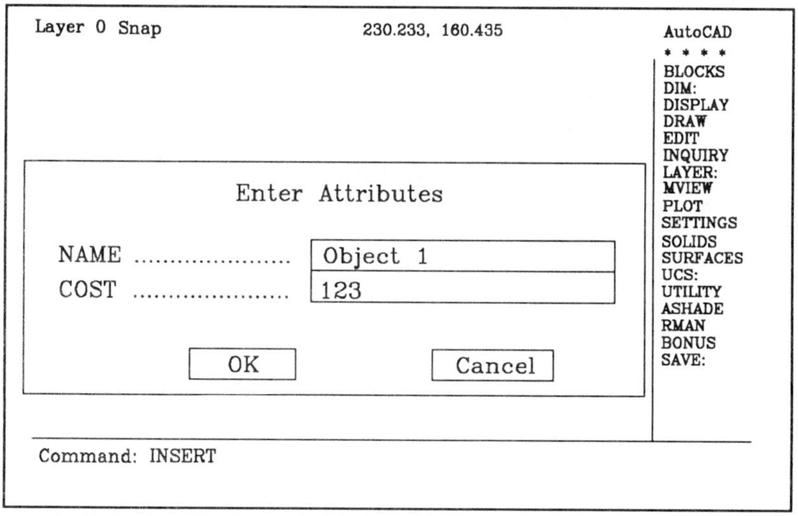

```
Layer 0  Snap                230.233, 160.435            AutoCAD
                                                         * * * *
                                                         BLOCKS
                                                         DIM:
                                                         DISPLAY
                                                         DRAW
                                                         EDIT
                                                         INQUIRY
                                                         LAYER:
              Enter  Attributes                          MVIEW
                                                         PLOT
                                                         SETTINGS
                                                         SOLIDS
       NAME  ......................  | Object  1 |       SURFACES
                                                         UCS:
       COST  ......................  | 123 |             UTILITY
                                                         ASHADE
                                                         RMAN
                                                         BONUS
                  | OK |       | Cancel |               SAVE:


    Command: INSERT
```

Figure 10.8   Insertion using a dialogue box

10.5.5 Visibility

The visibility of the attribute values after block insertion may be controlled by the ATTDISP command.

Command: ATTDISP
Normal/OFF/OFF <Normal>:

The Normal mode allows the visibility of each attribute to be as specified during the ATTDEF process. The On mode overrides this and makes all attributes visible. Similarly, the Off mode makes all attributes invisible.

10.5.6 Editing Attribute Values

If the *value* of an attribute is to be changed then the DDATTE or the ATTEDIT commands can be used.

Note: The editing functions cannot be applied to constant attributes.

The DDATTE command is dialogue box orientated and is very similar in operation to the insert dialogue box. When DDATTE is invoked, you will be prompted to select the block to be edited. Once chosen, a dialogue box will appear with the chosen block preset and/or variable attribute names and existing values. These values can then be modified as required, (see Figure 10.9).

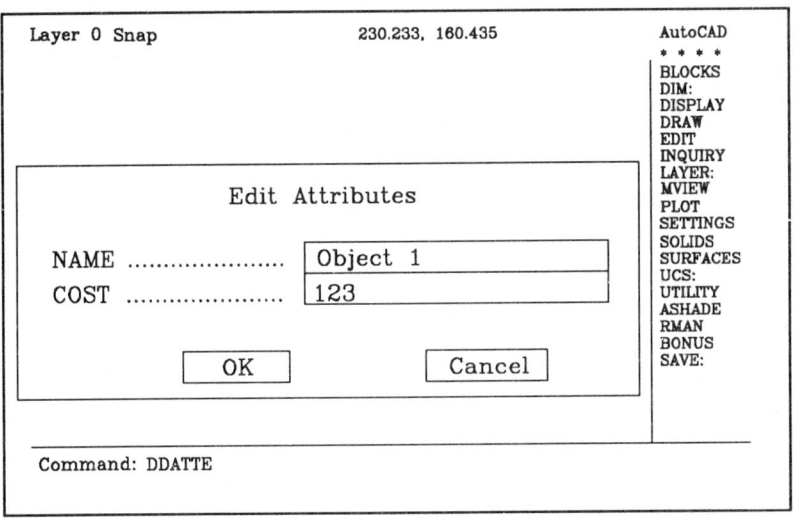

Figure 10.9 Edit Attribute dialogue box

The ATTEDIT command gives wide scope in the editing of attribute values. Thus, it allows you to edit *all*, or *selected*, attributes of all, or selected, blocks. The scope of the command is first set by specifying which attributes, or groups of attributes, are to be edited and which blocks are to be considered. AutoCAD then searches the drawing for all attributes which match this pattern and presents them for modification.

The ATTEDIT command can be applied either to individual attributes, or globally to all the attributes in the drawing. The command is very powerful and requires some practice to use effectively.

10.5.7 Individual Attribute Property Editing using ATTEDIT

If the individual attribute editing route is chosen, then in addition to changing the attribute value it is also possible to change other properties such as colour, layer, position etc.

Command: ATTEDIT
Edit Attributes one at a time? <Y>: Y
Block name specification <*>:
Attribute tag specification <*>:
Attribute value specification <*>:

These three questions allow you to specify the scope of the command. By returning the default wild card symbol * you can apply the ATTEDIT command to every attribute within the drawing.

Select attributes:

Point to individual blocks or use a window to select a number of blocks; those which satisfy the scope criteria may then be edited. The first attribute to be edited is marked with a cross X.

Value/Position/Height/Angle/Style/Layer/Color/Next <N>: V

These property options are largely self explanatory, but in the case of **Value** a subsidiary question is asked.

Change or Replace? <R>:

If you select **Replace** then you are allowed to change the complete attribute entry, whereas if you select Change then AutoCAD prompts

String to change:
New string:

which allows you to change *part* of the attribute string.

EXAMPLE

If the old attribute value represents a serial part number LS127649/341/000 then by selecting **Change:**

String to change: 341
New string: 678

a new attribute value of LS127649/678/000 is attained.

Other properties of the same attribute can be modified until the **Next** option is selected. The marker cross X then moves on to the next attribute to be edited.

> *Note:* Unlike the PEDIT Edit vertex option, it is not possible to return to an attribute once the **Next** option has been selected, i.e. there is no Previous option.

10.5.8 Global Attribute Editing using ATTEDIT

If the individual attribute editing route is not chosen then the global option is invoked. This allows the multiple editing of all the selected blocks in one operation. However, the only editing allowed is the changing of all or part of the *attribute value string* (as described above - **Change** option).

> **Command:** ATTEDIT
> **Edit Attributes one at a time? <Y>:** N
> **Global edit of attribute values.**
> **Edit only attributes visible on screen? <Y>:**

If you respond with a Y only attributes selected from the screen will be edited. If you respond with an N every attribute within the drawing which fits the scope will be edited

> **Block name specification <*>:**
> **Attribute tag specification <*>:**
> **Attribute value specification <*>:**
> **Select attributes:**

This prompt is displayed only when editing attributes visible on screen - use a suitable window

> **nnn attributes selected.**
> **String to change:**
> **New string:**

10.6 EXTERNAL REFERENCED DRAWINGS

When constructing a drawing, it is possible to incorporate other previously created component drawings as blocks using the INSERT command, as described in section 10.3.7. This useful facility is however limited, in that later changes to these component drawings do not affect the main drawing once insertion of the block has taken place. The result is that, if a number of draughtsmen are working on the components of a large master drawing, the master cannot be assembled until all the component drawings have been completed. Similarly, any change made to any one of the component drawings means that the master drawing has to be re-assembled.

If the XREF command is used instead of INSERT, then these problems are overcome. The component drawings may be referenced, (attached), to the master drawing but they are not permanently fixed; each time the master drawing is loaded the *latest version* of the component drawings is used. (See Figure 10.10.) There is no limit to the number of drawings which may be referenced from a single master, and these component drawings may themselves contain references to other drawings, resulting in several *nested* levels of references.

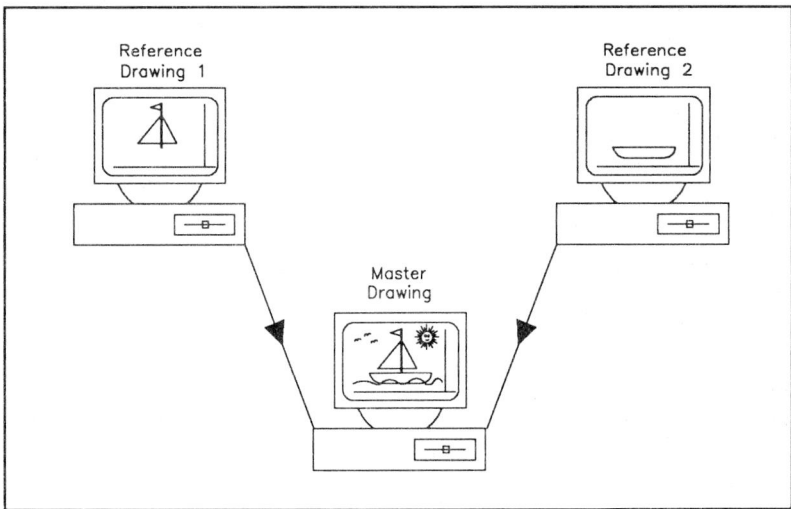

Figure 10.10   Referenced drawings

10.6.1 The XREF command

The XREF command may be accessed from the **Draw** pull down or from the **Draw** screen menu.

> **Command:** XREF
> **?/Bind/Detach/Path/Reload/<Attach>:** return
> **Xref to Attach:**   Give filename

Enter the name of the *drawing file* (.dwg) which is to be referenced (attached). This file name can also include a path if the file is not in the default directory. Alternatively, a tilde (~) response will call up the file dialogue box which will list available drawings, (see Section 2.7.3). AutoCAD will respond:

Attach Xref FILENAME: filename
FILENAME loaded.

After the file has been loaded, AutoCAD responds with the standard block INSERT responses:

Insertion point:
X scale factor <1> / Corner / XYZ:
Y scale factor (default=X):
Rotation angle <0.0000>:

Note: Once a component drawing has been loaded as a block you will not be allowed to load it as an XREF in the same drawing. The converse is also true.

When referencing a 3D or solid modelling drawing, the plan view of the WCS of the component drawing will be placed on the current UCS of the master drawing. It is advised that the master drawing coordinate system is set to WCS *before* a 3D or solid component drawing is referenced to it.

After a drawing has been attached it is treated as if it were a block except that *it can not* be EXPLODEd and hence none of its component entities can be edited. If you LIST the XREF, it will be identified as a BLOCK REFERENCE with a sub-heading "External reference".

Any *dependent symbols*, i.e. layers, linetypes, text styles, blocks and Dim styles associated with the component drawing, will remain with it after attachment to the master drawing, but they will not be available while the drawing remains referenced. To differentiate them from resident symbols, AutoCAD automatically prefixes their names with the file name and a | character.

EXAMPLE

When a drawing called TEST.DWG containing a layer called SAMPLE is referenced from a master drawing, then the layer becomes TEST|SAMPLE. Although its visibility, colour and linetype may be changed it may not be made current. (See Figure 10.11.)

If the Attach default is not taken there are a number of alternative options:

?/Bind/Detach/Path/Reload/<Attach>:

?   Returns a list of drawings already referenced within the current drawing together with their associated paths. This includes nested reference drawings.

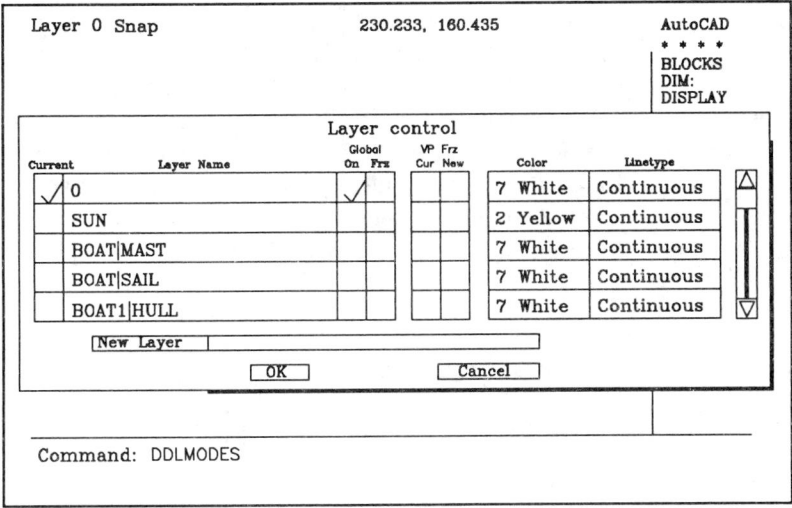

Figure 10.11   Layer dialogue box

Bind   This causes an existing referenced drawing to be permanently incorporated into the master drawing *as a block*. Once this has occurred, subsequent loading of the modified master drawing will not make reference to the component drawing and therefore will not incorporate any subsequent changes. Once a reference drawing has been bound as a block, it will have all the usual block characteristics, e.g. it will now be possible to EXPLODE it. The dependent symbols associated with the original reference drawing will now become available for use and their names will automatically be modified.

EXAMPLE

In the previous example, if the reference drawing TEST.DWG is bound to the master drawing, the layer TEST|SAMPLE becomes TEST0SAMPLE, where 0 replaces the | character and may be modified to 1 etc., if the name already exists. You are now free to edit this name if required. The layer is now available for use, i.e. it can be made current.

Detach

This *completely* removes a previously attached reference drawing from the master drawing. You cannot remove a nested reference drawing with this sub-command.

Path

If the name and/or the path of a reference drawing which has previously been attached to a master drawing is no longer valid, then, on re-loading the master drawing, the reference drawing will not be found. In place of the reference drawing, its name and path will written on the master drawing (error text) at the insertion point with its original scale and rotation angle, (see Figure 10.12). The **Path** option allows the name and path data to be corrected *within the master drawing*. The reference drawing will then be automatically re-loaded to replace the error text.

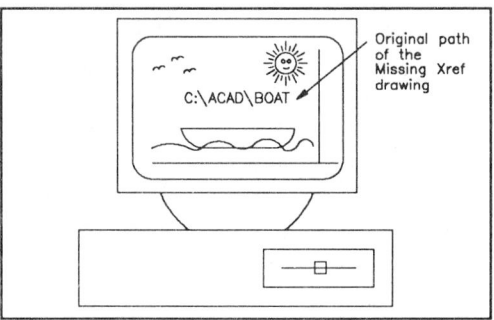

C:\ACAD\BOAT

Original path
of the
Missing Xref
drawing

Figure 10.12   Path error message

Reload

If you know that a reference drawing(s) has been modified *since* it was attached to the current master drawing, then you can force AutoCAD to update the master drawing by *Reloading* the latest version of the specified component drawing(s). This avoids having to save and re-load the entire master drawing to achieve the same effect.

10.6.2 The XBIND command

The *dependent symbols*, i.e. layers, linetypes, text styles, blocks and Dim styles associated with any referenced drawing will not normally become part of the master drawing unless the complete referenced drawing is bound to the master. However, if you wish to have access to any of these dependent symbols, it is possible to bind them selectively using XBIND *without* binding the referenced drawing.

Command: XBIND
Block/Dimstyle/LAyer/LType/Style:

As in the case of a bound reference drawing, the relevant name, e.g. TEST|SAMPLE becomes, after XBIND, TEST0SAMPLE.

The XBIND command allows you to inject a required dependent symbol, previously created in some other drawing, by simply attaching that drawing, XBINDing the required symbol(s) and then detaching the reference drawing.

11. Dimensioning

Dimensions may be added to a drawing by the rather tedious method of drawing each dimension line, finding its length, and then adding the dimension via the TEXT command. A much easier, more efficient method is to use AutoCAD's comprehensive in-built DIMension facility, accessed using the DIM or DIM1 commands. When using this facility, all the relevant lines, arcs and text features which go to make up a dimension are drawn automatically.

If these commands are selected from the screen menu or typed in directly from the keyboard, then all the dimension facilities will be available in their basic form. A more convenient and easier to use method of adding dimensions to your drawing is to use the icon menus available under Dim on the **Draw** pull down menu. (See Figures 11.1, 11.2 and 11.3.)

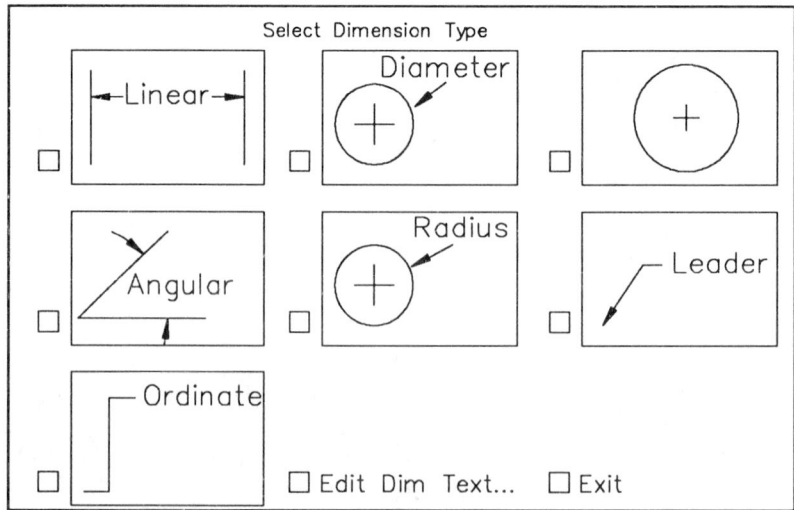

Figure 11.1   Dimension type icon menu

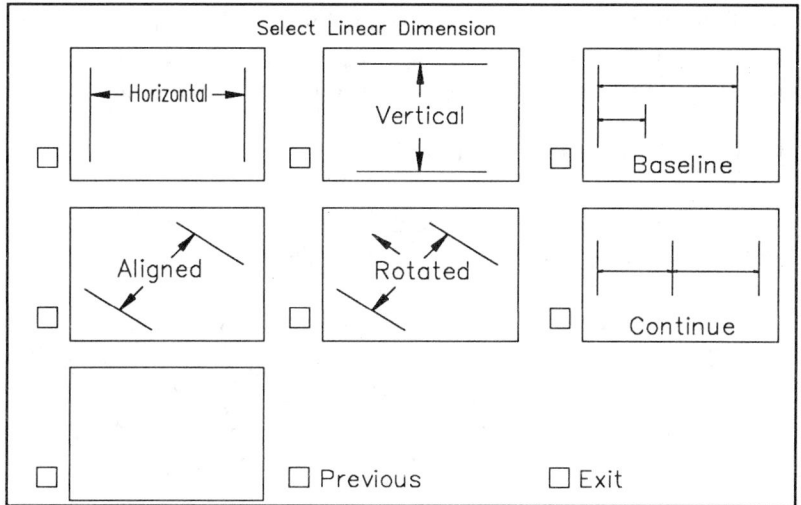

Figure 11.2 Linear dimension icon menu

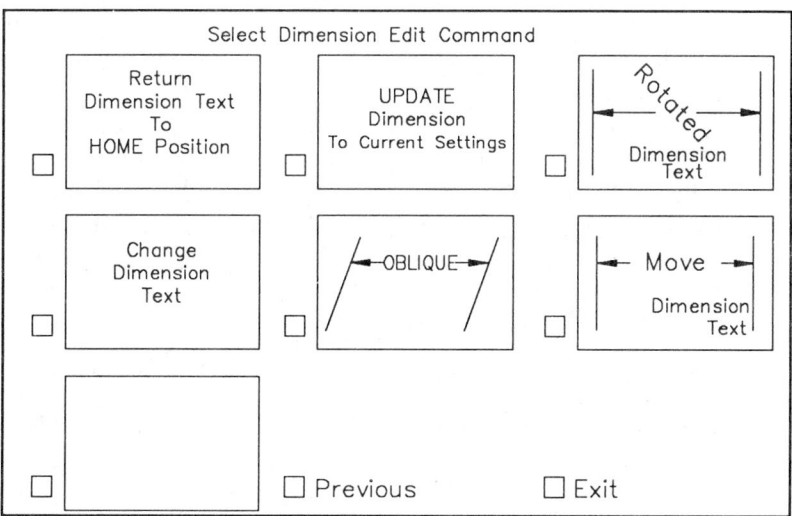

Figure 11.3 Dimension edit icon menu

There are five basic types of dimensioning available - linear, angular, diameter, radius and ordinate. These, plus a number of additional features such as centre marks and leader lines, are controlled by a large number of dedicated, user-controlled, dimension variables. The dimension variables control *every* aspect of the way in which a dimension is displayed and it is therefore possible to customise dimensions to suit individual applications. Any number of sets of user-defined selections of these dimension variables may be saved under various dimension *style names*.

11.1. DIMENSION TERMINOLOGY

There are various terms which are used to describe the way in which an entity can be dimensioned and it is essential to be familiar with these. (See Figures 11.4 and 11.5.)

- *Alternate units:* Two sets of units can be used simultaneously, e.g. the dimension text can be displayed in both inches *and* millimetres.
- *Arrows:* Different countries and professions have a variety of different draughting standards; for this reason AutoCAD allows the drawing of arrows, tick marks or an arbitrary arrow block (defining a symbol of your choice) at the end of the dimension line.
- *Centre mark/line:* The centre of a circle or arc can be shown by using either a centre mark (a small cross) or a centre line (a broken lines crossing at the centre and intersecting the circumference of the circle or arc).
- *Dimension line:* A line with arrows which marks out the dimension boundary; the dimension text is positioned either along-side the dimension line or it divides the dimension line in two. If the dimension is too small to include the text, then the dimension lines can be made to take the form of two arrows pointing inward to two short lines which mark the positions of the measured object.
- *Dimension text:* This is the text string which is used to indicate the measured dimension. AutoCAD will automatically compute the dimension text from the drawing (by default); this can be inserted directly into the drawing. Alternatively, this response can be over-ridden and the dimension text can be input from the keyboard. The dimension text will be in the current text style, and default units. These can be changed by invoking the UNITS command.
- *Extension lines:* If the dimension line is drawn outside the limits of the object being measured, then extension lines are drawn, perpendicular to the dimension line. They are used only with linear and angular dimensioning.
- *Leaders:* A leader is a line drawn from the object being measured to an area of the drawing free to take the dimension text; e.g. if a circle is too small to have the radius drawn within it, then a leader would be used to position the dimension text in a free area outside the circle.

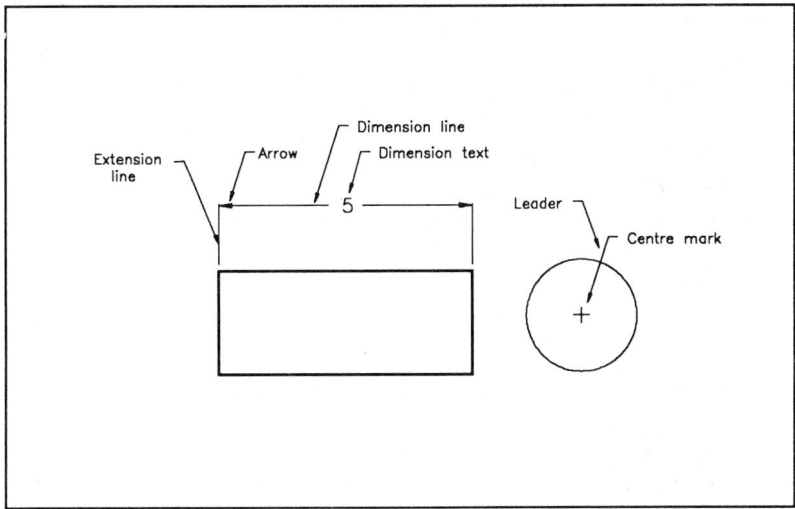

Figure 11.4 Dimension terminology

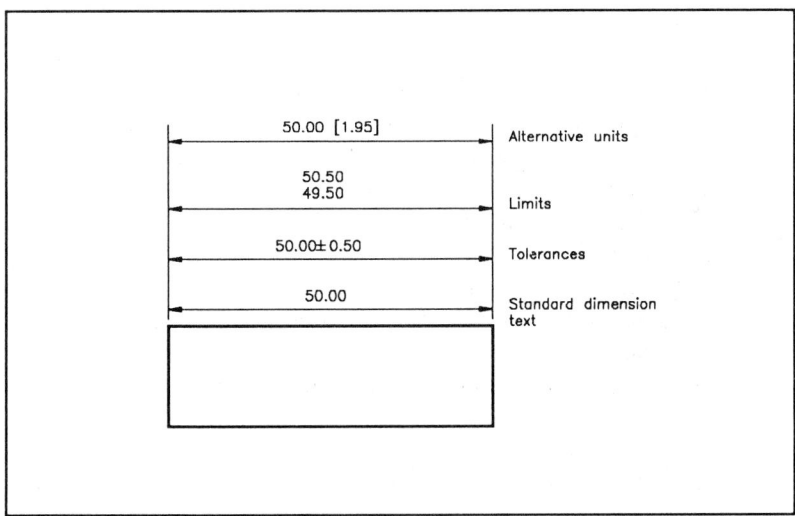

Figure 11.5 Dimension units

- *Limits:*   The tolerance values can be added and subtracted from the dimension value giving the limits for the measured line rather than the nominal value. The upper and lower limits will be displayed one above the other.
- *Ordinate:*   The X- and/or Y- coordinate of a point in the drawing.
- *Tolerances:*   Dimension tolerances can be appended to the dimension text automatically. The plus and minus quantities may be equal or may be different. If they are equal then AutoCAD will use the ± symbol, if they are different then they will be displayed one above the other.
- *Variables:*   The presentation of dimensions in a drawing is controlled by a set of dimension variables, some being simple On/Off types while others have numerical values. These can be changed at any time from within the drawing.

11.2. DIM AND DIM1

The two commands DIM and DIM1 are used to access the dimension function. DIM1 is used when a *single* dimension is to be added to the drawing, whereas DIM is used when a number of dimensions are to be added.

When using DIM, the **Command:** prompt is replaced by the **Dim:** prompt. To return to the **Command:** prompt select another command, use Ctrl C, or select EXIT from the DIM menu.

The screen menu which appears when either the DIM or DIM1 command is invoked is as follows:

AUTOCAD
* * * *
DIM:
DIM1:

angular
Dim Vars
leader
linear
oblique
ORDINAT:
radial
status
style
trotate
undo

TEdit
EXIT

next ----------------> **HOMETEXT**
UPDATE
NEWTEXT

Dimstyle
Save
Restore
Override
Variabls
?

11.3 ADDING DIMENSIONS TO A DRAWING

11.3.1 Linear dimensions

When the linear dimensioning option is chosen from the main dimension menu, the following new menu appears:

horiz
vertical
aligned
rotated

baseline
continue

There are four dimension options under **linear**: horizontal, vertical, aligned and rotated (See Figure 11.6).

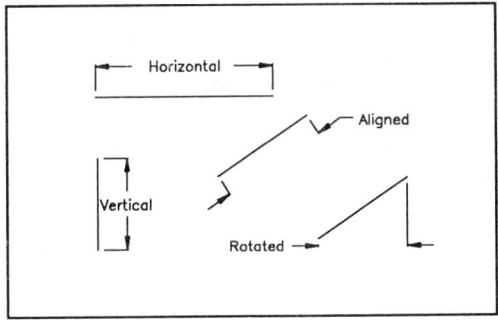

Figure 11.6   Dimension types

The only difference between these four options is the angle at which the dimension line is drawn.

- **horiz**   Draws the linear dimension line horizontally.
- **vertical**   Draws the linear dimension line vertically.
- **aligned**   Aligns the dimension line to the object being dimensioned.
- **rotated**   Allows the specification of an angle for the dimension line.

The two other dimension commands available under **linear** are **baseline** and **continue**, (see Figure 11.7).

- **baseline**   Continues the linear dimension from the first extension line (baseline) of the previous dimension, i.e. several points along a line can be dimensioned from the start of the line.
- **continue**   Continues the linear dimension from the last extension line defined in the previous dimension, i.e. the distance between points along a line can be dimensioned without having to specify the first point each time.

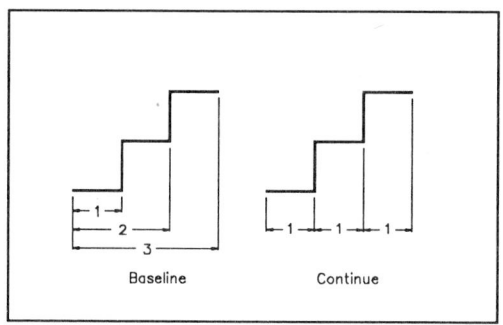

Figure 11.7   Further linear dimension options

The command sequence for linear dimensioning is as follows:

- Pick linear from the Dim screen menu or select the Dim icon found under the **Draw** pull down.

> **dim:**   Horiz or Vertical or Aligned or Rotated
> **First extension line origin or RETURN to select:**

There are two valid responses to the above prompt:

       i)   Specify a point on the drawing - the first extension line.

AutoCAD will then prompt:

Second extension line origin:

Specify the position of the start of the second extension line.

   ii)   A return (or pressing the space bar) allows you to choose a line, arc or circle for dimensioning. AutoCAD will then prompt:

Select line, arc or circle:

Specify the line, arc or circle to be dimensioned, either by pointing or by using a window. AutoCAD will locate the end points of lines or centres of the circles or arcs automatically.

● Once the extents of the dimension line have been given AutoCAD will ask for the position of the dimension line i.e a point through which the dimension line will pass.

Dimension line location:

● It then remains to specify the dimension text.

Dimension text <measured length>:

There are two ways of entering the dimension text:

   i)   AutoCAD will compute the distance between the two extension lines and give the value in drawing units. This is the default response and so pressing the return will automatically add this dimension to your drawing. If you wish to add a prefix or suffix to the computed value, then this can be achieved by typing the prefix followed by <>, or by typing <> followed by the suffix. The <> represents the computed value.

   ii)   Alternatively, you can input your own value by simply entering it as text at this point.

11.3.2 Angular Dimensioning

The dimension line in this case is an arc spanning the angle between the two extension lines. Normally the angle to be dimensioned will be between two intersecting lines but this is not essential. AutoCAD allows the dimensioning of the angle between two lines which do not touch.

dim: ANGULAR
Select first line:
Second line:
Enter the dimension line arc location:
Dimension text <measured angle>:
Enter text location:

The prompts above are similar to those used in linear dimensioning apart from the request **Enter text location.** A return at this point will cause AutoCAD to position the text across the dimension line, breaking the line first to allow room for the text. If there is not enough room for the text, AutoCAD will ask for a new location. If you specify a location for the text, AutoCAD will assume that there is enough room and will not check to see if it is overwriting other work. (See Figure 11.8.)

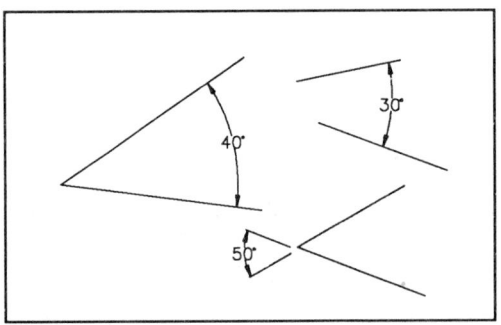

Figure 11.8   Angular dimensioning

11.3.3 Diameter Dimensioning

Both circles and arcs can be dimensioned using this command:

dim: DIAMETER
Select arc or circle:

The dimension line or leader will always go through the point used to select the circle. It is therefore important to select the point with care to ensure that the dimension line or leader is positioned correctly.

Dimension text <measured value>:

If the text will not fit inside the circle, then AutoCAD will prompt:

Text does not fit. Enter leader length for text:

Enter the leader line length; this will cause a line to be drawn from the point chosen on the diameter to the text.

11.3.4 Radius Dimensioning

The radius command is almost identical to the diameter command - a line may be drawn from the centre of the circle to the point used to specify the circle; the text is drawn along the radius line. If the text will not fit, then a leader will be drawn; this can be located at either end of the radius line, (see Figure 11.9.)

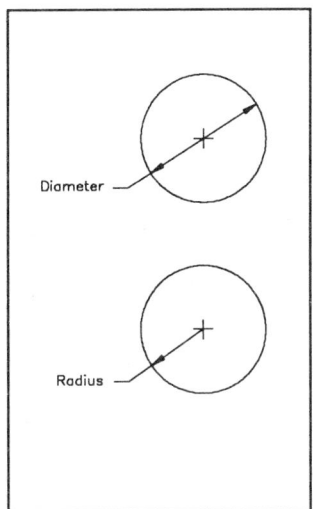

Figure 11.9   Radius and diameter
dimensioning

11.3.5 Ordinate Dimensions

The X- or Y-coordinate point of a feature within a drawing can be labelled using the ORDINATE dimension command. The default text will always be the true X- or Y-coordinate point relative to the current UCS, (see Figure 11.10).

Dim: ORDINATE
Select feature:
Leader endpoint (Xdatum/Ydatum):

If a leader endpoint is specified, then if the difference in X coordinates is greater than the difference in Y coordinates, a Y datum point will be labelled and visa versa. Alternately you may input an X or Y at this prompt to specify the desired datum point, AutoCAD will then prompt for the leader endpoint.

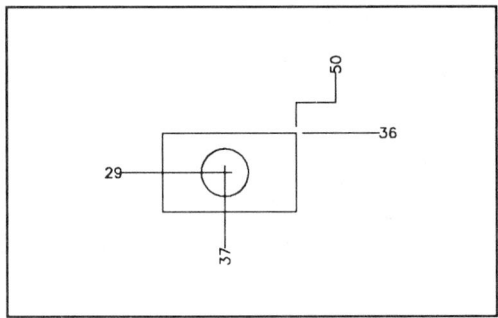

Figure 11.10   Ordinate dimensioning

11.3.6 Leaders

The main role of leaders is the positioning of dimension text in a free area of the drawing when the allowable space within the dimension line is insufficient. The command LEADER can be invoked independently of other DIM commands and allows the construction of complex leaders. When invoked you will be prompted:

Dim: LEADER
Leader start
To point:
To point:
.
.
To point: return
Dimension text<previous default>:

Leaders are very useful for labelling a drawing because they automatically produce an arrow head and line.

11.4 DIMENSION EDITING

Dimensions are considered to be single entities if the dimension variable DIMASO is On, i.e. the dimension is *associative*. If this is the case, then it is possible to use the following editing commands to change certain dimension features and text values.

11.4.1 HOMETEXT

If the dimension text has been positioned away from the dimension line, as is the case with angular dimensioning, then HOMETEXT causes the re-positioning of the dimension text to its "home" position. For example, if a dimensioned line has been stretched then the dimension text will be "out of position". Hometext places the dimension text correctly relative to the stretched line - at its centre point, (see Figure 11.11).

Dim: HOMETEXT
Select objects:

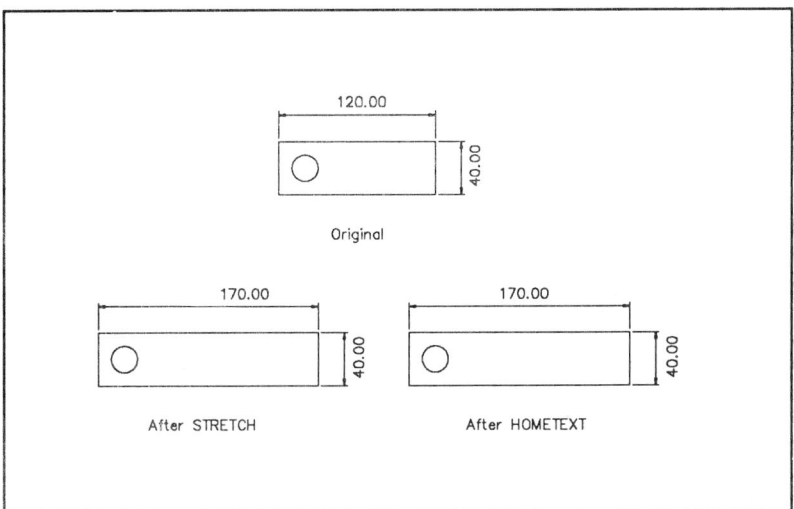

Figure 11.11   HOMETEXT

11.4.2 NEWTEXT

This is used to re-specify the text for a dimension entity without having first to erase the old dimension and then re-specify it.

Dim: NEWTEXT
Enter new dimension text:

Enter the new text or a return for the AutoCAD measured length.

Select objects:

The selected dimension's text will be replaced with the new text in the current text style and units.

11.4.3 OBLIQUE Dimensions

When creating a linear dimensions AutoCAD *always* generates the extension lines, perpendicular to the dimension lines. In complex drawings with many dimensions, this can cause problems of over crowding. The OBLIQUE dimension command allows the extension lines of a dimension to be reset to a user defined angle.

Dim: OBLIQUE
Select objects:
Enter obliquing angle (RETURN for none):

See Figure 11.12.

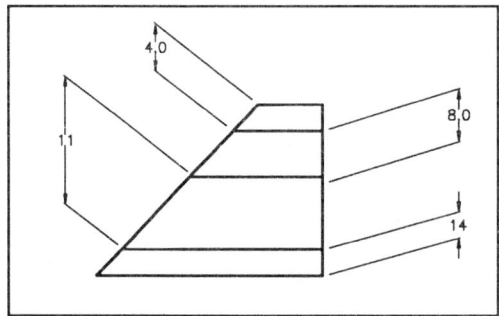

Figure 11.12   Oblique dimensions

11.4.4 OVERRIDE

If you wish to make a change to one or more dimensions currently in the drawing, without making a permanent change to the dimension variables, use the OVERRIDE command. OVERRIDE allows a number of variables to be modified for selected dimensions without changing the current variable setting.

Dim: OVERRIDE
Dimension variable to override:
Current value <default> **New value:**
Dimension variable to override:
Current value <default> **New value:**
Dimension variable to override: return to continue
Select objects:

11.4.5 Changing Dimension Text Position and Angle Using TEDIT

Dimension text can be re-positioned (by dynamic dragging), left or right justified or set to a user defined angle by using the TEDIT dimension command. (See Figure 11.13.)

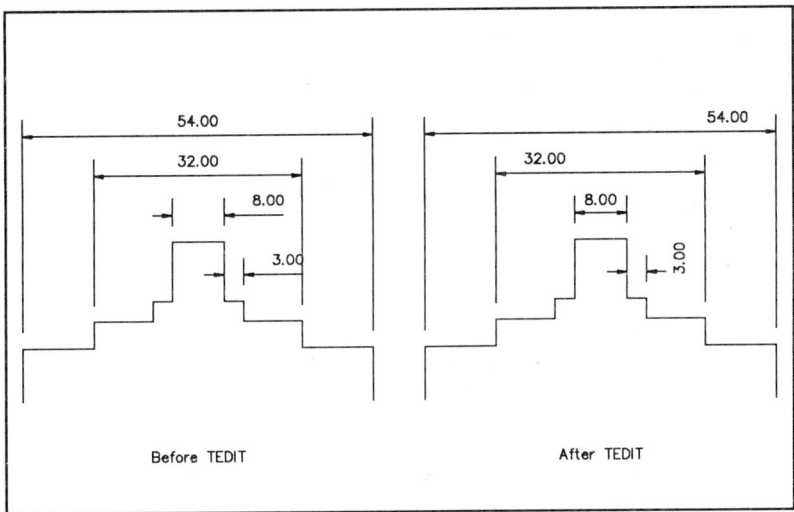

Figure 11.13   Example of TEDIT

Dim: TEDIT
Select dimension:
Enter text location (Left/Right/Home/Angle):

The home option sends the text back to its initial default position as with HOMETEXT.

Note: When dynamically dragging the dimension text, the *complete* dimension (including dimension lines, extension lines etc.) will seem to move. This is an illusion - only the text will be re-positioned.

11.4.6 UPDATE Dimensions

If it is decided that dimensions already added to a drawing are not displayed correctly, e.g. the dimension text size is too small, then it is necessary to change the desired dimension variable and update the old dimensions. To achieve this modification it is only necessary to change the desired dimension variable, invoke the UPDATE dimension command, select the dimensions to be updated and execute with a return.

Dim: UPDATE
Select objects:

> *Note:* Changes may also be made to the text style and dimension units by updating the dimension to a new *current* text style or unit setting.

11.5 UTILITY COMMANDS

There are a number of additional utility commands available:

- CENTER   Draws a centre mark or lines in a circle or arc; dependent on the setting of the DIMCEN variable.
- REDRAW   This redraws the entire drawing.
- STATUS   Gives a list of the dimension variables, their associated "status" and a brief description of each, as in the list of variables below.
- UNDO   Allows you to delete the last dimension command; by repeated use of UNDO you can step back through the dimension commands to the beginning of the sequence.
- STYLE   Allows the changing of the dimension text style (as with the standard text STYLE command)
- EXIT   Allows you to exit from the DIM command mode.

11.6 DIM VARIABLES

The appearance of dimensions in a drawing is governed totally by the setting of the dimension variables. Some variables are of the On/Off variety while the remainder represent sizes and distances.

Normally the dimension variables will be preset by the user in the prototype drawing, but occasionally it will be found necessary to change a particular one. This is achieved simply by selecting DIM VARS from the dimension screen menu, picking the variable name and making the required change.

This is simple enough; the main problem with the dimension variables is in remembering which is which. A series of diagrams in Figures 11.14 and 11.15 illustrate the functions of the different variables.

Some alternative versions of the AutoCAD menu supply similar diagrams as icons which also give access to each variable so that its value can be changed. This is the preferred method for editing dimension variables and you should enquire from your AutoCAD dealer whether such alternative menu software is available.

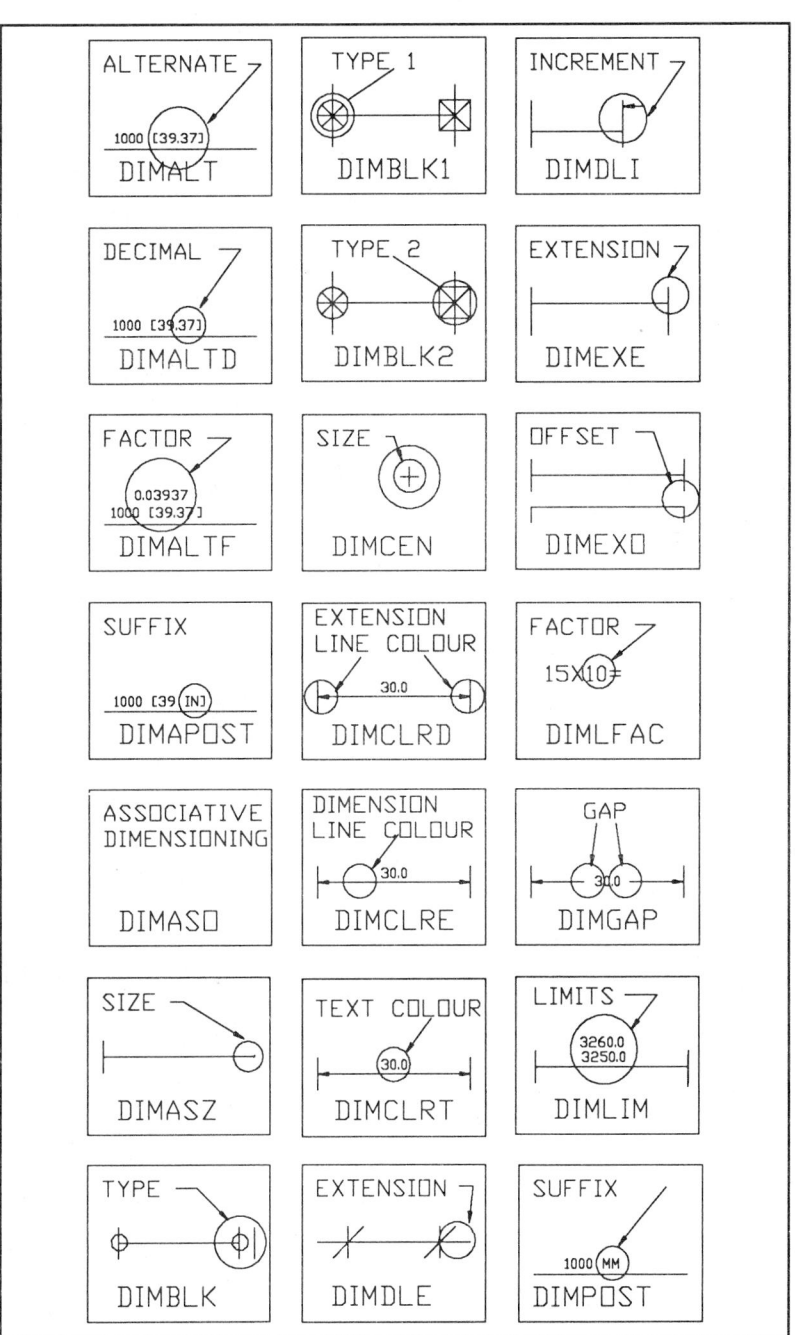

Figure 11.14 Dimension variables

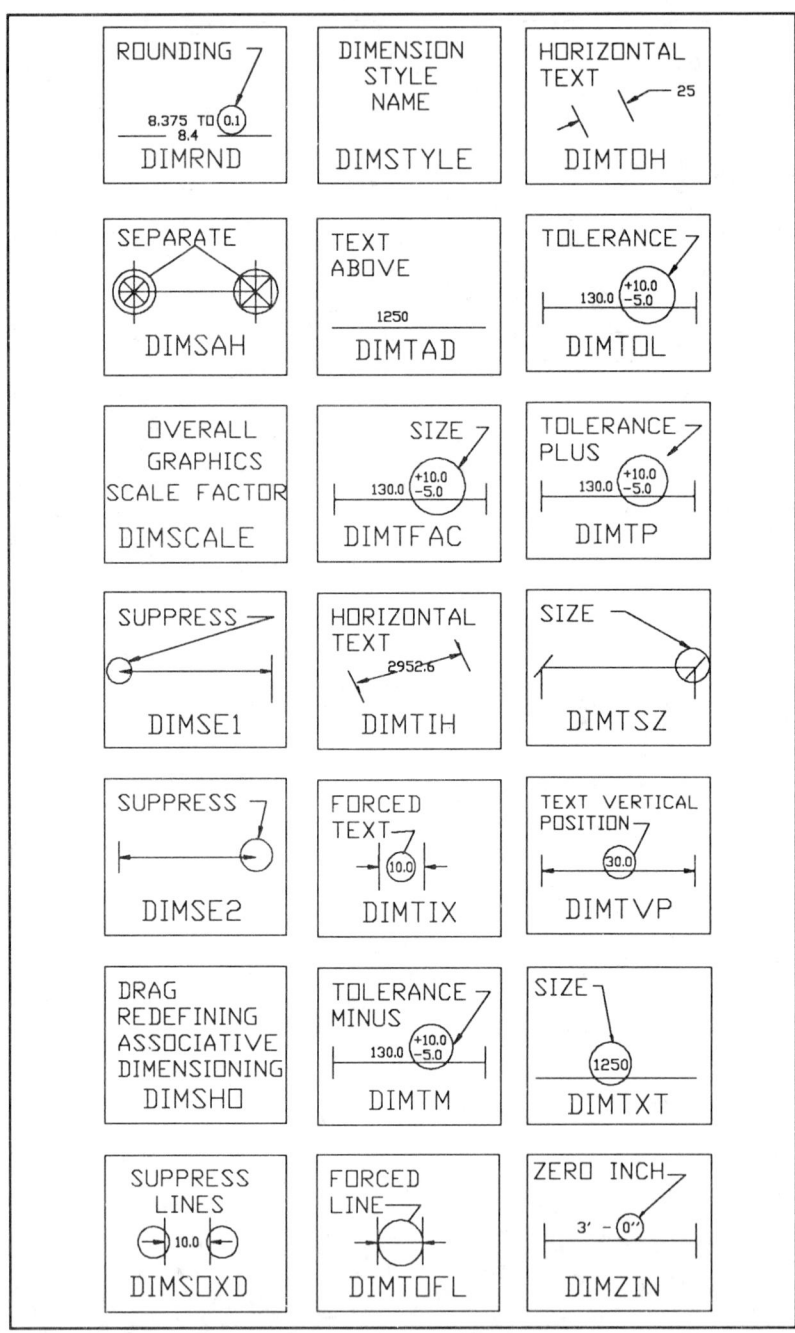

Figure 11.15 Dimension variables

The full list of dimension variables is given below together with the normal default settings:

DIMALT	Off	Alternate units selected
DIMALTD	2	Alternate units decimal places
DIMALTF	0.039	Alternate units scale factor
DIMAPOST		Default suffix for alternate text
DIMASO	On	Create associative dimension
DIMASZ	3.0	Arrow size
DIMBLK		Arrow block name
DIMBLK1		First arrow block name
DIMBLK2		Second arrow block name
DIMCEN	-3.0	Centre mark size
DIMCLRD	BYBLOCK	Dimension line colour
DIMCLRE	BYBLOCK	Extension line colour
DIMCLRT	BYBLOCK	Dimension text colour
DIMDLE	1.25	Dimension line extension
DIMDLI	10.0	Dimension line increment for continuation
DIMEXE	2.5	Extension above dimension line
DIMEXO	2.5	Extension line origin offset
DIMLFAC	1.0000	Linear unit scale factor
DIMGAP	1.5	Dimension line gap
DIMLIM	Off	Generate dimension limits
DIMPOST		Default suffix for dimension text
DIMRND	0.0000	Rounding value
DIMSAH	Off	Seperate arrow blocks
DIMSCALE	1.0000	Overall scale factor
DIMSE1	Off	Suppress the first extension line
DIMSE2	Off	Suppress the second extension line
DIMSHO	Off	Update dimensions while dragging
DIMSOXD	Off	Suppress outside extension dimension
DIMSTYLE		Dimension style
DIMTAD	Off	Place text above the extension line
DIMTFAC	0.75	Tolerance text scale factor
DIMTIH	Off	Text inside extensions is horizontal
DIMTIX	Off	Place text inside extensions
DIMTM	0.0	Minus tolerance
DIMTOFL	Off	Force line inside extension lines
DIMTOH	Off	Text outside extensions is horizontal
DIMTOL	Off	Generate dimension tolerances
DIMTP	0.0	Plus tolerance
DIMTSZ	0.0	Tick size
DIMTVP	1.5	Text vertical position
DIMTXT	3.0	Text height
DIMZIN	1	Zero inches/feet control

Note: To achieve certain dimension environments, it will be necessary to set a number of these variables at one time. This is particularly true for the positioning of text and dimension lines. (Figures 11.16 and 11.17.)

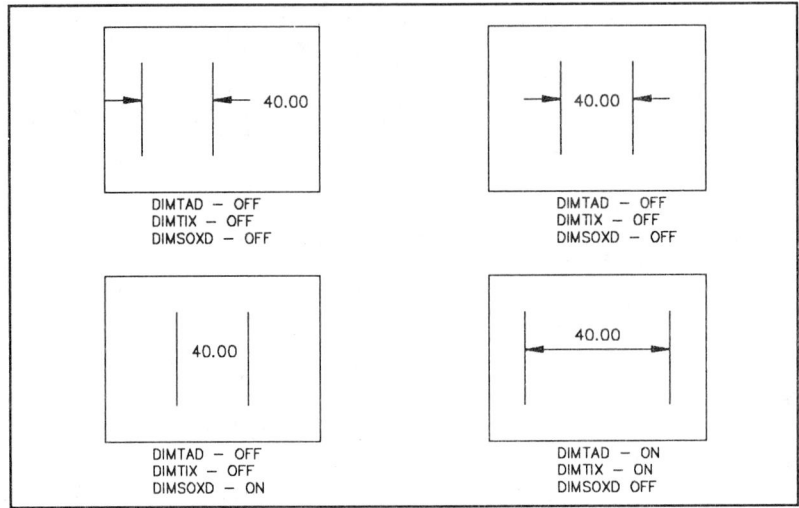

Figure 11.16 Linear dimension variables

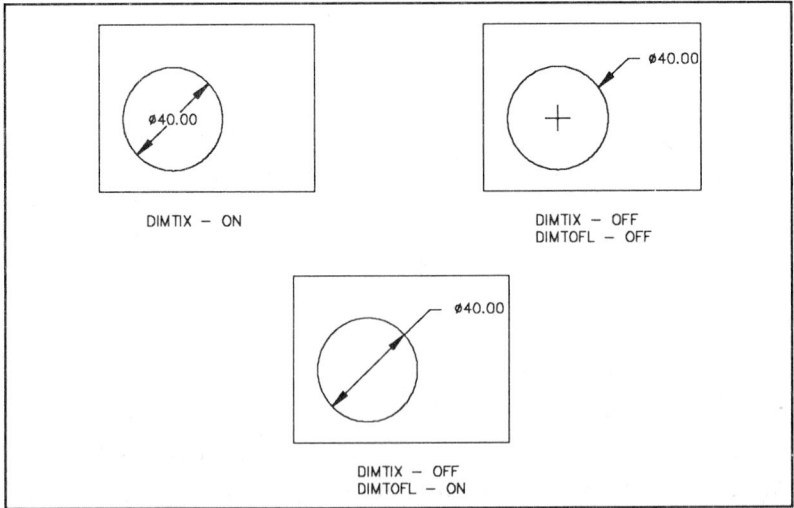

Figure 11.17 Diameter and radius dimension variables

11.6.1 Dimension Styles

Dimension styles allow the saving of any number of different combinations of dimension variable settings. This avoids the unenviable task of resetting a large number of dimension variables for each new requirement. The three commands used to access the dimension styles are:

- SAVE   Saves the current settings of the dimension variables as a new style.

    Dim: SAVE
    ?/Name of new dimension style:

    The **?** lists previously saved styles.

- RESTORE   Restores a previously saved dimension style with its associated dimension variable settings.

    Dim: RESTORE
    Current dimension style: STANDARD
    ?/Enter dimension style name or Return to select dimension:

    The **?** lists the previously saved styles. If you enter a return, then you will prompted: **Select entity**. The style of the dimension selected will become the current style.

- VARIABLES Lists the dimension variables associated with a dimension style. The prompts are identical to those of the RESTORE dimension command.

11.7 ASSOCIATED DIMENSION COMMANDS

There are various commands which automatically edit dimension entities, (if associated, see Section 11.5) automatically when changing a drawing. The dimension entities must be included in the selection set together with the drawn entities which are to be altered or edited. The commands are:

ARRAY	Polar array only
EXTEND	Linear dimensions only
MIRROR	
ROTATE	
SCALE	
STRETCH	Linear and angular dimensions only
TRIM	Linear dimensions only

The command EXPLODE can be used to split an associated dimension into its component parts which may then be edited individually.

12. Hatching

12.1 USING THE HATCH COMMAND

As with linetypes AutoCAD has a built-in library of hatch patterns stored in a hatch library file called ACAD.PAT. These are shown in Figures 12.1 and 12.2. It is possible to create your own hatch patterns and store them for future use, (see Section 18.6), or create simple patterns for *one time* use from within the HATCH command.

A hatch pattern is made of a number of hatch lines *of the current linetype* which have a particular angle and spacing.

> **Command:** HATCH
> **Pattern (? or name/U,style) <default>:**
> **Scale for pattern <1.0000>:**
> **Angle for pattern <0.0000>:**
> **Select objects:**

Note: The area which is hatched will, in all but the most simple cases, depend upon the method of selection used, i.e. if a window is used rather than picking individual entities, (see Figure 12.3).

?   Lists the standard hatch patterns stored in the library file ACAD.PAT together with their general use. When the desired pattern has been chosen, input its name to make it the default pattern for all subsequent hatching. If the name of the hatch pattern is followed by a comma, together with one of the letters N, O or I, then the hatch style will be changed, (see Section 12.3), e.g.

> **Pattern (? or name/U,style) <default>:** ESCHER,O

will change the default to the escher hatch with outermost style.

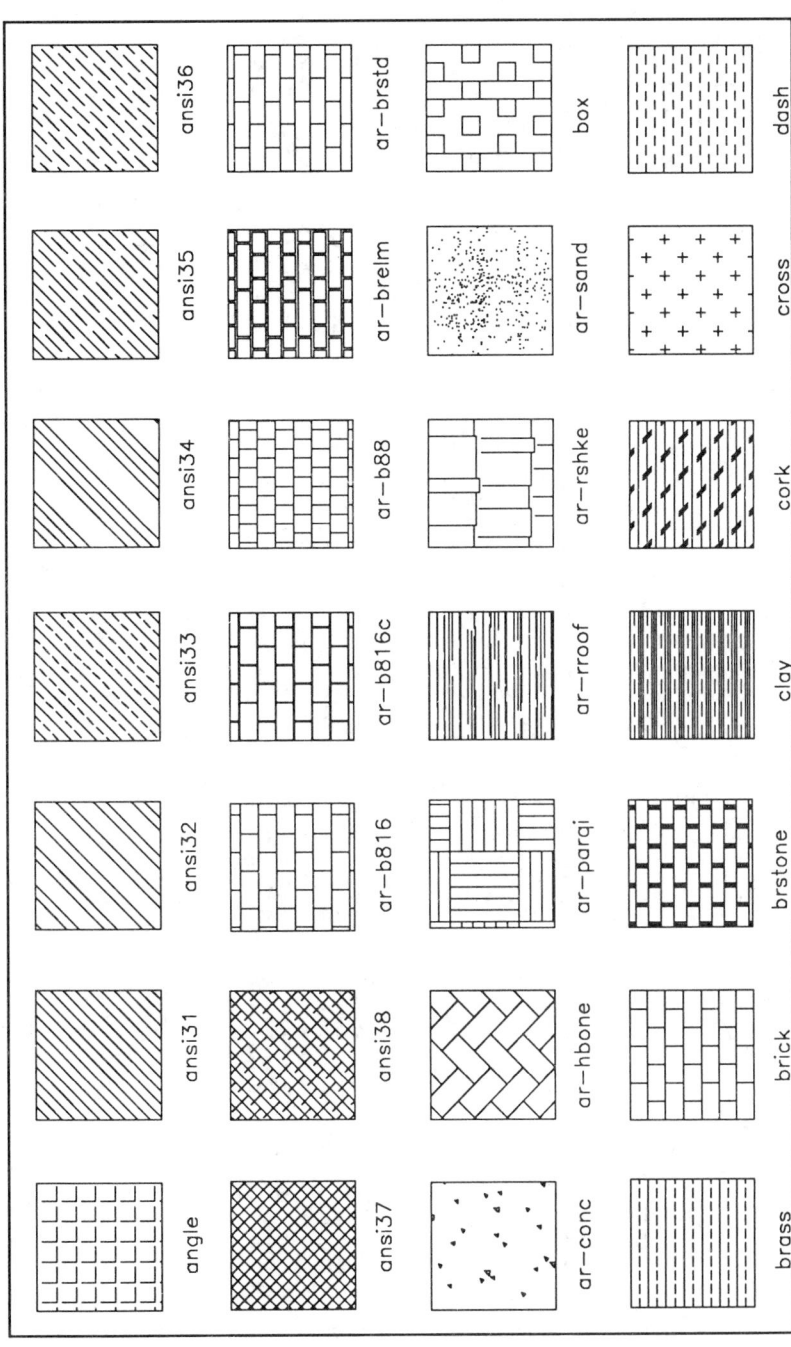

Figure 12.1 ACAD.PAT hatch library patterns

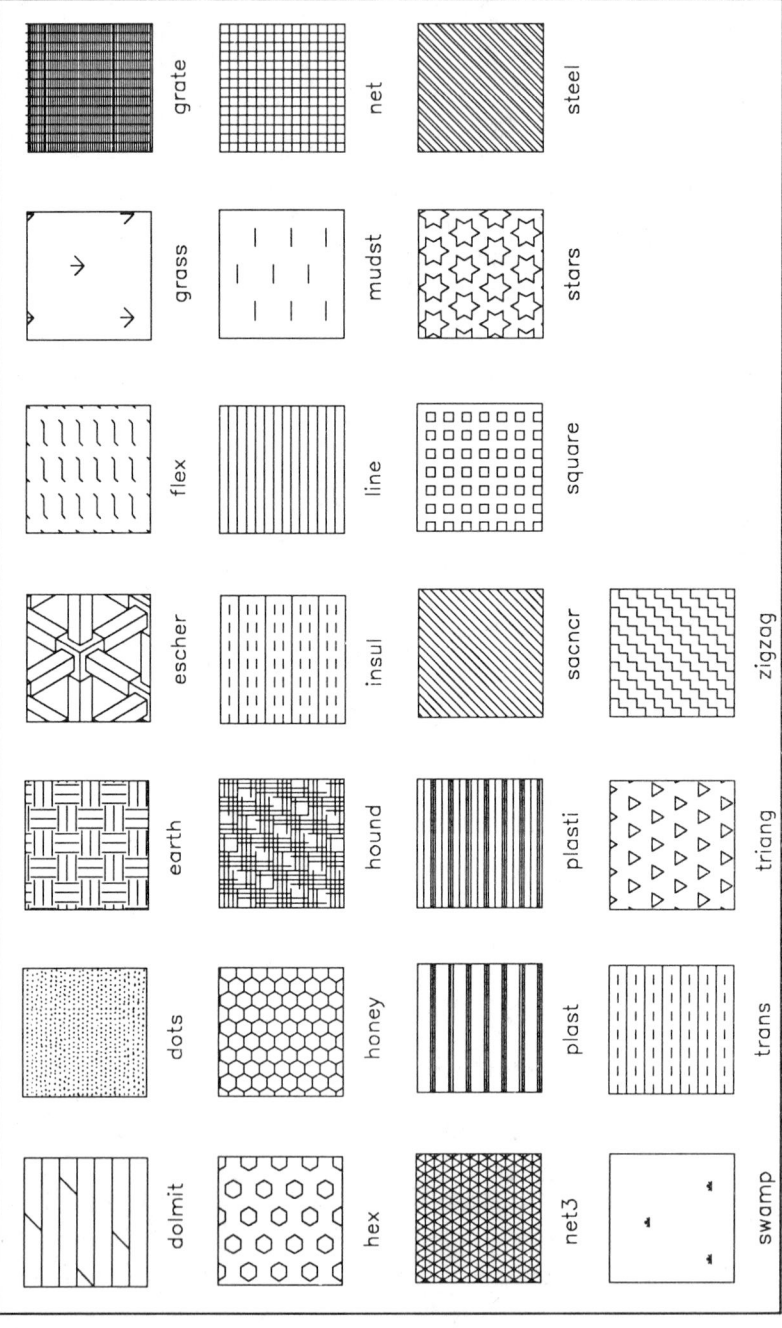

Figure 12.2 ACAD.PAT hatch library patterns

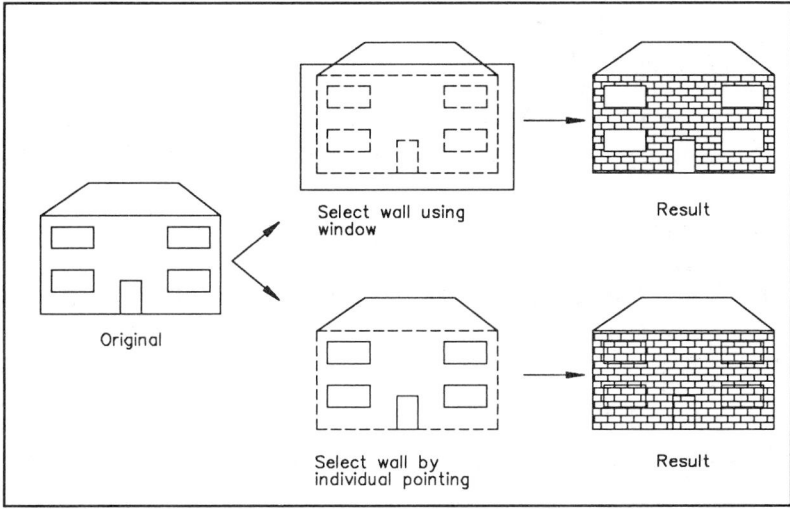

Figure 12.3   The effect of the selection method on the hatched area

U   User defined. Simple hatch patterns can be defined for immediate use only. AutoCAD will prompt:

> **Angle for crosshatch lines <0.0000>:**
> **Spacing between lines <1.0000>:**
> **Double hatch area? <N>:**

The double hatch area prompt requires a Y or N input; it refers to whether you require a second set of lines drawn at right angles to the original set of lines.

> *Note:*   If the HATCH command was the last command used, and it is recalled with a return then the previously used pattern, scale and angle will be assumed and you will be prompted only to select objects. If you need to re-specify any of these parameters, then you must give a fresh HATCH command.

It is possible to pre-set the hatch pattern, its style, scale and rotation angle by selecting HATCH OPTIONS from the **Options** pull down *before* entering the HATCH command from the **Draw** pull down menu. In this case, the corresponding prompts will not be given.

The hatch scale and rotation angle may be pre-set simply by selecting the Hatch Scale or Hatch Angle options. You will be prompted:

> **Enter default hatch scale or . to prompt each time <.>:**

or

> **Enter default hatch rotation angle or . to prompt each time <.>:**

A . response effectively cancels the preset.

The hatch pattern may be pre-set by selecting the Hatch Pattern... option. This causes an icon menu to be displayed. Selection of the relevant icon pre-sets the desired pattern.

Note: These presets remain in force within the current drawing when HATCH is selected from the **Draw** pull down. If HATCH is called from the keyboard or the screen menu, a separate set of defaults may be employed.

12.2 BOUNDARY OF THE HATCHED AREA

The boundary of the area to be hatched has to be specified and it is important that it is made up of single entities which join at their end points. If one of the entities overhangs the hatch area, then the hatch pattern may be generated incorrectly; the overhanging segment must therefore be removed or replaced by two separate entities.

If the areas ABFE and CDHG are to be hatched, then the lines AD and EH have to be broken into the separate segments AB, CD, EF and GH with invisible cuts, by applying the BREAK command at points B,C,F and G, (see Figure 12.4). Alternatively, lines AB, BC, CD, EF, FG and GH may be individually drawn.

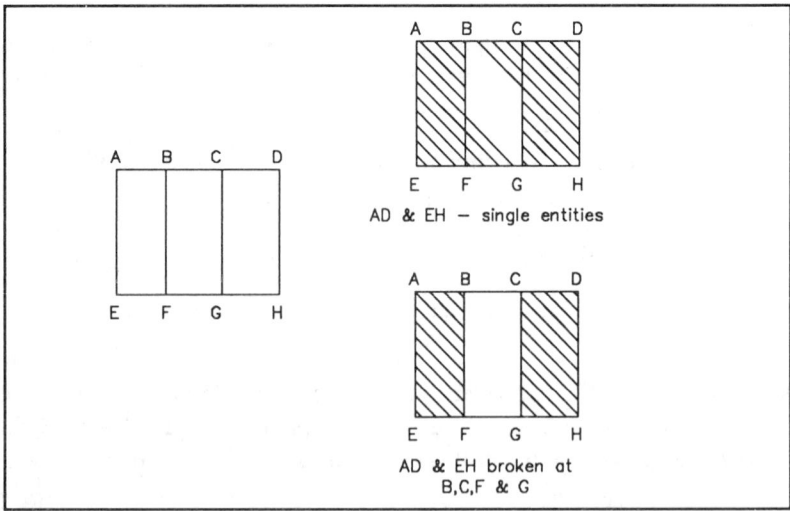

Figure 12.4   Boundary of hatched area

12.3 HATCH STYLES

When using HATCH, it is important that only the *required* area is cross-hatched. If the space inside the boundary chosen is empty, then there are no problems, but if there are separate entities within the boundary then it is necessary to specify which areas are to be hatched. There are various hatch styles which can be invoked to allow specification of the areas to be hatched, (see Figure 12.5).

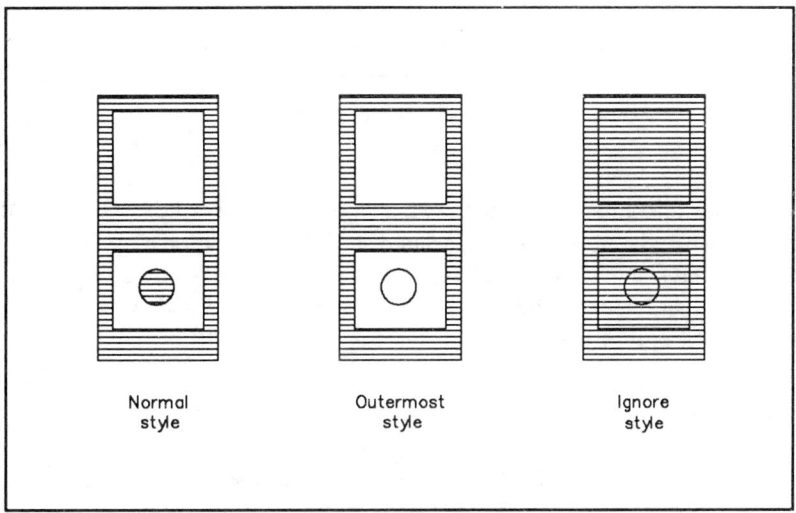

Figure 12.5   Hatch styles

- **Normal:** The default setting. It causes the hatch lines to extend from the outer boundary wall to the next intersecting line; the hatch line is then turned off until it meets the next intersecting line which reactivates the hatch line etc. If the boundary lines are numbered from the outermost inwards, areas which are surrounded by an odd numbered line will be hatched whereas areas surrounded by an even numbered line will not, (see Figure 12.6).
- **Outermost:**   This again hatches inward from the area boundary. If an intersecting line is encountered, then the hatch line is turned off and does not turn back on again as in the Normal case with the result that only the outermost area is hatched.
- **Ignore:**   Any entity within the boundary area is ignored, the hatch lines extending over them to the opposite boundary line.

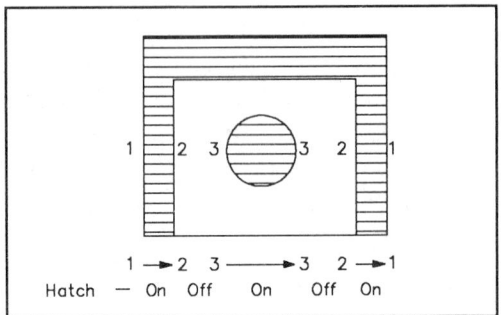

Figure 12.6 Normal hatch style mechanism

When hatch lines encounter attributes, text, shapes, traces or solids, then the hatch line is turned off. An invisible box exists around attribute, shape or text. If these entities are included in the selection of the objects to be hatched, either by using a window or by individual selection, then the entities will be recognised and will not be hatched (unless the Ignore option has been selected. See Figure 12.7.)

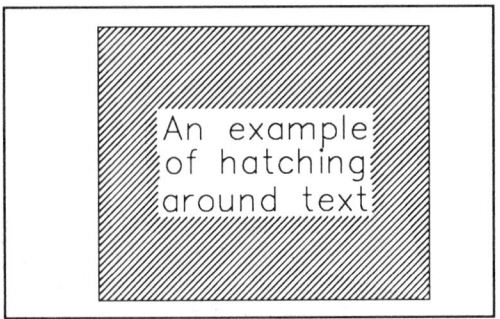

Figure 12.7 Hatching inhibited by text

13. The Paper Space Environment

13.1 THE CONCEPT OF PAPER SPACE

The concept of Paper Space allows the user to compose the layout and presentation of the drawing prior to printing. Multiple views of a single object or a collage made up of many different drawings can be handled with ease. Similarly, details of the drawing may be presented as insets at a precise scale and orientation. AutoCAD is now able to produce the sort of complex, composite drawings required by draughtsmen and designers worldwide. (See Figure 13.1.)

Paper Space can be thought of as one of two separate parallel worlds, the other world being called *Model Space*. Paper Space is used for composing the final printed output whereas Model Space is used to *create* the drawing entities. You are already totally familiar with Model Space; you have been using it to create your drawings; it is the standard AutoCAD draughting world.

The majority of AutoCAD's commands are available in both Paper Space and Model Space but each has a few special commands which cannot be used in the other world. AutoCAD will warn you if you try to use an illegal command.

13.1.1 TILEMODE

TILEMODE is a strangely named system variable which controls the presentation of viewports on the screen. With TILEMODE set to 1 you are only allowed to use viewports *which lie alongside each other* - as if tiled - produced by the VPORTS command, (see Section 5.5). This system places you under rigorous constraints. You cannot scale a viewport, you cannot freely re-position a viewport on screen and you can only plot the contents of the active viewport.

Setting TILEMODE to 0 frees you from all these constraints and automatically places you in Paper Space as indicated by a P appearing on the Status line and a new icon appearing within the drawing area.

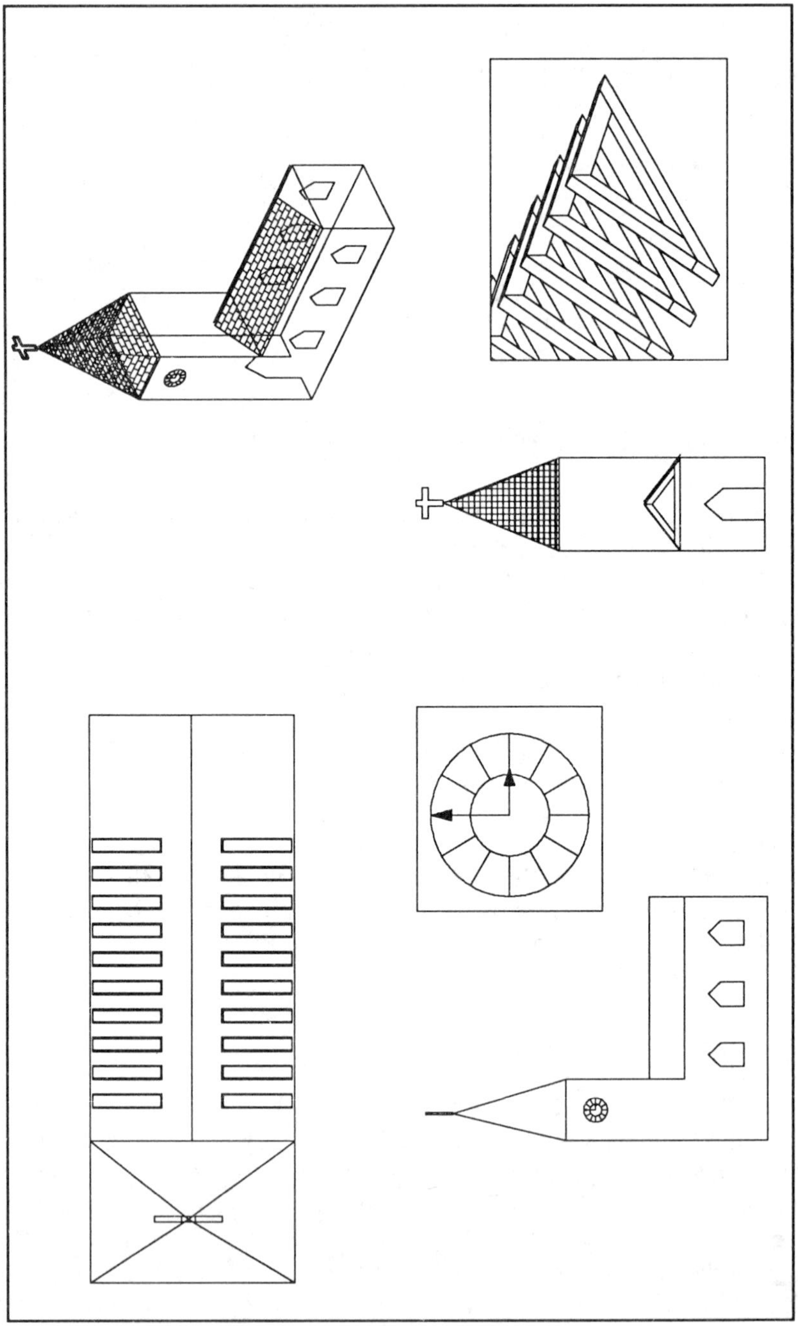

Figure 13.1 Composite paper space plot derived from a single drawing

Note: Because Paper Space is a totally separate world your Model Space drawing will disappear until you open a viewport window linking the two worlds by use of the MVIEW command.

TILEMODE must be set to 0 before you are allowed into Paper Space *but* it does not follow that TILEMODE must be set to 1 to enter Model Space. Model Space can be accessed with TILEMODE set to either 1 or 0.

13.1.2 The Paper Space Icon

When in Paper Space, an icon (Figure 13.2) appears - usually in the bottom left hand corner of the screen. This icon has some similarities to the UCS icon, (see Section 16.2.2). The Paper Space icon can be turned On/Off and positioned at the Paper Space origin using the UCSICON command.

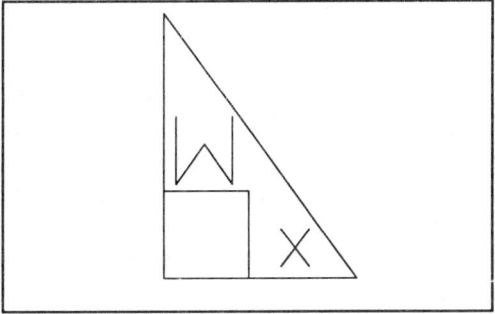

Figure 13.2   Paper space icon

Command: UCSICON
ON/OFF/All/Noorigin/ORigin <ON>:

ON and **OFF** control the Paper Space icon's visibility while **Noorigen** places the icon in the bottom left hand corner of the screen irrespective of the position of the Paper Space origin. **ORigin** places the icon at the Paper Space origin point *if* this is possible, in which case the icon is displayed with a + to indicate the 0,0 position, (see Figure 13.2). The **All** option is not relevant to the Paper Space icon.

13.1.3 Setting the LIMITS in Paper Space

Before creating viewports in the Paper Space environment it is *highly advisable* to set the Paper Space limits to equal the size of the paper upon which you wish to plot.

After setting the limits use ZOOM All to set the screen to the new limits and turn on the grid to display the actual paper area. You should find it very helpful to be able to visualise this area of the screen as if it were the paper while composing the final layout of your drawing.

13.1.4 MVIEW

The MVIEW command is fundamental to the use of Paper Space. It is used to create user-defined viewports within the Paper Space environment.

> *Note:* Until these windows have been created it is impossible to view any entities in Paper Space.

These windows give total flexibility to the layout of entities in Paper Space. Any number of viewports may be created, they can be of any size, in any position, may be separate or overlapped, may be scaled to the required size. *Viewports created in Paper Space are treated as single entities in their own right.* You can check this by using LIST when in Paper Space and picking a viewport border. The command will report that the selected entity is a viewport.

> *Note:* When a viewport has been created in Paper Space, the entities drawn in Model Space should become visible. The apparent size and the percentage of the drawing displayed in the viewport is primarily controlled by the viewport dimensions. In particular, the height of the viewport controls the apparent size while the shape (height/width ratio) of the window will determine whether the drawing will be truncated (clipped). See Figure 13.3. However, the viewport and its contents may always be edited subsequently to obtain the desired display. (See Section 13.2.1.)

MVIEW may be accessed from the screen or pull down menus. This command is specific to Paper Space and can only be used when TILEMODE is set to 0. However, if you select MVIEW from the **Display** pull down then TILEMODE will be automatically set to 0 before the MVIEW command is issued.

> **Command:** MVIEW
> **ON/OFF/Hideplot/Fit/2/3/4/Restore/<First Point>:**

First Point This is the default and prompts for one corner point of the viewport to be created. This can be specified by pointing or by numerical input from the keyboard. You will then be prompted for the **Other corner**. As soon as this viewport is created your Model Space drawing will become visible.

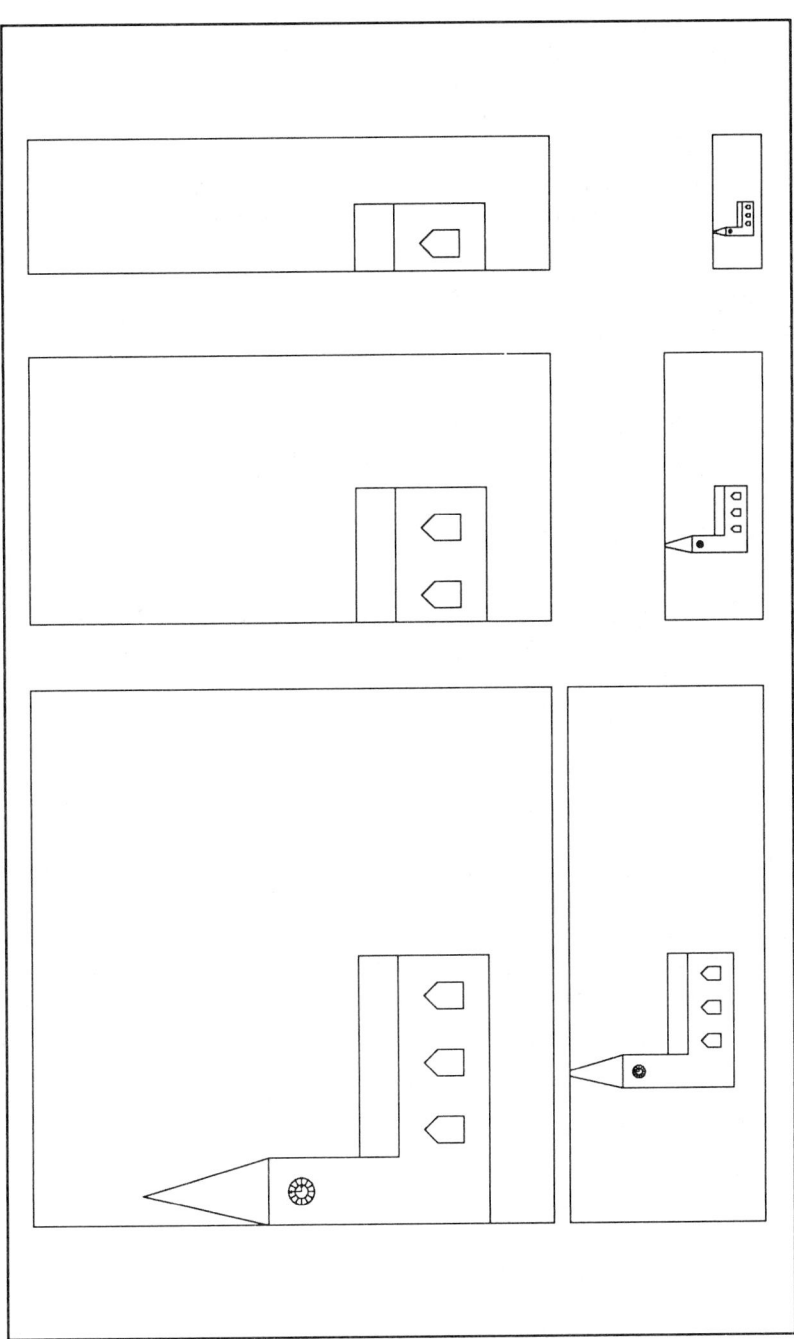

Figure 13.3 Paper space viewport clipping

ON/OFF When a viewport has been created, AutoCAD assumes that it is switched On (active), i.e. that the contents of the viewport are to be visible. It is only necessaryto turn viewports Off if you create a large number of viewports or you wish to speed up the REGENeration process. To turn a viewport On or Off you will be prompted to **Select objects:** - note that the objects to be selected are *the viewport windows* and NOT the entities displayed within the windows. The maximum allowed number of active viewports is set by the MAXACTVP system variable. This in turn has an absolute maximum imposed upon it by your choice of graphics hardware, e.g. a typical VGA system can support 15 active viewports (MAXACTVP=16). Remember, there is no limit to the number of viewports which can be created and plotted, MAXACTVP only controls their *visibility* on the screen.

Hideplot This applies only to plotting three-dimensional drawings and solids and is used for changing a wire frame representation to one with a solid appearance. (See Section 16.1.6). You will be prompted to select those *viewports* in which HIDE is to operate during plotting. (See Section 14.3.)

Fit This option allows the creation of a single viewport which exactly fills the screen display.

2/3/4 These create a number of viewports in a specified area of Paper Space. You will be prompted:

Fit/<First Point>:

These options operate in the same manner as described above but refer to the area to be divided into the specified number of viewports. The **2** option creates two horizontal or vertical viewports of equal size. If you choose the **3** option, you will be prompted:

Horizontal/Vertical/Above/Below/Left/<Right>:

(See the corresponding VPORTS command in Section 5.5.) Option **4** divides the specified area into four equal and symmetrical viewports.

Restore A viewport configuration which has been previously saved using the VPORTS command (which can only be used when TILEMODE is set to 1) can be introduced into Paper Space:

?/Name of window configuration to insert <*ACTIVE>:

The **?** response gives a list of any previously saved VPORTS configurations. The ***ACTIVE** default relates to the viewport configuration currently active in Model Space when TILEMODE=1.

13.1.5 MSPACE

The command MSPACE is used to switch from the Paper Space environment to the Model Space environment.

Command: MSPACE

> *Note:*   This command may only be used when TILEMODE=0.

This switch may be recognised by the disappearance of the full screen cross wires; they will now be displayed only in the active viewport (usually the last viewport to be created). You will also notice that the single Paper Space icon has been replaced by a separate UCS icon in *each* of the viewports - assuming that the icon is switched On, see Figure 13.4).

Assuming that you have a number of viewports created you are now able to treat them exactly as viewports created with the VPORTS command with TILEMODE=1. (See Section 5.5.) Thus, you may change the active viewport by picking, and use various display commands such as ZOOM, PAN, VPOINT etc., within the active viewport without affecting the display in the other viewports. You can make any necessary modifications to the drawing, working between viewports if required.

> *Note:*   If one viewport has been created inside another, then you may find it difficult to use picking to make this viewport active. In this case, use Ctrl V repeatedly until the required viewport becomes active.

13.1.6 PSPACE

This is the companion command to MSPACE and serves to switch back to the Paper Space environment. Again, TILEMODE must equal 1 before this command may be used.

Command: PSPACE

When setting the final drawing layout prior to plotting, you will find it useful to be able to alternate between Paper Space and Model Space using these two commands.

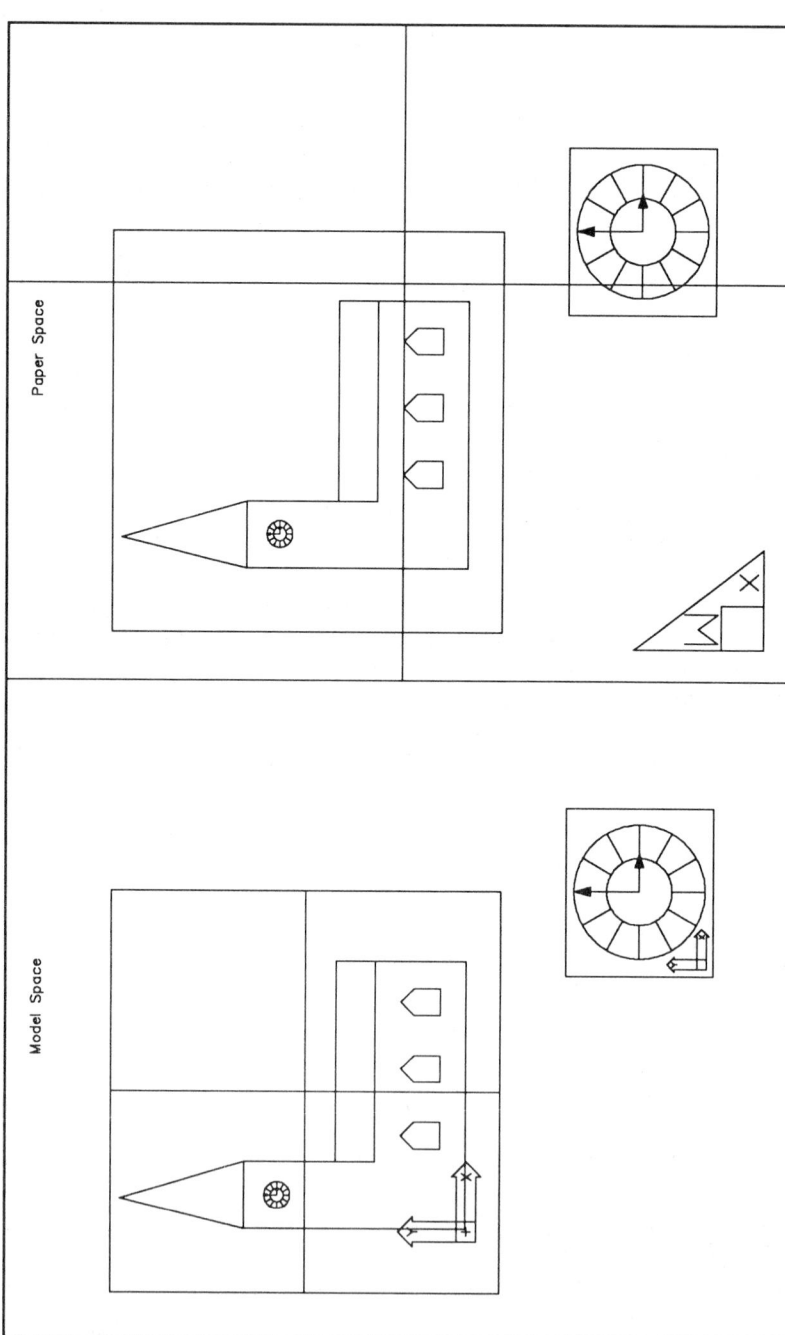

Figure 13.4 Comparison of paper space and model space screen displays

13.2 EXPERT USE OF PAPER SPACE VIEWPORTS

13.2.1 Editing a Viewport

When in Paper Space, the viewports are recognised by AutoCAD as entities in their own right, and as such they can be edited using the standard editing commands. These include ERASE, MOVE, COPY, SCALE, STRETCH and ARRAY. Other editing commands are either not allowed or will be executed imperfectly. The two most useful commands are MOVE and SCALE as these allow the modification of a viewport's position and size.

Similarly, all the 2D display commands may be used, e.g. ZOOM, PAN, VIEW etc., together with the constructional aids SNAP, GRID and ORTHO.

> *Note:* The snap, grid and ortho *settings* current in Model Space are independent of their settings in Paper Space.

13.2.2 Setting Different Scales in Paper Space

It is a common requirement for the different viewports in Paper Space to illustrate various details of the main drawing at an enhanced scale, (see Figure 13.5).

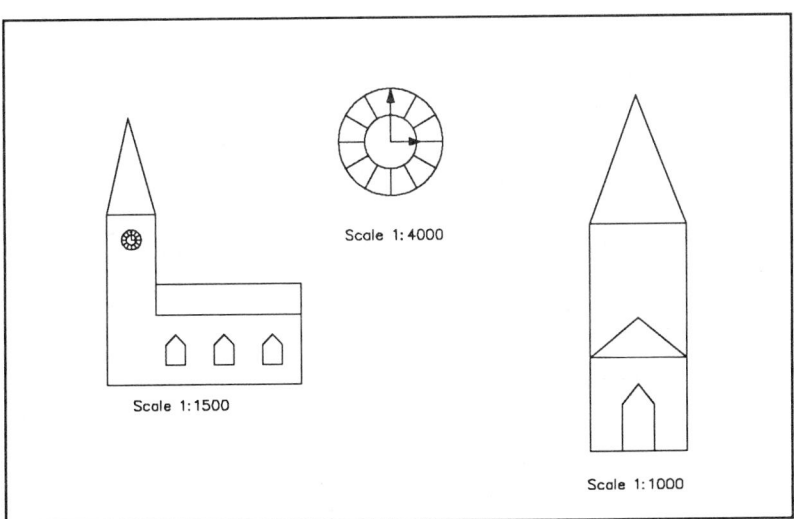

Figure 13.5 Example of scaled insets

This cannot be achieved by a true scaling operation - using the SCALE command applied to the object in Model Space - because the real dimensions of the object would be permanently changed. The "scaling" is performed by zooming the contents of the viewport when in Model Space to give the required "scale" so that, on transfer to Paper Space the drawing is depicted at precisely the correct size. This would be virtually impossible to achieve without the special command ZOOM <scale factor> XP. This command allows you to enter a zoom scale factor which expands or contracts the Model Space view of the object *relative to Paper Space.*

EXAMPLE

Consider the case where you wish to plot an overall view of the drawing at a scale of 1:50, i.e. one millimetre plotted on the paper corresponds to 50 millimetres in the real object. Remember, drawings should always be constructed full size, therefore in this case one drawing unit equates to one millimetre in the real object.

Set TILEMODE=0 to enter Paper Space and create a suitable viewport. You may find it helpful to create a viewport corresponding to the size of the paper on which you wish to plot. Switch to Model Space, using the MSPACE command to make this viewport active.

Now you must ZOOM to the required "scale":

Command: ZOOM

All/Center/Dynamic/Extents/Left/Previous/Vmax/Window/<Scale(X/XP)>:1/50XP

> *Note:* It is assumed here that the required scale of 1:50 is suitable to plot your particular drawing on the paper size which you have selected and set up in Paper Space. If you have made a mistake in deciding on this scale factor, or in the choice of paper size, then the drawing will appear too large or too small after zooming.

Return to Paper Space using the PSPACE command. If you wish, you can now check the "scale" of the entities within the viewport by using the LIST command and selecting the viewport frame. You will then see:

Scale relative to paper space: 0.0200xp

where 0.02 corresponds to a scale of 1/50.

> *Note:* If your scale factor is less than 1:10000, then the LIST command will always respond with a scale relative to Paper Space of 0.0000xp. Don't worry, the actual scale will still be valid.

If you wish, you may now make fine adjustments to the viewport's size, using SCALE, and position, using MOVE while still in Paper Space. Positioning of the drawing *within* the viewport may be achieved by returning to Model Space and using the PAN command.

You can now create other viewports as insets within the main viewport and repeat the above process to produce detailed aspects of the drawing at larger or smaller scales. (See Figure 13.6.)

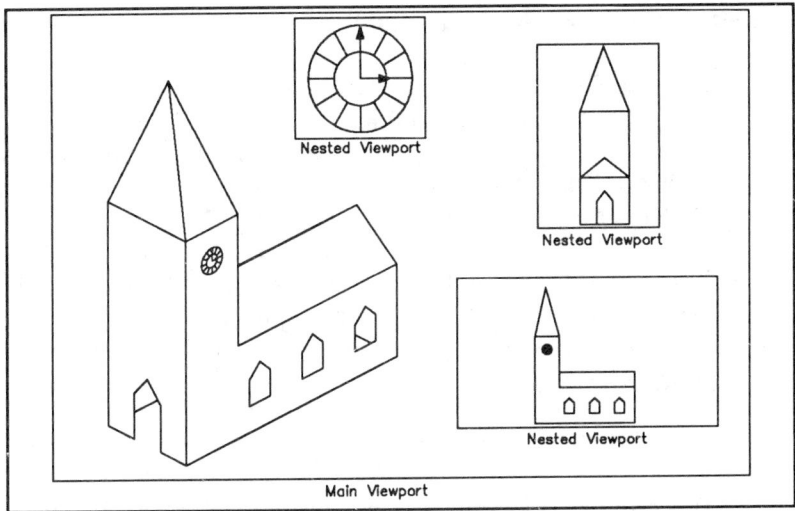

Figure 13.6   Nested viewports

> *Note:*   When setting up viewports in Paper Space, you may find it helpful to use the LISP program MVSETUP which you will find in the Bonus sub-directory of your AutoCAD package. See Appendix 5 for information on other LISP programmes found in Bonus.

13.2.3 Layer Control in Paper Space Viewports

It is not possible to control the visibility of layers in individual Paper Space viewports by using the LAYER command. This command acts *globally* in that all viewports will be equally affected.

The command VPLAYER, which may only be used when TILEMODE=0, overcomes this problem and allows the Freeze/Thaw state of a layer in any individual viewport or group of viewports to be controlled. This is a very useful facility which allows you to prepare multiple views of the drawing with different features emphasised in each viewport. When plotting a number of viewports, only those layers which are thawed in a particular viewport will be plotted. For example, descriptive text, although a part of the drawing and hence common to all viewports, will only be plotted in the viewport(s) in which the text layer is thawed.

Similarly, in a complex drawing containing too many dimension entities to be clearly displayed in a single viewport, these may be shared between two or more viewports by placing them on separate layers which may then be thawed or frozen as required.

Command: VPLAYER
?/Freeze/Thaw/Reset/Newfrz/Vpvisdflt:

?   This provides *a list of all layers which are frozen* in a selected viewport. If you are working in Model Space, AutoCAD will temporarily switch to Paper Space to allow you to select a single viewport. The frozen layers are then named and you are returned to Model Space.

Freeze   Freeze operates as the Freeze option of the LAYER command except that you are offered the choice of applying it to any combination of viewports. After specifying the layer(s) to be frozen you will be prompted:

All/Select/<Current>:

Thaw   This operates in exactly the same manner as **Freeze** with the exception that, whereas VPLAYER Freeze can freeze a layer which is globally thawed (through the LAYER command), VPLAYER Thaw *cannot* thaw a layer which has previously been globally frozen.

Vpvisdflt   When a new viewport is created, it is possible to preset the visibility (Freeze/Thaw state) of all existing layers within that viewport; this forms the *default visibility* state for all viewports subsequently created.

Reset   This returns all selected viewports to the default visibility state as set by **Vpvisdflt**. This includes viewports created before **Vpvisdflt** was applied.

Newfrz   This creates new layers which are already frozen in all existing and new viewports. This is very useful if you have many viewports and require the new layer to be visible in only one; it is quicker to Thaw this layer in one viewport than to Freeze it in all the others.

All of the above sub-commands, with the exception of **Newfrz**, can be set from the Layer Control... option of the **Settings** pull down (DDLMODES). (See Figure 13.7.)

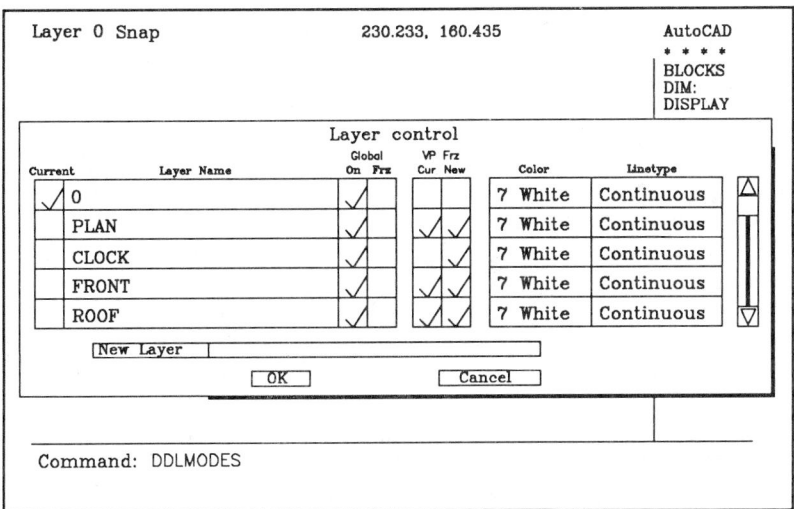

Layer 0 Snap			230.233, 160.435			AutoCAD

Figure 13.7   Access to the VPLAYER options from the Layer dialogue box

13.2.4 Dimensioning in Model Space and Paper Space

When constructing a drawing which requires a large number of dimensions to be added, these may of course be introduced while in Model Space with TILEMODE=1 before Paper Space viewports have been set up. However, it is preferable first to prepare the required viewports in Paper Space and then return to Model Space (TILEMODE=0) and place the dimension entities on suitable layers within the chosen viewport(s).

As mentioned above, one of the major features of Paper Space viewports is the ability to set different scales in various viewports prior to plotting. This causes problems with the dimension scale. Although the dimensions will be accurate in every case, it would be unacceptable to have each viewport containing dimension text, arrow heads etc., of different actual size, (see Figure 13.8). In other words, although the drawing may change its scale from viewport to viewport the dimension size should remain constant.

The dimension variable DIMSCALE, if set to 0.00, causes the actual size of the dimension entity to be directly related to the viewport scale relative to Paper Space, (see Section 13.2.2). All dimensions appear the *same size* in each viewport regardless of the viewport scale, (see Figure 13.9).

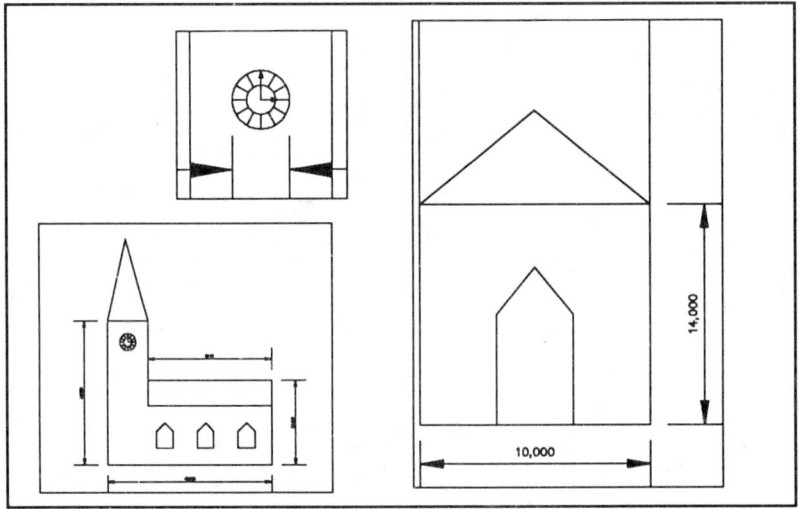

Figure 13.8 Various apparent dimension sizes

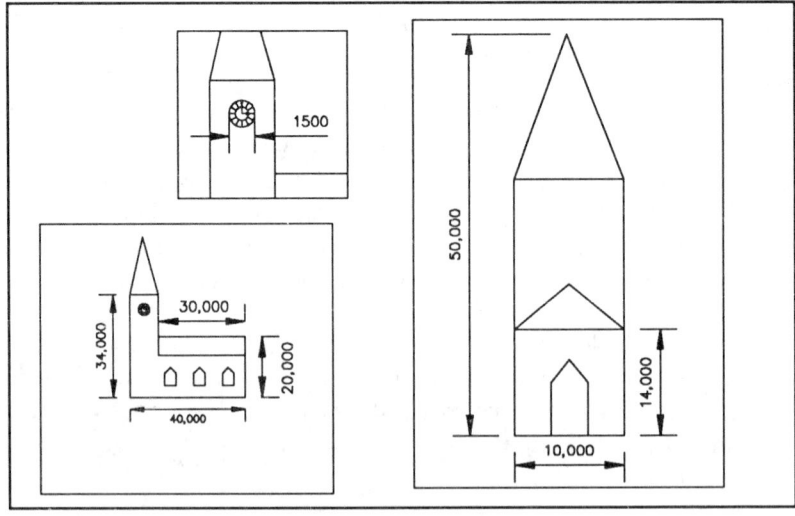

Figure 13.9 The effect of the DIMSCALE system variable

The following procedure is suggested when introducing dimensions into Paper Space viewports:

- Enter Model Space
- Set DIMSCALE=0.00
- Set up the dimension layer(s).
- * Enter the required viewport and scale the drawing using ZOOM (scale) XP.
- If drawing in three dimensions, check that the UCS is aligned with the viewport - use the UCS View option.
- Make *one* of the dimension layers *current* and visible in this viewport only.
- Add the required dimension entities.
- Repeat from * for dimensions in other viewports.

Figure 13.10 is a flow diagram to help you become proficient in the use of Paper Space.

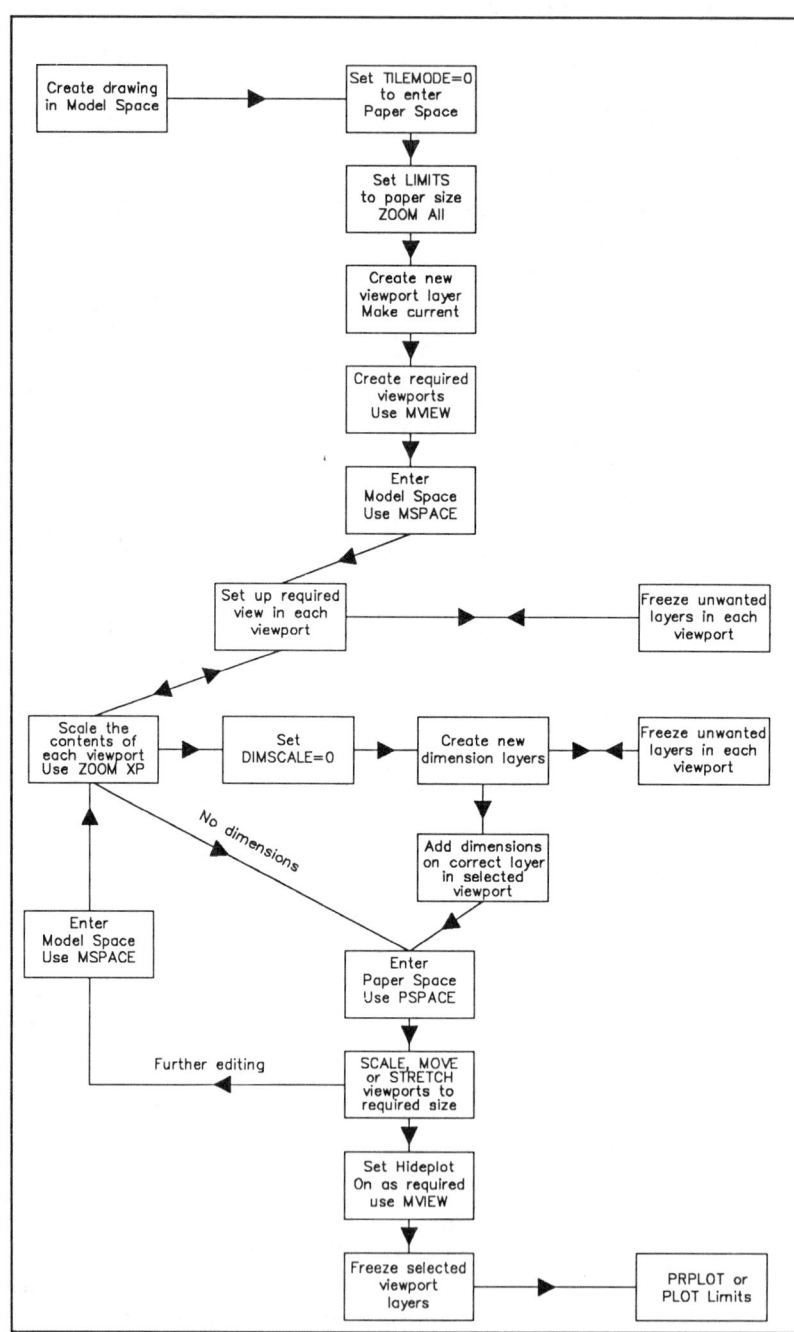

Figure 13.10   The use of paper space

14. Plotting

The end product of most drawings will be a "hard copy" or plot. Plotting may be performed using a plotter or printer. In general, the plotter will give a much more satisfactory result but the printer may possibly be cheaper and quicker. Most of the following, with the exception of the section covering pens and colours, will be applicable to both plotting and printer plotting.

Plotting may be initiated from main menu *Task 3* or from the PLOT command. The corresponding printer plot may be initiated from main menu *Task 4* or the PRPLOT command.

If you are plotting from the main menu, you must specify the drawing title. PLOT and PRPLOT are used with a drawing currently loaded. The advantage of the latter methods is that you have a visual choice of which sections of the drawing are to be plotted.

14.1 CHOOSING WHAT TO PLOT

When you have developed a drawing and wish to plot it, the golden rule is that, before you do anything else, *save the drawing*. It is possible for things to go wrong during plotting and you can find yourself in a situation where the computer "hangs up" - you can only switch off and then you will lose the drawing.

Command: PLOT
What to plot -- Display, Extents, Limits, View, or Window <D>:

This first prompt will occur with the drawing still on the screen. It is asking which part of the drawing should be plotted. The most likely response is the default response - **Display** - which results in the drawing being plotted as presently displayed in the active viewport on the screen (if in Model Space). This need not necessarily be the complete drawing, it could be a small view produced by ZOOM. The alternatives are reasonably self-explanatory:

Extents   Plots the whole drawing rather as Zoom Extents fills the screen with the drawing contents, leaving no surrounding space, (see Section 5.2).

Limits   Plots the entire drawing area as defined by the drawing limits, (see Section 2.3.3).

View   Plots a pre-defined and named view of the drawing, (see Section 5.4).

Window   Allows you to window a small section of the displayed drawing and plot that area only.

When you have chosen one of these alternatives, the drawing will be removed from the screen and the plotter menu will be displayed.

14.2 THE PLOTTER MENU

A plotter menu will typically look like:

> **Plot will NOT be written to a selected file**
> **Sizes are in millimetres**
> **Plot origin is at (0.00,0.00)**
> **Plotting area is 285.00 wide by 198.00 high (A4 size)**
> **Plot is NOT rotated**
> **Pen width is 0.25**
> **Area fill will NOT be adjusted for pen width**
> **Hidden lines will NOT be removed**
> **Plot will be scaled to fit available area**
>
> **Do you want to change anything? <N>**

Taking these one by one:

- **Plot will NOT be written to a selected file**
  It is possible to send your plotting data to a special plot file instead of to a plotter. This file, which carries a .PLT extension, (.LST in the case of printer plotting) needs special software not supplied with AutoCAD before it can be used. Its most likely application is with Desk Top Publishing where the plot file can be used to introduce the drawing into a mixed text/graphics format.
- **Sizes are in millimetres**
  The lengths of the lines plotted by the plotter are directly related to the drawing units at the top of the drawing. These units can be considered to be either inches or millimetres.

● **Plot origin is at (0.00,0.00)**

The plot origin is normally at 0,0 but it can be shifted by changing these coordinates. This allows you to position the bottom left hand corner of your plot on the paper. You should be aware that not all plotters use the corner of the paper as 0,0.

● **Plotting area is 285.00 wide by 198.00 high (A4 size)**

This is the plotting area - in millimetres in this case because of entry (2) - which is currently specified for the plot. The range of paper sizes offered will vary depending upon which plotter was specified at configuration.

● **Plot is NOT rotated**

The plotted drawing can be as it appeared on the screen, or rotated clockwise through 90°, 180° or 270°.

● **Pen width is 0.25**

This is only important when the plotter is filling in solid areas such as a doughnut or polyline. The finer the pen tip the more fill-in strokes will be needed to fill the area.

● **Area fill will NOT be adjusted for pen width**

This controls the area fill function as described above. When activated, it looks at the true width of a filled entity and adjusts the pen strokes to take into account the pen width to ensure accurate reproduction.

● **Hidden lines will NOT be removed**

This applies only to 3-D drawings and AME solid entities and is used for changing a wireframe model into one with a solid appearance. This need not be set to remove hidden lines when plotting from Pspace, the Hideplot sub-command will remove hidden lines from the required viewports.

● **Plot will be scaled to fit available area**

If the dimensions of the final plotted drawing are not critical, it is usually best to scale the drawing so that it fits the paper. The drawing units will not be faithfully reproduced as either inches or millimetres in this case, although relative sizes will of course be maintained (i.e. they will be scaled to some unknown value calculated by AutoCAD).

If you do not wish to change any of the above settings, then press return to accept the No default. The package will now give you a chance to set up the plotter. When all is ready, give another return. After the plot has been completed a further return will put the drawing back on screen.

A plot can be terminated at any time by a Ctrl C but the response may not be immediate because the plotter can store blocks of coordinates in its buffer and will insist on working through them before stopping. *Do not switch off the plotter while it is plotting* - you may hang up the computer and may lose your drawing if not previously saved!

14.2.1 Changing the Plotter Menu

If you *do* wish to change any of the plotter menu items, then return Y at the **Do you wish to change anything?** prompt. You will first of all be shown a pen/colour menu. You may ignore this using the No default, (see Section 14.2.2). You will then be prompted with each of the menu items above. Modify those which require it and return the others. The prompts are quite helpful.

In the case of the final item:

Plot will be scaled to fit available area

if you want to scale the drawing to fit the paper the response is F.

As AutoCAD expects all drawings to be constructed full size it is at this point that the required plotting scale should be specified. When the drawing was originally constructed, a drawing unit was considered as, say, 1 millimetre. This can now be related to a real plotted length.

Thus, to specify a true scale of drawing units to real millimetres or inches on the paper the response could be:

1=2

which means that 1 plotted millimetre (or inch if I is specified at item 2) is equal to 2 drawing units. Alternatively:

1=100

would give a scale of 1 plotted millimetre (or inch) = 100 drawing units.

You should always look carefully at the plotter menu. You will find that *AutoCAD remembers the last menu* and will reproduce the modified menu rather than the original the next time PLOT is entered, even when entering a new drawing.

> *Note:* When plotting a drawing from Paper Space, the scale should normally be set to 1=1. (See Section 14.3.)

14.2.2 Plotting in Different Colours

Most plotters, as distinct from printers, have the ability to change pens and plot in multi-colours. Thus, even if you have a monochrome display, it is possible to produce multi-coloured drawings if the colour options have been correctly invoked in the drawing.

Each colour with a colour number less than 16 can be separately assigned to a numbered pen in a multi-pen plotter. It is up to you to match the actual colours of the pens to the colours of the drawing in an acceptable way. Colours with numbers from 16-255 are automatically assigned to pen number 1.

To check on the current pen/colour configuration, request a plot and choose the required area of the drawing. AutoCAD will respond with the plotter menu described above. Respond with a Y at the end of the menu:

Do you want to change anything? <N> Y

You will then be shown the pen/colour menu which will depend upon the plotter configuration data:

Entity Color	Pen No.	Line Type	Pen Speed
1(red)	1	0	10
2(yellow)	2	0	10
3(green)	3	0	10
4(cyan)	4	0	10
5(blue)	5	0	10
6(magenta)	6	0	10
7(white)	7	0	10
8	8	0	10
:	:	:	:
:	:	:	:
15	1	0	10

Line types	0 = continuous line
	1 = ...
	2 = ...
	3 = -------------
	4 = - - - - - - - -

Do you want to change any of these parameters? <N>

Note: The above display will be influenced by the plotter which you have selected at configuration. For example, you will not be offered the linetype and pen speed options options if your plotter cannot handle these facilities.

If you wish to change anything you should respond with a Y. You will then be presented with each line of the menu separately and will be able to match each colour with a pen number. If you have only a few pens, you will have to assign the same pen to a number of different colours. When you have made all the adjustments that you need, you can exit to the main plotter menu with an X.

It is advisable for you to ignore the linetype and pen speed options (if offered) and leave them at their default values. This is particularly important if you have already introduced different linetypes into your drawing. The AutoCAD manual warns against mixing such software-defined linetypes with hardware-defined linetypes as found in this menu.

If your plotter supports only one pen, AutoCAD will recognise this and pause during plotting to allow you to change pens.

> *Note:* It is possible to specify different pen widths in your plot by assigning them to a particular (false) colour. For example, all "red" lines in the drawing could refer to a black pen with a width of 0.5 mm whereas all "green" lines could refer to a black pen with a width of 0.1 mm.

14.3 PLOTTING FROM PAPER SPACE

The Paper Space environment, which is described in detail in Chapter 13, greatly simplifies the plotting operation. The procedure for plotting from Paper Space may be summarized:

● Set the Paper Space limits to the plotting paper size and apply the ZOOM All command to represent the complete page on screen. Remember that enabling the grid will indicate the exact boundaries set by the LIMITS command.
● Create a special layer called, say, PAPERLAYER and make it current *before* any viewports are created in Paper Space. This allows you to freeze the viewports before plotting. This will not inhibit plotting of the viewport *contents* but will remove the viewport frames from the plot if required. If you do not wish all the viewports to be treated identically, you may place some on one layer and some on another. Nothing is irrevocable - you can use CHPROP to move viewports from layer to layer.
● Compose your drawing to be plotted by creating and editing the required viewports.
● Apply the Hideplot option of the MVIEW command to control the HIDE function in selected viewports.
● Apply the Freeze option of the VPLAYER command to suppress those layers which are not to be plotted *in each individual viewport*.
● Give the PLOT command and select the Limits option.

> *Note:* It is very easy, while switching between Paper Space and Model Space when setting up your final display, to initiate the plot from Model Space instead of from Paper Space. With the plot scale set to 1=1 this can result in a plot at totally the wrong scale.

- Remember that you *must* enable the **Hidden lines will be removed** option of the plot menu if you wish to use Hideplot in selected viewports.
- Do *not* use the Scale to Fit option of the plot menu. Set the scale to 1=1 for the plot to be reproduced at the desired size.

15. Isometric drawing

15.1 ISOMETRIC AXES

The isometric features of AutoCAD are provided simply as an aid to producing drawings with an isometric projection and should not be confused with the extensive three-dimensional facilities of the package. The features are closely linked with the SNAP command.

To commence a drawing in isometric projection, SNAP should be invoked and the Style option chosen.

> **Command:** SNAP
> **Snap spacing or ON/OFF/Aspect/Rotate/Style <5.00>:** S
> **Standard/Isometric <S>:** I
> **Vertical spacing <5>:**

You will now see that the cross wires on the screen are no longer at right angles but are set at 60° to each other. When making isometric drawings, surfaces may be represented on one of three planes, Left, Top and Right. Lines defining these surfaces will normally be drawn at 30°, 90° or 150° to the horizontal. The cross wires, in the isometric snap style, act as an aid in the construction of these lines. Cross wire pairs may be inclined at 90°,150° (Left-hand plane), 150°,30° (Top plane) and 90°,30° (Right-hand plane). These combinations and their associated planes are shown in Figure 15.1.

To switch from one pair of cross wires to another you may use the ISOPLANE command.

> **Command:** ISOPLANE
> **Left/Top/Right/(Toggle):**

Left plane, Top plane or Right plane cross wires may be specified by responding with L, T or R. Alternatively, the plane may be toggled from L to T to R to L etc., by repeatedly pressing return.

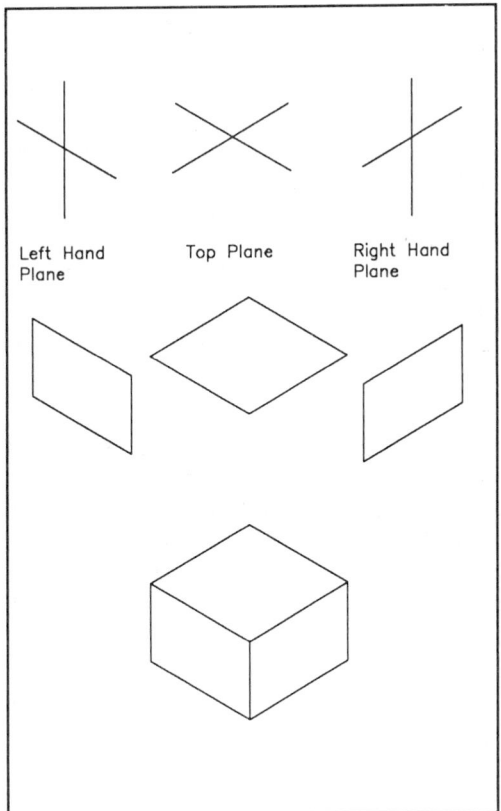

Figure 15.1   Isometric planes

However, you do not need to use the SNAP or the ISOPLANE commands to access the isometric drawing facilities:

- AutoCAD allows you to switch to isometric style by picking the **Isometric** box on the Drawing Tools... option of the **Settings** pull down.
- You can toggle between each isometric plane by using Ctrl E. This has the advantage of being transparent and so can be used within drawing commands.

ORTHO, GRID and SNAP commands, when used with isometric style, respond exactly in keeping with their normal functions but always with reference to the isometric planes rather than the normal orthogonal planes.

15.2 ISOCIRCLES

Most of the drawing commands such as CIRCLE, POLYGON etc., do not take account of the isometric style but there is one drawing facility which is specifically aimed at isometric drawing. This is the Isocircle section of the ELLIPSE command which is offered *only* when in isometric mode. A circular shape drawn on an isometric projection will, of course, be drawn as an ellipse. If it is assumed that the current drawing is in isometric style, then, to represent a circle :

> **Command: ELLIPSE**
> **<Axis endpoint 1>/Center/Isocircle: I**
> **Center of Circle:**
> **<Circle radius>/Diameter:**

You can then specify the position and size of the "circle" and the corresponding ellipse will be drawn with reference to the current isometric plane. Figure 15.2 displays a box drawn with the help of the isometric facilities of AutoCAD and shows isocircles inserted correctly into three of the plane surfaces. The angle of the cross hatching has been adjusted to match the isoplanes to enhance the effect.

Be careful not to insert the circle on some plane other than the current isoplane because the result will look "wrong." Figure 15.3 shows exactly the same isocircles as the previous figure, but inserted on the wrong faces. The illusion that they are circles has been totally lost.

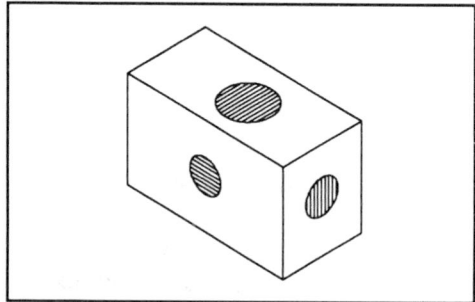
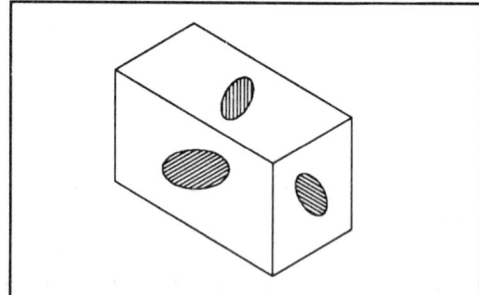

Figure 15.2   The illusion of circles   **Figure 15.3**   The illusion of circles destroyed

If you wish to produce the effect of a filleted corner in an isometric drawing, the normal FILLET command will not be satisfactory. It is possible to use sections of an Isocircle to TRIM away the unwanted portions to give the appearance of a true fillet.

Note: It is possible to produce very convincing three-dimensional representations using isometric drawing, (see Figure 15.4) but these are not recognised as three-dimensional drawings by AutoCAD. Any attempt to use the specialised 3-D commands such as VPOINT or HIDE on such a drawing will be unsuccessful and confusing.

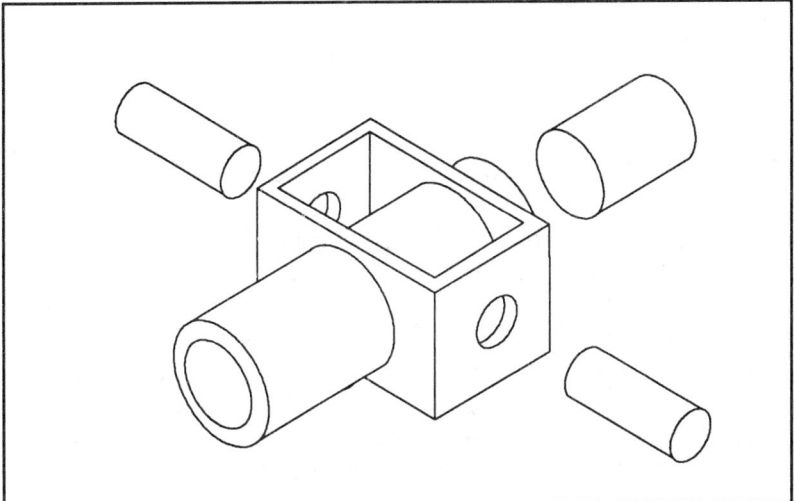

Figure 15.4 An example of an isometric drawing

16. Three dimensional drawing

16.1 SIMPLE THREE DIMENSIONAL CONSTRUCTION

AutoCAD's original three dimensional (3D) drawing facility could more accurately be referred to as 2½D drawing. Simple entities such as lines, circles or arcs could be "extruded" in the Z-direction (i.e. perpendicular to the X-Y plane). These parallel-sided 3D entities were of only limited use; they could be rotated *only* about the Z-axis and *only* extrusion lines parallel to the Z-axis could be constructed. This original AutoCAD 3D drawing facility relied upon the specification of both elevation and thickness.

To overcome the second limitation AutoCAD Release 2.6 introduced 2 additional commands, 3DLINE and 3DFACE, allowing non-parallel sided structures to be represented.

Although the original 3D facility was very limiting it has provided the basis upon which AutoCAD's extensive 3D features have been built.

16.1.1 ELEVation and Thickness

The simplest method of 3D realization is to construct the drawing as a 2D plan view, i.e. in the XY plane. If the plan is imagined to be drawn on a piece of paper, then the third dimension, the extrusion thickness, will extend either out of (above) or into (below) the paper's surface, i.e. in the positive or negative Z direction respectively. Other items may be added to the plan view which are at another height or ELEVation above or below the paper, although always parallel to it, (see Figure 16.1). Thus, before any 3D object is drawn, its elevation and thickness must have been specified using the ELEV command or by selecting Entity Creation under the **Options** pull down menu (DDEMODES). See Figure 16.2.

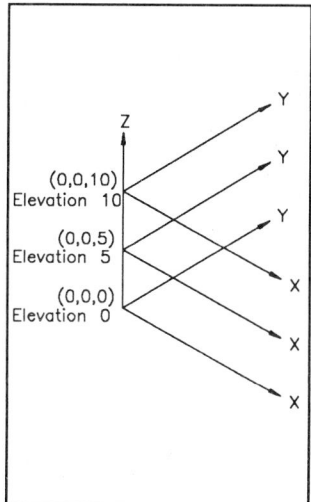

Figure 16.1 Different elevations

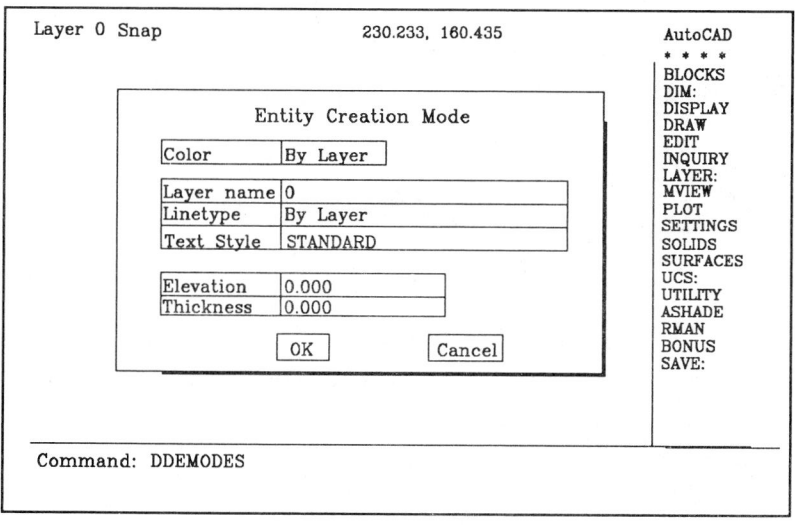

Figure 16.2 Entity Creation dialogue box

EXAMPLE

To draw a cylinder at elevation 0 and height 50 units:

Command: ELEV
New current elevation <0.00>: 0
New current thickness: <0.00>: 50

This sets the elevation and extrusion thickness of all subsequently drawn objects until these settings are re-specified.

Remember that you are looking at the cylinder in plan view so that it will appear as a simple circle. To view the cylinder from a point other than directly above, (see Figure 16.3), use the VPOINT command. (See Section 16.1.4.)

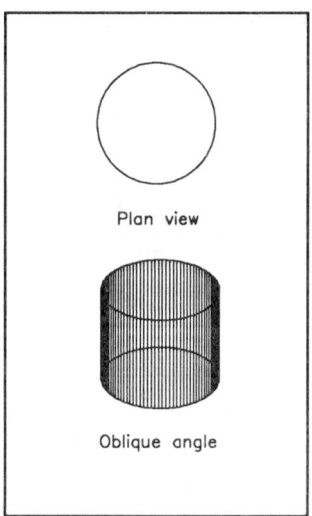

Plan view

Oblique angle

Figure 16.3 Changing the viewpoint

16.1.2 Varying the Elevation and Thickness

The single cylinder example, when viewed from some oblique angle, clearly demonstrates the effect of setting the extrusion thickness. The thickness determines the height of the object; in the above example this is 50 units. The effect of the elevation term will become clearer when extra objects are added to the drawing at various elevations.

> *Note:* Although it is possible to modify and extend drawings from other viewpoints it is always safest at this stage to return to the plan view before any changes are made.

EXAMPLE

The cylinder in the above example is based at elevation 0 and has a height of 50. To place another cylinder on top of the first the elevation must be changed before the second cylinder is drawn, (see Figure 16.4).

Command: ELEV
New current elevation <0.00>: 50
New current thickness <50>: 75

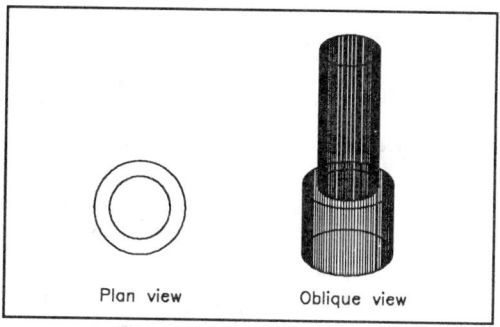

Plan view   Oblique view

Figure 16.4   Placing objects at different heights

16.1.3 Changing the Thickness of Existing Entities

The thickness of any existing entity in a drawing may be altered by use of the CHANGE or CHPROP commands. The entities are first selected in the normal manner and then, in the case of CHANGE, a P is returned to show that you wish to change one of the properties, followed by T for thickness.

16.1.4 VPOINT

To observe the 3D effect we need to change the viewpoint; there are various ways of achieving this although the icon method is the most convenient.

The viewpoint may be specified as a set of XYZ coordinates relative to the drawing which is assumed to be at the current origin. Remember that if perspective views are not generated then these coordinates specify only a *direction of view*, not a viewing distance. Thus the viewpoint 0,-1,0 will be interpreted as a view from the centre (X=0), front (Y=-1) and ground level (Z=0) but will give just the same view on screen as the more distant viewpoint 0,-10,0. A view from the left would be given by -1,0,0; from the right by 1,0,0; from the rear by 0,1,0 and from the top by 0,0,1. (See Figure 16.5.)

An isometric view from the right, front, top position would be obtained from viewpoint 1,-1,1 :

Command: VPOINT
Rotate/<View point> <0.00,0.00,1.00>: 1,-1,1

A "wireframe" model of the drawing is now displayed, (see Figure 16.6).

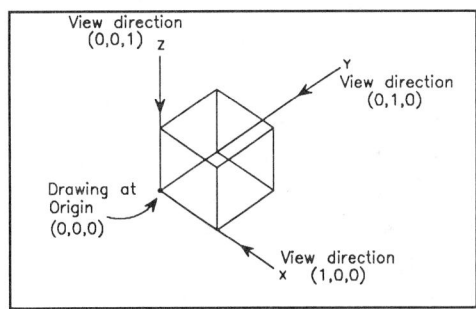

Figure 16.5   Specifying viewpoints   **Figure 16.6**   Wire frame representation

VPOINT may adjust the size of the display on screen, but the real dimensions and position of the object are not altered. To view the object from a different angle, repeat the VPOINT command and change the viewpoint coordinates.

An alternative means of setting the viewpoint is provided which is more convenient, although less precise, than specifying the coordinates. If a null response (return) is supplied at the VPOINT prompt, the screen will clear and an axes tripod and a compass are displayed, (see Figure 16.7). Either representation may be used to specify the viewpoint but the compass is probably easier to understand.

The compass is a two-dimensional representation of a globe as seen from above. Thus the centre point represents the north pole and if this position is picked with the pointing device the resulting display of the drawing will be a *plan view* (corresponding to coordinates 0,0,1).

The inner circle of the compass represents the equator and will always give a *ground level* (Z=0) view. "12 O'clock" on this circle represents a rear elevation (0,1,0), "3 O'clock" and "9 O'clock" represent side elevations (-1,0,0 and 1,0,0) and "6 O'clock" the front elevation (0,-1,0).

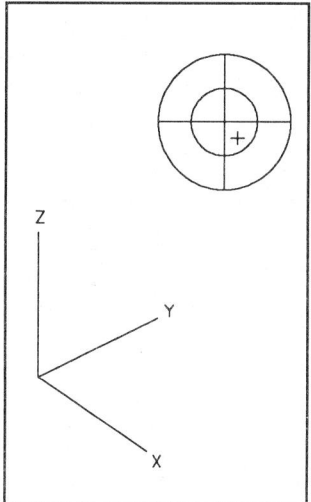

Figure 16.7 Viewpoint by compass

All points between the two compass circles represent points in the southern hemisphere and any corresponding viewpoint is from *below* (Z negative). The entire outer circle represents the south pole and gives a view from directly below (0,0,-1).

A third method of specifying the viewpoint is by defining the viewpoint angle.

Command: VPOINT
Rotate/<View point>: R
Enter angle in X-Y plane from X axis <270.0000>: 45
Enter angle from X-Y plane <90.0000>: 45

Imagine the object being drawn in the X-Y plane and extruded in the Z-plane; it would appear as in Figure 16.8. The viewpoint P is defined by setting the two angles shown.

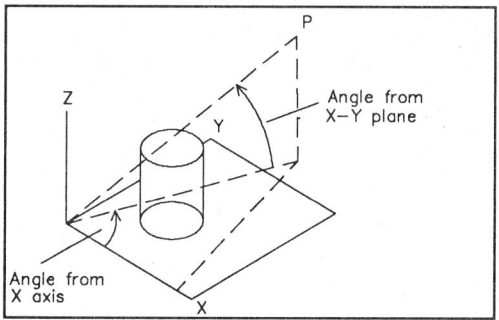

Figure 16.8 Viewpoint defined by angles

16.1.5 Viewpoint Selection by Icon Menu

The most convenient method of viewpoint selection is provided through the icons displayed by picking Vpoint 3D... from the **Display** pull down menu. The required direction of view may be chosen from the icons, (see Figure 16.9) and the viewpoint angle selected from the corresponding screen menu.

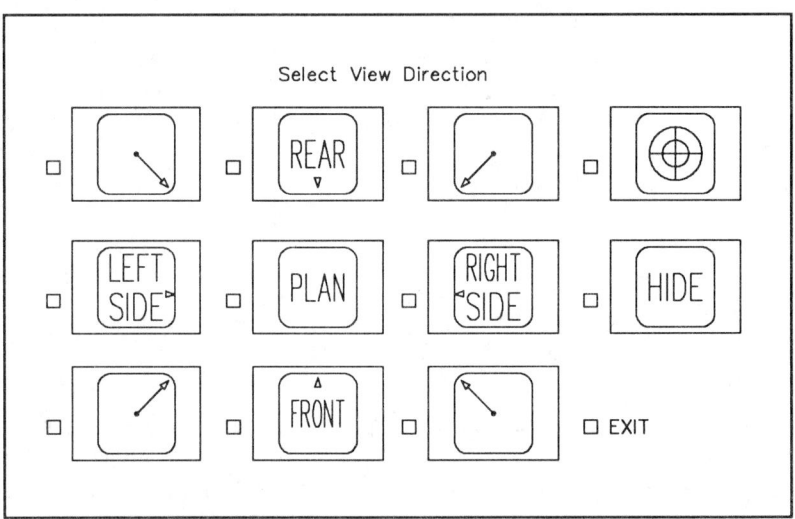

Figure 16.9   Viewpoint selection by icon menu

16.1.6 HIDE

3D drawings are normally displayed as wireframe models. This is acceptable for simple drawings but, as the complexity increases, the number of lines tends to obscure important features. The HIDE command takes a wireframe model as viewed on the screen and removes those lines which would be hidden from view in a solid object viewed from that angle. The process can be slow because each segment of each line must be treated separately. In a very complex drawing the time elapsed may extend to hours. Once the process is completed, the drawing is displayed on screen with hidden lines removed, (see Figure 16.10).

However, if you subsequently change the viewpoint *the drawing will revert to wireframe* because the HIDE operation was only relevant to the view current at the time HIDE was invoked.

The same is true for plotting. It is pointless going through the HIDE routine on screen if you wish only to plot the hidden line version. Normal plotting will usually result in a wireframe drawing. A plot with hidden lines removed *must be specified in the plotting menu* and the HIDE process will then be repeated, whether or not the display on screen has been processed by HIDE. (See Section 14.2.)

16.1.7 Solid and Hollow Entities

Following HIDE, wireframe cylinders are represented as cylindrical solids. In many cases this is desirable but it is possible that you may wish to represent a hollow cylinder and yet still use the hidden lines facility. The AutoCAD software has built in to it some (rather arbitrary) decisions of how a particular shape should be considered. It all depends on the original 2D shape that was used in the plan view. Thus a circle, when extruded into a cylinder, is always considered to be a solid, i.e. it has a top and a bottom. If a hollow cylinder is required, it must be derived from two arcs, (see Figure 16.11).

Similarly, a box derived from lines will be thought of as having no top or bottom.

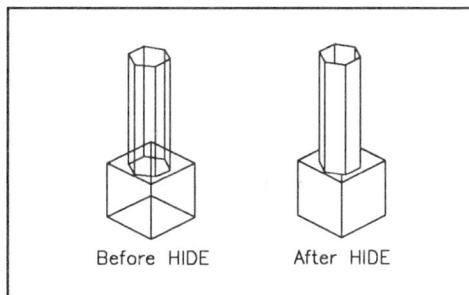

Before HIDE   After HIDE

Figure 16.10   The effect of HIDE

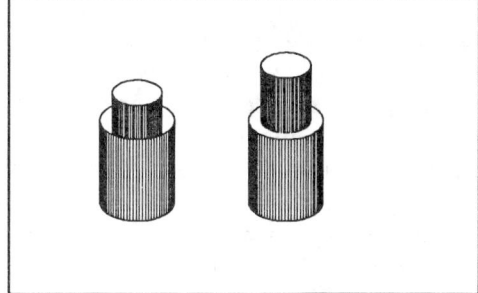

Figure 16.11   Hollow and solid cylinders

To avoid this the original rectangle in the plan view may have a 3DFACE placed on top of the box to act as a lid (See Figure 16.12 and Section 16.4.3). Circles, 2D solids and wide polylines are all treated, when extruded, as solids by HIDE. Any non-closed entity in the 2D plan view will result in an open 3D structure, (see Figure 16.13).

If SOLID is used as the basis of rectilinear structures, it will be treated on screen as a filled area on the plan view but not in any other projection. If this is inconvenient, the FILL facility can be turned off.

One of the problems with HIDE is that you cannot save a drawing in hidden form. This is not important for simple drawings but if the drawing is very large the time for a HIDE can be considerable and this must be endured each time a hidden version of the drawing is required.

One solution is to form a SLIDE of the drawing. (See Chapter 19.)

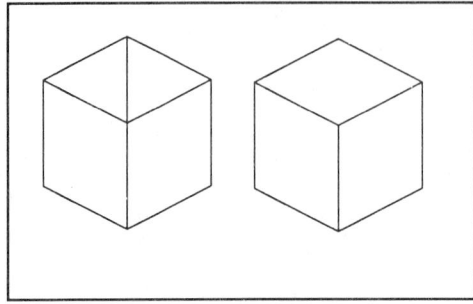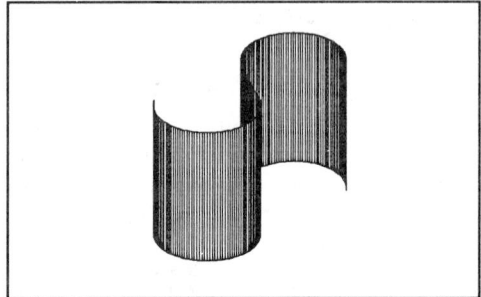

Figure 16.12   Open and solid boxes   **Figure 16.13**   An open hidden entity

16.1.8 Hiding Objects that Touch

The decisions taken by the HIDE routine on whether any given object is hidden by another are a matter of accurate calculation of the coordinates. When two objects are drawn to be exactly touching each other, the decision becomes almost arbitrary. Minute rounding errors in the calculation can have a disproportionate effect. Thus, in a drawing of a house, the line of an interior wall which exactly touches an exterior wall may sometimes "appear" on the outside hidden view. This is usually caused when, in the plan view, the two walls are "snapped" to the same position. In the case of point contacts this is rarely important but, with lines and surfaces in contact, care is required to achieve the desired result.

16.1.9 Displaying the Hidden Lines

It is sometimes useful if the hidden lines, instead of being completely suppressed, can be displayed on a separate layer and in a different colour. To achieve this it is necessary to create an additional special layer for each layer in the original drawing. The special layers must carry the same names as the original layers but prefixed with the word HIDDEN. Thus if the original drawing was on layers called PLANE1 and PLANE2 the new layers *must* be called HIDDENPLANE1 and HIDDENPLANE2. By setting new colours for these special layers the hidden lines are clearly displayed after a HIDE operation.

> *Note:*   If an object is drawn on a layer that is turned off, it is invisible on the screen but it can still be considered by the HIDE command and can thus obscure an object that would otherwise have been visible. If the unwanted layer is frozen instead of turned off, this problem will not arise.

16.1.10 Shading 3D Surfaces with the SHADE command

An alternative to the HIDE command is to use SHADE. This results in a shaded rendering of the original surfaces in their initial wireframe colours. The resolution or quality of the shading is determined by the quality of hardware of your graphic display. If this can support 256 colours, then a true shadowing effect may be generated, whereas lower quality hardware systems can only produce a rendered image with no shadowing. The shadowing simulates the effect produced by a combination of a single light source positioned behind the user together with a level of ambient light.

Command: SHADE
Regenerating drawing.
Shading nn% done.

The presentation of the SHADEd image is controlled by the two system variables SHADEDGE and SHADEDIF.

The optimum setting of SHADEDGE will depend on your display hardware. This system variable may take integer values from 0 to 3.

0   May be used to give a full shadowed image with the original face edges removed. This is the highest quality option but may only be used to full effect with 256 colour hardware. If this option is used on a lower quality display, then a grey featureless image will result.

1   This operates in exactly the same way as the previous option but the face edges are depicted in the screen background colour.

2   This option gives an effect similar to that of the HIDE command and may be used on all colour and monochrome systems. The surface of each face is always shown in black and the face edges take their wire-frame colour.

3   This operates as option 2 except that the surface of each face is shaded in the wireframe colour and the face edges are shown in the screen background colour.

The system variable SHADEDIF controls the ratio of directed to ambient light. The default setting of 70 represents 70% directed light and 30% ambient light. The higher the percentage of directed light the greater is the contrast in the shaded image.

Note: SHADE can only be used to produce an image on screen. If you attempt to produce a print or plot of a SHADEd object, you only obtain a wireframe representation. This is the reason for our lack of illustrations on this subject!

Because you cannot record or save a SHADEd image, the only way to preserve it is to make a slide. (See Chapter 19.)

It is impossible to use any editing command, such as ERASE, on a SHADEd object. If you wish to return to a wireframe model, or make modifications to the original 3D entity, either force a REGEN or change the ViewPOINT.

16.2 ADVANCED THREE DIMENSIONAL CONSTRUCTION

When constructing complex 3D entities, the above commands and techniques are now supplemented with a User-defined Coordinate System. This allows the standard 2D drawing commands to be used in conjunction with specialised 3D surface mesh commands.

16.2.1 The User Coordinate System (UCS)

The User Coordinate System (UCS) is fundamental to the treatment of 3D constructions.

Originally, AutoCAD made use of the static coordinate system, the coordinate point X=0, Y=0, Z=0 being fixed. All inputs were then made relative to this fixed origin and were therefore unique. This system is now known as the World Coordinate System (WCS). See Figure 16.14.

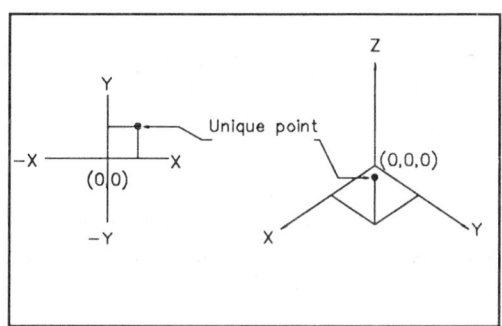

Figure 16.14 World Coordinate System

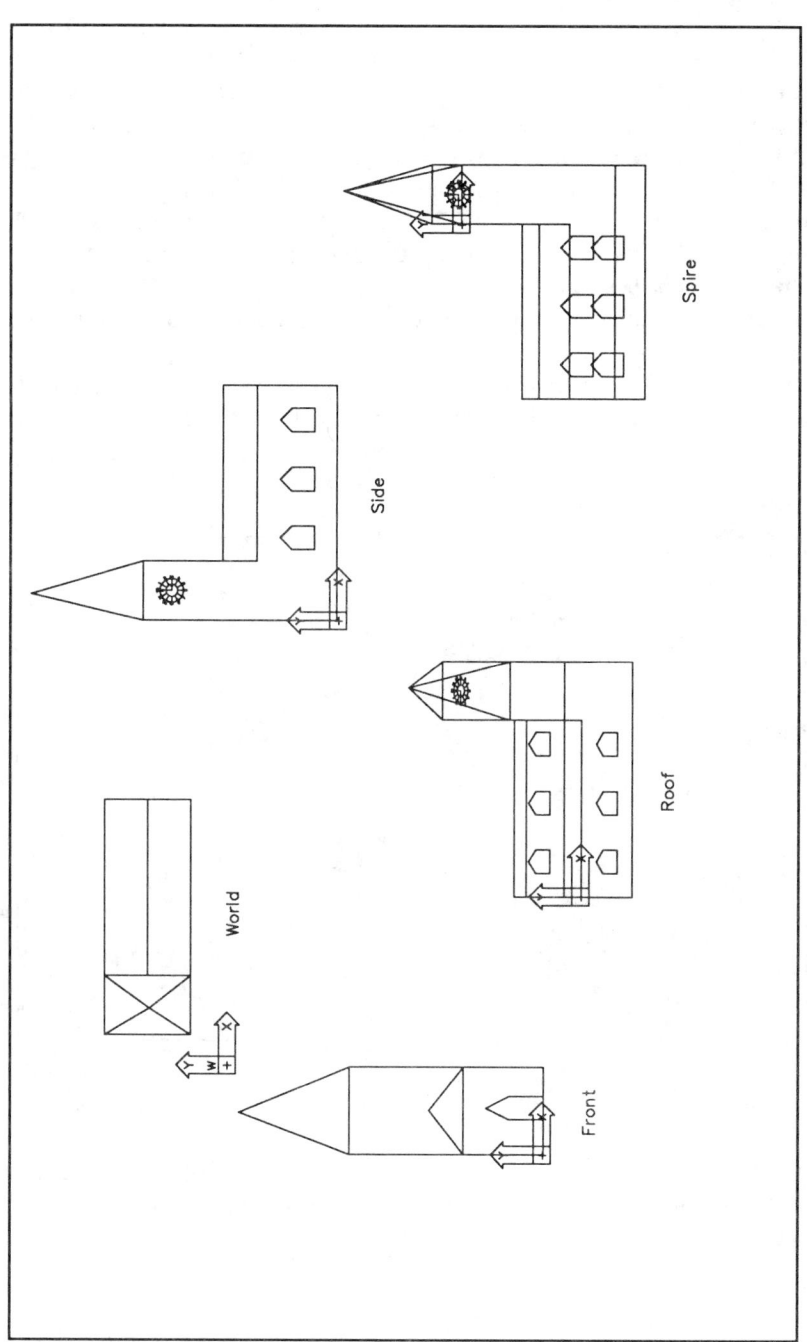

Figure 16.15 Various User Coordinate Systems

The UCS allows the 0,0,0 point to be re-positioned anywhere *with respect to the previously defined origin*. Any number of UCS's, together with their user defined 0,0,0 coordinate points, can now be defined within a drawing, (see Figure 16.15).

A UCS can be defined at any position and at any angle in space. This immensely simplifies the production of 3D drawings, allowing 3D objects to be constructed using standard 2D techniques. You should always draw on the plan view, i.e. on the XY plane of the current UCS, which may now be orientated at any angle and any position in space. Thus all the standard 2D entities such as circles, arcs, polygons etc., can be drawn on the current UCS X-Y plane. This is the *only* technique by which these 2D entities can be positioned anywhere in space. The exception to this rule is the LINE entity which has now been given full 3D properties, i.e. X-, Y-, Z- coordinates of the start and end points can now be specified to define uniquely its position in space. (See section 16.3.1.)

All the original (pre-Release 10) 3D techniques, such as setting the extrusion thickness, can be applied to entities drawn on any defined UCS. For example, it is now possible to construct cylinders at any orientation in space, (see Figure 16.16).

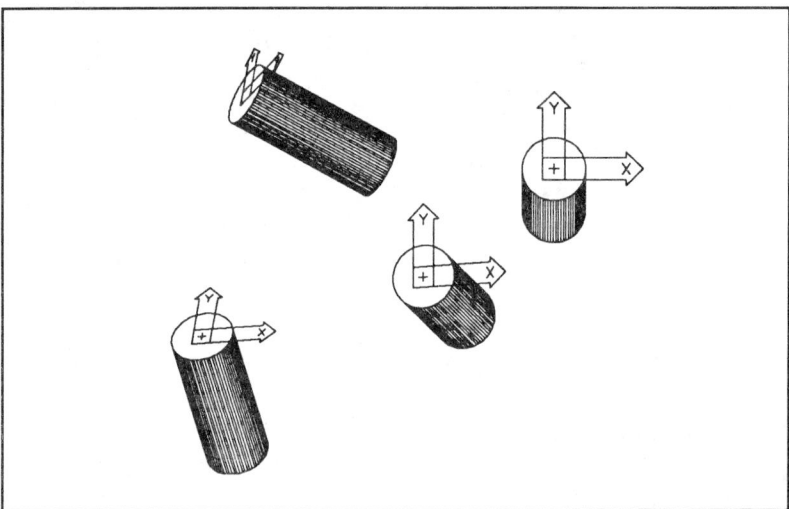

Figure 16.16 Cylinders at various orientations

Once a UCS has been defined and named, it can be recalled at any time and made the current UCS. All inputs will then be relative to the 0,0,0 origin defined by this current UCS.

> *Note:* Learning to create and manipulate User Coordinate Systems is fundamental to 3D drawing. You should persevere - it will be worth it eventually.
>
> The examples given in Appendix 7 have been structured to introduce you to the concept of the UCS and other advanced 3D techniques.

16.2.2 The UCS Icon

The UCS icon is an aid to visualising the position and angle of the current UCS *with respect to the previous UCS*. The icon consists of two orthogonal arrows pointing in the positive X- and Y- directions.

- If you are presently using the WCS, then a W will appear within the Y arrow.
- If the UCS icon is positioned at the origin of the current UCS then a + symbol will appear at the intersection of the arrows.
- If you are viewing the drawing from any position above the current UCS, (i.e. positive Z), then a square box will also appear at this intersection.
- If you are viewing the drawing exactly edge on (± 1°) to the current UCS, then the UCS icon will be replaced by a broken pencil symbol - accurate positioning of a coordinate point may now be impossible.

The various UCS icons are shown in Figure 16.17.

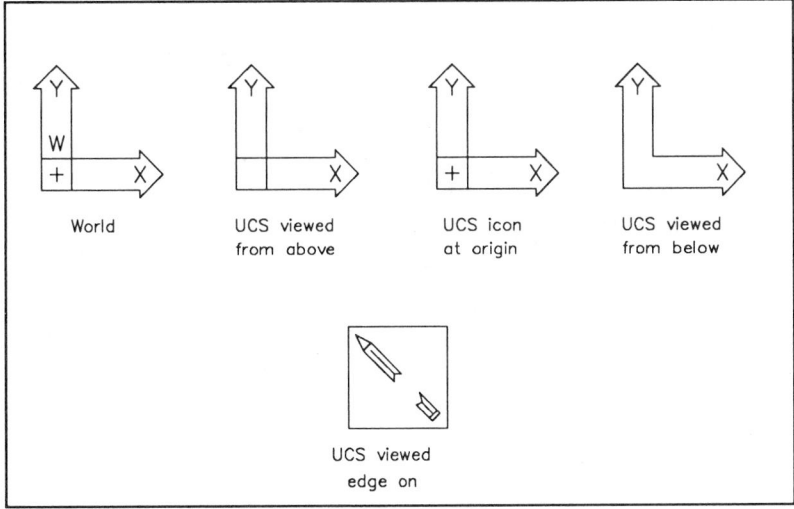

Figure 16.17 UCS icons

The UCS icon is controlled by the UCSICON command.

Command: UCSICON
ON/OFF/All/Noorigin/ORigin <current state>:

ON/OFF   Enables/disables the UCS icon in the current active viewport.

All   All is always used in conjunction with one of the other options. Thus All followed by ON will switch on the UCS icon in all the current viewports.

Noorigin   Positions the UCS icon at the bottom left hand corner of the screen regardless of the 0,0,0 position.

Origin   Places the icon at the user-defined origin of the current UCS. If the icon cannot be fitted at this position without being clipped by the viewport borders, it will be placed in the lower left hand corner of the screen.

Note: When the UCS icon is set to Origin and, due to the positioning of the drawing the 0,0,0 is not on the screen, then the icon will appear without the + at the intersection of the X and Y arrows.

16.2.3 Definition of a UCS

There are four principals by which a new UCS may be defined relative to the *active* coordinate system:

- By specifying a new origin, a new Z-axis or a new X-Y plane.
- By aligning with the orientation of an existing object.
- By aligning with the current view.
- By rotation about the X-, Y-, or Z- axis.

Note: It should always be remembered that, when defining a new UCS, it is done relative to the current (active) UCS.

Command: UCS
Origin/ZAxis/3point/Entity/View/X/Y/Z/Prev/Restore/Save/Del/?/<World>:

Origin   **Origin point <0,0,0>:**

Allows the definition of a new UCS origin relative to the current UCS, *leaving the orientation of the axes unchanged.* This can be achieved either by pointing or by the numerical input, *relative to the currently active UCS,* of the new origin point from the keyboard. Figure 16.18).

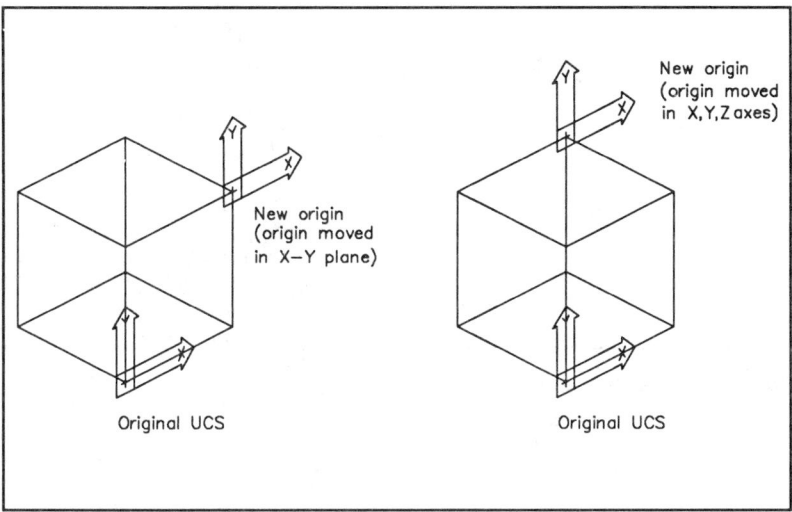

Figure 16.18   New UCS origin

ZAxis   **Origin point <0,0,0>:**
                 Point on positive portion of the Z axis <default>:

Allows the definition of a new UCS origin relative to the current UCS but with the Z- axis direction re-defined. AutoCAD specifies the directions of the X- and Y- axes for you. (See Figure 16.19.)

3point   **Origin point <0,0,0>:**
                 Point on positive portion of the X axis <default>:
                 Point on positive Y portion of the UCS X-Y plane <default>:

Allows the definition of a new UCS origin relative to the current UCS by specifying the origin, the direction of the new positive X-axis and the inclination of the X-Y plane. This is the most versatile method but does take a little practice. (See Figure 16.20.)

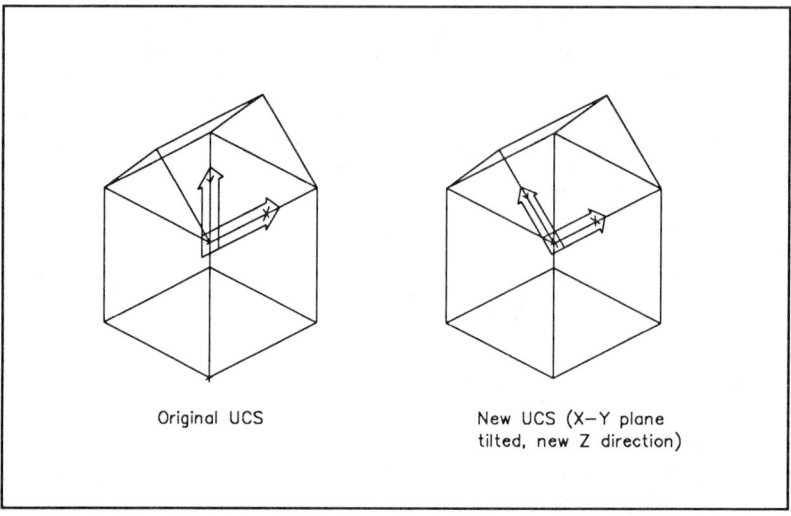

Figure 16.19 New UCS Z-direction

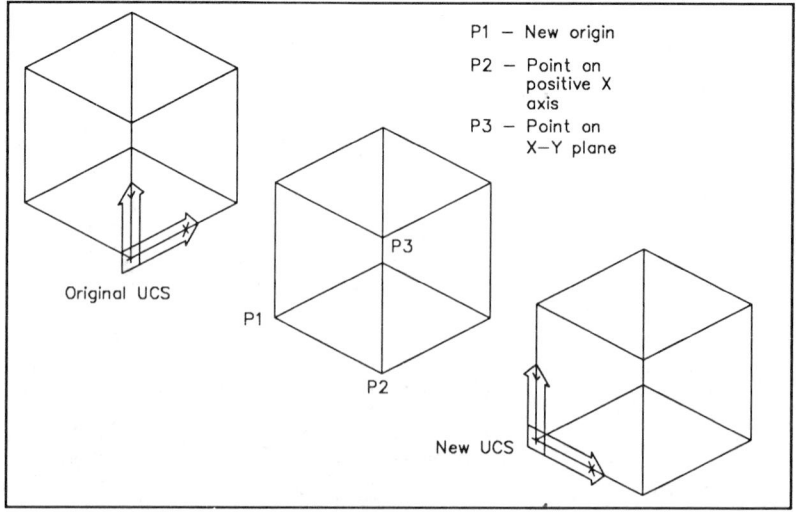

Figure 16.20 New UCS by three point selection

Entity   **Select object to align UCS:**

Allows the definition of a new UCS origin relative to the current UCS by selection of a particular entity. The new Z- axis will be aligned with the extrusion direction (positive Z) of the chosen entity. Figure 16.21.

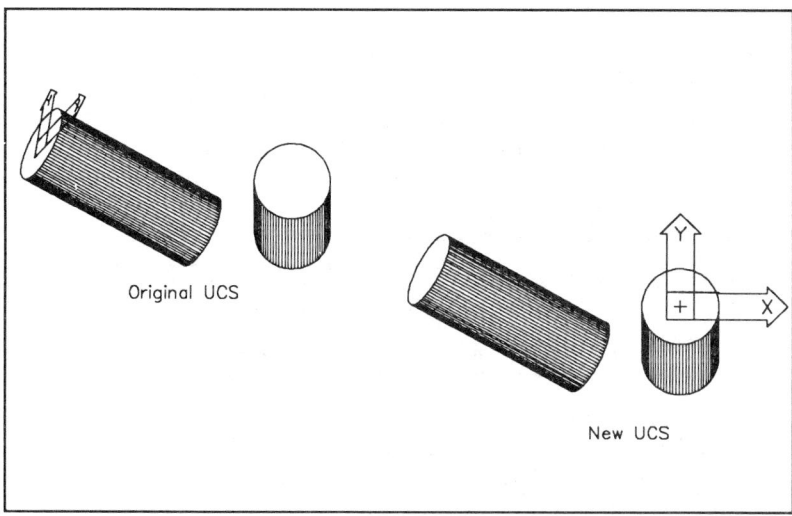

Figure 16.21   Align UCS with entity

The origin and the X- direction are derived by reference to the following set of rules:

- *Arc:*   Origin=centre point: X- axis passes through the end point of the arc.
- *Circle:*   Origin=centre point: X- axis passes through the pick point (radius or diameter).
- *Dim:*   Origin=centre point of dimension text: X- axis is parallel to the X- axis of the dimension.
- *Line:*   Origin=endpoint (the nearest endpoint to the picked point will be adopted): X- axis lies along the line and the X-Y plane remains unchanged.
- *Point:*   Origin=point location: X- axis is in an arbitrary direction!
- *2D Pline:*   Origin=start point: X- axis is in the direction of the next vertex.

- *Solid:* Origin=first definition point: X- axis lies along the line joining the first two points.
- *3D Face:* Origin=first definition point: X- axis lies along the line joining the first two points: the Y- axis lies along the line joining the first and fourth points.
- *Shape, Text, Block, Attribute:* Origin=insertion point: X- axis follows the line of rotation specified when the entity was inserted.

View

In this option the origin remains unchanged. The X-Y plane is rotated so that it is perpendicular to the current view direction; i.e. if a new view is selected, using the VPOINT command, which lies at a particular angle with respect to the original view, then the X-Y plane will be rotated through the same angle.

X/Y/Z

Rotation angle about the X (or Y or Z) **axis<0.0>:**

In this option the origin remains unchanged. If X is selected, the X- axis remains unchanged and the Y- and Z- axes are rotated through the specified angle. The direction of this rotation is governed by AutoCAD's right hand rule. This states that if you grip the selected axis and point your thumb in the positive direction then your curled fingers will indicate the positive direction of rotation. (See Figures 16.22 and 16.23.)

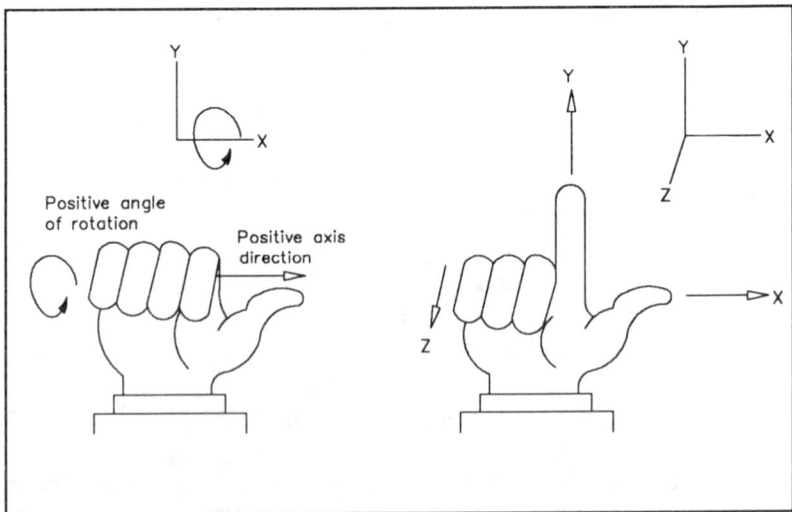

Figure 16.22 The right hand rule to define coordinate systems

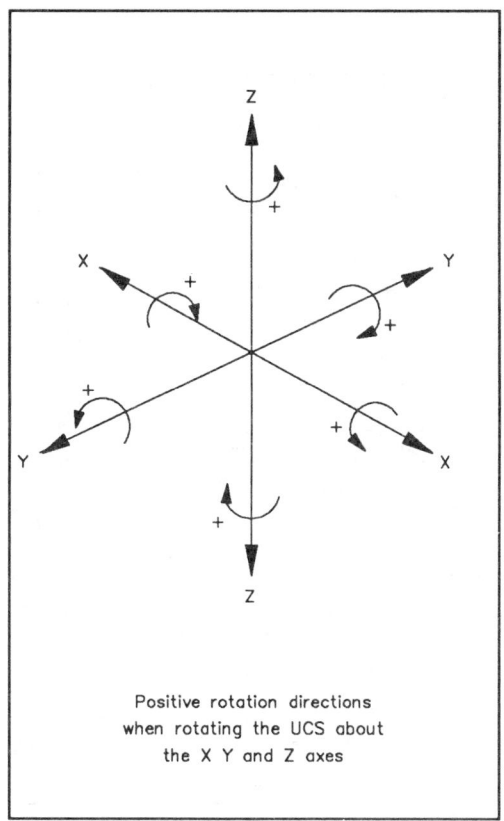

Figure 16.23 Positive rotation directions

Prev   Returns you to the previously used UCS. AutoCAD allows you to step back through the last 10 UCS definitions.

Restore   Allows you to return to a previously saved (named) UCS.

Save   Allows you to name (31 characters maximum) and save the current active UCS.

Del   Deletes a previously saved UCS. Wild card characters (? and *) can be used to delete more than one UCS.

?   Returns a list of all the previously saved UCS definitions.

World   Returns you to the World Coordinate System (WCS).

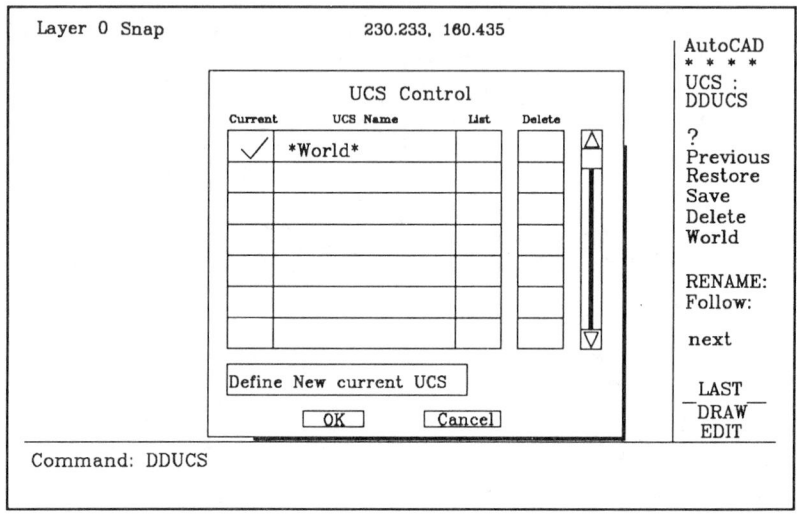

Figure 16.24 UCS dialogue box

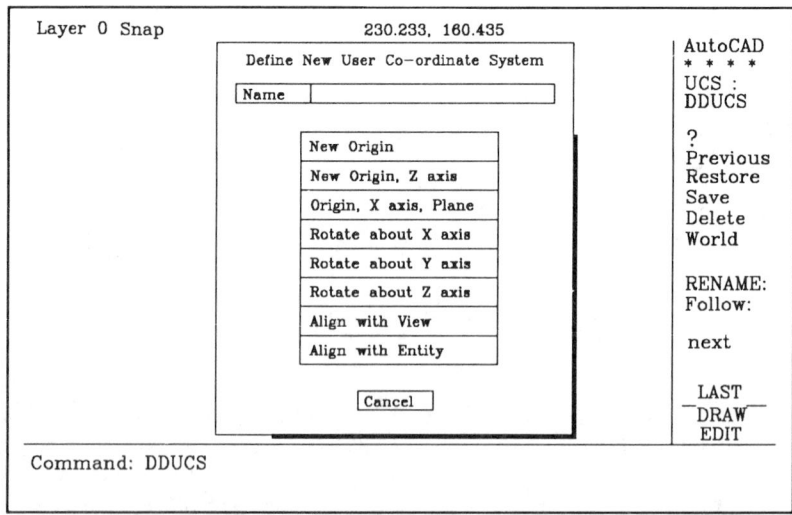

Figure 16.25 UCS definition dialogue box

16.2.4 The UCS Dialogue Box

The UCS dialogue box can be accessed from the pull down menu (under **Settings**), from the **UCS** screen menu option or from the command line by typing DDUCS. All the above-described options for defining and saving a UCS are available through this dialogue box. (See Figures 16.24 and 16.25.)

16.2.5 The UCS Options Icon Menu

This may be used to define a limited number (6) of standard UCS options (found under the **Settings** pull down menu). It also allows you to define a new UCS as with the View option of the UCS command, (see Figure 16.26).

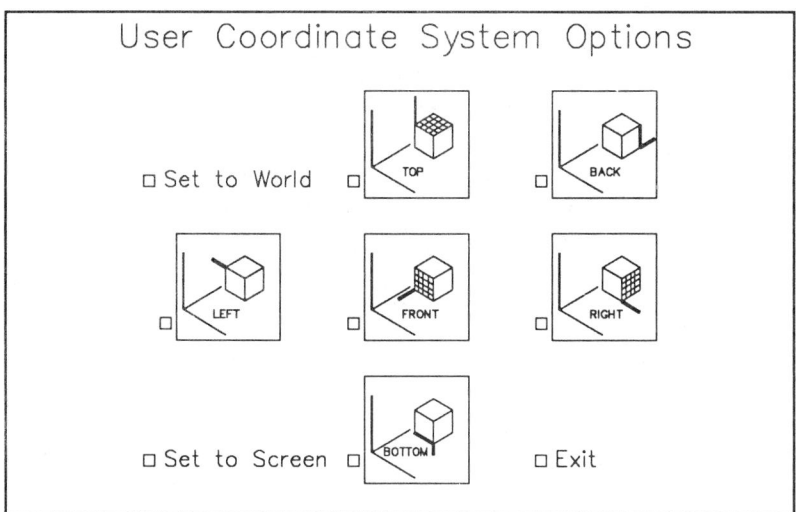

Figure 16.26   UCS options icon

16.2.6 PLAN

When changing from one UCS to another, the viewing direction remains unaltered. The PLAN command has been introduced as an easy way to change the viewpoint automatically to the plan view (viewpoint=0,0,1) each time the UCS is changed, (see Figure 16.27).

Command: PLAN
<Current UCS>/Ucs/World:

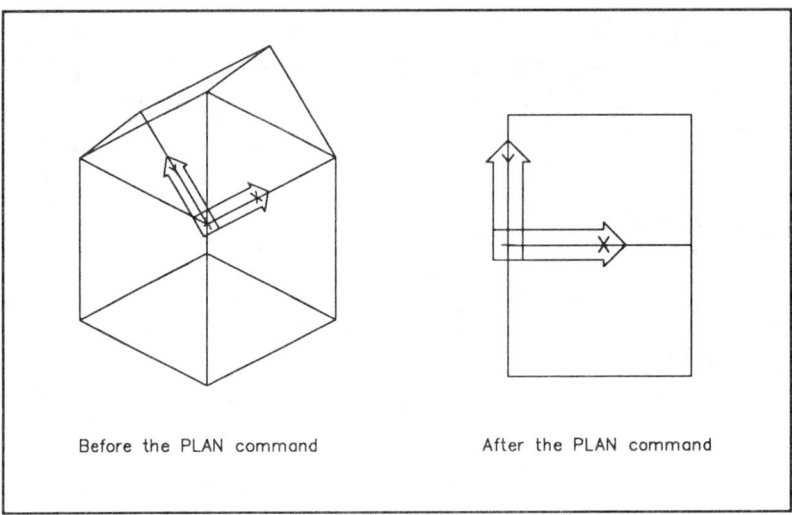

Before the PLAN command   After the PLAN command

Figure 16.27   Use of the PLAN command

The **Ucs** option allows you to generate a plan view of a previously saved UCS *while remaining in the current UCS*. Similarly, the **World** option gives a plan view of the WCS.

> *Note:*   It is an excellent general rule to construct *all* 3D objects while working in the plan view of the current UCS.

16.2.7 The UCSFOLLOW System Variable

If the UCSFOLLOW system variable is set to 1, then on changing from one UCS to another, the *plan view of the new UCS is automatically invoked*. UCSFOLLOW may be set from screen menu under UCS or by typing UCSFOLLOW at the command prompt. UCSFOLLOW may be set individually for each viewport.

> *Note:*   When constructing complex 3D objects, the most useful technique is to split the screen into two vertical viewports, set UCSFOLLOW to 1 in the first viewport (the viewport to be used for drawing - always in plan view) while the second viewport retains UCSFOLLOW=0. Set an oblique view in this second viewport. This combination of plan and oblique views of the same object greatly facilitates 3D construction. (See Appendix 7, Section A7.2.)

16.3. COORDINATES IN 3D

Any point in space can be specified by supplying the absolute (relative to the current UCS) X-, Y- and Z- coordinate points. Relative and polar coordinates may also be used and can greatly simplify the construction of 3D drawings. The basic rules are exactly equivalent to those outlined in Section 3.1.1.

In the case of relative coordinates, the Z- displacement is now required in addition to the X- and Y- displacements. As with absolute coordinates, this allows an entity to be positioned anywhere in 3D space.

Relative and polar coordinates can if required both be referred to the WCS whilst remaining in the active UCS. This is achieved by introducing an asterisk (*) after the @ symbol and before the displacement(s).

16.3.1 Spherical Coordinates

Spherical coordinates are the 3D equivalent of 2D polar coordinates and their specification is analogous to the angular method of specifying a viewpoint, (see Section 16.1.4), with the necessary addition of the distance from the current UCS origin. (See Figure 16.28.)

EXAMPLE

To place a point which is 122 drawing units from the current UCS origin at an angle of 56° from the X axis in the XY plane and at an angle of 23° from the XY plane:

> **Command:** LINE
> **From point:** 122<56<23

16.3.2 Cylindrical Coordinates

Cylindrical coordinates are again polar in form but in this case require the specification of the distance from the current UCS origin, the angle in the XY plane, and the Z-coordinate. (See Figure 16.29.)

EXAMPLE

To place a point which is 73.5 drawing units from the current UCS origin at an angle of 193° from the X axis in the XY plane and with a Z-coordinate of 15 drawing units:

Command: LINE
From point: 73.5<193,15

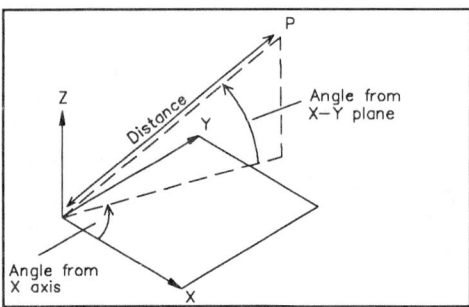

Figure 16.28 Spherical coordinates   **Figure 16.29** Cylindrical coordinates

16.4 3D DRAWING COMMANDS

The standard technique for constructing 3D drawings is to set the relevant UCS and then proceed to use the familiar 2D entity commands such as circle, arc, ellipse etc. Although this allows complex drawings to be constructed it is sometimes more efficient to be able to position 3D entities in 3D space by specifying their X-,Y- and Z-coordinates.

Note: This may be applied to any 2D entity BUT the entity will normally only be drawn parallel to the XY plane of the active UCS. The exception to this rule is the LINE command which has been given the properties of the old 3DLINE command allowing a line to be positioned at any orientation in space relative to the active UCS.

16.4.1 LINE in 3D

In standard 2D construction the Z- coordinate is omitted and is assumed to be zero (unless the ELEVation has been set to some other value). LINEs drawn in 3D normally require the specification of the Z- coordinate unless one end of the LINE lies on the current UCS. (See Figure 16.30.)

> **Command:** LINE
> **From point** 100,120,50
> **To point:** 50,20,150

Convenient alternatives to this rather laborious process are to use either point filters, (see Section 16.5.1), or object snap, (see Section 16.5.2).

16.4.2 3DPOLY

The 3DPOLY command is very similar to the 2D PLINE command but it has reduced capabilities - only straight line segments can be drawn, it is not possible to change the width and the editing facilities supplied by PEDIT are greatly curtailed.

> **Command:** 3DPOLY
> **From point:**
> **Close/Undo/<Endpoint of line>:**

If a 3DPOLYline is selected when in the PEDIT command, the following limited options are available:

> **Command:** PEDIT
> **Select object:**   Select a 3DPOLYline
> **Close/Edit vertex/Spline curve/Decurve/Undo/eXit <X>:**

These options work in the same way as for the editing of 2D polylines, (see Section 4.3) apart from the Spline curve option which produces a 3D curve as in Figure 16.31.

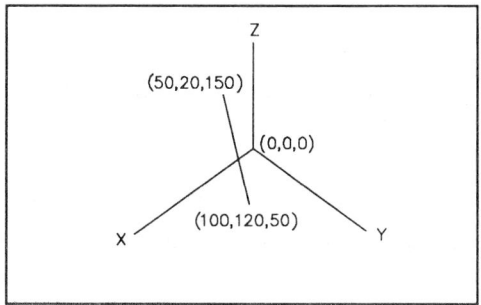

Figure 16.30   LINE in 3D

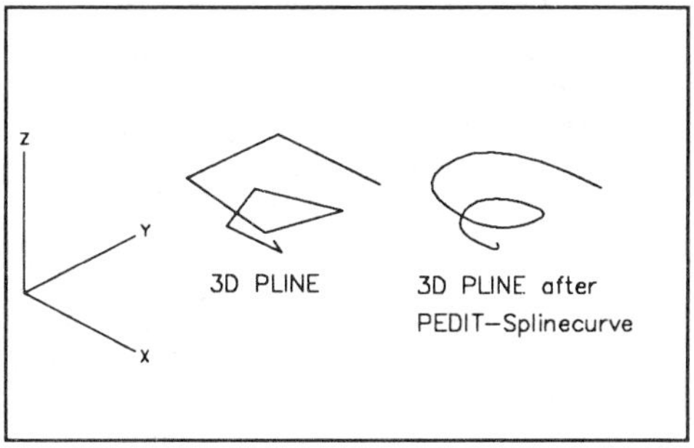

Figure 16.31   Editing a 3DPOLYline

16.4.3 3DFACE

If LINES or 3DPOLYlines are used to construct a 3D object, the result is always a wireframe model and the HIDE command will have no effect. It is for this reason that AutoCAD introduced the 3DFACE command, (see Figure 16.32). 3DFACE is now treated as the basic building block for the majority of 3D solid constructions and forms the basis of all the 3D polygon meshes.

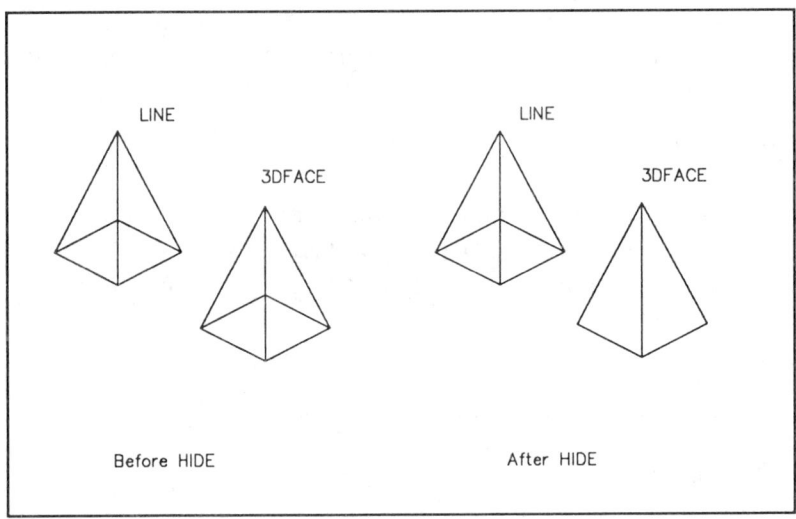

Figure 16.32   The effect of HIDE on LINE and 3DFACE

Command: 3DFACE
First point:
Second point:
Third point:
Fourth point:

If this is coincident with the first point, a triangle results; if it is a separate point an automatic close will be executed to produce a closed 4-sided face.

Third point:

This prompts for the third point of the next face, and assumes that the first two points have already been specified as points 3 and 4 of the previous face, (see Figure 16.33).

Fourth point: (see above)
Third point: "
Fourth point: "

.
.

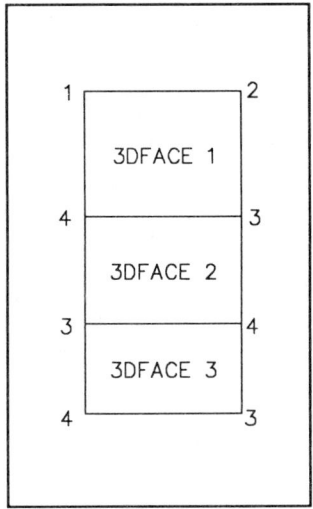

Figure 16.33   Definition points for
3DFACE

16.4.4 Invisible 3DFACE

One of the major problems associated with realistic 3D construction is that of representing a solid face containing an aperture, e.g. a house wall with a window. Although it is possible to represent this using simple line construction techniques it is not possible to make the wall appear solid by use of the HIDE command. This may be overcome by the use of 3DFACEs to make up the solid walls surrounding a hole (the window). This in turn creates the problem that the edges of the 3DFACEs are visible and tend to destroy the effect, (see Figure 16.34). One of the extra features of 3DFACE is specifically designed to overcome this problem - each edge as it is defined can be made *invisible*. (See Figure 16.35.)

To understand how the invisible feature may be used it is necessary to remember that the first point represents the first 3DFACE edge, the second point the second edge etc. Therefore, if you require the first edge to be invisible this must be specified when you are prompted for the first point by entering an I at the prompt followed by the coordinates of the point, (see Figure 16.36).

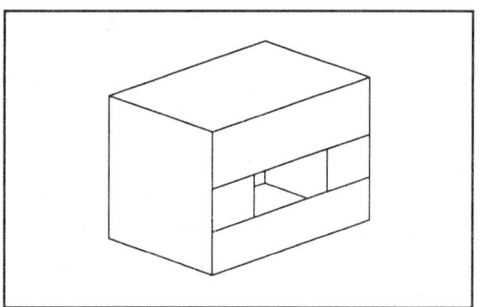 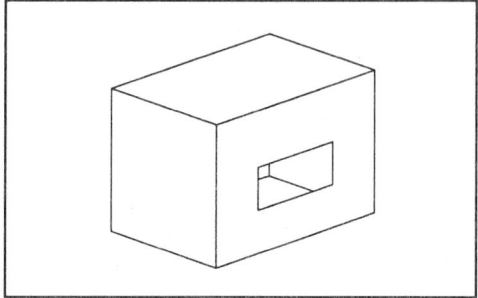

Figure 16.34 Window constructed with visible 3DFACE **Figure 16.35** Window constructed with invisible 3DFACE

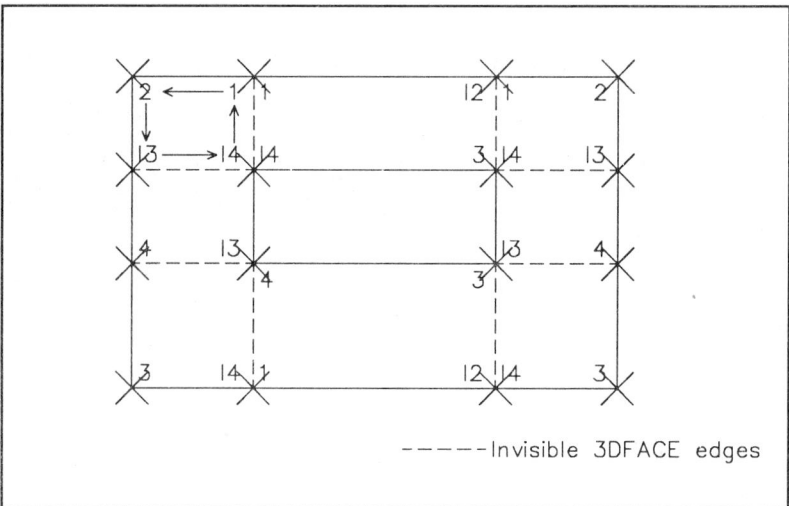

Figure 16.36 Invisible 3DFACE edge definition

Command: 3DFACE
First point: I   (Now enter the coordinates)
Second point:
Third point:
Fourth point:

The visibility of 3DFACE invisible edges is controlled by the SPLFRAME system variable; if SPLFRAME is set to any non-zero value then previously invisible edges will be displayed. This can also be achieved by picking Showedge from the 3DFACE option of the **Draw** screen menu followed by a REGEN. This can be useful when locating phantom 3DFACEs which have been created with all edges invisible.

16.5 AIDS TO 3D CONSTRUCTION

A common fault when constructing 3D drawings is to place entities by pointing to what appears to be the correct position on the screen. This will almost invariably cause the object to be incorrectly positioned because of the ambiguity inherent in presenting a 3D image on a two-dimensional screen. This problem may be reduced by presenting alternative views simultaneously in two or more viewports, (see Section 16.2.7). However it is still advisable wherever possible to use point filters and/or object snap to ensure the accurate location of all 3D coordinates.

16.5.1 Point Filters

If you wish to specify a 3D point using both the mouse, (for pointing), and the keyboard, (for coordinate entry), then you *must* use X/Y/Z point filtering. By choosing the appropriate filter it is possible to input say the X- component by pointing and the Y-, Z- components from the keyboard. Alternatively two coordinate components may be input by pointing leaving the remaining component to be supplied from the keyboard. The pointing component(s) must always be given first. Any combination of X followed by Y, Z; X,Y followed by Z; Y followed by X,Z etc., can be used.

There are three ways to choose the appropriate filter combination:

- By selecting FILTERS from the **Assist** pull-down menu.
- By selecting LINE, 3DPOLY or 3DFACE from the screen menu.
- From the keyboard by typing .X, .Y, .Z, .XY, .XZ or .YZ at the point prompt of the above three commands.

Command: LINE
From point: .XY   **of**   Point with mouse to X,Y position
(need Z)   Supply Z coordinate from the keyboard

16.5.2 Object snap in 3D

If simple pointing is attempted, the X-Y position will be accepted but the Z- coordinate will always default to the current value of the elevation. This may be altered to the required value during pointing either by transparently setting the ELEVATION system variable using 'ELEVATION or by using the Entity Creation dialogue box.

A better approach is to use object snap. If object snap is used to snap a 3D line to, say, the end of an existing line on a drawing the Z coordinate of the endpoint will also be taken into account and therefore the line will automatically start or finish at the correct elevation.

16.5.3 Basic 3D Objects

As a further aid to 3D construction, AutoCAD supplies a number of basic 3D shapes which may be accessed from the **Draw** pull down menu under Objects... (see Figure 16.37). These include boxes, wedges, pyramids, cones, spheres, hemispheres and toroids which are not resident in the AutoCAD main program but which are defined by an AutoLISP program called 3D (loaded automatically when the required object is selected from the icon menu). Alternatively, the AutoLISP program, (see Appendix 3), may be run directly from the keyboard:

Command: (LOAD"3D")

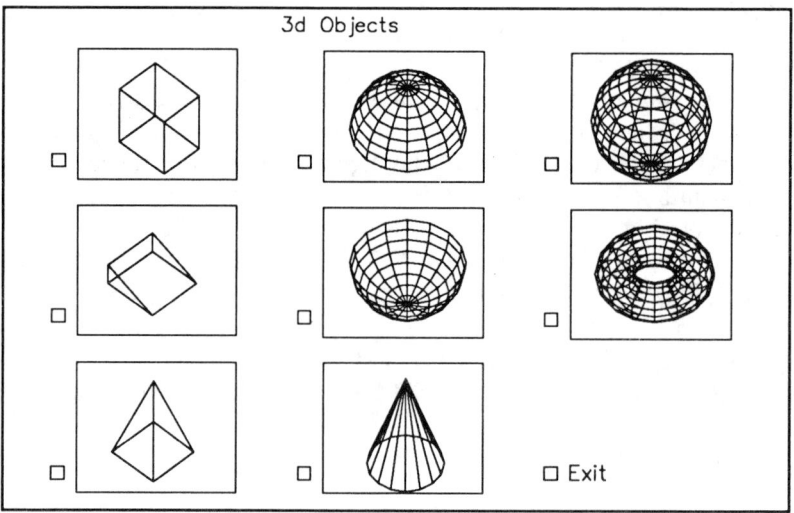

Figure 16.37   The 3D objects icon

16.6 3D POLYGON MESHES

One of the main 3D features of AutoCAD is the ability to represent complex 3D shapes by the use of polygon meshes consisting of columns and rows of 3DFACE elements in an M by N matrix, (see Figure 16.38).

The command 3DMESH allows the construction of a 3D mesh by specifying each individual element of the mesh through numerical input of each vertex position in 3D space. This process is extremely laborious and in practice is usually employed only within a Lisp programme.

The resolution of the 3D mesh is controlled by two system variables SURFTAB1 and SURFTAB2.

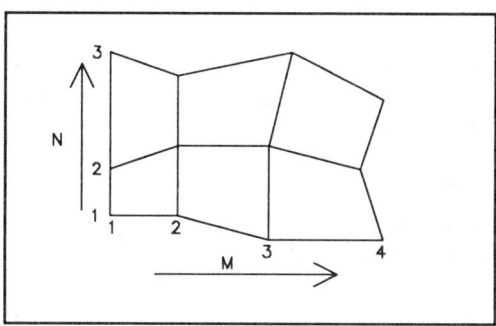

Figure 16.38 3DMESH M=4, N=3

AutoCAD provides four methods for the automatic generation of 3D meshes which avoid the pitfalls inherent in the 3DMESH command. These may be accessed either directly from the keyboard, from the **Draw** pull down menu under Surfaces....(see Figure 16.39), or from the screen menu.

Note: The further examples given in Appendix 7 demonstrate the versatility of these polygon mesh commands.

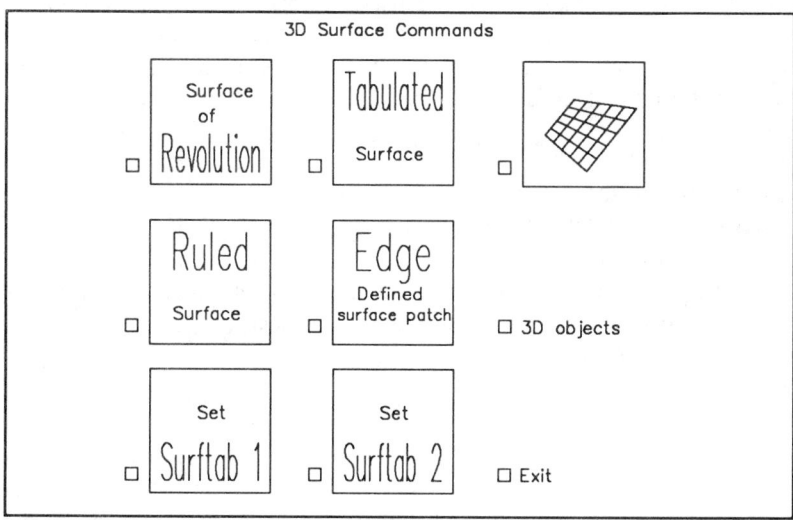

Figure 16.39 The 3D surfaces icon

16.6.1 RULESURF

RULESURF constructs a simple set of ruled lines between two specified objects. This is not a true mesh because it is made up of only two columns of N rows, N being controlled by the value of SURFTAB1.

> **Command:** RULESURF
> **Select first defining curve:**
> **Select second defining curve:**

A "defining curve" may be a line, point, arc, circle or polyline. If the first defining curve is closed, (e.g. a circle or closed polyline), then the second defining curve must also be closed.

> *Note:* A point is a special entity as it is treated as either open or closed, (see Figure 16.40).

When selecting the defining curves, the choice of selection point will affect the final shape of the ruled surface, (see Figure 16.41).

16.6.2 TABSURF

TABSURF allows the construction of a 3D parallel mesh by the specification of a path curve (an open or closed single entity constructed from a line, arc, circle or polyline) and a direction vector (derived from a line or polyline). Again, as in the case of RULESURF, this produces a 2 by N mesh, N being controlled by the value of SURFTAB1. (See Figure 16.42.)

> **Command:** TABSURF
> **Select path curve:**
> **Select direction vector:**

The length of the direction vector controls the *length* of extrusion and the position of the selection point (i.e. which end of the line it is closest to) controls the *direction* of extrusion, (see Figure 16.43).

16.6.3 REVSURF

A surface of revolution is represented by a true M by N mesh constructed from a specified path curve and an axis of rotation. The path curve may be an open or closed line, arc, circle or polyline while the axis is derived from a line or open polyline.

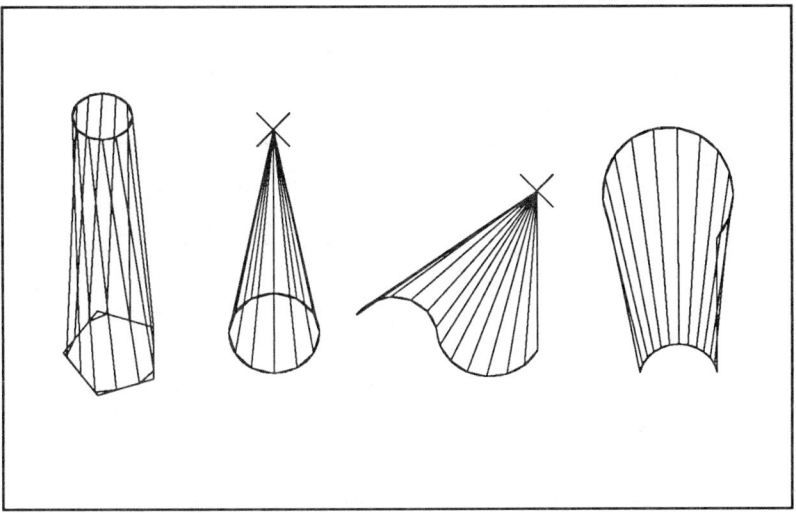

Figure 16.40   Examples of open and closed ruled surfaces

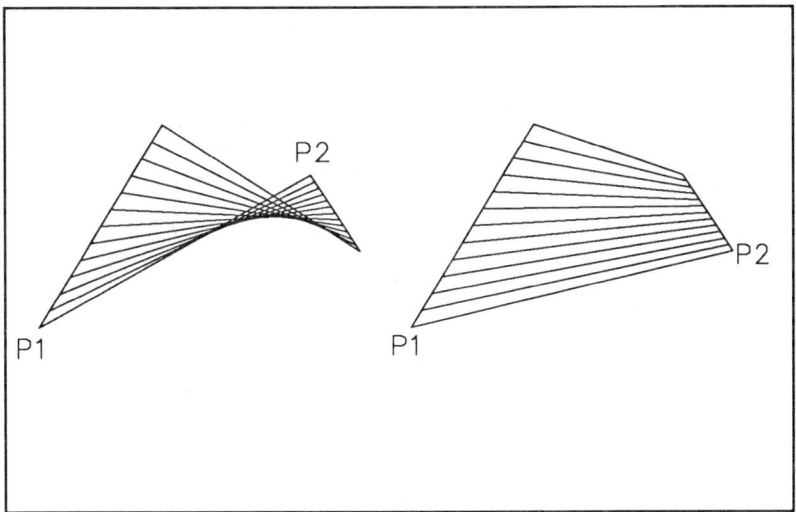

Figure 16.41   The effect of choosing different selection points when using RULESURF

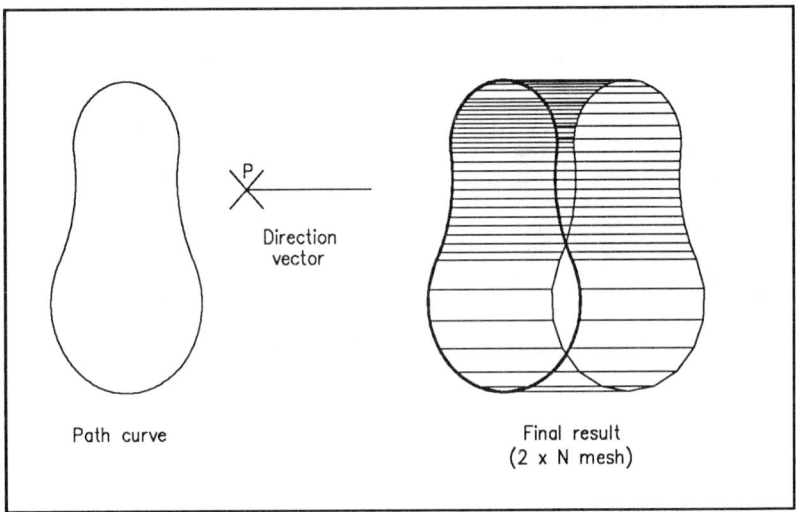

Figure 16.42 Use of TABSURF

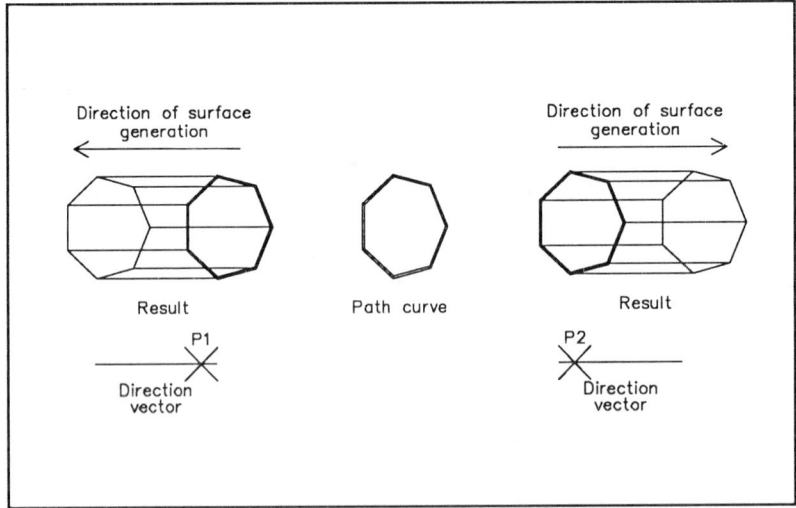

Figure 16.43 TABSURF generation direction

The axis of revolution determines the *M-* direction of the mesh. The mesh density is controlled by both SURFTAB1 (N- direction) and SURFTAB2 (M- direction).

Command: REVSURF
Select path curve:
Select axis of rotation:
Start angle <0>:

If non-zero, this specifies an initial offset from the path curve.

Included angle (+=CCW, -=CW)<Full circle>:

The angle through which the path curve is rotated.

See Figure 16.44.

16.6.4 EDGESURF

This produces a true *M* by *N* mesh bounded by four adjoining edges made up from lines, arcs or separate open polylines, their endpoints touching to form a *closed* quadrilateral. Again, the mesh density is controlled by SURFTAB1 and SURFTAB2.

Command: EDGESURF
Select edge 1:
Select edge 2:
Select edge 3:
Select edge 4:

The four edges may be selected in any order but the first selected edge defines the *M-* direction, (see Figure 16.45).

If the endpoints of the component edges do not touch, then AutoCAD will respond with:

Edge x does not touch another edge

A 3D mesh constructed using one of the above commands is treated as a single entity. Most of the standard editing commands may be used to modify the 3DFACE component of a mesh but it should be remembered that the mesh *must* be EXPLODEd first.

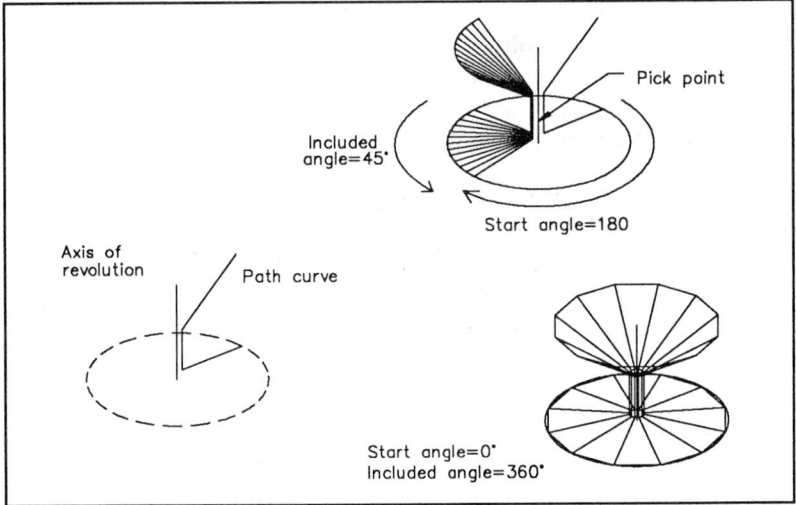

Figure 16.44   Use of REVSURF

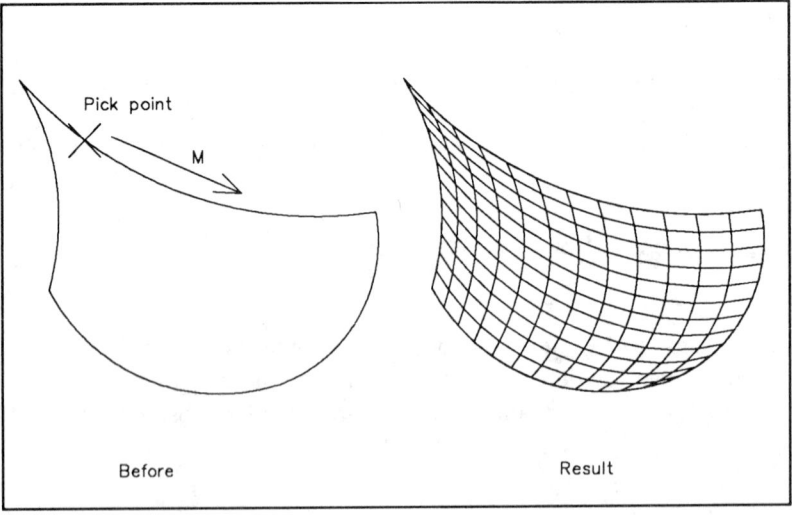

Figure 16.45   Use of EDGESURF

16.6.5 Editing 3D Polygon Meshes with PEDIT

The PEDIT sub-commands available for editing 3D polygon meshes are closely related to those used for editing 3D polylines. Before you attempt to edit 3D meshes it is strongly recommended that you familiarise yourself with polyline editing, (see Section 4.3).

Command: PEDIT
Select polyline: Choose a 3D mesh
Edit vertex/Smooth surface/Desmooth/Mclose/Nclose/Undo/eXit<X>:

Edit   Vertex(m,n). Next/Previous/Left/Right/Up/Down/Move/REgen/eXit <N>:

> A cross appears on the first vertex of the mesh. As in the case of polyline editing, this indicates the vertex which may be edited and it may be moved through the mesh by use of the commands Next, Previous, Left, Right, Up and Down. Next, Previous, Left and Right allow the cross to be moved in the *N*- direction. Up and Down move it in the *M*- direction. The **Vertex(m,n)** indicator shows the current coordinates of the cross within the mesh. When the cross has been positioned at the required vertex, the Move sub-command allows you to distort the mesh by re-positioning the marked vertex, (see Figure 16.46).

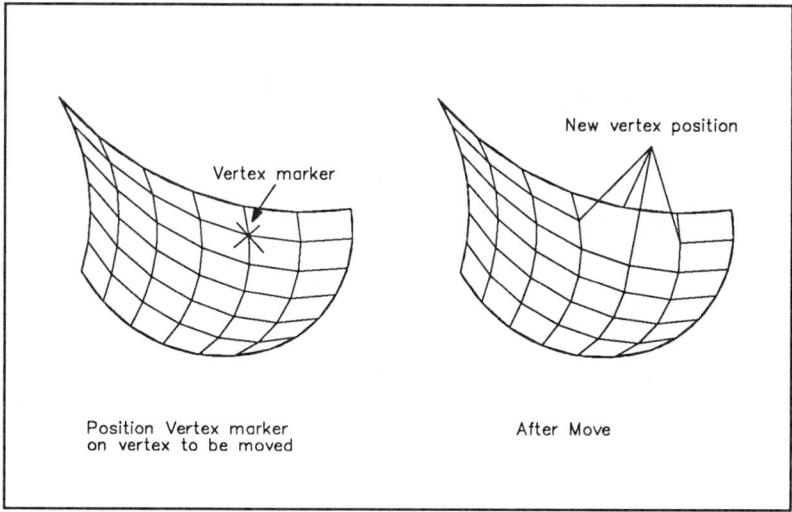

Figure 16.46   Vertex editing using PEDIT

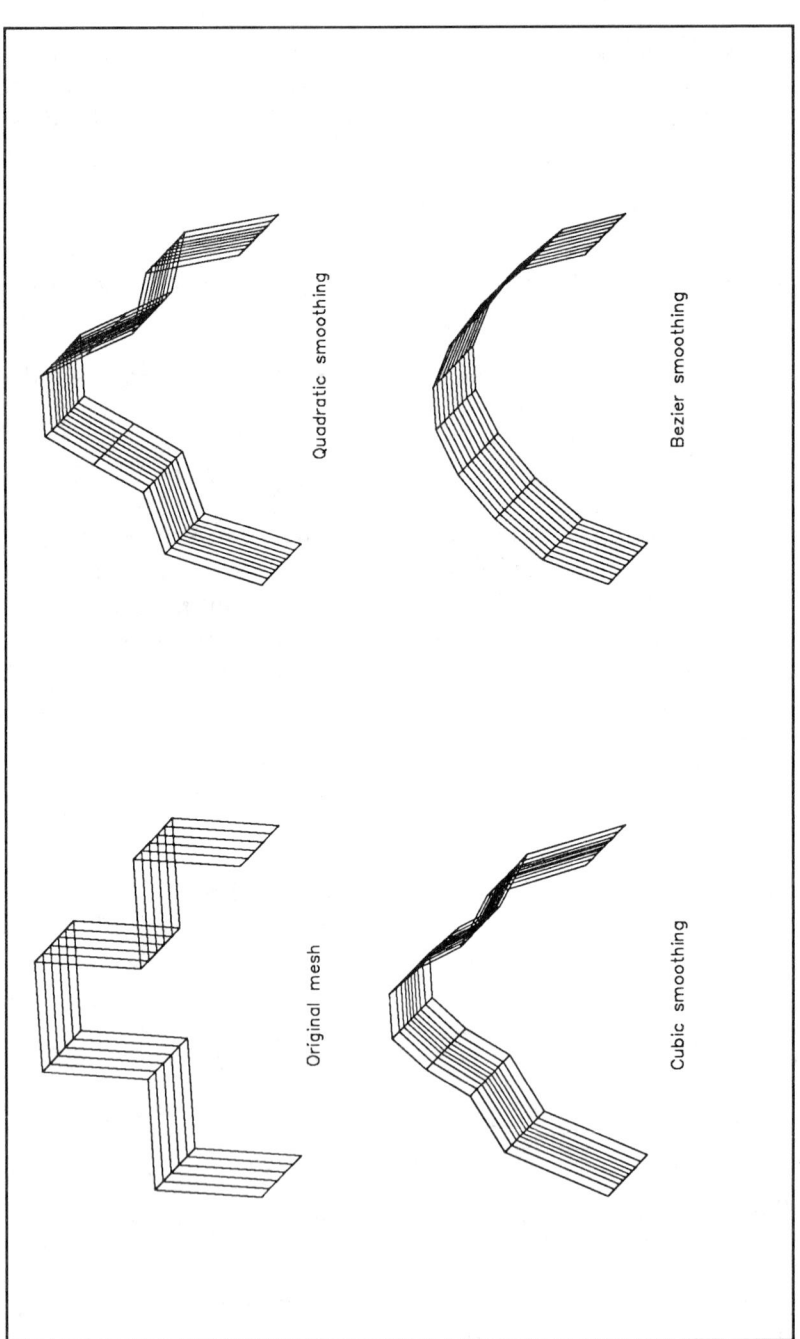

Figure 16.47 Polygon mesh smoothing functions

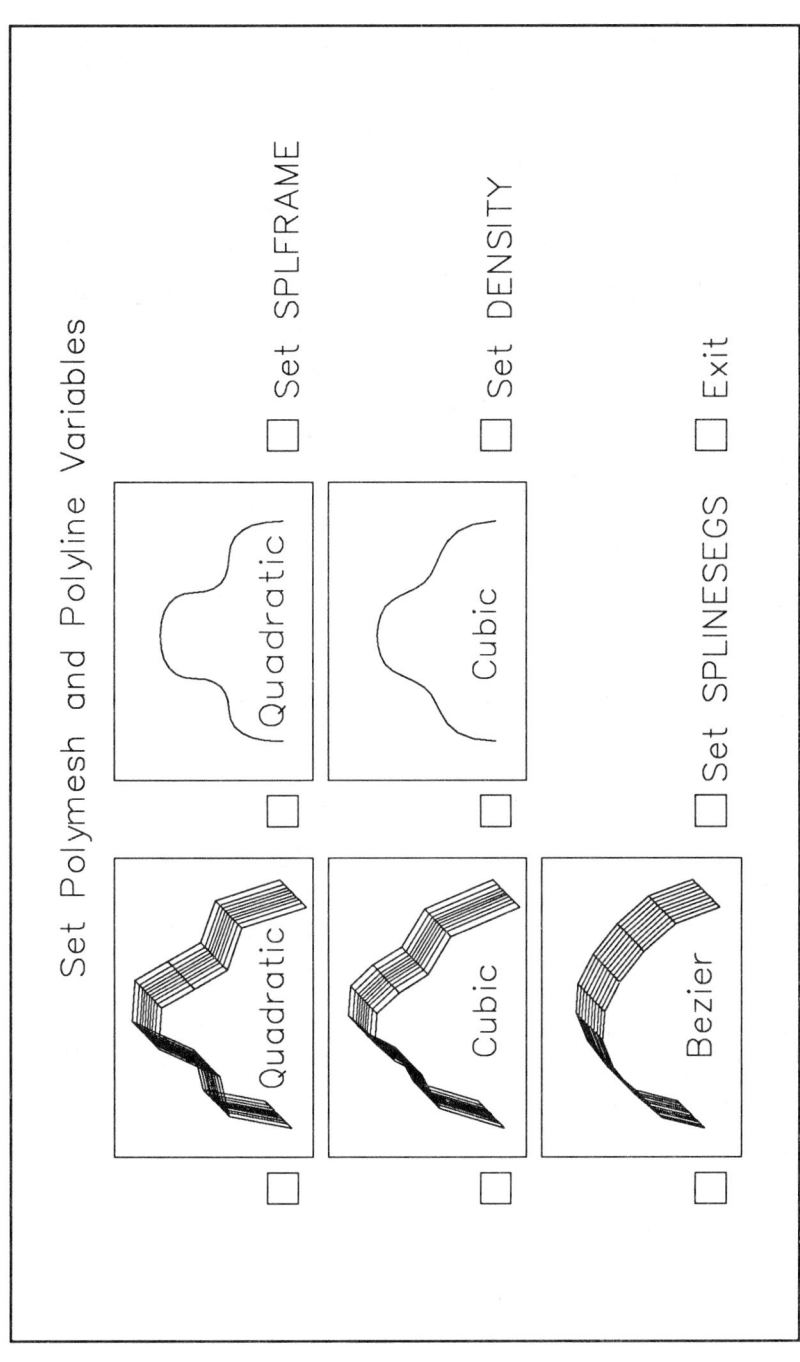

Figure 16.48   Polymesh and polyline variables

Smooth surface

This corresponds to the Spline sub-command in polyline editing. There are three smoothing functions available - the quadratic B-spline, the cubic B-spline and the Bezier function. (See Figure 16.47.)

The system variable SURFTYPE is used to select the required smoothing function - SURFTYPE may be set to 5 (quadratic), 6 (cubic) or 8 (Bezier) and the smoothing effect increases in the same order. There are limitations on which smoothing may be used; a quadratic may be used on meshes of 3 x 3 or more, a cubic on 4 x 4 or more and a Bezier requires more than 11 vertices in either the *M*- or *N*- direction. The density of the mesh is controlled by the two system variables SURFU and SURFV. SURFU controls the mesh density in the *M*-direction while SURFV controls it in the *N*- direction.

The choice of smoothing function and the values of mesh density variables may be set by selecting Polyvars from the PEDIT option under the **Edit** screen menu. This invokes an icon menu, (see Figure 16.48), which gives easy access to these variables and also to SPLFRAME and SPLSEGS.

Desmooth   Restores the *original* polygon mesh after smoothing.

Mclose   Closes the polygon mesh in the *M*- direction if open. If the polygon mesh is already closed, Mclose is replaced in the menu with Mopen.

Nclose   Closes the polygon mesh in the *N*- direction if open. If the polygon mesh is already closed, Nclose is replaced in the menu with Nopen.

Undo   Progressively reverses the actions of the PEDIT command.

eXit   Exits PEDIT and returns you to the command line.

16.7   PERSPECTIVE PROJECTION USING THE DVIEW COMMAND

AutoCAD, like most other CAD packages, makes use of parallel projection for viewing 3D objects. This, although satisfactory, does not always give a true visualization of the objects.

The DVIEW command allows a perspective projection to be constructed by specifying a target point and a camera (observer) position, i.e. a viewing vector, (see Figure 16.49). The default positions of the camera and target are initially set by AutoCAD.

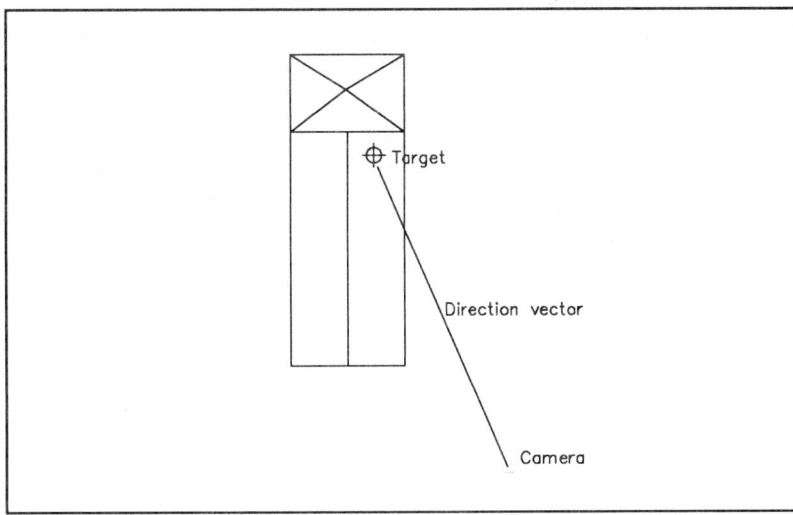

Figure 16.49   Plan view of target and camera positions

DVIEW incorporates a clipping function which allows "cut-away" sections to be produced. A cutting plane is specified and the visibility of objects on either side of this plane can be controlled to give a "clipped" view, i.e. a section through a 3D drawing, (see Figure 16.50).

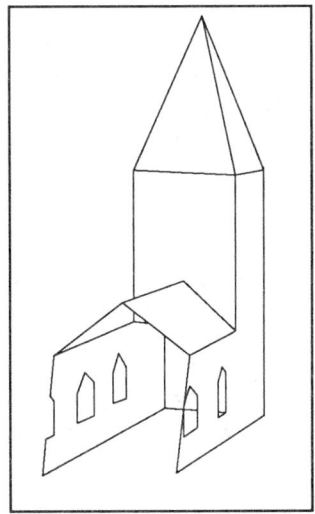

Figure 16.50   A section produced by
the clipping function

DVIEW makes use of *slider bars* which appear whenever a scale factor or angle is requested. As the cursor is moved along the slider bar, (see Figure 16.51) the drawing is dynamically dragged to show automatically the effect of the new scale or angle.

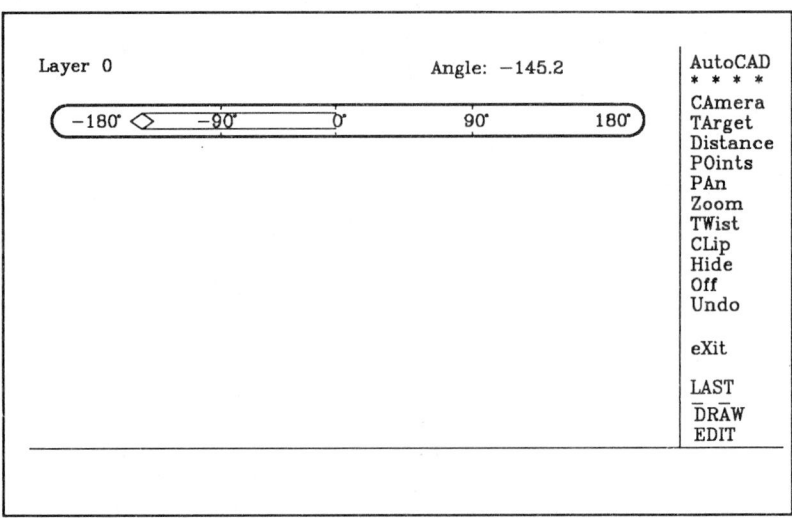

Figure 16.51   DVIEW slider bar (camera angle)

Command: DVIEW
Select objects:

Select *with care* a number of objects which will give a good representation (preview) of the complete drawing, (see Figure 16.52). AutoCAD will use these objects to give a *perspective preview*. If too many objects are chosen, then generation of the perspective preview is slow and sometimes frustrating. When exiting the DVIEW command, the complete drawing is regenerated based on the preview settings.

CAmera/TArget/Distance/POints/PAn/Zoom/TWist/CLip/Hide/Off/Undo/<eXit>:

CAmera   A slider bar will appear on screen which allows rotation of the camera about the target point, firstly in the Z- direction (-90° = looking straight down, 0° = looking along the X-Y plane, +90° = looking straight up) and secondly in the X-Y plane (0° = looking straight along the X axis, 90° = looking along the Y axis). See Figure 16.53.

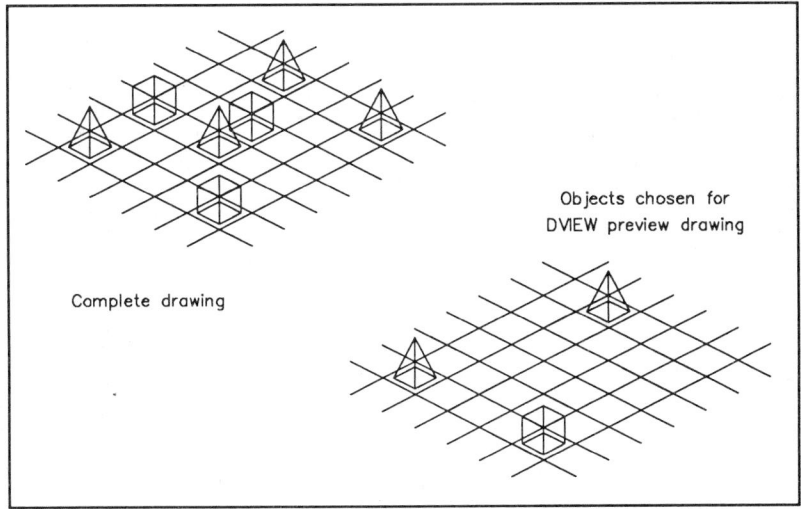

Figure 16.52   Selected representative objects

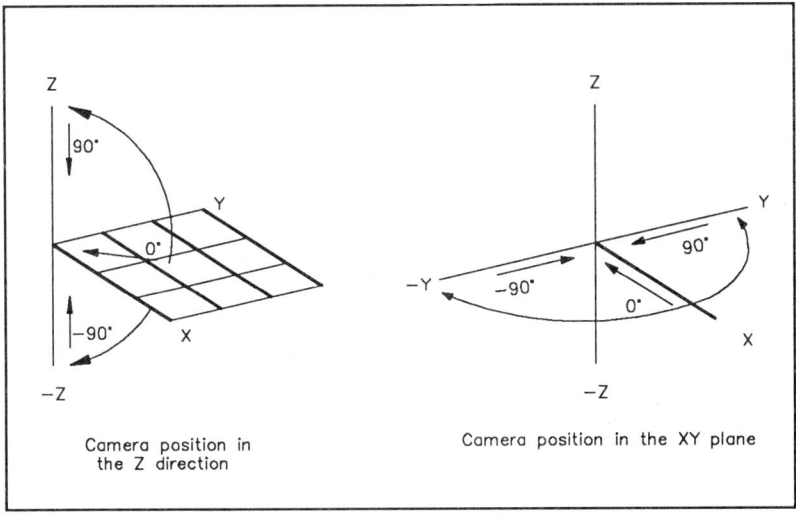

Figure 16.53   Rotating camera position

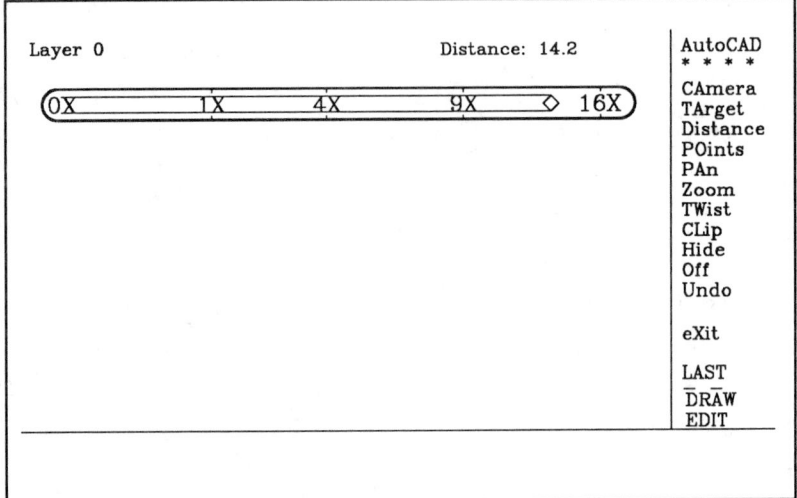

Figure 16.54 DVIEW slider bar (distance)

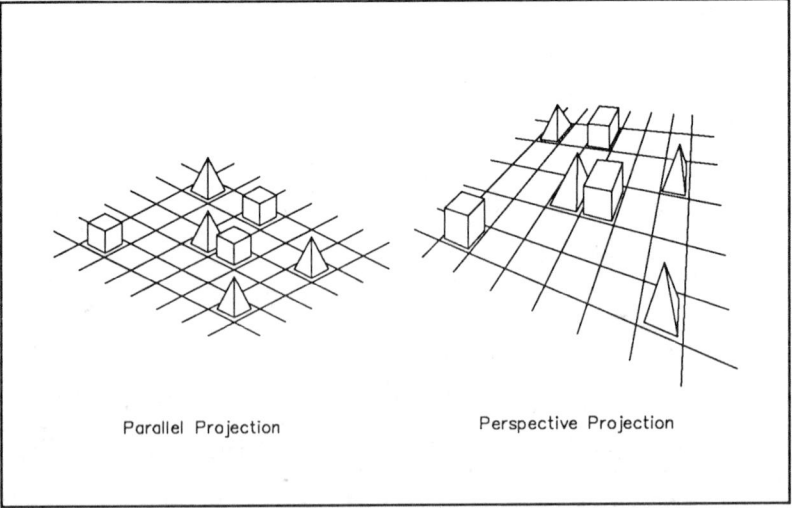

Figure 16.55 Two types of projection

TArget   A slider bar will appear on screen which allows the rotation of the target point about the camera point. The angle specification is the same as for CAmera.

Distance   This option allows the distance between the camera and target to be adjusted. A slider bar allows scaling of the viewing distance from 0x to 16x where 1x represents the current distance (originally set by AutoCAD). See Figure 16.54.

> *Note:*   Perspective viewing is turned on only when this option is taken. (See Figure 16.55).

The Perspective Icon, (see Figure 16.56), is displayed in the bottom left-hand corner of the screen when perspective viewing mode is on.

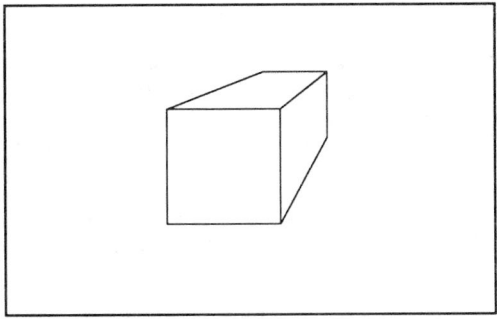

Figure 16.56   Perspective icon

POints   The positions of the target and camera can be specified by input of their X-, Y- and Z- coordinates; point filters and object snap can be used. The target point is specified first followed by the camera position which is connected to the target point by means of a elastic band (the view direction) to help place the camera.

PAn   This is the same as the command PAN and moves the image without changing the magnification. This option works slightly differently depending whether or not you are in perspective viewing mode.

Zoom   The way in which zoom works depends on whether perspective viewing mode is On or Off. If perspective is Off, then AutoCAD performs a ZOOM Centre and presents a slider bar to allow the setting of the zoom scale factor. If perspective is On, then zoom allows the changing of the camera "lens", the default being 50mm. A 35mm lens would allow a wider field of view to be seen, whereas a 200mm lens would act as a telephoto lens narrowing the field of view.

TWist   Allows tilting of the objects about the view direction. This is equivalent to rotating the camera about the view direction vector.

CLip   This option allows the positioning of front or back clipping planes. AutoCAD temporarily "erases" portions of the drawing which are behind a back clipping plane or in front of a front clipping plane. Clipping can be performed on both parallel and perspective projections and remains active when Dview is exited.

AutoCAD prompts: **Back/Front/<Off>:**

Back   **ON/OFF/<Distance from target>:**
A positive distance places the clipping plane between the target point and the camera whereas a negative distance places the clipping plane beyond the target point. If the slider bar is used, then the clipping plane is dynamically dragged through the objects, (see Figure 16.57).
ON/OFF enables/disables Back clipping.

Front   **Eye/ON/OFF/<Distance from target>:**
This option works in the same way as Back except for the Eye feature, which allows the clipping plane to be placed at the camera (its default position). See Figure 16.58.

Off   Turns clipping off.

Hide   Operates in the same way as the command HIDE and removes hidden lines from the preview drawing.

Off   Disables perspective mode and returns the preview drawing to parallel projection.

Undo   Undoes the last DVIEW sub-command. By repeating this command you are allowed to step back through the DVIEW sub-commands.

eXit   Ends DVIEW and causes a regeneration of the whole drawing to match the preview drawing. An example of a hidden perspective view is shown in Figure 16.59.

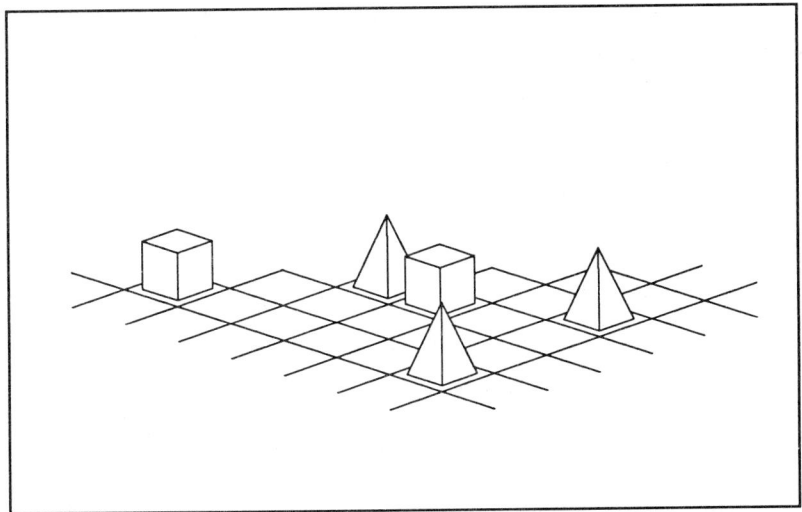

Figure 16.57   Back clipping

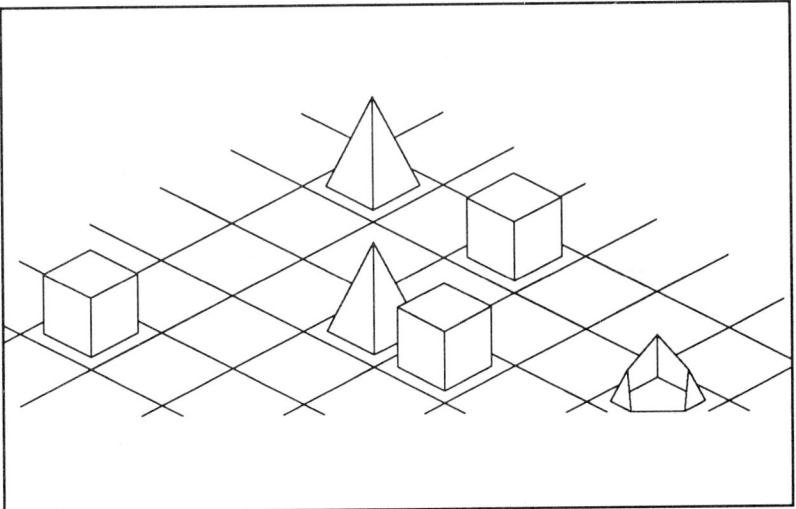

Figure 16.58   Front clipping

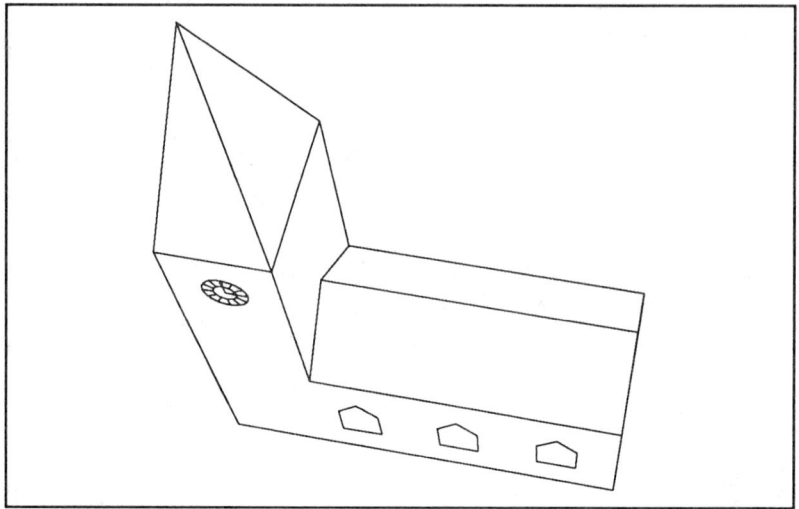

Figure 16.59   A hidden perspective view

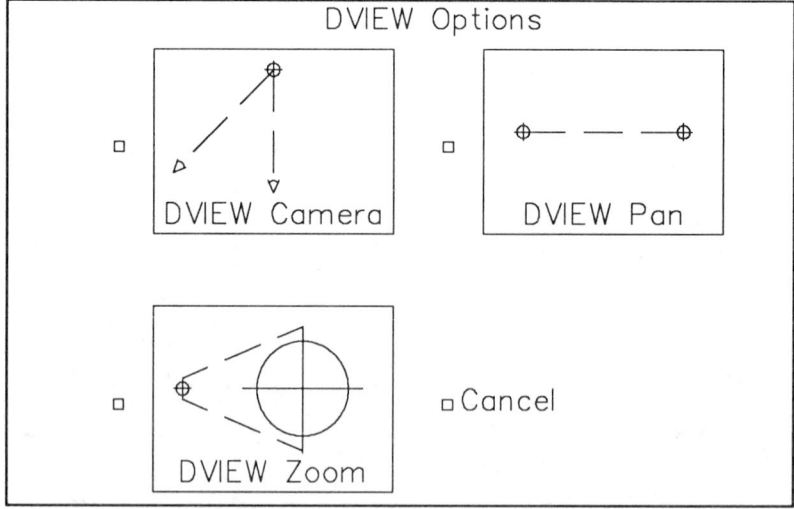

Figure 16.60   DVIEW options icon

When the final perspective view has been invoked from the preview drawing, then certain dynamic view options may easily be selected using the **Dview Options...** icon, found under the **Display** pull down. This avoids the necessity of returning to the DVIEW command. (See Figure 16.60). These options include changing the camera angle, the zoom lens and drawing position on screen using DVIEW Pan.

Note: When a perspective view has been invoked, it is not always possible to edit the drawing. The display controls such as ZOOM and PAN are not allowed unless you use the special versions of these commands which may be accessed through the DVIEW command or via the Dview Options... icon.

17. AME - the advanced modelling extension

17.1 WHAT IS A SOLID?

An AutoCAD AME solid is a 3D representation of a physical entity which can in principle be constructed, i.e. it is not an "impossible figure". This entity has associated with it real physical and material properties - surface area, volume, density, Young's modulus, thermal conductivity etc. As a result, analysis can compute physical parameters such as mass, centre of gravity, moment of inertia, radius of gyration etc.

Complex solids may be created by combining or subtracting simpler *primitive* solids. A range of primitives is supplied and you are given the facility to construct your own primitives from basic AutoCAD 2D circle and polyline entities - remember that ellipses and polygons are treated as polylines.

Primitives and combined solids may be varied in size, shape, attitude and colour, they may be modified by filleting and chamfering, and they may be sectioned in a specified plane to give cut-away drawings. Shading and rendering may be applied to the completed solid to enhance its visual effect.

17.2 AMELITE

AMElite is an attenuated version of AME. It allows you to generate the basic solid primitives - box, cone, cylinder, sphere, torus and wedge - together with user-defined solid primitives derived from circles or polylines.

The final solids may be rendered or shaded. AMElite and AME use the same menus but with AMElite you are *not* allowed to use the more powerful commands provided with AME, even though they appear to be available from the menu. If you choose a command which is not allowed, the following message will be displayed:

Requires the solid server - it's not available.

17.3 LOADING AND RUNNING AME FOR THE FIRST TIME

AME is in effect separate from AutoCAD with its own commands and its own system variables. It can be loaded from the **Solids** pull down or screen menus or from the keyboard:

Command: (XLOAD"AME")

The *first time* that you load AME you may be requested for the AutoCAD AME Authorization Code supplied with the disks. Without this code it is *impossible* to initiate the AME software. Loading AME may take some time during which you will notice that the crosswires have temporarily disappeared from the screen.

> *Note:*   Once AME has been loaded it is not necessary to reload unless you either leave AutoCAD completely or you unload AME using the command (XUNLOAD"AME") or by picking Unload from the **Sol - Utility** pull down.

After loading is complete both the pull down and screen **Solids** menus are replaced by the first of five special AME menus - Primitives, Modify, Inquiry, Display, Utility - which give access to all the AME commands. (See Figure 17.1.)

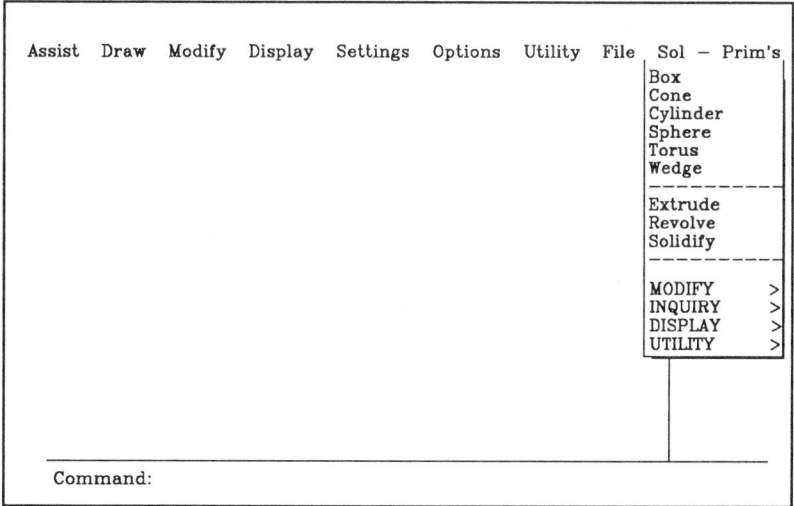

Figure 17.1   The AME pull down menu

Note: The functions listed on the pull down menus do not always correspond closely with the AME command subsequently issued, e.g. picking Change Primitive from the **Sol - Modify** pull down issues the command SOLCHP.

17.4 PRIMITIVE SOLIDS SUPPLIED WITH AME

The primitives supplied with AME, i.e. box, cone, cylinder, sphere, torus and wedge, are at first glance, similar to those provided for 3D construction under the 3D Objects icon accessed from the **Draw** pull down, (see Section 16.5.3). The construction prompts are very similar in both cases, with the primitive being drawn in plan on the current UCS. (See Figure 17.2.)

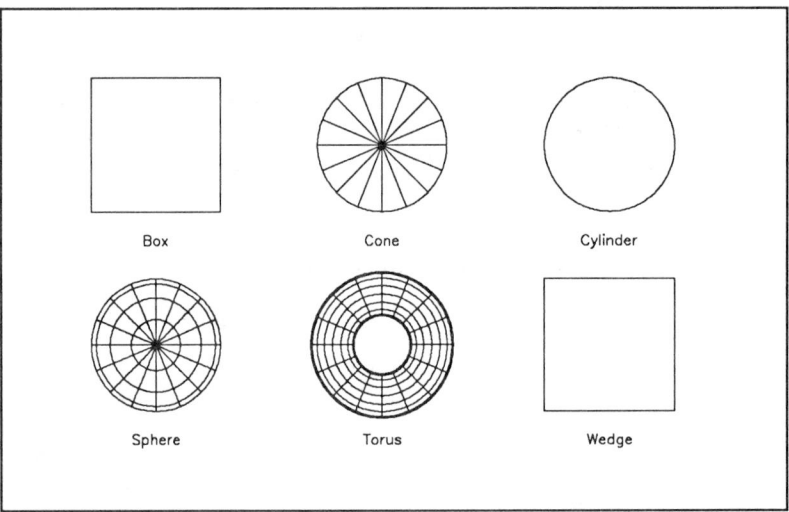

Figure 17.2 Plan view of primitive entities

17.4.1 Solid Box Creation - SOLBOX

Picked as Box from the **Sol - Prim's** pull down.

> **Command:** SOLBOX
> **Corner of box:**   Select point
> **Cube/Length/<Other corner>:**   Select opposite corner
> **Height:**

The above default option creates a box with a square section and a user-defined height. The **Cube** option prompts for a single side length, while the **Length** option prompts for length, width and height.

As the solid box is being created, AutoCAD reports on the progress with the following messages:

> **Phase I - Boundary evaluation begins.**
> **Phase II - Tessellation computation begins.**
> **Updating the Advanced Modeling Extension database.**

The solid box will then be drawn, (see Figure 17.3).

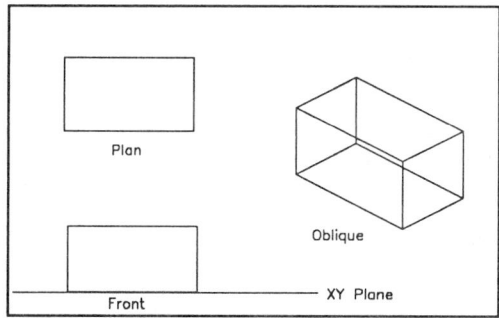

Figure 17.3   Solid box

17.4.2 Solid Cone Creation - SOLCONE

Picked as Cone from the **Sol - Prim's** pull down.

> **Command:** SOLCONE
> **Elliptical/<Center point>:**
> **Diameter/<Radius>:**
> **Height of cone:**

The default route creates a solid cone of circular section (parallel to the current UCS) with the specified height and base positioned on the Z=0 plane. The **Elliptical** option responds with prompts similar to those of the standard AutoCAD ELLIPSE command. (See Figure 17.4.)

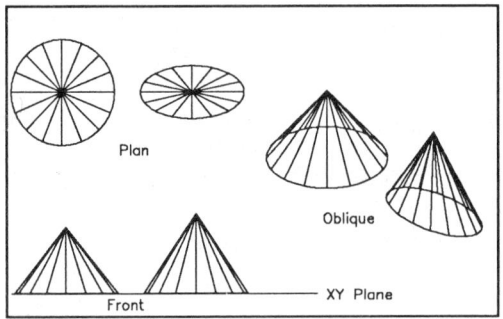

Figure 17.4 Circular and elliptical cones

Elliptical/<Center point>: E
<Axis endpoint 1>/Center:
Axis endpoint 2:
Other axis distance:
Height of cone:

17.4.3 Solid Cylinder Creation - SOLCYL

Picked as Cylinder from the **Sol - Prim's** pull down.

Command: SOLCYL
Elliptical/<Center point>:
Diameter/<Radius>:
Height of cylinder:

This command is identical in format to the SOLCONE command, (see Figure 17.5).

17.4.4 Solid Sphere Creation - SOLSPHERE

Picked as Sphere from the **Sol - Prim's** pull down.

Command: SOLSPHERE
Center of sphere:
Diameter/<Radius> of sphere:

The centre of the solid sphere lies on the Z=0 plane of the current UCS. Figure 17.6.

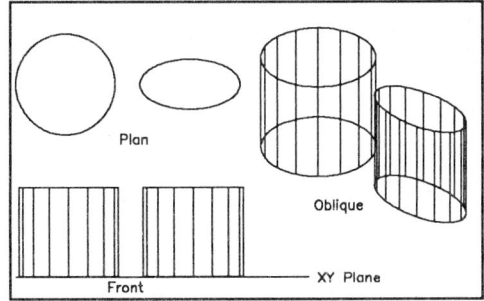

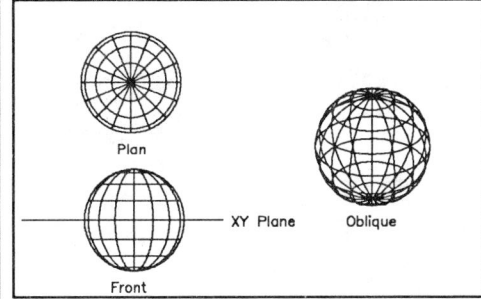

Figure 17.5   Circular and elliptical cylinders   **Figure 17.6**   Solid sphere

17.4.5 Solid Torus Creation - SOLTORUS

Picked as Torus from the **Sol - Prim's** pull down.

> **Command:** SOLTORUS
> **Center of torus:**
> **Diameter/<Radius> of torus:**
> **Diameter/<Radius> of tube:**

> *Note:*   The radii requested here are equivalent to those required to create a 3D torus but *not* to those required to create a DOUGHNUT.

The centre of the solid torus lies on the Z=0 plane of the current UCS. Figure 17.7.

17.4.6 Solid Wedge Creation - SOLWEDGE

Picked as Wedge from the **Sol - Prim's** pull down.

> **Command:** SOLWEDGE
> **Corner of wedge:**
> **Length/<Other corner>:**
> **Height:**

The default route results in a square section wedge parallel to the current UCS at Z=0. The **Length** option prompts for length, width and height. Whichever way you specify these dimensions, the solid wedge is always created with the taper in the positive X-direction of the current UCS. (See Figure 17.8)

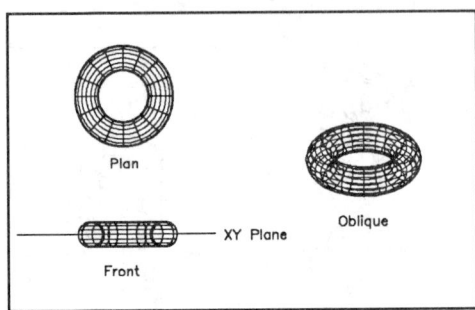

Figure 17.7 Solid torus

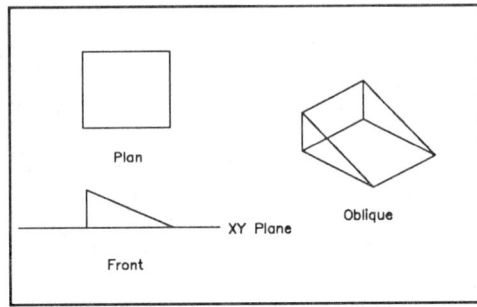

Figure 17.8 Solid wedge

17.5 CREATING USER-DEFINED SOLIDS

AutoCAD gives you the facility to construct your own primitives from basic 2D circle and polyline entities. This frees you from the limitation imposed, when constructing solids, of having only six constituent solid primitives available. Polylines having finite width are converted to zero width before solid entity creation.

There are three simple techniques which may be used; a simple extrusion process, revolution about a specified axis or solidifying an existing 3D entity. These three techniques allow virtually any solid primitive entity to be created.

It is interesting to note that, because the extrusion and revolution processes are both based on polyline path curves, it is possible to produce solids incorporating surfaces defined by mathematical functions. (See Figure 17.9.)

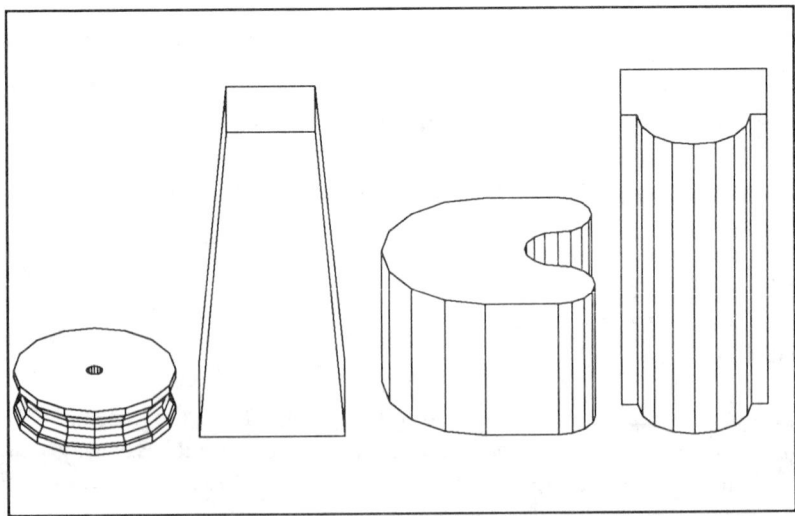

Figure 17.9 User-defined solids

17.5.1 Solid Creation by Extrusion - SOLEXT

Extrusion may be applied to circles and polylines and may be perpendicular to the XY plane or tapered in, at a specified angle. Polylines may be either 2D or 3D and include ellipses and polygons. The number of vertices must lie between 3 and 500. The polyline need *not* be closed as the command will automatically perform a close operation before extrusion.

> *Note:*   If the closing line crosses the polyline, then the extrusion will be aborted as this would create an "impossible solid", (see Figure 17.10.)

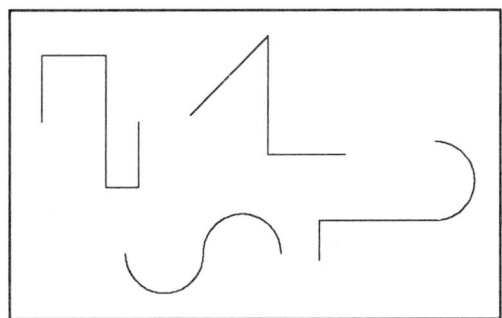

Figure 17.10   Shapes which would produce impossible
solids

If SOLEXT is applied to a 3D polyline, then the Z- coordinates of the polyline are ignored and set to zero; it is then treated as a 2D polyline.

Command: SOLEXT
Select polylines and circles for extrusion...
Select objects: Assemble the selection set
Height of extrusion:
Extrusion taper angle from Z <0>:

The zero default taper angle creates a perpendicular extrusion in the Z- direction. The allowed angle of taper must be between 0° and 90°. The angle will *always* be interpreted as an inward taper to give a convergent solid, (see Figure 17.11).

17.5.2 Solid Creation by Revolution - SOLREV.

The SOLREV command can be thought of as the AME version of the 3D REVSURF command. It allows the creation of a solid entity by the revolution of a circle or polyline path curve about an axis. The rules which apply to SOLEXT concerning

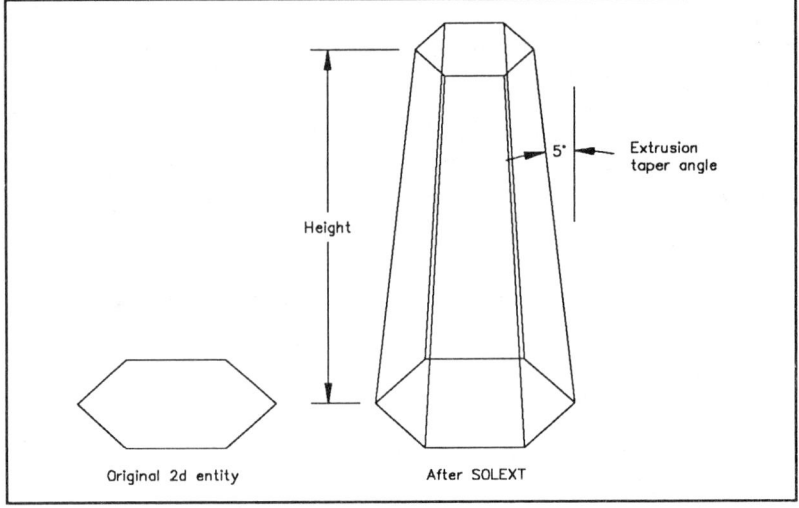

Figure 17.11 Solid extrusion

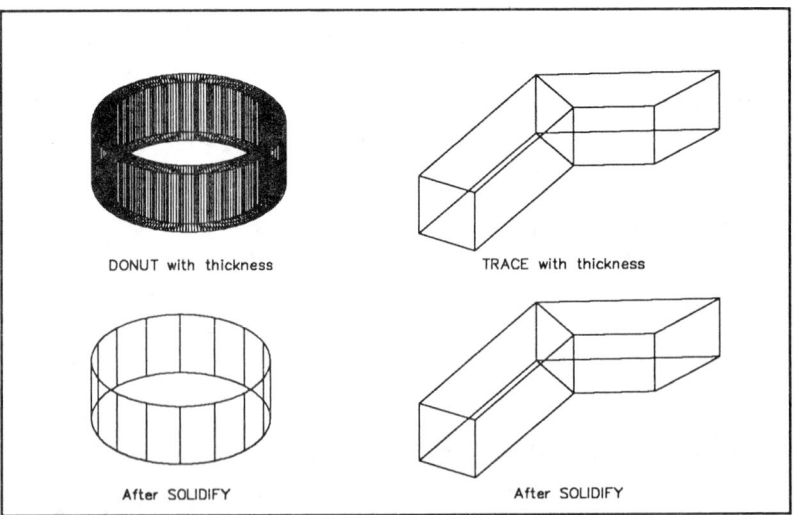

Figure 17.12 Solids created from 2D entities

polyline segments which cross, the permitted number of vertices, etc., also apply to SOLREV.

Command: SOLREV
Select polyline or circle for revolution...
Select objects: Select a *single* polyline or circle entity
Axis of revolution - Entity/X/Y/<Start point of axis>:
Endpoint of axis:
Included angle <full circle>:

There are four different ways of specifying the axis of revolution:

- **Start point of axis:** this default method requires the input of two coordinate points, from the keyboard or the mouse.
- **Entity:** this *must* be a line or *single* polyline segment. You will be prompted:

    Entity to revolve about:

- **X or Y**   selection of X or Y specifies the current UCS X or Y *axis* as the axis of revolution.

Once you have specified an axis of revolution you will be prompted for an included angle. The default response is 360°. In the case of angles less than 360° it is important to remember that the AutoCAD 3D right hand rule applies. (See Figure 16.22.)

Note: When using the **Start point of axis** route to specify the axis of revolution, the order in which the coordinates are specified determines the *direction* of revolution. Similarly, when specifying the axis by **Entity**, the *position of the selection point* controls the direction. This is similar to the rules applying to the AutoCAD 3D TABSURF command, (see Section 16.6.2).

17.5.3 Solid Creation using SOLIDIFY

Any circle or 2D polyline entity *which has associated thickness* may be directly converted to a true solid by using the SOLIDIFY command. In addition you may SOLIDIFY doughnuts and traces. In the case of a doughnut a solid entity, similar to that derived from a circle, will be created with a radius equal to the difference between the inside and outside radii. A trace may only be solidified if the *width* is finite. (See Figure 17.12.) Neither 2D nor 3D lines may be solidified.

Command: SOLIDIFY
Select objects:

17.6 SYNTHESIZING COMPOSITE SOLIDS

AME supplies three commands which allows you to use primitives as building blocks with which to synthesize a single complex solid entity. With these commands you are able to:

● combine primitives in a truly additive manner
● subtract one primitive from another
● overlap two solids and retain only that volume which is common to both.

Any complex solids so formed can themselves be used as building blocks for even more intricate solid entities.

The three commands are located on the **Sol - Modify** pull down which may be activated by selecting MODIFY from the any of the other AME pull downs.

17.6.1 Joining two solids - SOLUNION

Picked as Union from the **Sol - Modify** pull down.

The SOLUNION command allows two or more separate solids to be joined to form a single solid entity.

The individual component solids may be touching or separate but in either case they will be considered as a single solid after union. Overlapping solids will, after union, be considered as a single solid entity but the total volume will be the sum of the volume of the component solids minus the volume in common, (see Figure 17.13).

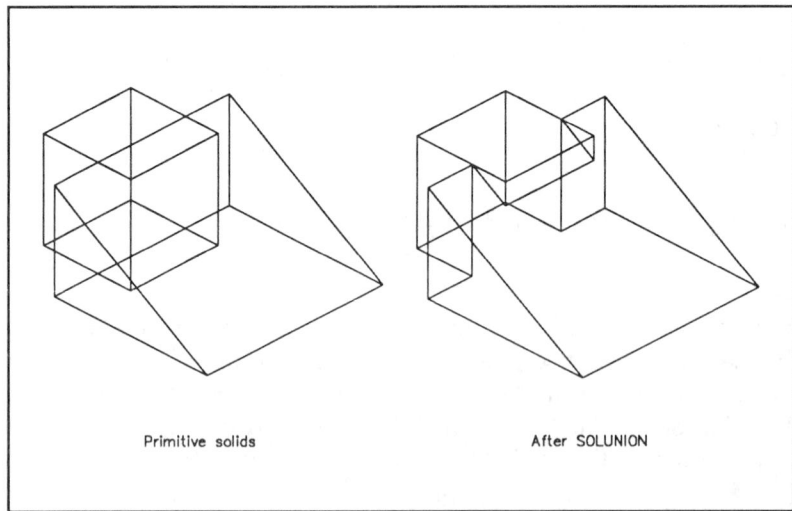

Primitive solids   After SOLUNION

Figure 17.13 Union of two solid primitives

Command: SOLUNION
Select objects: Select all solids to be united
n **solids selected.**

Phase I - Boundary evaluation begins.
Phase II - Tessellation computation begins.
Updating the Advanced Modeling Extension database.

This command allows the creation of single entity solids with shapes which are far more complicated than those of the primitives of which they are composed.

17.6.2 Subtracting two solids - SOLSUB

Picked as Subtract from the **Sol - Modify** pull down.
   The SOLSUB command allows the assembly of two solid selection sets. Solids from the second set are then subtracted from those of the first. Before subtraction takes place, the solid entities within the first selection set are automatically joined (as if with a hidden SOLUNION command) with the result that the final solid after subtraction is a *single* solid entity.
   Any solids or parts of solids within the second selection set which do not intersect with solids from the first set are discarded, (see Figure 17.14).

Command: SOLSUB
Source objects...
Select objects: Pick solids for first selection set
n **solids selected.**
Objects to subtract from them...
Select objects: Pick solids for second selection set
m **solids selected.**

Phase I - Boundary evaluation begins.
Phase II - Tessellation computation begins.
Updating the Advanced Modeling Extension database.

A useful application of this command is the "drilling" of holes in solid entities by the subtraction of a number of cylinders, (see Figure 17.15).

17.6.3 Intersection of two solids - SOLINT

Picked as Intersect from the **Sol - Modify** pull down.
   Two or more solids may be combined together but *only* the *common volume* is retained.

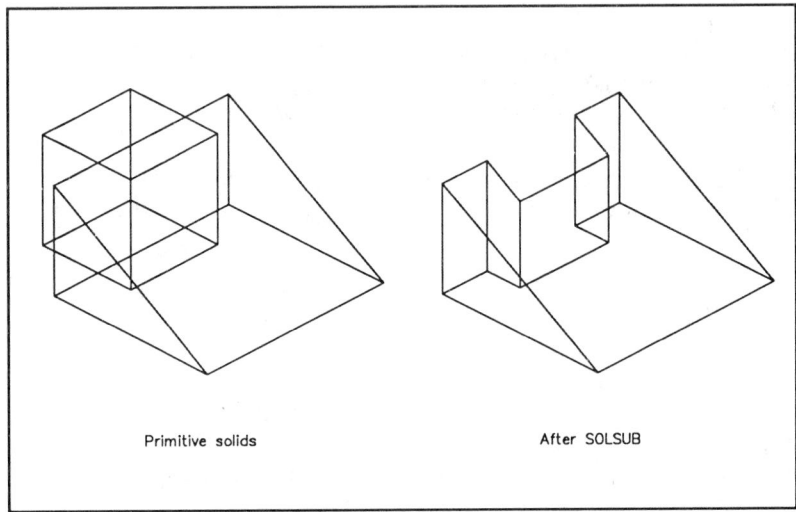

Figure 17.14 Subtraction of two solid primitives

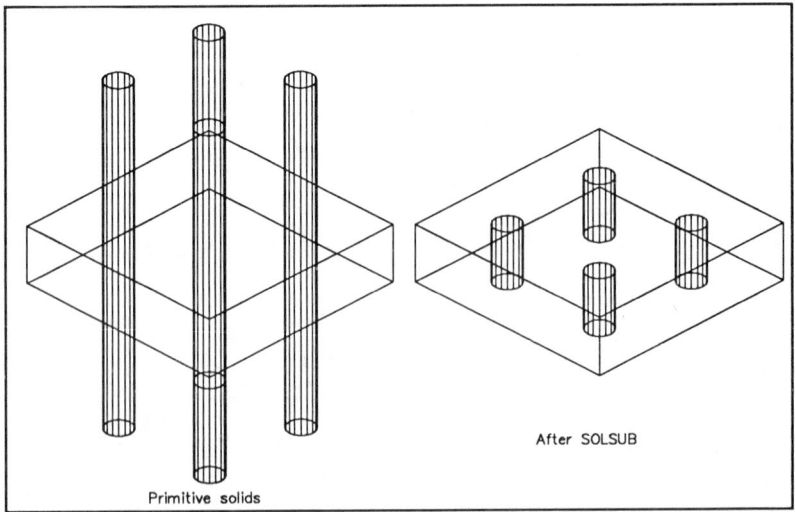

Figure 17.15 Creating "holes" in solid entities

Command: SOLINT
Select objects: Select all solids to be considered
n solids selected.

Phase I - Boundary evaluation begins.
Phase II - Tessellation computation begins.
Updating the Advanced Modeling Extension database.

This command allows the combining of two or more different surface profiles into a single solid object, e.g. the production of a solid cylinder with radiused end faces (see Figure 17.16).

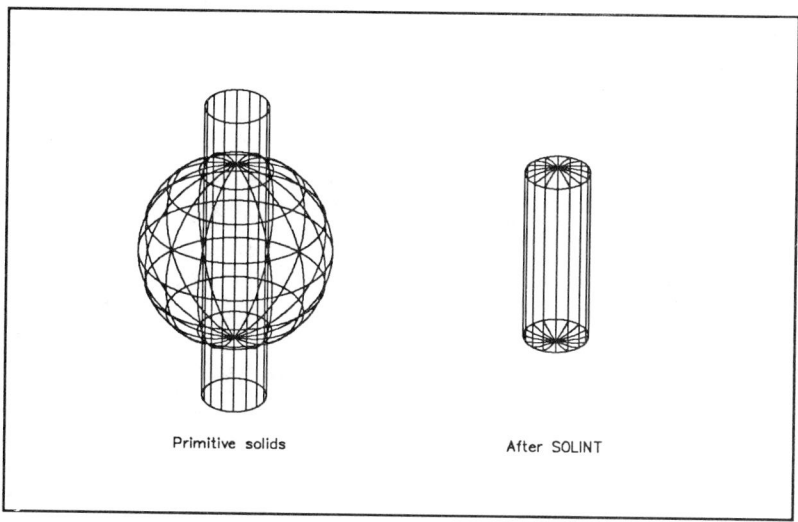

Primitive solids   After SOLINT

Figure 17.16   Intersection of two solid primitives

17.6.4 Separating Solids - SOLSEP

Picked as Separate from the **Sol - Modify** pull down.
    Any solid entity which has been synthesized using the above commands may be returned to its components using SOLSEP. If a number of commands have been used in the synthesis, then SOLSEP may be applied repeatedly until all the commands have been undone.

Command: SOLSEP
Select objects: Select the composite solid to be undone.

17.7 SOLID EDITING

Compared with AutoCAD, AME offers only a limited number of commands for editing existing solid entities. You may move, chamfer or fillet a composite single solid entity. In addition it is possible to modify the properties of primitive solid elements *within* a composite solid such as their colour and to alter their size and position. Many of the AutoCAD editing commands, such as SCALE and MOVE, may be used with solids.

17.7.1 Chamfering Solids - SOLCHAM

Picked as Chamfer from the **Sol - Modify** pull down.
    The SOLCHAM command creates both internal and external chamfers on both straight and curved solid edges. All adjacent edges to be chamfered must be part of a single solid.

> **Command:** SOLCHAM
> **Select base surface:**

It is not possible to select a surface by picking, so you must select one of the edges of the required surface. As this edge will be common to two surfaces there is an ambiguity and AME will highlight only one of them. The selected surface *must* be bounded by *all* the edges to be chamfered, (see Figure 17.17). If the highlighted edge is not the one you require, you may enter:

<OK>/Next: N   the alternative surface will be offered.

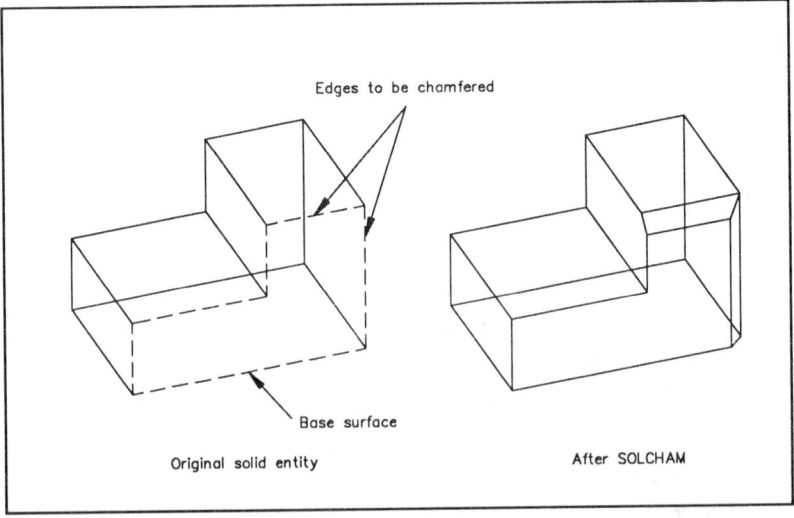

Figure 17.17   Boundary of solid for chamfering

Select edges to be chamfered (Press ENTER when done):
n edges selected.
Enter distance along first surface:
Enter distance along second surface:

Phase I - Boundary evaluation begins.
Phase II - Tessellation computation begins.
Updating the Advanced Modeling Extension database.

Note: The chamfer command operates by creating a new solid in the shape of the chamfer. This solid is automatically added (SOLUNION) in the case of an internal chamfer or subtracted (SOLSUB) in the case of an external chamfer.

It is interesting to note that, if SOLSEP is applied to the chamfered solid, these solid entities are re-created and may be separated from the composite. It is then possible to evaluate their mass etc., to calculate the quantity of material added or subtracted when making the chamfer. (Figure 17.18).

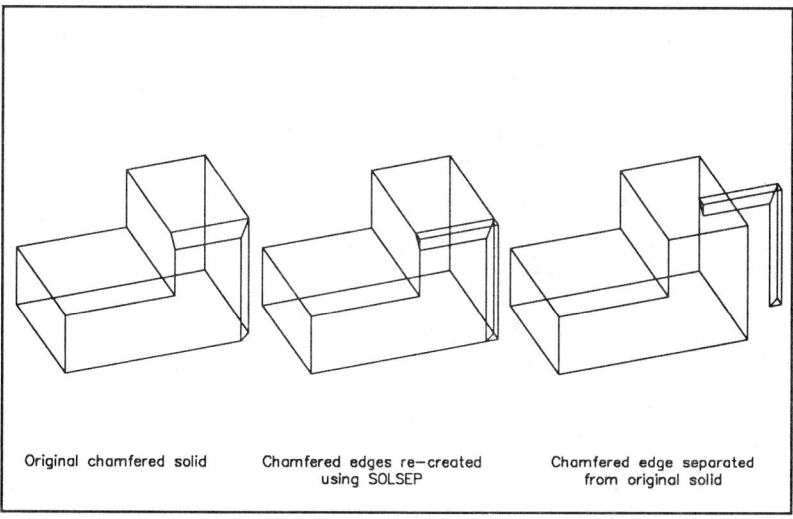

| Original chamfered solid | Chamfered edges re-created using SOLSEP | Chamfered edge separated from original solid |

Figure 17.18 SOLSEP applied to a chamfered solid entity

Single edge chamfering is a simple process and you need only ensure that the faces to be chamfered are planar, (see Figure 17.19).

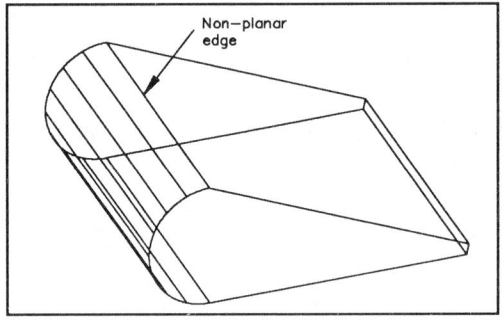

Figure 17.19   Single edge chamfering

When chamfering two or more adjacent edges, it is important to observe the following:

● When chamfering two adjoining edges, it is only possible to form a correct chamfer if the chamfer is on totally external or totally internal edges. Chamfers formed on one internal edge and one adjacent external edge will be incorrectly formed, (see Figure 17.20). Chamfers on two adjoining edges may be formed by the individual chamfering of each edge.
● When chamfering three adjoining edges, which must be totally external or totally internal, two separate chamfer operations must be employed, (Figure 17.21).

17.7.2 Filleting Solids - SOLFILL

Picked as Fillet from the **Sol - Modify** pull down.

The SOLFILL command creates internal and external fillets on both straight and curved solid edges. All adjacent edges to be filleted must be part of a single solid.

> **Command:** SOLFILL
> **Select edges to be filleted (Press ENTER when done):**
> **n edges selected.**
> **Diameter/<Radius> of fillet:**
>
> **Phase I - Boundary evaluation begins.**
> **Phase II - Tessellation computation begins.**
> **Updating the Advanced Modeling Extension database.**

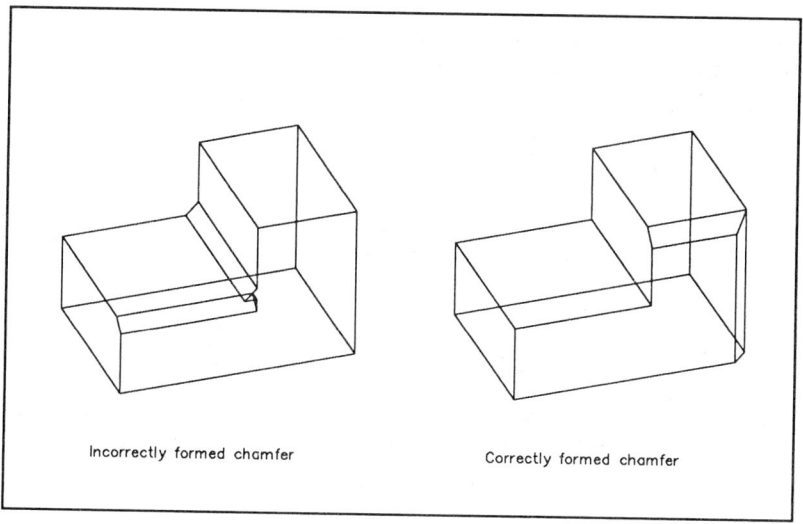

Figure 17.20 Correctly and incorrectly formed chamfers on two adjoining edges

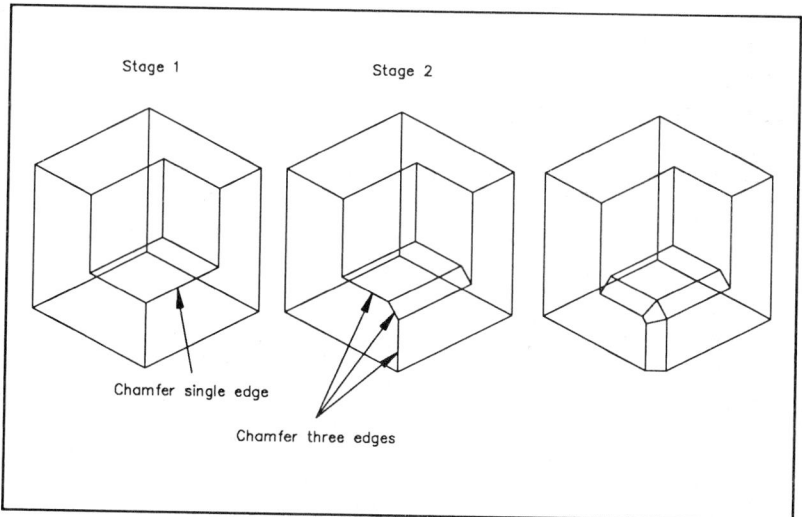

Figure 17.21 Chamfering three adjoining edges

The SOLFILL command operates in the same manner as SOLCHAM in that a new solid is created in the shape of the fillet. This solid is automatically added (SOLUNION) in the case of an internal fillet or subtracted (SOLSUB) in the case of an external fillet.

As with chamfering, single edge filleting is a simple process and you need only ensure that the faces to be filleted are planar, (see Figure 17.22).

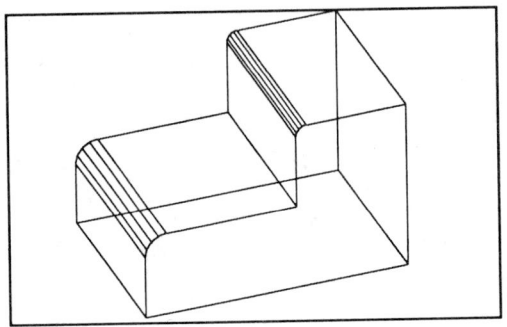

Figure 17.22   Single edge filleting

When filleting two or more adjacent edges, it is important to observe the following:

- When filleting two adjoining edges, it is only possible to form a correct fillet if the fillet is on totally external or totally internal edges. Fillets on one internal edge and one adjacent external edge will be incorrectly formed, Figure 17.23.

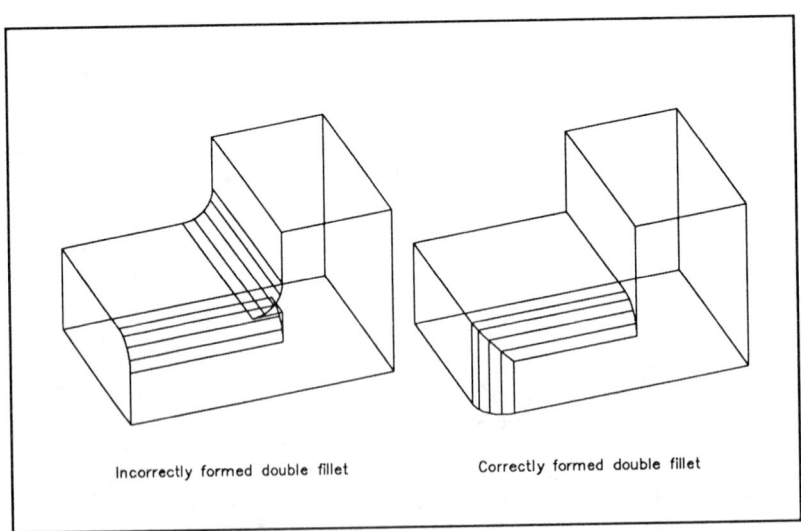

Incorrectly formed double fillet   Correctly formed double fillet

Figure 17.23   Correctly and incorrectly formed fillets on two adjoining edges

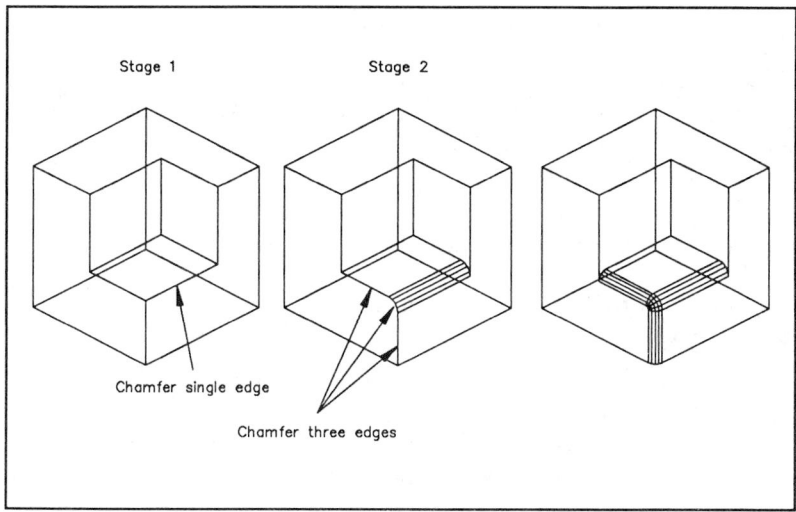

Figure 17.24   Filleting three adjoining edges

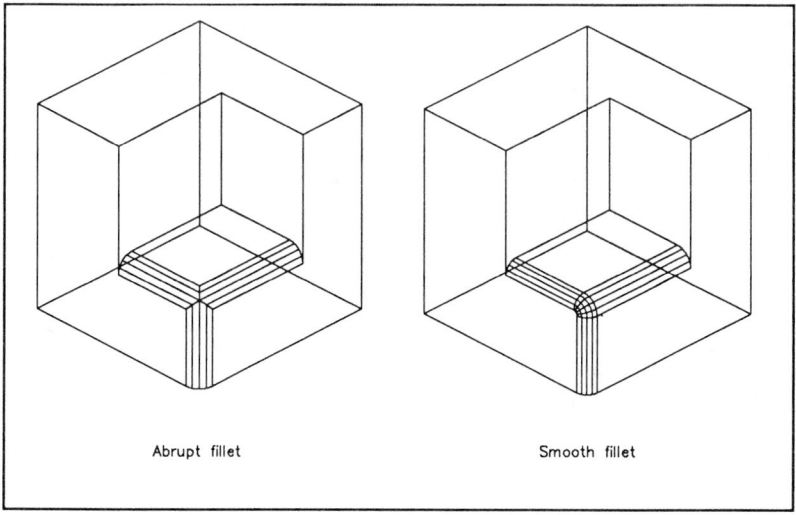

Figure 17.25   Alternative fillets formed on three adjoining edges

● When filleting three adjoining edges, two separate fillet operations may be employed, (see Figure 17.24). If all three edges are selected in one fillet operation, then the interface between the three fillets will be curved yet abrupt, (see Figure 17.25).

> *Note:*   The filleting and chamfering operations do not always give the expected result. Only prolonged practice will allow you to predict the outcome with confidence.

17.7.3 Translating and Rotating Solids - SOLMOVE

Picked as Solid Move from the **Sol - Modify** pull down.

The SOLMOVE command combines the functions of MOVE and ROTATE and thus allows solids to be translated along a defined direction or rotated about a specified axis.

A new coordinate system icon defines the current Motion Coordinate System (MCS). The icon acts as a signpost which indicates the MCS X- axis by a single tipped arrow, the Y- axis by a double tipped arrow and the Z- axis by a triple tipped arrow (see Figure 17.26).

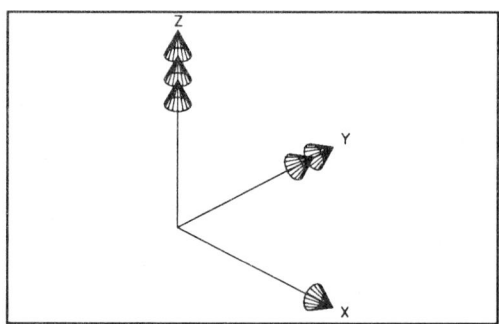

Figure 17.26   The Motion Coordinate System icon

Movement of the selected solids is subsequently defined with reference to the MCS. The MCS may be re-defined as often as required and aligned to either the current UCS, the WCS or an edge or surface of an existing solid.

Command: SOLMOVE
Select objects: Select solid(s) to be moved
<Motion description>/?:   Enter code letter(s)

The last prompt is repeated indefinitely to allow complex movements to be synthesized, a final return terminating the command. The possible code letters are:

- **E**   Aligns the MCS to the selected edge of a solid.
- **F**   Aligns the MCS to the selected face of a solid.
- **U**   Aligns the MCS with the current UCS.
- **U**   Aligns the MCS with the WCS.
- **O**   Returns the objects moved within the present command to their original positions.
- **AE**   Aligns the selected solids and the MCS icon with an edge of solid. You must first place the MCS on the edge or face of one of the solids to be moved using the **E** or **F** codes.
- **AF**   Aligns the selected solids and the MCS icon with an face of solid. You must first place the MCS on the edge or face of one of the solids to be moved using the **E** or **F** codes.
- **AU**   Aligns the selected solids and the MCS icon with an the current UCS. You must first place the MCS on the edge or face of one of the solids to be moved using the **E** or **F** codes.
- **AW**   Aligns the selected solids and the MCS icon with the WCS. You must first place the MCS on the edge or face of one of the solids to be moved using the **E** or **F** codes.
- **R(X** or **Y** or **Z)angle**   Rotates the solid objects about the nominated axis through the specified angle, e.g. RY30 will cause the solids to be rotated by 30° about the Y axis, observing the normal right hand rule convention.
- **T(X** or **Y** or **Z)distance**   Translates the solids along the nominated axis e.g. TZ230 will cause the solids to be moved 230 units along the Z-axis.

Note: Any number of motion description codes can be issued in combination to produce complex movements. Each code group must be separated from the others by commas, e.g. TX22,TZ-50,RY45.

17.7.4 Changing the Properties of Solids - SOLCHP

Picked as Change Prim. from the **Sol - Modify** pull down.

It is possible to modify the colour, size and position of solids and primitive solid elements *within* a composite solid.

> **Command:** SOLCHP
> **Select Solid:**   Select a primitive or composite solid

if a composite solid is chosen then AME will temporarily separate this composite into its component primitive elements and you will be prompted:

Select primitive:
Color/Delete/Evaluate/Instance/Move/Next/Pick/Replace/Size/eXit <N>:

Color　　　　Allows the colour of the solid to be changed.

Delete　　　　If the selected primitive is not part of a composite solid, then *it will be deleted*. A primitive which forms part of a composite may be deleted from the composite but retained as a separate primitive.

Evaluate　　　Forces an immediate update of the AME database.

Instance　　　This option allows the creation of a *separate* solid primitive by copying one of the component primitives of the solid. This copy is placed directly over the original and is therefore virtually impossible to see.

Move　　　　Identical to the AutoCAD MOVE command and prompts for points of displacement.

Next　　　　Selects the next component primitive in a composite solid.

Pick　　　　Allows the user to select, by picking, another primitive from the composite solid.

Replace　　　The selected component primitive may be replaced by another primitive or composite solid which already exists in the drawing.

Size　　　　As with SOLMOVE, the MCS icon is used to indicate the X-, Y-, Z-axes. You will be prompted to supply new values of the basic dimensions of the primitive to re-define its size.

eXit　　　　Exits the COLCHP command and re-forms the composite solid.

17.8 DISPLAYING SOLID ENTITIES

The default representation of all solid entities is controlled by the AME system variable SOLDISPLAY. This variable may be set to give either wireframe or mesh representation to all newly created solids.

Command: SOLDISPLAY
Display type Mesh/<Wire>:

17.8.1 Applying a mesh to a solid - SOLMESH

Picked as Mesh from the **Sol - Display** pull down.

A solid can be presented as either a wireframe or a mesh. Before a solid can be rendered using the SHADE command, (see Section 16.1.10), or hidden using the HIDE command, (see Section 16.1.6), it is first necessary to "mesh" it. This involves applying a series of polyface mesh entities to the surface of the solid. The process is approximate and some detail will inevitably be lost but the rendered image often gives a more realistic impression of a true solid.

> **Command:** SOLMESH
> **Select objects:**
> n **solids selected.**
> **Surface meshing of current solids is completed.**
>
> **Creating block for mesh representation...**
> **Done.**

The mesh density is controlled by the AME system variable SOLWDENS which may be accessed by picking Set Wire Dens. from the **Sol - Display** pull down. The following will be displayed:

> **Command:** SOLVAR
> **Variable name or ?:** SOLWDENS
> **Wireframe mesh density (1 to 8) <4>:**

The value 1 results in the lowest resolution of wireframe or mesh: 8 gives the highest resolution.

Note: If you wish to make modifications to a solid which is in mesh representation and has been SHADEd, you must first remove the shading using REGEN.

17.8.2 Returning a Solid to Wireframe Form - SOLWIRE

Picked as Wireframe from the **Sol - Display** pull down.

The SOLWIRE command returns a meshed solid to a wireframe solid.

> **Command:** SOLWIRE
> **Select solids to be wired ...**
> **Select objects:**
> n **solids selected.**

Again, the system variable SOLWDENS controls the accuracy of the wireframe representation. This is most noticeable on curved surfaces.

17.8.3 Copying a Solid Face or Edge - SOLFEAT

Picked as Copy Feature from the **Sol - Display** pull down.

Any solid face or edge may be copied using SOLFEAT to form a non-solid representation constructed from lines, polylines, arcs and circles in the form of an unnamed block.

> **Command:** SOLFEAT
> **Edge/<Face>:** F
> **Select a face...**

If the choice of face is ambiguous, you will be prompted:

> **<OK>/Next:**

After execution of this command the new copy will lie directly on top of the selected face or edge and, although highlighted, will be difficult to differentiate from the original. To separate this copy it may be moved using the AutoCAD MOVE command - SOLMOVE may not be used because the *copy* is not a solid. (See Figure 17.27.)

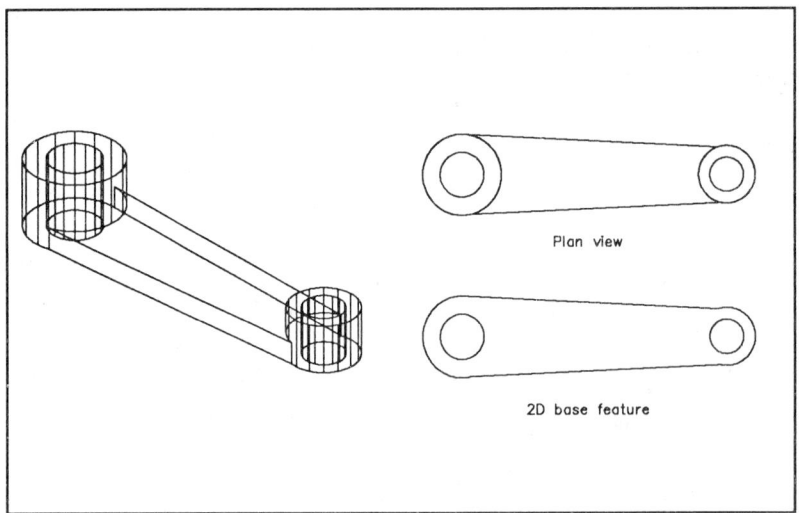

Figure 17.27 The SOLFEAT command

Note: It is not possible to create a copy of a face or an edge if the solid entity is meshed.

17.8.4 Creating a Two Dimensional Cross Section - SOLSECT

Picked as Cut Section from the **Sol - Display** pull down.

This command produces a two dimensional cross section through any selected plane passing through one or more solid entities.

The cross section plane is selected by positioning the X-Y plane of the current UCS to cut the solid, (see Figure 17.28).

> **Command:** SOLSECT
> **Select objects:**
> n **objects selected.**

This command operates in a very similar fashion to SOLFEAT; the newly created cross section is a block which is embedded inside the solid. As with the copy produced by SOLFEAT, this entity may be separated from the solid by the MOVE command.

The section created by the SOLSECT command may be hatched automatically using the SOLHPAT, SOLHANGLE and SOLHSIZE AME system variables. (See Figure 17.29.) This feature is enabled by nominating a hatch pattern to be stored in SOLHPAT and is subsequently disabled by replacing the hatch pattern name with NONE.

> *Note:*   When separating a hatched section from a solid entity, remember to select *both* the section and the hatch pattern.

17.8.5 Creating a Surface Profile - SOLPROF

Picked as Profile from the **Sol - Display** pull down.

The profile of a solid entity may be created which is view-specific. This profile may only be created when the TILEMODE system variable is set to zero and you are working in Model Space, (see Chapter 13).

When a profile is created, AME produces two special layers - one for the hidden line profile and one for the visible line profile. These layers take their names from the layer upon which the solid was created and from the viewport number. For example, if the solid was created on layer CONCRETE and you are working in viewport number 3 then the hidden layer will be named CONCRETE-PH-3 and the visible layer will be named CONCRETE-PV-3. If the linetype named Hidden has previously been loaded, then the special hidden PH layer will take this linetype. The resulting display will then show visible lines in the Continuous linetype and hidden lines in the Hidden linetype. This gives a very realistic representation of the solid.

> **Command:** SOLPROF
> **Select objects:**
> **Display hidden profile lines on separate layer ? <N>** Y

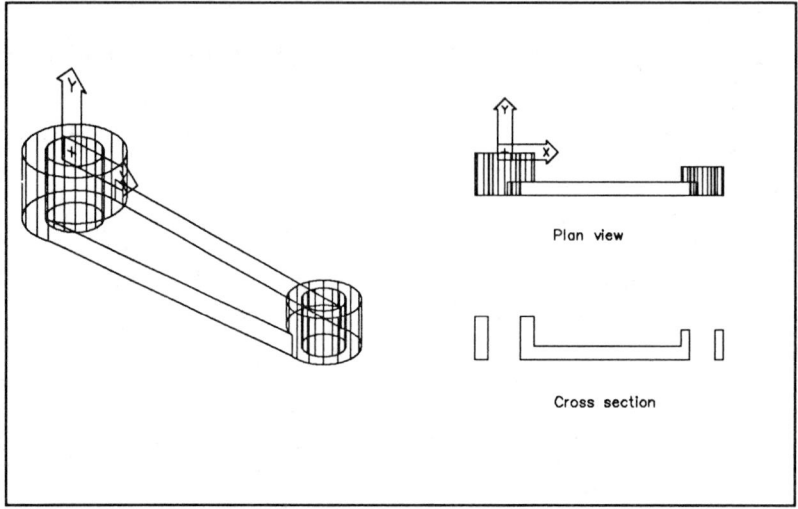

Figure 17.28   Cross section formed by SOLSECT

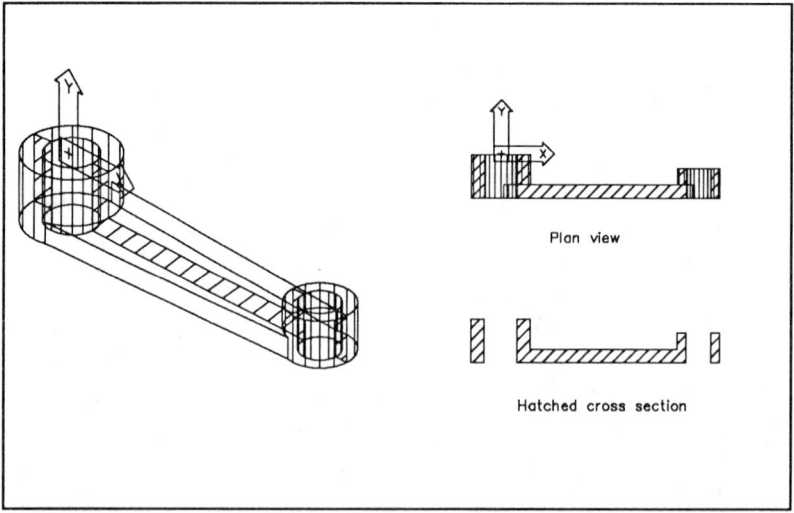

Figure 17.29   Hatched cross section

A Y response allows you to segregate the hidden lines on to the special hidden PH layer. If you give an N response, the hidden and visible lines will *both* be placed on the PV layer as a single block.

n solids selected.

Phase I of hidden line removal computation of current solid has started.

Phase II of hidden line removal computation of current solid has started.

Phase III of hidden line removal computation of current solid has started.

Hidden line removal computation of current solid is completed.

See Figure 17.30.

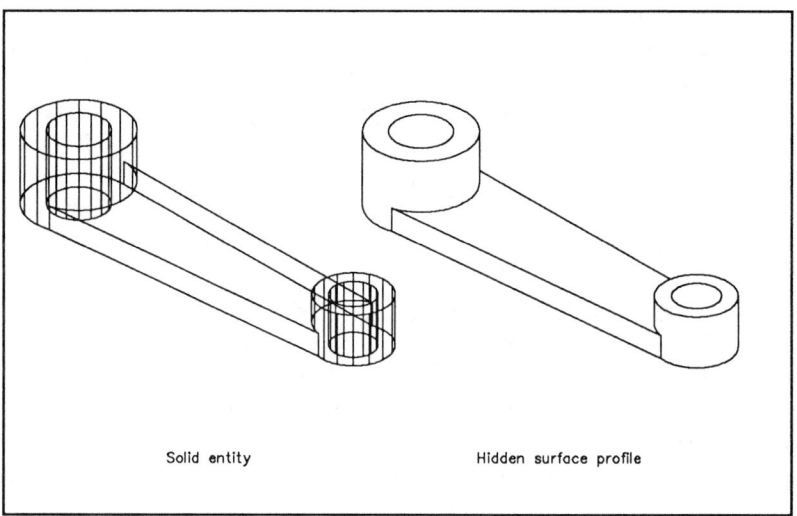

Solid entity   Hidden surface profile

Figure 17.30 Surface profile created with SOLPROF

17.9 INQUIRY COMMANDS

A range of commands under the **Sol - Inquiry** menu is designed to report various attributes of AME solids.

17.9.1 Listing Solid Properties - SOLLIST

Picked as List Solid from the **Sol - Inquiry** pull down.

The AutoCAD LIST command will invariably see every solid as a block reference and only report its insertion point and scale factor. The AME SOLLIST command gives information about, for example, the solid's dimensions and coordinates, primitive component composition and whether wireframe or mesh representation is employed.

> **Command:** SOLLIST
> **Edge/Face/Tree/<Solid>:**
> **Select** ....

<Solid> This default option gives information about the selected solid. For example, for a primitive box you will be informed about the solid type, its dimensions, the material of construction, its handle and whether wireframe or mesh representation is employed. If the solid is a composite, you will in addition be told how it was formed, e.g. union, subtraction etc., and the handles of its component primitives.

Edge Gives information about the selected edge. For example, for a circular edge you will be informed about the edge length, radius and centre coordinates.

Face Gives information about the selected face. For example, for a planar face you will be informed about the plane upon which the face sits.

Tree This option provides a full history of the processes by which a composite solid was created. This includes all the information given under the **Solid** option but is extended to *all* the component primitives. The node level indicates the order in which the various operations were performed.

17.9.2 Listing Solid Mass Properties - SOLMASSP

Picked as Mass Property from the **Sol - Inquiry** pull down.

Various mass properties of selected solids are detailed as follows: Mass, Volume, Bounding box, Centroid, Moments of Inertia, Products of Inertia, Radii of Gyration, Principal moments and X-, Y-, and Z- directions about the centroid.

Command: SOLMASSP
Select objects:
Updating solid...
Done
n **solids selected.**
Calculating mass properties.

The properties listed above will be displayed on screen and you will be prompted:

Write to file <N> ?

If you reply with a Y, then you will be prompted:

File name <filename>**:**

The data will be saved in ASCII format in a file with a .MPR extension.

17.9.3 Listing the Area of a Solid - SOLAREA

Picked as Solid Area from the **Sol - Inquiry** pull down.

SOLAREA reports an approximate surface area for selected solids. When calculating the area, AME divides the surface of the solid into Pmesh entities and sums their surface area. Again, the system variable SOLWDENS controls the density of the Pmesh elements and hence the accuracy of the calculation. This is most noticeable on curved surfaces.

Command: SOLAREA
Select solids for surface area computation ...
Select objects:
n **solids selected.**
Surface meshing of current solid completed.
Creating block for mesh representation...
Done.
Surface area of solids is xxxx **sq cm**

The units quoted are controlled by the SOLAREAU AME variable, i.e. Imp - mass in lb, area in sq ft, volume in cu ft.; CGS - mass in gm, area in sq cm, volume in cu cm.; SI - mass in kg, area in sq m, volume in cu m.

17.10 UTILITY COMMANDS

A range of commands under the **Sol - Utility** menu facilitate control of various attributes of AME solids and the solid creation process.

17.10.1 Specifying the Solid Material - SOLMAT

Picked as Material from the **Sol - Utility** pull down.

All AME solids have associated with them some of the physical attributes of the material of construction. The default material is MILD_STEEL. AME supplies data on ten materials in an ASCII file ACAD.MAT - nine metals plus glass. You may supplement this list with your own data. The quoted parameters are density, Young's modulus, Poisson's ratio, Yield strength, Ultimate strength, Thermal conductivity, Linear expansion coefficient and specific heat. The only parameter used by AME's SOLMASSP command is the density.

> **Command: SOLMAT**
> **Change/Edit/<eXit>/LIst/LOad/New/Remove/SAve/SEt/?:**

Change   Allows you to change the material of the selected solid(s) to any of the materials available in the ASCII file ACAD.MAT. The selected material is loaded into the drawing automatically.

Note: When using the **Change** option, the default material reported is *always* the default material (initially mild steel), even if the actual material is one of the other materials available. if in doubt, use the SOLLIST command.

Edit   The above mentioned properties of any material previously loaded into the drawing may be edited. The modifications will be incorporated into the current drawing and you will be prompted:

> **Save the material to a file <N> ?**

A Y response will redefine the materials file for future use.

eXit   Exits the SOLMAT command and executes any changes.

List   Allows you to list the properties of any material in the ACAD.MAT materials file whether or not it is loaded into the current drawing.

LOad   Loads a material into the current drawing.

New Allows the user to define a new material for use in the current drawing. You will also be prompted:

    Save the material to a file <N> ?

  A Y response will add the new material to the materials file for future use.

Remove Removes a material from the current drawing.

SAve Saves a material previously defined (using the **New** option) in the current drawing to the materials file.

SEt Allows the setting of a new default material in the current drawing.

17.10.2 Altering AME System Variables - SOLVAR

Picked as Solvars from the **Sol - Utility** pull down.
  This command is exactly equivalent to the AutoCAD SETVAR command and as such need only be invoked when an AME variable takes the same name as an AME command.

  Command: SOLVAR
  Variable name or ?:

  The ? response yields a list of all AME system variables together with their current values and a brief description of their function.

17.10.3 Invoking Additional UCS features within AME - SOLUCS

Picked as SolUCS from the **Sol - Utility** pull down.
  This command allows the UCS to be aligned to a specific edge or face of an AME solid.

  Command: SOLUCS
  Edge/<Face> : F
  Select a face...

  The UCS will now be moved to the specific position relative to the selected face as defined by AME, (see Figure 17.31). In the case of ambiguity of choice you will be prompted:

  <OK>/Next:

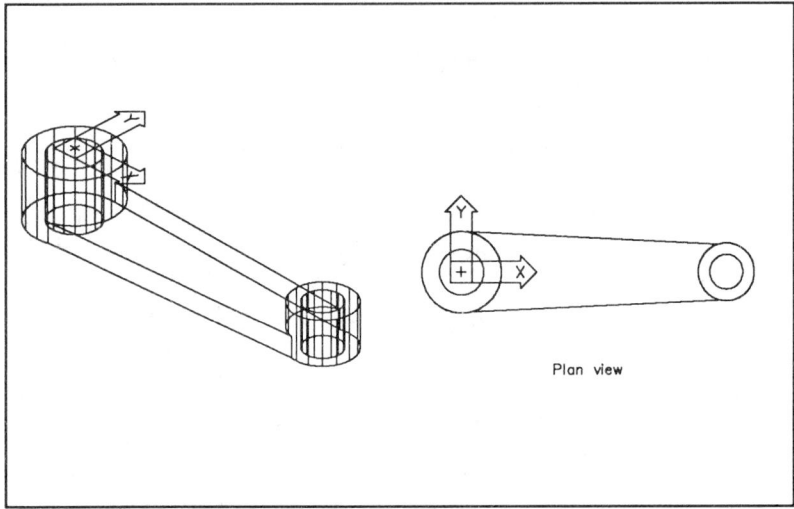

Figure 17.31   UCS positioning relative to a solid face using SOLUCS

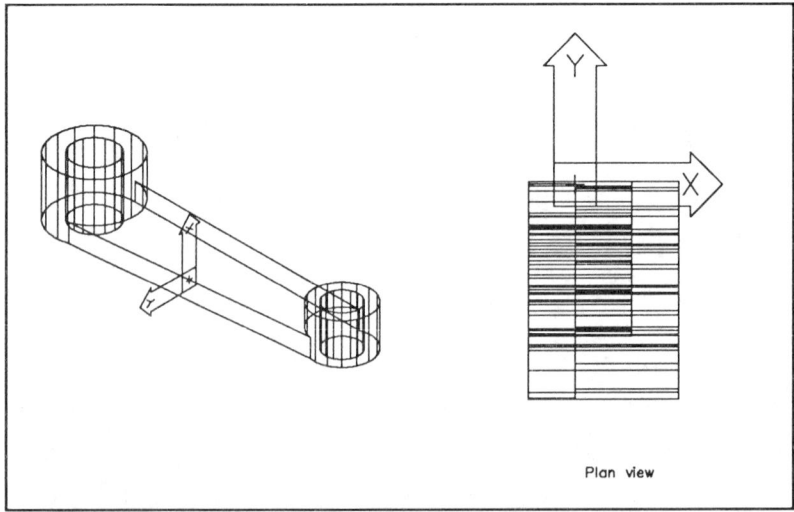

Figure 17.32   UCS positioning relative to a solid edge using SOLUCS

If an **Edge** is selected:

> **Select an edge...**

The UCS will now be moved to the specific position relative to the selected edge as defined by AME, (see Figure 17.32).

17.10.4 Importing and Exporting solids - SOLIN and SOLOUT

Picked as SOL in   .asm and SOL out .asm from the **Sol - Utility** pull down.

These commands are for the export and import of solids between an AME drawing and another solid modelling package such as AutoSOLID. You will be prompted for a file name with an implied .ASM extension.

17.10.5 Memory Management - SOLPURGE

Picked as Purge Solids from the **Sol - Utility** pull down.

This command allows you to clear the computer's memory of unwanted solids data and to reduce the size of the current drawing file.

> **Command:** SOLPURGE
> **Memory/Bfile/Pmesh/<Erased>:**

<Erased> When a complex solid is erased from the drawing, significant quantities of data remain. The drawing size may therefore be reduced by purging the remains of these entities with this option.

Memory This option clears the working memory of data used in the creation of the solids in the current drawing. This does not affect the solid entities in any way and they will still be available for all editing functions.

Bfile If the Bfile entities are purged from the drawing, then this will result in a significant reduction in the size of the drawing file.

Pmesh All existing Pmeshes in the drawing, whether visible or not, will be removed by this command. If *both* the Bfile and the Pmesh options are invoked, then a *50% reduction* in drawing size may be anticipated.

18. Customized lines, hatchings and shapes

18.1 CREATING TEXT FILES

When creating your own linetypes, hatch patterns, shapes, menus etc., you will need to be able to create text files to be saved within a selected directory. AutoCAD provides a facility to do this:

> **Command:** EDIT
> **File to edit:**

This makes use of a simple text editor called Edlin. Although Edlin is capable of producing the relatively simple text files required by AutoCAD, many people find it unfriendly and difficult to use. It is often easier to use a word processor to write these files. In some respects this is "overkill" because you will not make use of many of the more sophisticated features of the word processor package. However, a word processor is usually easy to work with and, particularly when you come to write longer text files such as menus, life can be much easier with a word processor than with a simple text editor.

There is one problem. Word processors produce text documents within which are embedded a large number of control characters. These characters are used to indicate text features such as underlined words, emboldened words, paragraph indentations, etc. Such characters can only be recognised by the particular word processor package on which the text was written. They cannot be understood by AutoCAD and will cause trouble if they are included in the text files. Almost all word processor packages will allow you to save the text with these characters removed - such text files are usually known as DOS text files or ASCII text files - and it is essential that you *always* save your AutoCAD text files in this format.

18.2 EXTERNAL COMMANDS AND THE ACAD.PGP FILE

It can be rather a laborious process to switch between AutoCAD and the word processor. If you are working on a drawing, you must save it, exit AutoCAD, enter the word processor, write your text file, save it, exit the word processor, enter AutoCAD, re-load the drawing and then continue.

AutoCAD has a mechanism for calling up an *external* software package without leaving the drawing. A ProGram Parameters file called ACAD.PGP is supplied with AutoCAD. This is a text file which controls both the external software accessible from the drawing editor and command alias definitions. When supplied, it probably looks like:

```
; acad.pgp - External Command and Command Alias definitions

; External Command format:
; <Command name>,[<DOS request>],<Memory  reserve>,[*]<Prompt>, <Return code>

; Examples of External Commands for DOS

CATALOG,DIR /W,33000,File specification: ,0
DEL,DEL,      33000,File to delete: ,0
DIR,DIR,      33000,File specification: ,0
EDIT,EDLIN,   42000,File to edit: ,0
SH,,          33000,*DOS Command: ,0
SHELL,,       127000,*DOS Command: ,0
TYPE,TYPE,    33000,File to list: ,0
```

The remainder of the ACAD.PGP file refers to command aliases which are covered in Section 18.3.

It is important to understand the structure of this file. The lines prefixed by semicolons are simply comments and have no executive effect. Each of the external command specification lines defines a single command recognised by AutoCAD which activates an external command which AutoCAD would not otherwise accept. Each of these lines consists of 5 fields, separated by commas. The fields are:

- *Command name:*   The first field gives the command which will be recognised as a valid AutoCAD command. This must not duplicate an existing AutoCAD command.
- *File command:*   The second field gives the external command which AutoCAD will issue as a result. The command name and the file command may be the same or they may differ. The file command must be a valid command which you would use to call up the external software at the DOS prompt. As in DOS, the command may include paths and parameters.
- *Memory reserve:*   When AutoCAD boots up, it normally "grabs" all the available RAM memory for its own use. If you wish to run external software, AutoCAD must be made to give up some of this memory for the external

software's own use. This may be an area of conflict and you should aim to minimise the memory reserve to avoid hampering AutoCAD's operation. You should allow a minimum of 24000 bytes and at least 4000 bytes in excess of the size of the external software itself. This can end up as a process of trial and error to find a suitable number.

● *Prompt:* This is an optional prompt which appears in addition to any prompt generated by the external software itself. If not needed, this field can be left blank. If the first character of this field is a * then you will be allowed to include spaces in your response, otherwise the space will be interpreted as a return.

● *Return code:* Each command in ACAD.PGP switches the display to text mode. The most important function of the final field dictates whether, on returning to AutoCAD's drawing editor, you remain in text mode (field set to 0) or switch back to graphics mode (field set to 4) - this is assuming that you were originally in graphics mode when you issued the external command.

This all seems very complicated but is actually quite easy to use. A glance at the above ACAD.PGP file will show that AutoCAD is able to respond to the DOS commands DIR, DEL and TYPE and can call up Edlin. It can also return to DOS, either for a single DOS command or, if you respond to the SHELL or SH prompt with a return, you can remain in DOS indefinitely until you type the command EXIT.

Once you understand the purpose of this section of the ACAD.PGP file then you can experiment with some modifications. For example, the TYPE command will list out a text file on the screen, but if the file is longer than can be shown on a single screen it will scroll without giving you the chance to read it all. The DOS command MORE allows you to type the file on screen but will pause after each full screen to allow you time to read the information. Pressing return will give you the next full screen, and so on. If you wish to incorporate this feature into your system, start up your word processor and load in the ACAD.PGP file as a DOS text file. Then modify the line:

```
        TYPE,TYPE,    33000,File to list: ,0
to:
        TYPE,MORE<,   33000,File to list: ,0
```

Save this modified file in DOS text format as ACAD.PGP to replace the original file. Whenever you subsequently give the command TYPE from the AutoCAD command line, the new version including the MORE feature will be executed.

Note: You may have trouble if your word processor cannot accommodate the long comments in ACAD.PGP on a single line without it forcing a wrap around on to the next line. If you save the file in this format, AutoCAD will register an error next time you enter the drawing editor. You can avoid this problem either by increasing the page width of your word processor or by adding an extra ; at the start of the wrapped around text line.

It is advisable to keep a copy of *any* original AutoCAD file before experimenting with any modifications.

The location of any external software (such as MORE.COM) to be accessed through the ACAD.PGP file *must* be included in the DOS PATH set up *before* entering AutoCAD.

The really useful thing about ACAD.PGP is that you can add to it.

EXAMPLE

You can add a line which will allow you to call up your word processor from the drawing editor. Thus, if your word processor is normally started with the command WP, and takes up 200000 bytes, you could add the line:

```
WORDPRO,WP,     205000,,4
```

and again save this modified file in DOS text format as ACAD.PGP

This effectively adds the new command WORDPRO to your AutoCAD package. When you type this command, AutoCAD will issue the file command WP. You must be sure that the word processor directory is mentioned in the DOS Path, (See Appendix 1), so that the WP file can be found. When you have finished word processing, you exit the package in the usual way and you will be returned immediately to your original AutoCAD drawing.

Note: It is advisable to save your drawing before entering any external software.

18.3 COMMAND ALIASES AND THE ACAD.PGP FILE

A very useful aid to speeding up your use of AutoCAD is to define a list of short form commands or *aliases*, each representing a frequently used command. This list is incorporated into the ACAD.PGP file. In use, an alias command is given from the keyboard, and as in the case of an external command, it will not be recognised as an AutoCAD command and therefore the ACAD.PGP file will be consulted. If the alias is found in the ACAD.PGP file, the corresponding AutoCAD command will be issued. An alias can be composed of one, two or more alpha-numerics. A typical fragment from the alias section of the ACAD.PGP file is as follows:

```
A,      *ARC
C,      *CIRCLE
CP,     *COPY
DV,     *DVIEW
E,      *ERASE
L,      *LINE
LA,     *LAYER
M,      *MOVE
MS,     *MSPACE
P,      *PAN
PS,     *PSPACE
PL,     *PLINE
R,      *REDRAW
Z,      *ZOOM
```

You may add further aliases to the above list as required. You may also delete or modify existing aliases. The alias structure is:

<Alias>,*<Full command name>

You may add extra spaces between the comma and the star to make the list easier to read.

Aliases may be created for any valid AutoCAD or AME command including transparent commands (don't forget to include the apostrophe before the command name), system variable (which does not bear the same name as a command) or AutoLISP command.

18.4 MULTIPLE CONFIGURATION

When you use the AutoCAD package for the first time, you will be told that the system must first be configured. You must then embark on the configuration routine, which is a lengthy ritual informing the package about the display cards and monitors, the mouse and/or digitiser and the plotter and/or printer which are to be used. Once this has been done there is usually no need to repeat it. However, if the package is run with several different sets of equipment the configurator would normally have to be run each time a change was made. This can be avoided if the configuration data files are separately retained.

The configuration data are normally stored in a file called ACAD.CFG. This is looked for on a separate directory called the Configuration Directory. In most cases this directory does not have a separate existence but is the same as the system directory - the directory on which the AutoCAD program files are located.

It is, of course, not possible to have more than one file called ACAD.CFG in the same directory, but it is possible to create them and keep them in separate directories. If AutoCAD is first told which of these directories is to be considered as the configuration directory, it becomes easy to switch between the different configuration files.

The name of the configuration directory may be set from DOS *before* AutoCAD is started. This is done by using the DOS command SET to set a special environment variable called ACADCFG.

Thus, suppose that you wish to keep the first configuration file in a configuration directory called, say, MYCONF. Before starting up AutoCAD, you must issue the DOS command

C>SET ACADCFG=C:\ACAD\MYCONF   or whatever is the correct path for
                                                             your system

On start up, AutoCAD will be unable to find an ACAD.CFG file anywhere (you should have removed any old versions of ACAD.CFG before you start) and so will enter the configurator as normal. As a result of the information which you supply, the configurator will then write an ACAD.CFG file into the configuration directory, in this case, MYCONF.

If you now exit AutoCAD and repeat the whole process with a second Configuration Directory called, say, HISCONF you can create a second ACAD.CFG file. (See Figure 18.1.) This may be repeated for as many different configurations as you require.

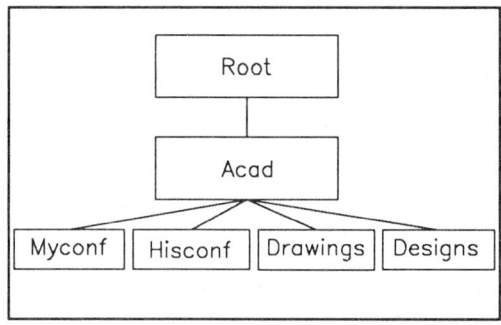

Figure 18.1   Multiple configuration directories

At any future time, before starting AutoCAD, you simply SET the Configuration Directory to MYCONF, HISCONF, etc and AutoCAD will then search the specified directory during its start up routine and will configure the package accordingly.

18.4.1 Changing the Configuration from a Batch File

This setting of the configuration directory may conveniently be performed within a batch file, (see Appendix 1, Section A1.3), and will then become automatic. This file may also be used to set any selected directory as the default. It is often convenient to create separate directories to accommodate all the drawings and associated files belonging, say, to one user or covering one topic etc.

Suppose that you wish to keep all your drawing files in a sub-directory called MYFILES. You should first create this directory - usually as a sub-directory of the AutoCAD system directory. You must then write a batch file; this will usually be located in the root directory. The tasks of the batch file are:

- To set MYFILES to be the default directory.
- To set MYCONF to be the configuration directory.
- To start up AutoCAD.
- To default to the root directory when AutoCAD has finished.

In order for the computer to be able to find the ACAD system files you should also include the AutoCAD system directory in the PATH. This may also be done from the batch file.

EXAMPLE

The batch file referred to in Section 2.2.1 may thus be modified :

```
PATH=C:\ACAD\MYFILES;\
CD\ACAD\MYFILES
SET LISPHEAP=42000
SET LISPSTACK=2500
SET ACADCFG=C:\ACAD\MYCONF
SET ACAD=C:\ACAD\SUPPORT
ACAD
CD\
```

If this batch file is saved on the root directory as MYDRAW.BAT, then to start AutoCAD with your personal configuration and your personal drawing directory you need only type MYDRAW.

18.5 CUSTOMIZED LINETYPES

AutoCAD contains a library of various linetypes which can be called at any time during the drawing execution. The standard AutoCAD linetypes are kept in a library file called ACAD.LIN. It is relatively simple to create your own linetypes (containing only dots and dashes) and add them to the supplied library file (ACAD.LIN) or create your own library file (which must have the .LIN extension).

Linetypes can be modified or created in two ways; by using an external text editor or by using the Create option from within the LINETYPE command. Both methods produce linetypes which are stored in a library file the contents of which must be loaded into the drawing file before subsequent use.

18.5.1 Linetypes Created from Within AutoCAD

Command: LINETYPE
?/Create/Load/Set: C
Name of linetype to create: EXAMPLE
File for storage of linetype <ACAD>:

Enter the linetype name and the name of the library file where the linetype is to be stored. AutoCAD will then request a description of the new or modified linetype. This should preferably be a representation made up of dots and dashes, e.g.

Descriptive text: --- ... --- ... --- ... --- ... --

AutoCAD will now require the pattern to be entered:

Enter pattern (on next line):
A,

The **A** represents the "alignment" field which deals with the way in which lines, arcs and circles join or end, always with a dash. As there is only one alignment definition supported by AutoCAD it can be ignored!

The line pattern is made up of "pen down" and "pen up" segments, each of a certain length. Positive values represent "pen down" whilst negative values represent "pen up". A zero represents a dot.

Twelve dash length specifications can be entered per linetype providing they fit on one 80-character line.

EXAMPLE

A,40,-20,0,-4,0,-4,0,-20

would represent a dash of length of 40 drawing units, followed by a space of 20 drawing units, followed by a dot, followed by a space of 4 drawing units etc.

18.5.2 Linetype Creation using an External Text Editor

Linetypes can be formulated using an external text editor or word processor.

EXAMPLE

The following will create a linetype identical to the example above.

```
*EXAMPLE,--- ... --- ... --- ... --- ... --- ... ---
A,40,-20,0,-4,0,-4,0,-20
```

> *Note:* Do *not* forget the * or the A.

If this Example is now saved as a DOS text file with the file extension .LIN, it will act as a library file in which AutoCAD can be directed to search when looking for the linetype. Any number of other linetype definitions may be contained within the same file

18.6 CUSTOMIZED HATCH PATTERNS

In addition to being able to create very simple patterns for one-time use from within the HATCH command, it is also possible to create your own hatch patterns and store them for future use. You will need an external text editor and a lot of patience.

The new hatch pattern can be stored in AutoCAD's hatch library file ACAD.PAT or in an individual hatch pattern file having a file name which must be the same as the hatch pattern name and which must have the extension .PAT. *It is not possible to compile your own hatch pattern library files.*

The format specified by AutoCAD for writing the file containing the new hatch pattern is:

*pattern name[,description]

where [,description] is optional. It is used to describe in words the pattern to be generated. *Do not forget the comma!*

angle,<space>X-origin,Y-origin,<space>delta-X,delta-Y<space>[,dash-1,dash-2......]

Each pattern consists of one or more sets of parallel lines (no limit) specified by the above format, (see Figure 18.2).

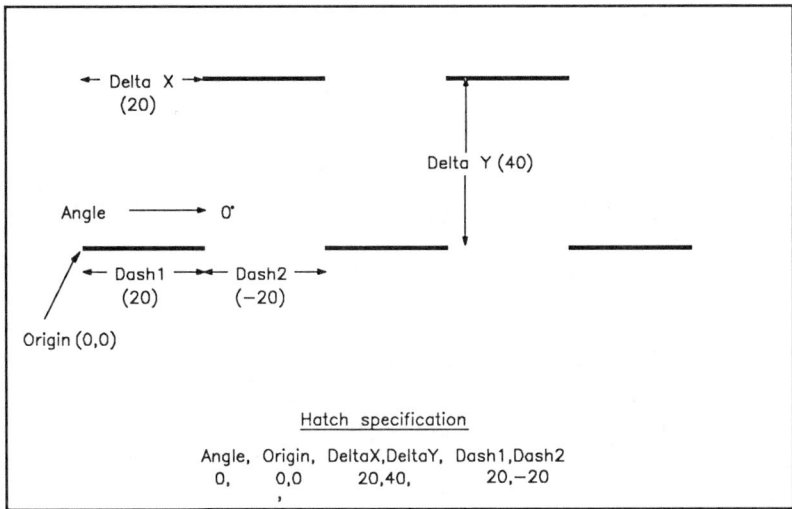

Figure 18.2 HATCH pattern specification

- *Angle:* The angle parameter denotes the angle *and also the vector starting direction* at which the hatch pattern line will be drawn. Angles are measured in a counter-clockwise direction with 3 O'clock = 0°, 12 O'clock = 90°, 9 O'clock = 180°, and 6 O'clock =270°.
- *X-origin:* This is an arbitrary X-origin representing the beginning of a hatch line. All lines then relate to this origin.
- *Y-origin:* This is an arbitrary Y-origin representing the beginning of a hatch line. All lines then relate to this origin.
- *delta-X:* This is the displacement of the line in the X- direction. When AutoCAD hatches a designated area, the specified hatch line will be regenerated a number of times until the area is filled. The delta-X parameter denotes the offset (in drawing units) in the X- direction of the line each time it is generated with respect to the previously drawn line. *The X- direction is always the direction in which the line is drawn.*

- *delta-Y:* This represents the corresponding displacement of the line in the Y-direction, i.e. the spacing between the generated lines, in drawing units.
- *dash-1,dash-2...* These parameters represent the line specification. The same rules apply as for drawing customized lines, i.e. a positive value represents "pen down", a negative value represents a space/"pen up", while a zero represents a dot.

Note: When designing your own hatch lines, it is essential to include all the required spaces and commas.

EXAMPLES

Simple Hatch Pattern Definitions:

1. *LINE1,straight line horizontal hatching
    0, 0,0, 0,20

angle=0, X-origin=0, Y-origin=0, delta-X=0, delta-Y=20

The hatch pattern called LINE1 will be a horizontal straight line pattern with a line spacing of 20 drawing units. As there are no dash parameters AutoCAD will assume a single straight line.

2. *LINE45,straight line at 45° to the horizontal
    45, 0,0, 0,20

angle=45, X-origin=0, Y-origin=0, delta-X=0, delta-Y=20

This will produce an identical pattern to the above but it will be drawn at 45° to the horizontal.

3. *DASHED,horizontal dashed line drawn beneath each other
    0, 0,0, 0,40, 20,-20

angle=0, X-origin=0, Y-origin=0, delta-X=0, delta-Y=40, dash1=20, dash2=-20

This will produce a hatch pattern consisting of dashed lines, each dash being 20 drawing units long separated by 20 drawing units. Each hatch line will be 40 drawing units apart and drawn directly beneath each other.

4.   *DASHED1,horizontal dashed lines offset by 20 drawing units
       0, 0,0, 20,40, 20,-20

angle=0, X-origin=0, Y-origin=0, delta-X=20, delta-Y=40,dash1=20, dash2=-20

This will produce a hatch pattern consisting of dashed lines, each dash being
20 drawing units long separated by 20 drawing units. Each hatch line will be
40 drawing units apart and drawn with an offset of 20 drawing units with
respect to the previous line.

5.   *T,lines of T's drawn with a 20 offset
       0, 0,0, 20,20, 20,-20
       270, 10,0, 20,20, 20,-20

angle=0, X-origin=0, Y-origin=0, delta-X=20, delta-Y=20,dash1=20, dash2=-20

angle=270, X-origin=10, Y-origin=0, delta-X=20, delta-Y=20, dash1=20,
dash2=-20

This is a hatch pattern made up of two lines. Both are dashed lines but the
second is rotated by 270° and has a starting point of 10 drawing units from the
X-origin. Each line of T's is offset by 20 drawing units from the previous line.

These examples are illustrated in Figure 18.3.

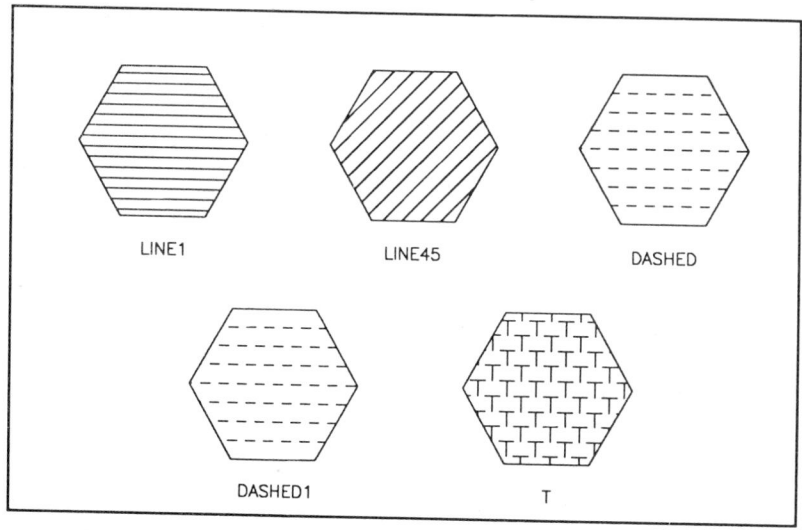

LINE1   LINE45   DASHED

DASHED1   T

Figure 18.3 HATCH examples

18.7 SHAPES

Shapes are special entities made up of lines, circles and arcs which have been defined numerically. They can be inserted into any drawing at any required scale and rotation angle. Shapes are stored in a special shape library file (which has the extension .SHX) which must be loaded into the current drawing file before the desired shapes can be used. Once a shape library file has been loaded, its shapes can be used any number of times. Shapes are superficially similar to blocks. While blocks are more versatile and easier to define, AutoCAD uses shapes more efficiently with considerable savings in memory.

18.7.1 The LOAD Command

Before a shape can be used the file in which it is stored must first be loaded into the current drawing.

> **Command: LOAD**
> **Name of shape file to load (or ?):**

The **?** input gives a list of the *currently loaded shape library files.*

18.7.2 The SHAPE Command

Once the shape definition file has been loaded into the current drawing, shapes from within this file can be positioned in the drawing by using the SHAPE command.

> **Command: SHAPE**
> **Shape name (or ?):**
> **Starting point:**
> **Height <1.00>:**
> **Rotation angle <0.0000>:**

The shape can be dynamically dragged to its starting point and dragged to the required height and rotation angle.
    ? will give a list of the *currently loaded shapes.*

18.7.3 Compiling Shape Files

To compile a shape file it must first be written using a text editor and saved with the extension .SHP. The .SHP file is then compiled using *Task 7* from the AutoCAD main menu. If there are no syntax errors in the text file, the compilation is declared to be successful and the compiled file is given the extension .SHX. It is then ready to be loaded into your drawing using the LOAD command. A shape file may contain many shape definitions, *all* of which become available once the file has been loaded.

18.7.4 Preparing a Shape Text File

Shape files are written using an external text editor. This file acts as a library of shapes (maximum number of shapes 255) which must be loaded into a drawing before the shapes can be used.

The first line of each shape definition *must* follow the following syntax *exactly*:

> *shapenumber,defbytes,shapename

- *shapenumber:*   Each shape definition saved in a shape file is given its own unique number between 1 and 255.
- *defbytes:*   The number of data bytes used in the subsequent shape definition (maximum of 2000). This number has to be supplied *after* the shape definition has been written.
- *shapename:*   The name assigned to the shape. This name must be written *IN UPPER CASE.*

18.7.5 Defining simple straight line shapes

The simplest shapes can be defined by using basic line elements orientated along one of the 16 pre-defined directions - each direction has its own specific code number/letter, (see Figure 18.4).

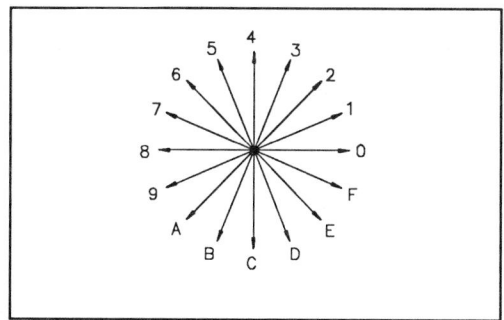

Figure 18.4   The sixteen pre-defined vector directions

Each shape definition byte contains information about vector length and direction. The maximum length of any line is 15 units. For convenience, a diagonal of a unit sided box is considered to be also of unit length (but it will be drawn as its true length of 1.414), e.g. if a vector is defined 014 then it will be one drawing unit long in the vertical (4) direction but if it is defined 016 it will be stretched to 1.414 units long in the (6) direction.

18.7.6 Special Codes for defining complex shapes

Apart from the standard vector definition there are various special codes to assist in the definition of more complex shapes:

000	End of shape definition.
001	Activates draw mode (pen down).
002	De-activates draw mode (pen up).
003	Divide vector lengths by next byte.
004	Multiply vector lengths by next byte.
005	Push (save) current location onto stack.
006	Pop (restore) current location from stack.
007	Draw sub-shape number given by next byte.
008	X-Y displacement given by next two bytes.
009	Multiple X-Y displacements, terminated by (0,0).
00A(10)	Octant arc defined by next two bytes.
00B(11)	Fractional arc defined by next five bytes.
00C(12)	Arc defined by X-Y displacement and bulge.
00D(13)	Multiple bulge-specified arcs, terminated by (0,0).
00E(14)	Process next command only if text style is vertical

- *Code 0 - End of shape:* Marks the end of a shape definition.
- *Codes 1 and 2 - Draw mode:* This corresponds to "Pen Up" and "Pen Down". Draw is On at the start of each shape and therefore any specified vectors will be drawn. If Draw mode is set Off (code 002), then the move to the next specified location is made without drawing. Issuing the code 001 re-activates the draw mode.
- *Codes 3 and 4 - Size control:* These set the relative size of each vector. When the SHAPE command is invoked and the height specified, it is assumed by AutoCAD that this height is the orthogonal vector, i.e. directions 0, 4, 8 or C. The byte following the code 3 or 4 contains the new scale factor - (initial height multiplied by new scale), e.g. 4,5 would multiply the current scale by 5. Scale factors are cumulative and therefore you must be careful to reset the scale when necessary: AutoCAD does not automatically reset the scale for you.
- *Codes 5 and 6 - Location save/restore:* Codes 5 and 6 are used to save and restore the current position within the shape so that it can be returned to at a later stage in the shape definition. Any location saved must later be restored.

The stack is only four deep and if the stack overflows the following message will appear:

Position stack overflow in shape nnn

Similarly if you try to restore more locations than have been saved the following will appear.

Position stack underflow in shape nnn

You must remember that locations are restored from the stack in the reverse order to that in which they were saved - last on, first off.

● *Code 7 - Sub-shape:*   The vector following code 7 specifies the number of another shape which is saved in the *same shape file.* The shape with this number will be incorporated into the current shape.

Note: You should ensure that the draw mode is set ON before this code is issued.

● *Codes 8 and 9 - X-Y displacement:*   The existence of only 16 pre-defined directions can be very limiting. To overcome this, codes 8 and 9 can be used to specify X-Y displacements.

Code 8 is used to specify a single X-Y displacement and must be followed by two bytes in the following format:

8,X-displacement,Y-displacement

X-Y displacements can be in the range -128 to 127.
e.g. 8,(5,8) would result in a vector being drawn 5 units to the right and 8 units up.

+ve up and right, -ve down and left

Note: The brackets are an optional aid to clarity and are not recognised by AutoCAD.

Code 9 is used where a *sequence* of nonstandard vectors is required:

e.g.   9,(5,-6),(3,2),(-4,1),(0,0)

The sequence must be terminated with (0,0)

● *Codes 00A (10) - Octant arc:*   Octants are arcs which span one or more 45° angles, starting and ending on an octant boundary. Octants are numbered counter-clockwise from the 3 o'clock position and are specified as follows:

10,radius,(-)0SC

The radius can be any value between 1 and 255.

S represents the number of the starting octant, 0 to 7.

C represents the number of octants to be drawn, 0 to 7, 0 representing a full circle.

A negative sign represents an octant being drawn in the clockwise direction while a positive sign (or no sign) represents an octant drawn in the counter-clockwise direction.

See Figure 18-5.

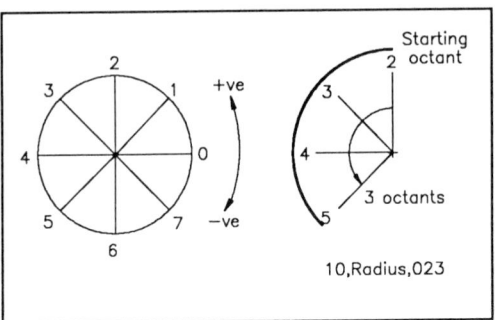

Figure 18.5   Octant arc definition

● *Code 00B (11) - Fractional arc:*   This is used to draw arcs which do not finish on an octant boundary and are defined as follows:

11,start-offset,end-offset,high-radius,low-radius,(-)0SC

The start and end offsets represent the amount that the arc is displaced from the octant boundary. The high radius is zero unless the radius is greater than 255. The low radius is any radius below 255. S and C are the same as for octants.
    To calculate the start-offset, find the difference between the starting octant boundary and the start of the arc, multiply this by 256 and divide the answer by 45. If the arc ends on an octant boundary, then the end-offset will be zero.

● *Codes 00C and 00D (12 and 13) - Bulge-specified arcs:* These codes are similar to codes 8 and 9 but have the added facility of a "bulge" factor which is applied to the displacement vector. Code 00C (12) draws one arc segment while code 00D (13) draws multiple arc segments (which must be ended with 0,0).

The format for code 12 or 00C is:

12,X-displacement,Y-displacement,bulge

The X- and Y- displacements are defined in the same way as for codes 8 and 9, and may be in the range -127 to 127. The bulge is the curvature of the arc and may be in the range -127 to 127. It is calculated by taking the distance D between the two arc ends, the perpendicular height H from the mid point of this line to the arc, dividing H by D and multiplying the answer by 254.

i.e. bulge = (H/D)*254   (see Figure 18-6).

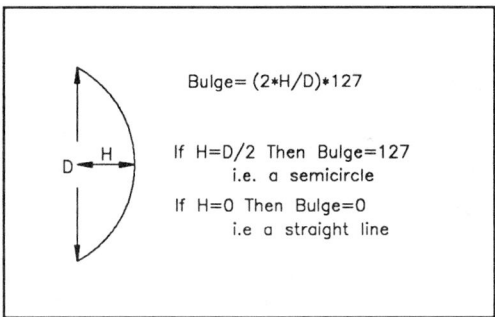

Figure 18.6   Bulge definition

This is negative if the direction of the arc is clockwise.

A bulge of 127 or -127 represents a semicircle, whereas a bulge of zero represents a straight line.

The format for 00D (13) is the same as for 00C (12) but multiple X-, Y- and bulge specifications are defined, terminated with (0,0).

EXAMPLES

Simple Shape Definitions:

1. A triangle could be defined as follows:

    ```
    *165,4,TRIANGLE
    014,01E,018,0
    ```

    The final zero in the shape definition marks the end of the shape. This shape may now be saved within a file with extension .SHP, and compiled into an .SHX file using *Task 7* from the main menu.

2. The following will draw a circle with two diametric lines at right angles to each other (north-south and east-west).

    ```
    *101,11,WOTSIT
    3,5,10,1,000,028,002,012,001,02C,0
    ```

    The constituent parts are:

3	represents "divide vector by next byte"
5	the division factor
10	octant arc defined by next two bytes
1	octant arc radius of 1
000	draw a circle
028	draw a line 2 units long in the 8 direction
002	pen up - deactivate draw mode
012	move 1 unit in the 2 direction
001	pen down - activate draw mode
02C	draw a line 2 units in the C direction
0	end shape definition

3. To draw an arc from 65° to 100° with a 3 unit radius:

    ```
    *28,7,ARC
    11,(114,57,0,3,012),0
    ```

11	Fractional arcs.
114	Start-offset = $((65-45)*256/45)$
57	End-offset = $((100-90)*256/45)$

0	High radius
3	Low radius of 3 units
012	The 1 is the starting octant S, the 2 is the octant count C.
0	end shape definition

4.   To draw a crude letter S:

*58,10,S
13,(0,5,127),(0,5,-127),(0,0),0

13	multiple bulge specification
0,5,127	semicircle with a displacement of 0 in the X-direction and 5 in the Y- direction, drawn counter-clockwise.
0,5,-127	semicircle with a displacement of 0 in the X-direction and 5 in the Y- direction, drawn clockwise.
0	end shape definition

These examples are illustrated in Figure 18.7.

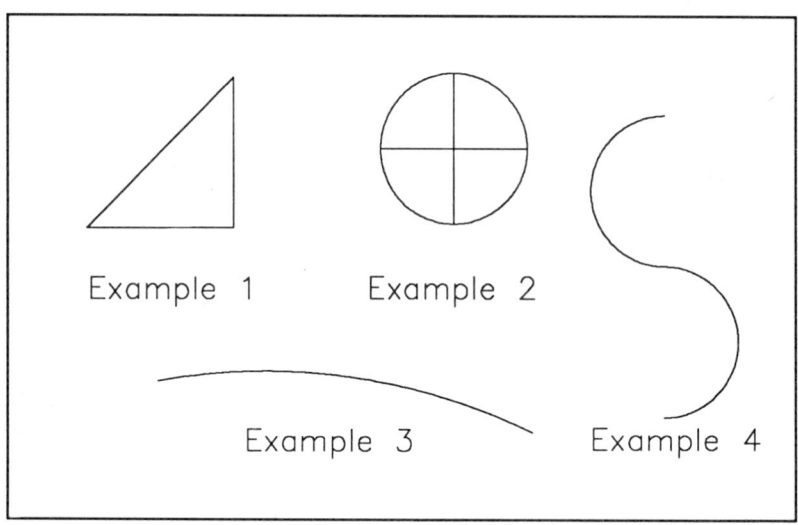

Figure 18.7   SHAPE examples

18.7.7 Using Shapes in Font Files

Text font files are used when text is to be added to a drawing. The text style used incorporates one of the font files, e.g. Simplex or Italic. These files are prepared in essentially the same way as are shape files.

Two fragments of the Simplex font file are shown below:

```
*0,4,Roman Simplex 1/20/86
21,7,2,0
*10,9,lf
2,8,(0,-36),14,8,(30,36),0
*32,9,spc
2,8,(19,0),14,8,(-19,-30),0
*33,38,kexc
2,14,8,(-1,-21),8,(1,21),1,02B,9,(1,-12),(1,12),(0,0),025,2,
02C,1,06C,2,0BC,1,01A,01E,012,016,2,8,(12,-2),14,8,(-12,-10),0
:
:
*65,27,uca
2,14,8,(-8,-21),1,8,(8,21),8,(8,-21),2,8,(-13,7),1,0A0,2,8,
(9,-7),14,8,(-14,-10),0
*66,46,ucb
2,14,8,(-7,-21),1,8,(0,21),090,8,(3,-1),01E,02D,02C,02B,01A,
8,(-3,-1),2,098,1,090,8,(3,-1),01E,02D,03C,02B,01A,8,(-3,-1),
098,2,8,(21,0),14,8,(-14,-10),0
```

This becomes a bit more comprehensible when you remember that

- lf stands for line feed and has an ASCII value of 10
- spc stands for space and has an ASCII value of 32
- uca stands for upper case A and has an ASCII value of 65 etc.

A font file must carry the special header:

```
*0,4,font name
above,below,mode,0
```

Where "above" and "below" refer respectively to the number of vector lengths that the upper case letters extend above the base line and to the number of vector lengths that the lower case letters extend below the base line. These effectively scale the font characters. Mode may be set to 0 for a horizontally oriented font or 2 for a dual orientation (horizontal or vertical font). The special command code 00E (14) is obeyed only when mode is set to 2.

The font characters are referenced by AutoCAD through their shape number only, *never by name*. The name should therefore always be written in *lower case* - this makes it visible to the reader but it is not recognised by AutoCAD. The shape number used for a text font character must always be the ASCII code (American Standard Code for Information Interchange) for that character. Within these restrictions, the font character is then defined exactly as any other shape.

It is possible to use standard shape definition techniques to add non-standard characters and symbols to an existing font. You must assign them code numbers between 130 and 255 to avoid interference with the standard characters.

To use these extra characters within a TEXT or DTEXT command you must include the string

%%nnn

within the text, where nnn represents the three digits of the code number which you have assigned to the character. (See Section 9.3.)

19. Slides and presentations

19.1 PREPARING AND VIEWING SLIDES

The SLIDE command in effect takes a snapshot of the drawing as it appears on the screen and saves this for future viewing. The slide is not a drawing and can only be viewed; it can not be modified in any way nor can it be plotted or printed.

When creating a slide in Model Space, the slide will depict the drawing as displayed *in the current active viewport* but when creating a slide in Paper Space *the complete screen display, together with all the viewports,* is included in the slide.

A slide is created with the MSLIDE (MakeSLIDE) command when the required display is already on the screen.

Command: MSLIDE

The file dialogue box, (see Section 2.7.3), will automatically appear if FILEDIA is switched On. This will allow you to specify the filename (and directory) under which the slide will be saved. The filename may be chosen from the list of existing files - *Caution: this will overwrite the chosen file* - or it may be typed in from the keyboard by selecting the **Type it** box.

The current drawing name comes up as the default and may be selected by choosing the **OK** box. The slide will be saved on the specified directory with an .SLD extension.

Slides can be viewed at any time while in the drawing editor by using the VSLIDE command. It does not matter if you already have a drawing on screen, the slide will replace it *temporarily* and the drawing will be restored when the slide is cancelled with a REDRAW.

Command: VSLIDE

The file dialogue box will again appear and will allow you to select the filename (and directory) of the required slide.

> *Note:* When operating in Model Space, a slide will be displayed in the current active viewport *only*; whereas, when operating in Paper Space, a slide will occupy the *entire screen*.

19.1.1 Slide Libraries

Slides may conveniently be collected together into slide libraries. A slide library is created using AutoCAD's SLIDELIB.EXE utility program from DOS. The best way to use this program is first to use a word processor or text editor to prepare a simple DOS or ASCII file, with a TXT extension, containing a list of the slides you wish to include, (see Section 18.1). This list should consist of *one slide name per line*. The SLIDELIB program then calls upon this slide file list when compiling the library.

EXAMPLE

To compile a library called MYLIB containing 3 slides, a slide file list called, say, MYSLIDES.TXT is first prepared and would look like :

```
SLIDE1    you do not need the .SLD file extension
SLIDE2
SLIDE3
```

The SLIDELIB program is then called from DOS :

```
C> SLIDELIB MYLIB <MYSLIDES.TXT
```

It is important not to forget the re-direction character < before the slide file list name, otherwise SLIDELIB thinks that you have supplied two library names, and wil "crash".

> *Note:* The slide library so formed carries an .SLB extension. It is not a text file and may not be inspected or altered. If you wish to make any changes, you *must* alter the slide file list, before re-compiling the library using SLIDELIB.

To view a particular slide (say slide1) from a slide library, the library name is specified (without the .SLB extension), and the slide name is included in round brackets :

Command: VSLIDE

The file dialogue box will appear. Select the **Type it** box:

Slide file <default>: MYLIB(SLIDE1)

> *Note:*   You will *not* be allowed to enter this response from within the
> file dialogue box.

19.2 SCRIPT FILES

A script file acts rather as a batch file in DOS or as a Macro in Lotus 1-2-3, in that
any number of AutoCAD commands can be written into the file and are then executed
sequentially when the file is used. Script files may be used for performing repetitive
tasks such as setting up units, automatically setting up the plotter menu for different
paper sizes etc. A delay between operations may be introduced by incorporating a
DELAY command and specifying the delay in milliseconds.

19.2.1 Slide Presentations using SCRIPT Files

Script files are particularly effective when used with a series of slides to present an
automated slide show.
   A typical script file, called SLDSHOW1.SCR (written on a text editor), to display
a sequence of 3 slides could be as follows:

```
VSLIDE SLIDE1
DELAY 2000
VSLIDE SLIDE2
DELAY 2000
VSLIDE SLIDE3
DELAY 2000
```

To run this script file:

Command: SCRIPT

Use the file dialogue box to enter the required script file (SLDSHOW1).
   This script file will show each slide for a period of 2 seconds. When the script file
is running, each DELAY 2000 instruction gives a delay of 2000 milliseconds or 2
seconds. The last slide will remain on the screen until a REDRAW command is given.
   The sequence of commands in the file may be repeated indefinitely if the script file
is terminated with RSCRIPT. The process may be interrupted by a Ctrl C or a Ctrl H

and started again with the command RESUME.

There may also be an unwanted delay between slides as the new slide is loaded from the disk prior to display. This can be eliminated by loading the next slide while the present slide is being viewed. When the next VSLIDE command is encountered, the previously loaded slide is displayed. Pre-loading is achieved by adding a * to the slide name.

These modifications are shown in SLDSHOW2.SCR:

```
VSLIDE SLIDE1
VSLIDE *SLIDE2
DELAY 2000
VSLIDE
VSLIDE *SLIDE3
DELAY 2000
VSLIDE
DELAY 2000
RSCRIPT
```

Script files can even be used from DOS to run AutoCAD and select *Tasks* from the main menu. The following script file, called AUTOSHOW.SCR, selects main menu *Task 2* and then loads a particular drawing called MYDRAWNG. It then calls two slides with a display time of 5 seconds, redraws MYDRAWNG, quits the drawing editor, and finally exits AutoCAD with a main menu *Task 0*.

```
2
MYDRAWNG
VSLIDE SLIDE1
DELAY 5000
VSLIDE SLIDE2
DELAY 5000
REDRAW
QUIT Y
0
```

To run AUTOSHOW from DOS requires the command:

C> ACAD X AUTOSHOW

The X is a dummy default drawing name which is replaced by MYDRAWNG as soon as AUTOSHOW is run.

The above command assumes that you are already in the AutoCAD directory. The ultimate in showing off can be achieved by incorporating the command into a batch file called SHOWOFF.BAT, (see Appendix 1), which can be run from the root directory. It changes directory to the AutoCAD directory (ACAD), starts up AutoCAD, runs AUTOSHOW and finally returns you to the root.

The contents of SHOWOFF.BAT would be:

```
C:
CD\ACAD
ACAD X AUTOSHOW
CD\
```

The entire sequence of events can be initiated by typing the single command:

C> SHOWOFF

Go on! Show off!

19.2.2 Presentations Combining Slides and other AutoCAD Commands.

A particularly effective use of script files is to combine drawing, editing and display commands to produce a completed drawing on screen.

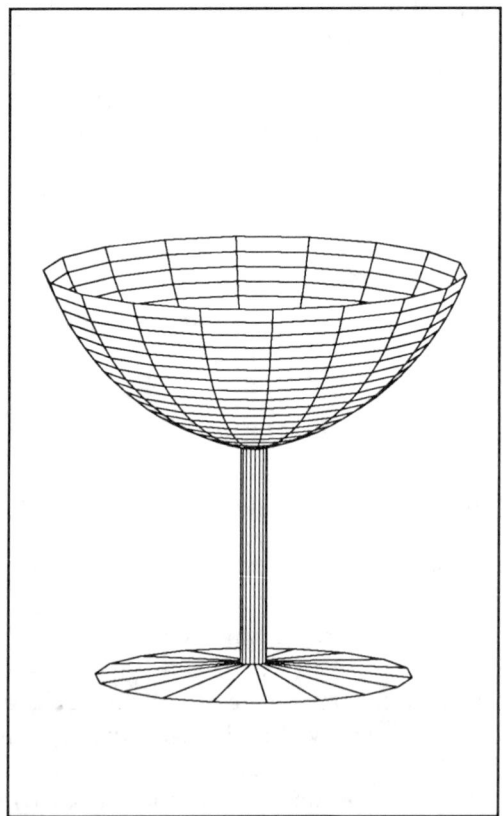

Figure 19.1 Automatic generation of a drawing using a SCRIPT file

EXAMPLE

The following simple script file, called WINE.SCR, will draw the wine glass shown in Figure 19.1, by rotating a polyline path curve about an axis of revolution. The glass is then viewed from an appropriate viewpoint after changing the UCS. If interspersed with suitable explanatory slides and viewing delays, this can form the basis of a useful tutorial or demonstration.

```
PLINE
100,100              Draw in the path curve
@60,0                       "
@-55,5                      "
@0,80                       "
A                    Set to arc mode
S                    Request second point
140,200              Draw in the path curve
180,250                     "
                     Return to terminate the path curve

PLINE
100,100              Draw in the axis of revolution
@0,200                      "
                     Return to terminate the axis of revolution

REVSURF
180,250              Point to path curve
100,300              Point to axis of revolution
                     Return to accept default start angle of 0°
                     Return to accept full circle included angle

ERASE
100,300              Point to axis of resolution
                     Return to terminate ERASE

UCS
O                    Request new UCS Origin
100,100,0            Move origin to base of glass
UCS
X                    Request new UCS by rotation about X axis
-90                  Rotate 90°
PLAN
                     Return to request Plan view of new UCS

VPOINT
0.70,-0.70,0.17      Set new view point
HIDE                 Apply HIDE to final view
```

20. Creating screen and tablet menus

Although AutoCAD may be driven exclusively from the keyboard the majority of users will be familiar with and will employ the screen, pull down and tablet menus. All these menus are set up within the package from a single menu file called ACAD.MNU. This is written as a DOS text file and can be examined and modified using a word processor. The file used by the drawing editor is ACAD.MNX, which is a compiled version of ACAD.MNU. If ACAD.MNX is not available, or if the corresponding .MNU file is newer, the package will automatically compile ACAD.MNU and store the result as ACAD.MNX for future use.

When a new drawing is started, it depends for its parameters on the values specified in the prototype drawing. It will also use *the menu specified by the prototype drawing*, which is usually the standard menu ACAD.MNX. Because of this, all drawings will normally be produced and saved with the standard menu.

However, it is possible to write alternative menu files for specific applications and these can be used with and attached to any drawing.

Note: Whatever menu is associated with a drawing when it is saved will remain with the drawing when it is subsequently retrieved.

In order to be able to write specific menu files it is helpful to understand the structure of the ACAD.MNU file.

Note: Although it is instructive to modify the ACAD.MNU file to observe the effect, you are strongly advised to retain an unmodified version in case of accidents!

20.1 STRUCTURE OF THE STANDARD MENU

The standard menu file can actually contain twenty two menus - one for the screen, four for the four separate tablet areas of the digitiser, four alternative menus for the same areas, one for the buttons on the mouse, one for the buttons of an auxiliary function box, up to ten pull down menus and one icon menu.

Looking at the beginning of the file with a text editor you will see a copyright comment followed by:

```
***BUTTONS
;
$P1=*
^C^C
^B
^O
^G
^D
^E
^T
***AUX1
;
$P1=*
^C^C
^B
^O
^G
^D
^E
^T

***POP1
[Assist]
[Help!    ]'?
[~--]
[Cancel   ]^C^C
[~--]
[Osnap: <mode>]^C^C$P1= $P1=* OSNAP \
[CENter]CEN
[ENDpoint ]ENDp
INSert
[INTersection]INT
MIDpoint
NEArest
NODe
[PERpendicular]PER
QUAdrant
[Quick,<mode> ]QUICK,^Z$P1=*
TANgent
NONE
[---]
[(REF) point  ]^P$S=X(if (not c:ref)+
(defun ref () (initget 1)(setvar "LASTPOINT" (getpoint "Reference
pt:"));+
(prompt (chr 10))(initget 1)+
```

```
(getpoint "Enter relative/polar coordinates (with @): "))(ref);^P
[---]
[FILTERS    >]$p1=filters $p1=*

**filters
[Filters]
.X
.Y
.Z
.XY
.XZ
.YZ
[---]
[ASSIST >]$p1= $p1=*
```

etc., etc.

Further down the same menu you will find the screen menu section:

```
***SCREEN
**S
[AutoCAD]^C^C^P$S=X $S=S (setq T_MENU 0)(princ) ^P$P1=POP1
$P2=P2DRAW $P4=P4DISP $P6=P6OPT $P8=POP8
[* * * *]$S=OSNAPB
[BLOCKS]$S=X $S=BL
[DIM:]$S=X $S=DIM ^C^CDIM
[DISPLAY]$S=X $S=DS
[DRAW]$S=X $S=DR
[EDIT]$S=X $S=ED
[INQUIRY]$S=X $S=INQ
[LAYER:]$S=X $S=LAYER ^C^CLAYER
[MVIEW]$S=X $S=MV
[PLOT]$S=X $S=PLOT
[SETTINGS]$S=X $S=SET
[SOLIDS]^C^C^P(progn(setq m:err *error*)(princ))+
(defun *error* (msg)(princ msg)(setq *error* m:err m:err nil f
nil)(princ))+
(if (null c:solbox)(progn (menucmd "S=X")(menucmd "S=SOLLOAD"))+
(progn (menucmd "S=X")(menucmd "S=SOLIDS")))(princ);^P
[SURFACES]$S=X $S=3D
[UCS:]$S=X $S=UCS1 ^C^CUCS
[UTILITY]$S=X $S=UT
```

This is at first sight pretty incomprehensible - and it is over 115 pages long! (This is where a good word processor is essential.) However, it is possible to split it up into more digestible portions.

The 22 menus are each identified by ***. Thus, on line 1, ***BUTTONS marks the start of the menu which defines the functions of the buttons on the mouse. Similarly, on line 11, ***AUX1 denotes the auxiliary function box button menu and on line 22 is the first pull down menu ***POP1. The screen menu starts on page 29 with ***SCREEN and the first of the four tablet menus is much further down, on page 83.

20.2 WRITING SIMPLE SCREEN MENUS

A menu item may consist of a command, a parameter or a sequence of commands and parameters. Normally, each menu item resides on one line of the menu file.

EXAMPLE

Suppose we require a simple screen menu for drawing lines and circles:

```
***SCREEN
LINE
CIRCLE
[BYE]quit
```

You can use either capitals or lower case letters for menu items but you may find it helpful to reserve capitals for titles and screen display items, leaving lower case letters for commands.

The first line, which identifies the screen menu, is not strictly necessary here because, in the absence of a *** label, AutoCAD assumes that the first menu item of the file is the Screen menu.

The above menu is easy to understand. The words LINE and CIRCLE will appear in the screen menu position (on the right of the screen) and when picked will result in the execution of the simple LINE and CIRCLE commands. [BYE]quit shows how to put a label on the screen (identified by square brackets - maximum label length 8 characters) which, when picked, will cause the execution of the corresponding command specified in the menu - in this case, QUIT.

> *Note:* The label must not itself be a valid AutoCAD command.

The file can now be saved (in DOS text format) with any legal name of your choice but it must carry the .MNU extension, e.g. MYMENU.MNU. The new menu file may be kept either in the same directory as ACAD.MNU or in the current working directory. Start up AutoCAD and commence a new drawing. Once in the drawing editor, the standard menu will appear on the screen as specifies by the prototype drawing. You can now load the new menu:

Command: MENU
Menu file name or . for none: <default> MYMENU

The new menu will now replace the standard menu.

> *Note:* A . response will replace the old menu with no menu at all.

20.2.1 Sub-Menus

The AutoCAD standard menu frequently employs sub-menus. In such cases, on picking a screen menu item, the original menu is replaced by a totally separate sub-menu.

A sub-menu is identified by ** followed by a name not exceeding thirty-one characters in length.

EXAMPLE

```
***SCREEN
LINE
[DRAWCIRC]$S=MYCIRCLES
[BYE]quit
**MYCIRCLES
[CIRCLE10]circle \10;
[CIRCLE20]circle \20;
[CIRCLE30]circle \30;

[MAINMENU]$s=SCREEN
```

With this menu in operation the screen menu display looks similar to the previous one. However, if you pick DRAWCIRC the menu is replaced by the sub-menu called MYCIRCLES. The sub-menu is specified by the $S= menu command immediately following the [DRAWCIRC] label. S here refers to the Screen menu so that $S=MYCIRCLES has the effect of making the sub-menu MYCIRCLES replace the current menu on the screen.

This sub-menu provides circles with pre-determined radii of 10, 20 or 30 drawing units without the need to supply these parameters from the keyboard. Supplying pre-determined parameters to commands is one of the strengths of a well designed menu.

20.2.2 Inputs within Menu Items

The back slash \ after the circle command in the above MYCIRCLES sub-menu is prompting for an input from the pointer or the keyboard; in this case it is prompting for the centre point of the circle. When this has been received, the command proceeds with the radius parameter provided by the menu.

The final semicolons are important; they act as the returns which are needed to execute the commands. In some menu lines you can make the command work without the semicolon because the fact that AutoCAD has reached the end of the menu line is sufficient to execute the command, but this is not a reliable technique. Get into the habit of *always* using a semicolon where a return would be the normal response if you were executing the same command from the keyboard. Try writing the menu line:

[LINES]line 100,50;150,20;200,30;;

and observe the effect of missing out the various semicolons.

When writing such menu items, you must make yourself completely familiar with the sequence in which the command expects its parameters!

> *Note:* This sequence, including any returns, must be reproduced exactly in the corresponding line of the menu otherwise AutoCAD will not respond as you might expect.

Conversely, if you are trying to disentangle an existing menu item which contains many semicolons and control characters, run through the same command manually within AutoCAD and take careful note of all the spaces, returns and other responses that you use.

20.2.3 Returning from the Sub-Menu

There remains the problem of returning from the sub-menu to the main menu. This is achieved in the last line of the sub-menu example. Just as the sub-menu was entered with $S=MYCIRCLES, so $S=SCREEN always returns you to the start of the screen menu. In this command the $ sign signifies that the menu is to be changed and the S refers to the screen menu. Similarly:

B	Refers to the button menu.
T	Refers to the tablet menus.
A	Refers to the auxiliary box menu.
P	Refers to the pull down menus.
I	Refers to the icon menu.

Menus can be "nested" one inside the other up to a maximum of 8. Thus a sub-menu can lead to a further sub-menu etc. When exiting a nested sub-menu, $S= will always return you to the previous menu. In the example, the previous menu is the main screen menu but this would not necessarily be the case if further nesting levels had been used.

20.2.4 Menu Blanks

When one menu is replaced by another, the new menu is simply written on top of the old - the old is not erased first. This would cause no problems if all menus were of the same length but a short menu written over a long one will leave the last few lines of the original menu still visible. You will find that MYMENU suffers from this problem

- the label MAINMENU refuses to disappear after you have left the MYCIRCLES sub-menu.

The problem may be overcome by adding blank lines to "pad out" a short menu to the full length. Alternatively, a special blanking menu consisting almost entirely of blank lines may be called up and then succeeded by the desired short menu. This approach is used in ACAD.MNU, where the blanking menu (on page 31 of the menu) is called **X.

Do not be tempted to make your menus too long. A sub-menu may theoretically be of any length, but any items which will not fit on the screen will be completely inaccessible - use further sub-menus instead.

If a sub-menu title is accompanied by a number:

**MYCIRCLES 2

then the sub-menu, when activated, will start at the position of Item 2 of the previous menu rather than at the top. This allows part of an old menu to be retained and used.

20.2.5 Control Characters

Control characters can be included in menus by the use of the ^ symbol. Thus Ctrl C (cancel), Ctrl B (snap toggle), Ctrl O (ortho toggle) may be represented as ^C, ^B, ^O etc. Examples of this may be seen in the Button menu of ACAD.MNU.

20.2.6 Long Menu Items

If a menu item is very complicated, it may not be possible to fit it on to one line of the menu. If it were allowed to wrap over on to the following line AutoCAD would try to interpret it as two separate menu items; probably with undesired results. To overcome this a long line should be broken and terminated with a + sign. The following line will then be considered as a continuation. This may be used to include as many lines as necessary. In practice, multi-line items are likely to be needed only if you are using AutoLISP to perform complex menu tasks.

20.3 PULL DOWN MENUS

The pull down menus may be written in a manner similar to that of the screen menu. Up to 10 pull down menus can be accommodated under the headings ***POP1 to ***POP10. If a POP section is absent from the menu, it will simply be omitted from the menu bar at the top of the screen.

The first item in square brackets on the pull down menu will be treated as the title and will appear on the menu bar. If this title is picked, the remaining items will be displayed in pull down form.

The title may be up to 14 characters long but, since most screen displays are only 80 characters wide and since up to 10 pull down menus may be used, it is usually advisable to restrict titles to 8 characters.

EXAMPLE

We can incorporate the MYCIRCLES routine from the screen menu onto a pull down menu by "stealing" the instructions from the MYCIRCLES screen subroutine and including them in a POP section:

```
***POP1
[DRAWCIRC]
[CIRCLE10]circle \10;
[CIRCLE20]circle \20;
[CIRCLE30]circle \30;


***SCREEN
LINE
[CIRCLES]$S=MYCIRCLES
[BYE]QUIT


**MYCIRCLES
[CIRCLE10]circle \10;
[CIRCLE20]circle \20;
[CIRCLE30]circle \30;

[MAINMENU]$s=SCREEN
```

20.3.1 Pull Down Sub-menus

Sub-menus can be added to pull downs and are handled very much as screen sub-menus. It is possible for an item on one pull down sub-menu to be used to call another pull down sub-menu. This *menu swapping* is controlled by the $P command.

EXAMPLE

Suppose a pull down menu, say ***POP2, consisted of three sub-menus called P2A, P2B and P2C.

```
***POP2
**P2A
[DRAW]
[BIGCIRCLE]$P2=P2B $P2=*
[ELLIPSES]$P2=P2C $P2=*


**P2B
[BIGCIRCLE]
[CIRCLE50]circle \50;
[CIRCLE60]circle \60;
[CIRCLE70]circle \70;
[EXIT]$P2=P2A
**P2C
[ELLIPSES]
[ELLIP10]ellipse \\10;
[ELLIP20]ellipse \\20;
[ELLIP30]ellipse \\30;
[EXIT]$P2=P2A
```

In this case, P2A, being the first sub-menu encountered, behaves as the main menu of POP2 and is pulled down when POP2 is called from the menu bar. DRAW, being the first item on the menu becomes the menu bar title of POP2. On selecting DRAW the items BIGCIRCLE and ELLIPSES are displayed.

If BIGCIRCLE is picked, then the menu commands $P2=P2B and $P2=* are executed.

$P2=P2B makes sub-menu P2B the main menu of POP2, and its first item, BIGCIRCLE, becomes the menu bar title.

$P2=* is a separate command which forces a pull down of this current POP2 menu without the need to pick the menu bar title. CIRCLE50, CIRCLE60, CIRCLE70 and EXIT are thus displayed.

If any of the CIRCLE items is picked, its commands are executed as normal and the pull down menu subsequently disappears - but P2B remains in effect as the main menu so that the POP2 menu bar title remains as BIGCIRCLE.

If EXIT is picked, the command $P2=P2A resets P2A as the main menu of POP2 and the menu bar title returns to DRAW.

A similar sequence of operations pertains to the ellipse sub-menu, P2C.

> *Note:* The EXIT items do not include the $P2=* command so that the POP2 menu is not pulled down until it is next picked from the menu bar.

20.4 ICON MENUS

A powerful feature of AutoCAD is the use made of icon menus. A number of small pictorially descriptive icons may be displayed on the screen and selection is made by picking the small box by the side of each icon. When an icon is picked, the corresponding command in the icon menu is executed and the icon display is removed.

Icons are composed of slides which have previously been prepared from AutoCAD drawings and stored in an accessible directory. The slides may be individuals or may be stored in a single slide library - the latter approach is neater and quicker in operation, (see Section 19.1.1).

EXAMPLE

A typical Icon menu for inclusion in MYMENU would be as follows:

```
***ICON
**MYSLIDES
[These are my slides]
[Mylib(Fig1)]
[Mylib(Fig2)]
[Fig3]
[ HIS SLIDES]$I=HISSLIDES $I=*
[ EXIT]^C^C

**HISSLIDES
[These are his slides]
[Hislib(Fig5)]
[Hislib(Fig6)]
[Fig7]
[ MY SLIDES]$I=MYSLIDES $I=*
[ EXIT]^C^C$I=MYSLIDES
```

This menu contains two sub-menus to permit the display of two sets of slides - MYSLIDES and HISSLIDES. The mechanism for displaying the Icon menus closely follows that of the pull down menus. Thus, MYSLIDES, being the first sub-menu, is the one normally displayed when picked. The first text item (in this case, **These are my slides**) forms the title and is printed at the top of the icon display.

Subsequent items are the names of the slides which form the individual icons. In the case of MYSLIDES there are three icons (Fig1, Fig2 and Fig3). The first two are contained in a slide file library called MYLIB. The third is a separate slide which is not in a library. Both the library and the free slide should be resident in the current directory.

The icons are automatically displayed on the screen at a position and magnification commensurate with the number of icons in the menu. The maximum is 16 icons, which are displayed in 4 columns of 4 rows.

The final items in the sub-menu are the words HIS SLIDES and EXIT. Text items like this may be displayed instead of icons if the first character of the text is a space. EXIT simply cancels all actions and removes the icon menu from the screen. HIS SLIDES, when picked, performs a menu swap to the HISSLIDES sub-menu followed by a forced display ($I=*) of that icon menu.

> *Note:* Both these sub-menus are incomplete because, with the exception of EXIT and HIS SLIDES, there is no command issued when an item is picked.

To call up this Icon menu a call line must appear in a pull down, a screen or a tablet menu. A typical pull down entry would be:

```
***POP3
[SLIDES]
[MY SLIDES]$I=MYSLIDES $I=*
[HIS SLIDES]$I=HISSLIDES $I=*
```

This allows direct access to either the MYSLIDES or HISSLIDES sub-menus. The $I= command sets the current menu and $I=* forces its display.

20.5 TABLET MENUS

When using the standard menu, ACAD.MNU, you are in a position to make use of the tablet template (assuming that you are using a digitiser and not a mouse). However, you may not be aware of this, particularly if the digitiser is acting as a simple pointing device with the whole tablet area being used to point to different positions on the screen.

A tablet template, (see Chapter 1), is supplied with AutoCAD for use with the standard tablet menu contained within ACAD.MNU.

To activate the tablet menu you must first configure the working areas of your digitiser.

Attach the template firmly to the digitiser tablet so that it will not slide around. It is sensible to position it to be as central and as square as possible, although AutoCAD will compensate for any slight misalignment.

Then invoke the configuration routine from the keyboard:

```
Command: TABLET
Option (ON/OFF/CAL/CFG): CFG
Enter number of tablet menus desired (0-4): 4
Do you want to re-align tablet menu areas? <N>: Y
```

Digitise upper left corner of menu area 1:   Point to indicated spot
Digitise lower left corner of menu area 1:   Point to indicated spot
Digitise lower right corner of menu area 1:   Point to indicated spot

This task is made easy when using the standard template because the requested corner points are clearly marked with small black circles, (see Figure 20.1).

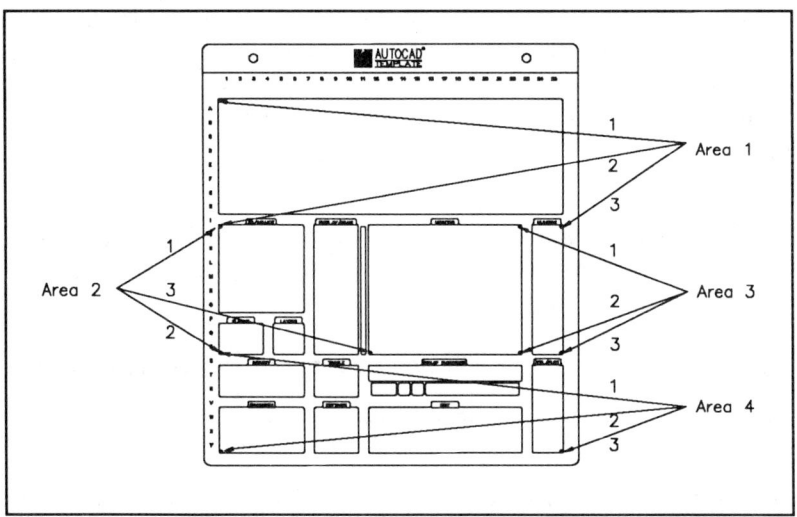

Figure 20.1   The four standard tablet menu areas

Enter the number of columns for menu area 1: 25
Enter the number of rows for menu area 1: 9

This ritual is repeated for the other three menu areas. To use the standard template you *must* respond to the questions about rows and columns as follows:

Menu Area	Columns	Rows
1	25	9
2	11	9
3	9	13
4	25	7

Finally, the configuration routine asks you to specify the screen pointing area.

Do you want to respecify the screen pointing area? <N>: Y
Digitise lower left corner of screen pointing area: point to spot
Digitise upper right corner of screen pointing area: point to spot

This is the end of the tablet configuration process.

This elaborate ritual may be shortened considerably if you enter configuration through the screen menu. Select the screen menu item **SETTINGS** followed by TABLET and finally config. The questions about rows and columns will then be answered for you. You will, however, still need to pick the corners of the menu areas on the tablet as before. For subsequent tablet configuration select re-cfg from the same screen menu.

> *Note:*   If your pointing device is a mouse, or it is not a recognised digitiser tablet, the following error message will appear in response to the TABLET command:
>
> **Your pointing device cannot be used as a tablet.**

The tablet has now been divided up into invisible "boxes". The first 225 boxes are in tablet menu area 1, menu area 2 contains a block of 99 boxes, menu area 3 has 117, menu area 4 has 175 and the remainder of the tablet is allocated to the screen pointing area. The size of each box is determined by the physical size of each menu area divided by the number of rows and columns. The above procedure results in standard sized boxes for menus 1, 2 and 4 but smaller boxes for menu area 3.

At the end of the procedure you will find that the tablet is active but that the screen pointing area has been reduced from the whole tablet to a small area identified by the heading **MONITOR** (on the template). If you now point to one of the marked areas on the template, and press the pick button the corresponding command will be issued.

20.5.1 Alternative Tablet Menus

AutoCAD provides an alternative set of tablet menus which can be *swapped* for each of the standard menus in areas 1,2,3 and 4. This may be achieved by selecting the relevant tablet swap icon(s) found on the template immediately below the screen pointing area. Each menu area has its own icon, identified by the dark shaded area. Any combination of menu areas may be swapped. You may toggle between the alternative and standard menus by repeated selection of the icon. The menu areas which are currently not in the standard mode are indicated by the stars at the top of the screen menu (under the word AutoCAD). Thus, if menu area 1 is not in the standard mode then the first star is replaced by a figure 1. If menu area 3 is non standard, then the third star is replaced by a 3 etc. If you wish to return all four menus to standard mode in a single action then pick the word AutoCAD at the top of the screen menu.

> *Note:* If you are in the habit of selecting the word AutoCAD to cancel a current command, or to return you to the root screen menu, then you must remember that this will in addition return all the tablet menus to standard mode.

Of the four alternative menus supplied, menus 2 and 4 are identical to the standard menus 2 and 4. Menu area 1 in standard mode includes the commands necessary for AME and AUTOSHADE. The alternative menu area 1 is completely blank. Menu area 3 provides for either imperial (fractions) or metric (decimal) numerical inputs.

20.5.2 Writing Alternative Tablet Menus

The areas of menu 1 which are blank on the template will not respond with any commands. If you examine the corresponding tablet section, (e.g. ***TABLET1ALT) of ACAD.MNU you will see:

```
***TABLET1ALT
[A-1]
[A-2]
[A-3]
[A-4]
.
.
.
[A-24]
[A-25]
[B-1]
[B-2]
[B-3]
[B-4]
.
.
.
[I-24]
[I-25]
```

These items correspond to the 225 "boxes" of menu area 1. If you are using the standard tablet menu 1, then boxes [A-1] to [A-10], [B-1] to [B-10] .... [I-1] to [I-10] are occupied by the AME and AUTOSHADE commands.

 If you wish to use one of the empty boxes, then after the item in square brackets (which is a label and has no function) add the relevant command using the same syntax as discussed for the screen and pull down menus. Similarly, you can utilise the alternative menus 2 and 4 by deleting the existing commands (which are duplicates of the commands on the corresponding standard menus) and adding your own.

EXAMPLE

Suppose that, using the techniques described in Chapter 18, you have designed 8 shapes which you have called SH1 - SH8 and located in a shape file called MYSHAPES. These may be allocated to 8 boxes in tablet area 1 by modifying the ***TABLET1ALT section of ACAD.MNU:

```
***TABLET1ALT
[A-1]load MYSHAPES;shape SH1 \1 0
[A-2]load MYSHAPES;shape SH2 \1 0
[A-3]load MYSHAPES;shape SH3 \5 0
[A-4]load MYSHAPES;shape SH4 \1 0
[A-5]load MYSHAPES;shape SH5 \1 0
[A-6]load MYSHAPES;shape SH6 \1 45
[A-7]load MYSHAPES;shape SH7 \1 0
[A-8]load MYSHAPES;shape SH8 \1 0
[A-9]
[A-10]
 .
 .
```

Note that in this example shape SH3 will be inserted at a magnification of 5 and shape SH6 will be inserted at a rotation of 45°. All other shapes will take up the size and orientation specified in their design.

As an alternative to including the command to load the shape file in every box, it is possible to allocate this command to a separate box of its own. This box *must* be picked before any of the shapes contained within the file may be used.

```
***TABLET1ALT
[A-1]load MYSHAPES
[A-2]shape SH1 \1 0
[A-3]shape SH2 \1 0
[A-4]shape SH3 \5 0
[A-5]shape SH4 \1 0
[A-6]shape SH5 \1 0
[A-7]shape SH6 \1 45
[A-8]shape SH7 \1 0
[A-9]shape SH8 \1 0
[A-10]
 .
 .
```

If you always use the standard AutoCAD template, you are restricted to the four menu areas and to the specified number of boxes in each area. If you wish to write your own tablet menus, then of course you are free to define the menu areas to suit your own requirements.

To return the tablet to a simple pointing device you should call TABLET from the keyboard, specify the number of menus to be zero and then redefine *the whole tablet* as the screen pointing area:

Command: TABLET
Option (ON/OFF/CAL/CFG): CFG
Enter number of tablet menus desired (0-4): 0
Do you want to respecify the screen pointing area? <N>: Y
Digitise lower left corner of screen pointing area:

Point to lower left corner of the whole tablet

Digitise upper right corner of screen pointing area:

Point to upper right corner of the whole tablet

The entire surface of the tablet may now be used for pointing.

21. Extracting data from a drawing

21.1 DRAWING INTERCHANGE (DXF) FILES

The information contained in an AutoCAD drawing is stored in a form which is very difficult to interpret or alter. Within the AutoCAD system this does not matter but there are occasions when drawing data needs to be extracted and transferred to other software for analysis. In such cases AutoCAD can produce a drawing interchange file (DXF) which is a file in simple ASCII text format which can easily be read.

Such files are comprehensive. They contain every detail of a drawing so that if necessary the drawing may be re-constructed exactly within another system. Even a blank drawing contains a large amount of data - everything contained within the prototype drawing. As a result the DXF file can appear fearsomely complicated. In fact, because the data is presented in a rigid format with every type of entry identified by a code number, it is relatively easy to read or alternatively to use a simple computer program - in BASIC for instance - to sift through the data and pick out only those bits which you require.

For instance, if you are interested in line elements, then the coordinates of the start and end points of all lines within a drawing may be extracted. Similarly, any other entities may be picked out, or any blocks or shapes, or only those appearing on certain layers etc. The DXF file contains all the information you need; it is just a matter of identifying the right codes to extract the required data.

21.1.1 DXFOUT - Writing a DXF File

Making a DXF file from the current drawing is very simple:

Command: DXFOUT
File name <default>:

The default name here is the current *drawing* name. The file will automatically be given a .DXF extension

Enter decimal places of accuracy (0-16)/Entities/Binary <6>:

This sets the number of decimal places of the coordinates of any points specified in the file. If you select **Entities,** you are prompted to select the required entities from the drawing; only those selected will be transferred to the DXF file. The **Binary** option allows the extraction of the same data in the same format but it is saved in binary not ASCII text format. This gives a more accurate and compact file but is much more difficult to read and edit.

The file will then be assembled and written (on the default directory if no other directory was specified with the file name.)

21.1.2 DXF File Structure

The DXF file is composed of 4 sections - header, tables, blocks, and entities. The header section contains the current values of the system variables; approximately 150 items in all covering everything from the snap setting to the current polyline width. The tables section covers viewports, line types, layers, text styles, views, UCS's, dimstyles and data relating to currently running applications software such as AME.

The blocks section gives full details of all blocks in the drawing including block attributes, whether constant, variable or preset, and also full data on the entities of which the blocks are composed, e.g. lines, circles, polylines etc.

The entities section covers everything else. All entities not included in any blocks are detailed together with their coordinates in the drawing and the layer on which they appear. Also, when relevant, data is given on the entities' thickness, linetype and colour. Any AME solids will also be detailed in this section.

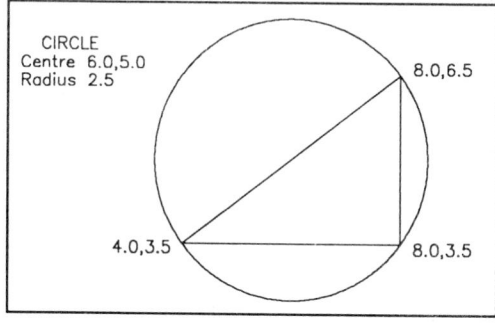

Figure 21.1   DXF extraction: example drawing

Figure 21.1 shows a simple diagram composed of three lines and a circle. The relevant part of the entities section of the corresponding DXF file is shown below together with some added comments.

ENTITIES	(start of entities section)	
.		
.	(Data concerning disposition of viewports and model space	
.		
.		
0	(label preceding 1st entity - LINE 1)	
LINE	(entity type)	
8	(label preceding layer name)	E
GEOMETRY	(layer name)	N
10	(label preceding X primary coordinate)	T
4.0	(X primary coordinate - start of line 1)	I
20	(label preceding Y primary coordinate)	T
3.5	(Y primary coordinate - start of line 1)	Y
30	(label preceding Z primary coordinate	
0.0	(Z primary coordinate - start of line 1)	
11	(label preceding X secondary coordinate)	
8.0	(X secondary coordinate - end of line 1)	1
21	(label preceding Y secondary coordinate)	
3.5	(Y secondary coordinate - end of line 1)	
31	(label preceding Z secondary coordinate)	
0.0	(Z secondary coordinate - end of line 1)	–
0	(NEXT ENTITY - LINE 2)	
LINE		
8		E
GEOMETRY	(layer name)	N
10		T
8.0	(Primary X)	I
20		T
3.5	(primary Y)	Y
30		
0.0	(primary Z)	
11		
8.0	(secondary X)	2
21		
6.5	(secondary Y)	
31		
0.0	(secondary Z)	
0	(NEXT ENTITY - LINE 3)	–
LINE		
8		E
GEOMETRY	(layer name)	N
10		T
8.0	(primary X)	I
20		T
6.5	(primary Y)	Y
30		

0.0	(primary Z)	
11		
4.0	(secondary X)	3
21		
3.5	(secondary Y)	
31		
0.0	(secondary Z)	–
0	(NEXT ENTITY - CIRCLE)	
CIRCLE		E
8		N
GEOMETRY	(layer name)	T
10		I
6.0	(primary X - centre of circle)	T
20		Y
5.0	(primary Y - centre of circle)	
30		
0.0	(primary Z - centre of circle)	
40	(label preceding radius)	4
2.5	(radius)	
0		–
ENDSEC	(end of entities section)	
0		
EOF	(end of DXF file)	

At first sight this is confusing but a little study soon reveals the file structure.

The entity name, LINE or CIRCLE in this case, is always preceded by a zero which acts as a label. The 8 in the next line is another label and announces the layer title, GEOMETRY. The labels 10, 20 and 30 precede the X-, Y- and Z- primary coordinates; here the start point of the lines and the centre of the circle. Similarly, labels 11, 21 and 31 precede any secondary coordinates - the end points of the lines. The circle does not have an end point but it does have a radius, and this is given in the file after the identifying label 40. ENDSEC indicates the end of the entities section and EOF denotes the End Of File.

The point to bear in mind about DXF files is that they define the drawing *totally* - so whatever information you wish to extract from a drawing *must* be represented in the DXF file.

21.1.3 DXFIN - Loading a Drawing from a DXF File

It follows from the above that a DXF file can be used to re-construct an entire drawing. This, like DXFOUT, is a simple operation:

Command: DXFIN
File name: Enter the name of the DXF file to be loaded

If you wish to load a complete DXF file, including all the sections - header, tables, blocks and entities - this can only be done with a *new* drawing - i.e. one which has just been started from *Task 1* of the main menu. If this is not the case, then only the entities section of the DXF file will be loaded.

> *Note:* If AutoCAD insists that the drawing is not a new one, when you know that it is, then take a look at your prototype drawing to see if it has had any entities incorporated into it.

If you wish to load only entities, then there is no need to use a complete DXF file. A file containing only the required entities set out in DXF format together with the end of file (EOF) marker will be accepted. The resultant drawing will merge the entities from the DXF file with the header data derived from the prototype drawing. Such a drawing can be edited and saved just as a drawing created with the drawing editor.

21.1.4 DXF File Code Numbers

The identifying codes used within a DXF file are given below:

Code	Function
0	The start of an entity, table entry or file separator
1	The primary text value for an entity
2	A name; attribute tag, block name etc.
3-4	Other textual name values
5	Entity handles as hexadecimal strings
6	Line type name (fixed)
7	Text style name (fixed)
8	Layer name (fixed)
9	variable name identifier (used only in header section)
10	Primary X coordinate (e.g start of line, centre of circle)
11-18	Other X coordinates
20	Primary Y coordinate (immediately following primary X coord)
21-28	Other Y coordinates
30	Primary Z coordinate (immediately following X and Y coords)
31-37	Other Z coordinates
38	The entities elevation if non-zero (fixed)
39	The entities thickness if non-zero (fixed)
40-48	Numerical floating point (radii, text height, scale factors..)
49	Repeated value
50-58	Angles
62	Colour number (fixed)
66	"Entities follow" flag (fixed)
70-78	Integer values (repeat counts, flag bits, modes etc.)
210,220	
230	X, Y, Z components of extrusion direction

999	Remarks
1000	ASCII string - 255 bytes maximum
1001	Application name - 31 bytes maximum
1002	Xdata control string
1003	Xdata layer name
1004	Chunk of bytes - up to 127 bytes long
1005	Xdata database handle
1010, 1020	
1030	Xdata X-, Y- and Z- coordinates
1011, 1021	
1031	Xdata X-, Y- and Z- coordinates of 3D WCS position
1012, 1022	
1032	Xdata X-, Y- and Z- coordinates of 3D WCS displacement
1013, 1023	
1033	Xdata X-, Y- and Z- coordinates of 3D WCS direction
1040	Xdata floating point value
1041	Xdata distance value
1042	Xdata scale factor
1070	Xdata 16-bit integer
1071	Xdata 32-bit signed long

21.1.5 Programs to Extract Data from DXF Files

Because of the rigidly defined structure of a DXF file, it is relatively easy to write programs to extract selected data.

A simple program written in BASIC to extract the start and end coordinates of all LINE entities in the file is given in the AutoCAD manual. A modified version which will additionally extract the centre points and radii of any circles in the DXF file is shown below :

```
500 CLS
1000 REM
1010 REM Extract lines from DXF file
1020 REM
1030 LINE INPUT "DXF file name: ";A$
1040 A$=A$+".dxf"
1050 OPEN "i",1,A$
1060 REM
1070 REM Ignore until section start encountered
1080 REM
1090 GOSUB 1320
1100 IF G% <> 0 THEN 1090
1110 IF S$ <> "SECTION" THEN 1090
1120 GOSUB 1320
1130 REM
1140 REM Skip unless ENTITIES section
1150 REM
1160 IF S$ <> "ENTITIES" THEN 1090
1170 REM
1180 REM Scan until end of section processing LINEs
1190 REM
1200 GOSUB 1320
```

```
1210 IF G% = 0 AND S$="ENDSEC" THEN END
1220 IF G%=0 AND S$="LINE" THEN GOSUB 1270:GOTO 1210
1225 IF G%=0 AND S$="CIRCLE" THEN GOSUB 1570:GOTO 1210
1230 GOTO 1200
1240 REM
1250 REM Line co-ordinates extract
1260 REM
1270 GOSUB 1320
1280 IF G%=10 THEN X1=X: Y1=Y
1290 IF G%=11 THEN X2=X: Y2=Y
1300 IF G%=0 THEN PRINT"IINE from (";X1;",";Y1;") to (";X2;",";Y2")":RETURN
1310 GOTO 1270
1320 REM
1330 REM Read group code and following value
1340 REM
1350 INPUT #1, G%
1360 IF G%<10 THEN LINE INPUT #1, S$ :RETURN
1370 IF G%>= 38 AND G%<= 49 THEN INPUT #1, V :RETURN
1380 IF G%>= 50 AND G%<= 59 THEN INPUT #1, A :RETURN
1390 IF G%>= 60 AND G%<= 69 THEN INPUT #1, P% :RETURN
1400 IF G%>= 70 AND G%<= 79 THEN INPUT #1, F% :RETURN
1410 IF G%>= 20 THEN PRINT"Invalid group code ";G% :STOP
1420 INPUT #1,X
1430 INPUT #1,G1%
1440 IF G1% <> (G%+10) THEN PRINT"Invalid coord code ";G1% :STOP
1450 INPUT #1,Y
1460 RETURN
1550 REM
1560 REM Extra extract routine for circles
1565 REM
1570 GOSUB 1320
1580 IF G%=10 THEN X1=X: Y1=Y
1590 IF G%=40 THEN R=V
1600 IF G%=0 THEN PRINT"CIRCLE    (Centre ";X1",";Y1;" Radius ";R;")":RETURN
1610 GOTO 1570
```

Corresponding flow diagrams are shown in Figures 21.2 and 21.3. A study of these in conjunction with the table of code numbers shows that the extraction technique is very simple.

Once this technique is mastered it should be possible to perform virtually any extract required.

> *Note:*   It is always useful to make a test drawing containing the entities, blocks etc. to be extracted and then to study the format of the corresponding DXF file before starting to write the extraction program.

21.1.6 HANDLES

Programmes such as the above enable you to identify and extract *classes* of entities such as lines, circles etc. It is not possible to identify *individual* entities. The HANDLES command allows you to attach a *unique* label - called a handle - to every entity created within a drawing.

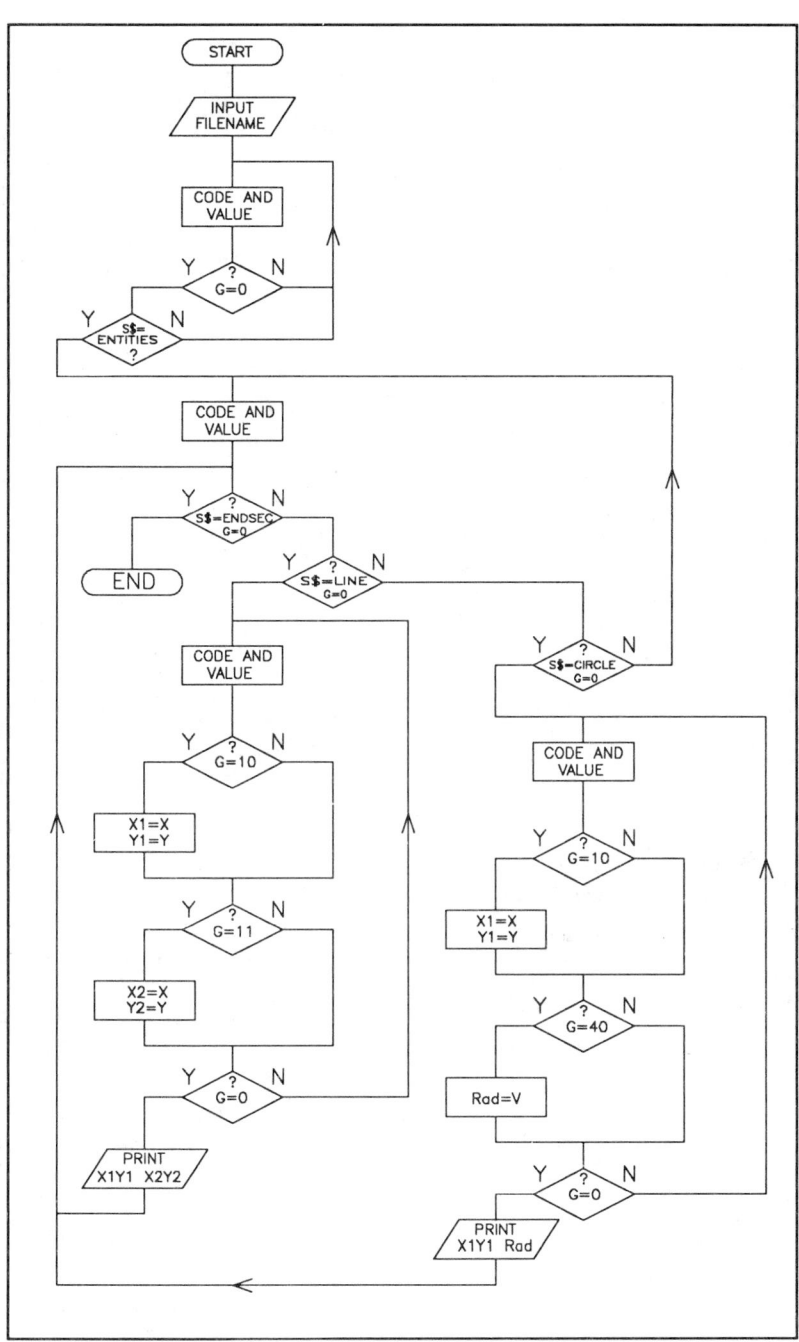

Figure 21.2 DXF entity coordinate extraction for lines and circles

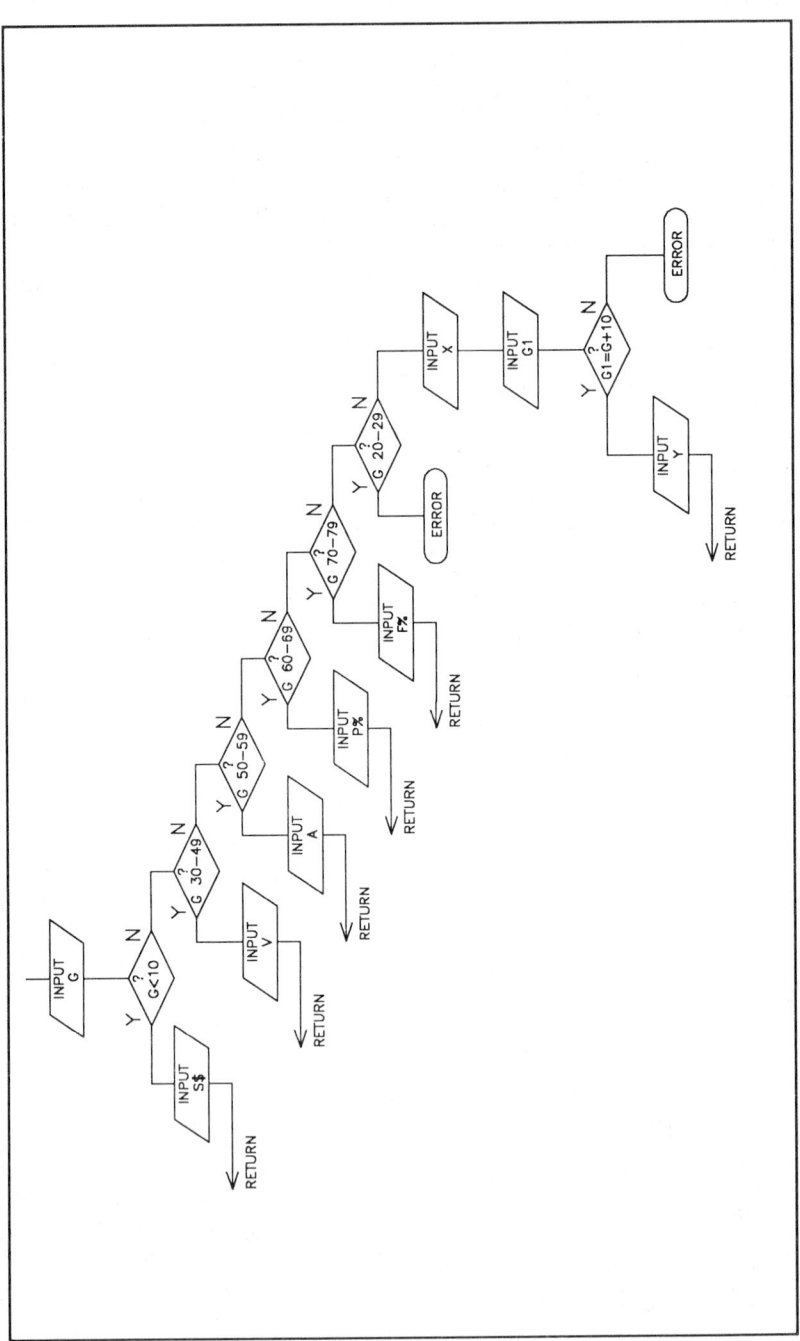

Figure 21.3 Code and value subroutine

The HANDLES system variable controls whether HANDLES is operative or not but this variable is "read only" and is controlled only via the HANDLES command.

Command: HANDLES
ON/DESTROY:

Handles is ON by default when entering a new drawing - HANDLES system variable=1. If you wish to turn handles off, then you must respond with DESTROY. This *must* be typed in full. You will then be prompted to type in one of six messages to confirm that you wish to destroy all existing handles.

You may not believe this - the requested response will be chosen at random from the following list:

**I AGREE
GO AHEAD
PRETTY PLEASE
MAKE MY DATA
UNHANDLE THAT DATABASE
DESTROY HANDLE**

Whichever message is requested must be typed in full.

21.2 TRANSFERRING DATA TO DBASE III+ - ATTRIBUTE EXTRACTION

The key to extracting data from an AutoCAD drawing and transferring it to another package such as dBASE III+ is in the use of blocks.

Attributes contained within the blocks of a drawing may be extracted and transferred to dBASE III+ where they can be manipulated and analyzed. The basis for this is an *extract file*. This file is written by AutoCAD and read by dBASE III+. The attributes to be transferred are selected by their tag names. Attributes with a selected tag occupy a field in dBASE III+, although the field name does not have to be the same as that of the tag. (See Section 10.5.)

21.2.1 Template Files

The tags of the attributes to be transferred are specified in a separate file called a *template file*. This file must be created, using a text editor or a word processor, *before* you initiate the transfer, (see Figure 21.4).

In its simplest form the template file lists the tag names of the attributes to be transferred.

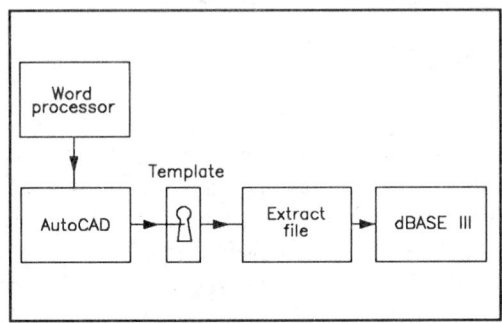

Figure 21.4   Use of template file

For each tag name listed the template file must also specify:

- The corresponding database field type, i.e. a *character* field or a *numeric* field.
- The field width.
- In cases where the field is numeric, the number of places after the decimal point.

Suppose that some of the blocks in your drawing contained attributes with tag names ITEM and COSTWHSL, the first containing a descriptive name and the second the numerical wholesale cost of the item. A template file written to extract only these two attributes could look like:

```
ITEM        C012000
COSTWHSL  N010002
```

> *Note:*   Do not use TABS when writing this file. To separate the columns (for improved readability) use only space characters.

The first non-space character after the tag name ITEM is a C indicating that the corresponding database field is a character field. This is followed by 012 to give a field width of 12 characters. The final 3 digits refer to the number of decimal places and are always zeros for a character field. Similarly, COSTWHSL is to be transferred into a numeric field with 10 places before the decimal point and 2 after it.

> *Note:*   If a numeric field is specified, but the attribute contains non-numeric characters, then errors will occur. A warning message will be displayed when such an error is detected.

When AutoCAD uses this template file to extract the attributes, it will apply the template to each block. Those blocks which contain one or both of the nominated tag names will have their corresponding attribute *values* written into the extract file. If a block contains one, but not both, of the tag names, the values for the absent one will be filled in with blanks (if character) or zeros (if numeric). Blocks containing neither of these tag names will be ignored.

A template file must obviously contain at least one attribute tag name but it can also contain optional special names which will result in more detailed data being extracted from blocks containing a nominated tag name.

These special names may occur in any order but they *must* be written in this exact form:

BL:NAME	Cwww000	(This extracts the block name)
BL:LEVEL	Nwww000	(This extracts the block nesting level)
BL:X	Nwwwddd	(This extracts the X- coordinate of the block)
BL:Y	Nwwwddd	(This extracts the Y- coordinate of the block)
BL:LAYER	Cwww000	(This extracts the block insertion layer name)
BL:ORIENT	Nwwwddd	(This extracts the block rotation angle)
BL:XSCALE	Nwwwddd	(This extracts the X- scale factor of the block)
BL:YSCALE	Nwwwddd	(This extracts the Y- scale factor of the block)

where www and ddd represent the field width and decimal place data respectively.

When completed, the template file must be saved with a .TXT extension, e.g. MYTEMPL.TXT.

21.2.2 Data Extraction

To extract data from a drawing:

Command: ATTEXT
CDF, SDF or DXF Attribute extract (or Entities)? <C>:

This prompt refers to the format to be adopted in the extract file. CDF stands for Comma Delimited Format - the file contains fields separated by delimiters (commas by default) and character fields are enclosed in single quotes. SDF stands for Space Delimited Format - the fields are of fixed width and so no delimiter characters are needed. DXF stands for a variant of AutoCAD's normal Drawing Interchange File format which contains only block reference, attribute and end of sequence entities. dBASE III+ can read extract files in either CDF or SDF format.

The **Entities** prompt is used if you do not wish to extract attributes from every block in the drawing - it allows you to prepare a selection set of those blocks whose attributes you wish to extract. Once you have done so the CDF, SDF or DXF prompt re-appears.

AutoCAD next prompts for the name of the template file to be used and also for a name to be given to the extract file which is about to be generated:

Template file: MYTEMPL
Extract file name: MYEXTRAC

If you reply with a simple return, the extract file name will default to that of the drawing, but it will be given a .TXT extension

The extract file MYEXTRAC.TXT will then be written on the default directory. Because this file is to be used by the dBASE package, you may prefer to direct it to some other directory by specifying the appropriate path.

EXAMPLE

Extract file name: C:\DBASE\MYEXTRACT

> *Note:* By using a number of different template files it is possible to derive multiple extract files from a single drawing.

It will be found that CDF is the most flexible format for the extract files but it does result in all character fields being enclosed in single quotes 'like this'. This can be annoying. The single quote can be replaced by another character, e.g a " symbol, by including:

C:QUOTE   "

in the template file, but this is not likely to be any more acceptable.

SDF format does not suffer from this problem but you must be certain to match the dBASE field widths and decimals *exactly* with those of the template file. If you fail to get this right, the dBASE records will be hopelessly jumbled and impossible to use.

A typical CDF format extract file is shown below:

```
"Desk","Mr Jones","Mahogany"
"Desk","Mr Brown","Teak"
"Desk","Mr Green","Plywood"
"Chair","Mr Jones","Leather"
"Chair","Mr Brown","Plastic"
"Chair","Mr Green","Wood"
"Telephone","Mr Jones","Radio"
"Telephone","Mr Brown","Digital"
"Telephone","Mr Green","Standard"
```

The same file in SDF format would be:

Desk	Mr Jones	Mahogany
Desk	Mr Brown	Teak
Desk	Mr Green	Plywood
Chair	Mr Jones	Leather
Chair	Mr Brown	Plastic
Chair	Mr Green	Wood
Telephone	Mr Jones	Radio
Telephone	Mr Brown	Digital
Telephone	Mr Green	Standard

The order in which the attribute values are written in the extract file follows the order in which the tag names are specified in the template, *not* the order in which the tag names are written in the block definition. Similarly, the order of tag names in the template file *must* follow the order of the fields in the database.

21.2.3 Reading an Extract File into dBASE III+

A database file must first be created with the desired field structure. Field widths must be large enough to accept the corresponding data from the drawing and field types must be specified which are suitable for the data which they will contain and for the analysis which is later to be performed. It is not necessary for the dBASE field names to match the AutoCAD attribute tag names - the tag names are not transmitted by the extract file and are unknown to dBASE III+.

> *Note:* If SDF format is to be used in the extract file, it is essential that the field widths specified in the database and in the template file match exactly.

The transfer of data from the extract file into the database is controlled from the dBASE III+ package. For a database called MYDBASE the commands would be:

.USE MYDBASE

If CDF format is to be used, the transfer command is:

.APPEND FROM MYEXTRAC.TXT DELIMITED

If SDF format is to be used, the transfer command is:

.APPEND FROM MYEXTRAC.TXT SDF

Data from the extract file will immediately be appended to the dBASE file and from then on can be treated and analyzed by the full range of dBASE III+ commands.

> *Note:* If you wish to repeat the transfer, say as a consequence of making some changes to the drawing, you must remember that the transfer is an APPEND process and so you must clear the original data using DELETE and PACK before the new data is transferred.

See Appendix 10 for an introduction to dBASE III+, and Appendix 11 for an example describing the transfer of attributes from an AutoCAD drawing into a dBASE III+ database.

Appendices

Appendix 1
An Introduction to DOS

DOS stands for Disk Operating System. Using DOS allows communication between the computer, disk drives, printer, etc. There are various versions of DOS - the commands outlined in this appendix refer to all versions up to and including DOS 3.3.

When "booting up" a computer, i.e. switching on from cold, the user needs a SYSTEM or DOS disk to load the computer operating system instructions into the machines memory. These files are interpreters that take written English commands and turn them into machine code. There are three operating system files, which are retained in the computer's memory for as long as the computer is switched on. Two of these files are known as *hidden files* and do not appear on any file directories or listings, and the third is called the COMMAND.COM file.

In the general formats listed in this section, items in [ ] (square brackets) are optional.

The following symbols are used:

d: represents the disk drive to be used, e.g. A:, B:, C:, etc.

Filename   represents the name of the file to be used.

.ext   represents the filename extension - a part of the filename which may be used to label a group of files collectively. For example, all program files written in the basic language are given the extension .BAS.

DOS commands such as COPY, ERASE, RENAME etc., can be entered in any combination of UPPER CASE or lower case letters.

Filenames and extensions may incorporate or be replaced by *global characters* or *wild cards*. The symbols used are ? and *.

?   replaces any single character.

*   replaces any number of characters up to the end of the filename or extension.

Note: The * should be used with care - particularly with the DELETE or ERASE commands !

A1.1 CHANGING THE DEFAULT DRIVE

The default drive is the disk drive (A, B, C etc.,) which the system will use in the absence of a particular drive being specified. The current default drive can be identified by the prompt symbol, e.g. **C>** ,which appears at the left hand edge of the screen when DOS is operating.

To change the default drive simply type the new drive letter followed by a colon:

e.g.

A> C: This changes the default drive from A to C with the result that the new prompt is now C>.

A1.2 SOME COMMON DOS COMMANDS

A1.2.1 DIRectory

Lists the files resident on a disk. The syntax is:

DIR [d:][filename][.ext][/P][/W]

- the suffix /P means   list the files a page at a time with a pause between pages.
- the suffix /W means   list the files by width, i.e. print their names across the screen instead of in a single column. This takes up less screen space but some information about the files is suppressed.

e.g.

C> DIR   DIRectory of default drive (C).

A> DIR C:/P   DIRectory of drive C by page.

C> DIR A:*.COM   DIRectory of the files on drive A with
                                          extension .COM.

A> DIR/W   DIRectory of drive A by width.

C> DIR *.   Lists all the directories on drive C.

A1.2.2 RENAME

Used to rename files. Can be used to change the filename, the extension or both. The
syntax is:

RENAME [d:]Filename.ext Newname.ext

e.g.

C> RENAME A:FILES.123 FILES1:LOT

                                          Changes the filename FILES to FILES1
                                          and the extension 123 to LOT.

┌───┐
│ *Note:*   The RENAME command can be shortened to REN.   │
└───┘

A1.2.3 FORMAT

Before a new disk can be used it has to be configured to the computer's particular
format.

****

WARNING!!!

****

*Formatting a disk whether new or used erases any information resident on that disk!
Therefore great care must be taken when using this command. This is particularly
important to users of hard/fixed disk machines where it is possible to wipe out over
100 Megabytes of data with this single command.*

The basic syntax is:

FORMAT [d:][/S][/V]

- /S = format disk with system files. This allows the disk to be used to "boot up" the system from cold.
- /V = volume name - this allows you to label your disk with your name or some other identifier. This can be changed at a later date (if necessary) by using the LABEL command.

e.g.

A> FORMAT A: FORMAT disk in default drive A.

A> FORMAT C: FORMAT disk in drive C.

****
DO NOT EXECUTE THIS COMMAND UNLESS ABSOLUTELY SURE -
ALL INFORMATION STORED ON THE HARD DISK C DRIVE WILL BE
ERASED!!!
****

C> FORMAT A:/S   FORMAT disk in drive A with system (hidden files) + COMMAND.COM.

A> FORMAT A:/S/V   FORMAT disk in drive A with both system files and volume name.

Note: If you wish to FORMAT a disk to another capacity, e.g. to format a 3½" disk to 720Kbyte instead of 1.4Mbyte, the syntax would be FORMAT A:/T:80/N:9. See your DOS manual for more information.

A1.2.4 COPY

Copies one or more files from one location to another. The syntax is:

COPY [d:]filename.ext [d:][filename.ext]

e.g.

C> COPY A:ANYFILE.COM C: COPY the file named /ANYFILE.COM from drive A to drive C.

C> COPY C:ANYFILE.COM A: COPY same file from C to A.

C> COPY A:*.* C: COPY ALL FILES on drive A to C.

C> COPY C:*.BAS A: COPY all file names with extension .BAS
                                     from C to A.

Note: Filenames and extensions can be changed when copying from
one location to another:

C> COPY A:ANYFILE.COM C:MYPROG.RPS

Copies file ANYFILE.COM from A to C and changes name to
MYPROG.RPS.

A1.2.5 DISKCOPY

Copies the total contents of one disk to another. This is generally used to make disk
backups on twin floppy machines - it is very rarely used with hard disk machines. The
syntax is:

DISKCOPY [d:][d:]

e.g.

A> DISKCOPY A: B: Copy all files from A to B, formatting B
                                     while copying.

A> DISKCOPY A: A: Copies from one floppy disk to another
                                     when only one floppy drive is available.
                                     You will be prompted to insert and
                                     remove disks as required.

A1.2.6 DELete or ERASE

These commands are used to delete files from the disk. The syntax is:

DEL [d:]filename.ext

e.g.

C> DEL A:FILENAME.COM   DELetes the file FILENAME.COM
                                     from drive A.

C> DEL A:FILENAME.*   DELetes   all   files   with   filename

FILENAME from drive A.

C> DEL A:*.*   DELetes all files from drive A.

A> DEL FILENAME.COM   DELetes file FILENAME.COM from default drive A.

Note: When using the *.* wild card with the DELete command, you will be prompted to confirm that you really do wish to delete *all* the files.

A1.2.7 TIME and DATE

Displays current time or date settings (in American format) on the screen, and allows either to be reset. This is useful, as both are stored with a file when it is saved. The syntax is:

TIME   This is followed by a prompt for you to supply the date. Don't forget the colons (:) but you can ignore the seconds if you wish. Responding with a return accepts the current time as displayed.

DATE   Again, you will be prompted to supply the date (in American format, i.e. month first). Don't forget the hyphens (-). Responding with a return accepts the current time as displayed.

A1.2.8 TYPE

Displays the contents of any ASCII file on the screen. Used mainly to check the contents of batch and text files. The syntax is:

TYPE [d:]filename.ext

e.g.

C>TYPE A:AUTOEXEC.BAT   Lists   the   contents   of   the   file AUTOEXEC.BAT

A1.2.9 MORE

The MORE command is used to display a single screen of information at a time. When used with the TYPE command, long files can be viewed one screen at a time.

C>TYPE A:AUTOEXEC.BAT | MORE

A1.3 BATCH FILES

A batch file allows a number of commands or programmes to be run automatically. The batch filename always contains the extension BAT. There is a special file called AUTOEXEC.BAT which is automatically executed when the computer is switched on. All other batch files have to be executed manually.

To create a batch file use the following syntax:

COPY CON <filename>.BAT

enter desired batch of commands followed by F6 and return.

e.g.

```
COPY CON AUTOEXEC.BAT
CD BASIC                 - Call directory BASIC
KEYBUK                   - Run file KEYBUK
CD\                      - Go back to root directory
^Z                       - Terminate batch file (this symbol results from
                           pressing the F6 key which terminates the file)
```

Whenever a batch filename is used, the batch of commands contained within the file will be executed.

Batch files may also be created using a word processor or text editor instead of the COPY CON command shown above.

A useful application within an AutoCAD framework is to use a batch file to set up the AutoCAD environment. The batch file could be used to set up the relevant path, (see Section A1.5), set the working directory to be default, set the relevant environment variables, (see Appendix 2), and start up AutoCAD. Such a batch file would look something like:

```
PATH=C:\ACAD;\FILES;\
CD\ACAD\FILES
SET ACADCFG=c:\ACAD\SUPPORT
ACAD
CD\
```

See Sections 2.2.1 and 18.4.1 for further uses of batch files with AutoCAD.

A1.4 DIRECTORIES

When a hard or floppy disk is formatted, a single *root* directory is created. *Sub-directories* can be created branching out from the root directory, and any of these can branch out to further directories, and so on. Therefore access is always gained to all sub-directories from the root.

The following commands are used in association with *sub*-directories:

- **MD**   Make Directory.   This allows the setting up of a new sub-directory either in the root or any other sub-directory. Directory names obey similar rules to the eight letter filenames. The syntax is:

    MD [d:]dirname

    e.g.
    C> MD C:WORDPERF

    > Creates a new sub-directory   called WORDPERF. Shown on ROOT directory as WORDPERF <DIR>.

- **CD**   Change Directory.   Used to change from the directory *in use* (default) to a new directory. The syntax is:

    CD [d:]dirname1[\dirname2][\].....

    e.g.
    C> CD C:WORDPERF

    > Changes from current directory to new directory called WORDPERF.

    C> CD C:WORDPERF\FILES

    > Changes from current directory through directory WORDPERF to directory FILES.

    C> CD\

    > \ (backslash) is a special command used to return to the root directory.

    C> CD..

    > The .. is used to return to the directory immediately above the current directory (the *parent* directory).

- **RD**   Remove Directory. Used to delete an *empty* directory. All files within the directory *must* be erased and all sub-directories must be removed before the directory can be deleted. The syntax is:

RD [d:]dirname

e.g.

C> RD C:WORDPERF

> Removes the directory WORDPERF from the disk (assuming that it contains no files or sub-directories).

A1.5 PATHWAYS

Pathways are used to permit the operator to call files from different sub-directories without the need to leave the current directory. Pathways are usually opened in the batch file used to start up a particular software package. The syntax is:

PATH [d:]\dirname1;\dirname2;\ etc.....

e.g.

C> PATH C:\WORDPERF;\WORDPERF\FILES

> Allows direct access to the files in both the WORDPERF directory and the FILES directory at the same time.

A1.6 THE SYSTEM ENVIRONMENT AND THE SET COMMAND

Approximately 200 bytes of memory is allocated to what is known as the system environment, this memory is checked by AutoCAD and other applications packages during initialization for information regarding environment variables.

Many packages require the setting of environment variables before the package will run efficiently; it is therefore good practice to include them within a start up batch file.

The SET command is used to set up an environment variable within the system environment. The syntax is:

SET variable name=value

| *Note:* Do not leave spaces either side of the = sign. |

A1.7 SHIPDISK, DPARK, PARK ETC

It is important to check the manufacturers instructions with regard to the moving of your computer. The hard disk and disk reading head can be damaged if the head is not properly parked. Some computer systems supply a programme called SHIPDISK or DPARK which parks the disk reading head. This *must be run* before the computer is moved.

A1.8 GLOSSARY OF DOS COMMANDS

Backup floppy disks	DISKCOPY
Change date	DATE
Change directory	CD
Change disk drive	d:
Change time	TIME
Copy files	COPY
Copy disks	DISKCOPY or COPY
Delete directory	RD
Delete files	DEL or ERASE
Display contents of file	TYPE
Display date	DATE
Display files on disk	DIR
Display time	TIME
Enter an Environment Variable	SET
Format new disks	FORMAT
Make new directory	MD
Move files	COPY
Rename files	RENAME or REN

Appendix 2
AutoCAD environment variables

There are a number of environment variables which AutoCAD will inspect during start up. If the variables have not been set, then AutoCAD will assign default values but will not run at its most efficient.

The variables fall into two groups; those which control memory allocation and those which tell AutoCAD where to find support and configuration files.

The environment variables must all be set from DOS *before* AutoCAD is run and should therefore be included in a batch file.

A2.1 ENVIRONMENT VARIABLE ACAD

This variable specifies one directory containing support files such as text fonts, menus, AutoLISP files etc., which are not resident in the AutoCAD system directory. AutoCAD will first search for such files in its system directory. If they are not found, then only if the ACAD environment variable has been correctly set will AutoCAD search for them in the nominated directory.

====

EXAMPLE

If the support files are resident in a directory called SUPPORT, a sub-directory of the ACAD system directory, then the ACAD environment variable may be set as follows:

   C> SET ACAD=C:\ACAD\SUPPORT

====

A2.2 ENVIRONMENT VARIABLE ACADCFG

AutoCAD's hardware configuration data are stored in a file called ACAD.CFG. This is assumed to be in a separate directory called the configuration directory. If this directory is not specified by the environment variable ACADCFG, then AutoCAD will search for the ACAD.CFG file in the system directory.

By specifying a separate configuration directory it is possible to maintain multiple configuration files for use as required. (See Section 18.4.)

EXAMPLE

To nominate a directory called MYCONF, a sub-directory of the ACAD system directory, as the configuration directory:

> **C>** SET ACADCFG=C:\ACAD\MYCONF

A2.3 ENVIRONMENT VARIABLE ACADALTMENU

If you are using a digitiser, then it is possible to specify the path and name of an alternative menu which can be substituted for the standard AutoCAD menu by picking the Change Template square (X25) on the tablet. A *complete* new menu will be loaded which will affect not only the tablet but the screen menu, pull down menus, buttons etc.

This is a one way process unless the corresponding square on the alternative menu is defined to return you to the standard menu.

EXAMPLE

To allow access to an alternative menu called MYMENU resident in MYDIR then the ACADALTMENU environment variable may be set as follows:

> **C>** SET ACADALTMENU=C:\ACAD\MYDIR\MYMENU

A2.4 ENVIRONMENT VARIABLES ACADXMEM AND ACADLIMEM

These variables control the amount of extended and expanded memory which may be used by AutoCAD. Refer to your DOS and hardware manuals for full details relevant to your computer installation.

If ACADXMEM is not set, then AutoCAD will use *all available* extended memory. The following SET options are available:

C> SET ACADXMEM=<start>	specifies the starting memory location
C> SET ACADXMEM=<start,size>	specifies the starting location and the size of reserved memory
C> SET ACADXMEM=<size>	specifies the size of reserved memory
C> SET ACADXMEM=NONE	
C> SET ACADLIMEM=<value>	

EXAMPLE

To set aside 128kbytes of extended memory starting at 1664k:

C> SET ACADXMEM=1664k,128k

To limit the available expanded memory to 20 pages (320kbytes):

C> SET ACADLIMEM=20

A2.5 AUTOLISP ENVIRONMENT VARIABLES LISPHEAP AND LISPSTACK

AutoLISP requires two independent areas of memory to be allocated for its use. The first stores all functions and variables and is called the heap while the second, called the stack, is the working memory.

The maximum total allocation for the heap and stack must not exceed 45000 bytes. The default settings are:

Heap = 40000
Stack = 3000

The two environment variables are called LISPHEAP and LISPSTACK respectively. If insufficient memory is allocated to the heap, the error message will be displayed:

Insufficient Node Space or **Insufficient String Space**

If insufficient memory is allocated to the stack the error message will be displayed:

Lispstack overflow

EXAMPLE

C> SET LISPHEAP=41000
C> SET LISPSTACK=3500

A2.6 ENVIRONMENT VARIABLES ACADPLCMD AND ACADPPCMD

Only one of these environment variables may be used at any given time. ACADPLCMD refers to plotting and ACADPPCMD refers to printer plotting. The setting of one of these variables allows you to plot or print a drawing "in the background" while you continue to use AutoCAD as normal.

To achieve this it is necessary to:

● create a directory called \SPFILES to accept the spooler file.
● modify the ACAD.PGP file by the addition of:

> PRINT,PRINT,   24000,,0

● set either ACADPLCMD or ACADPPCMD as follows:

> **C>** SET ACADPLCMD=PRINT %S

> **C>** SET ACADPLCMD=PRINT %S

● configure AutoCAD to recognise the spooler file directory and a default spooler file name. From the configuration menu select option **8. Operating parameters**. From the option 8 sub-menu select option **3. Default plot file name** and option **4. Plot spooler directory**.

Appendix 3
Loading and running AutoLISP programs

A3.1 A BRIEF INTRODUCTION TO AUTOLISP

AutoLISP is a simple programming language developed by AutoCAD from the artificial intelligence language LISP. There are many features associated with AutoLISP but the most important is the ability to write simple programmes which can fully customize the AutoCAD package to individual needs. This can include the customisation of commands and entity creation and also control of the AutoCAD system variables.

There are several specialist books already published covering AutoLISP programming which is beyond the scope of this book.

Before AutoLISP programs can successfully be executed, the two environment variables, LISPHEAP and LISPSTACK, must be set to suitable values, (see Appendix 2).

A3.2 LOADING AND UNLOADING AN AUTOLISP PROGRAM

Many AutoLISP programs are run automatically by AutoCAD; for example the shapes which may be selected from the 3D Objects icon accessed by picking Objects... from the **Draw** pull down menu. Similarly, the pseudo command Rectang on the **Draw** pull down menu loads the RECTANG.LSP program.

Other AutoLISP programs may be loaded from the **Command:** prompt.

EXAMPLE

To load and run a LISP program called SPIRAL on the SUPPORT sub-directory of ACAD:

Command: (LOAD"SPIRAL")
C:SPIRAL
Command: SPIRAL
Center point:
Number of rotations:
Growth per rotation:
Points per rotation <30>:

Each time an AutoLISP program is loaded it remains memory resident and therefore occupies valuable node space (heap memory). Because node space is limited, it is advisable to remove or unload programs which are no longer required. To unload the above program, use the following syntax:

Command: (setq SPIRAL nil)

A3.3 AUTOMATIC LOADING OF AUTOLISP PROGRAMS

If you have an AutoLISP program which is always required, you can ensure that it is loaded automatically each time the drawing editor is entered. The AutoLISP program must be saved in a text file which *must* be called ACAD.LSP and which may be located in the system directory. It is possible to include a number of AutoLISP programs within this file and all will be run automatically at the start of each drawing.

Appendix 4
AutoCAD and AME system variables

A4.1 AUTOCAD SYSTEM VARIABLES

NAME	*READ ONLY*	*FUNCTION*
ACADPREFIX	R	Directory and path set by environment variable ACAD
ACADVER	R	AutoCAD version number
AFLAGS		Attribute type
ANGBASE		Direction of zero angle
ANGDIR		Positive angles clockwise or anticlockwise
APERTURE		Object snap target box size
AREA	R	Computed area
ATTDIA		Calls attribute dialogue box
ATTMODE		Attribute display visibility
ATTREQ		Control of attribute prompts
AUNITS		Units of angular measurement
AUPREC		Number of decimal places (angles)
AXISMODE		Axis control (ON/OFF)
AXISUNIT		Axis marker spacing
BACKZ	R	Position of back clipping plane
BLIPMODE		Construction blips control (ON/OFF)
CDATE	R	Current date and time
CECOLOUR	R	Current entity colour
CELTYPE	R	Current linetype
CHAMFERA		First chamfer length
CHAMFERB		Second chamfer length
CLAYER	R	Current layer
CMDECHO		AutoLISP function display control
COORDS		Coordinate display presentation
CBPORT		Active viewport identification number
DATE	R	Current date and time (in days and fractions of days)
DIMxxx		Dimension variables (see section 8.2.8)

DISTANCE		Computed distance between digitised points
DRAGMODE		Drag feature ON/OFF
DRAGP1		Resolution of drag display
DRAGP2		Resolution of fast drag display
DWGNAME	R	Drawing name
DWGPREFIX	R	Full path of current drawing
ELEVATION		Elevation value (current UCS)
ERRNO		Error code number for applications software
EXPERT		Controls "safety net" prompts
EXTMAX	R	Upper right drawing extents
EXTMIN	R	Lower left drawing extents
FILEDIA		File dialogue box feature ON/OFF
FILLETRAD		Current fillet radius
FILLMODE		Fill ON/OFF
FRONTZ	R	Position of front clipping plane
GRIDMODE		Grid ON/OFF
GRIDUNIT		Current grid spacing
HANDLES	R	Handles feature ON/OFF
HIGHLIGHT		Selected entities identified ON/OFF
INSBASE		Insertion basepoint
LASTANGLE	R	Final angle of last drawn arc
LASTPOINT		Coordinates of last entered point
LENSLENGTH	R	Perspective viewing zoom lens focal length
LIMCHECK		Allows drawing to transgress limits
LIMMAX		Upper right drawing limits
LIMMIN		Lower left drawing limits
LTSCALE		Linetype scale
LUNITS		Units of linear measurement
LUPREC		Number of decimal place (linear)
MAXACTVP		Maximum number of regenerated viewports
MAXSORT		Maximum value of files to be alpha-sorted
MENUECHO		Menu command echo control
MENUNAME	R	Active menu name
MIRRTEXT		Controls presentation of mirrored text
ORTHOMODE		Ortho ON/OFF
OSMODE		Current object snap mode
PDMODE		Representation of point entities
PDSIZE		Size of point entities
PERIMETER	R	Computed perimeter
PFACEVMAX	R	Maximum number of vertices per face
PICKBOX		Selection box size
POPUPS	R	Pull down and icon menus and dialogue boxes ON/OFF
QTEXTMODE		Quick text feature ON/OFF
REGENMODE		Automatic regeneration ON/OFF
SCREENSIZE	R	Size of active viewport
SHADEDGE		Shading mode number
SHADEDIF		Ambient/diffused light ratio
SKETCHINC		Sketch resolution
SKPOLY		Defines sketch elements as lines of polylines
SNAPANG		Angle of snap and grid relative to current UCS
SNAPBASE		Origin of snap and grid relative to current UCS
SNAPISOPAIR		Current isometric plane

SNAPMODE		Snap ON/OFF
SNAPSTYL		Standard or isometric snap
SNAPUNIT		Current snap resolution
SPLFRAME		Controls visibility of polyline after smoothing
SPLINESEGS		Resolution of smoothed polyline
SPLINETYPE		Quadratic or cubic smoothing function (pline)
SURFTAB1		Mesh density in M direction
SURFTAB2		Mesh density in N direction
SURFTYPE		Quadratic, cubic or Bezier smoothing function (mesh)
SURFU		Surface density in M direction
SURFV		Surface density in N direction
TARGET	R	Dynamic view target point coordinates
TDCREATE	R	Start time and date of current drawing
TDINDWG	R	Total time spent on current drawing
TDUPDATE	R	Time and date of last update
TDUSRTIMER	R	Time currently spent in drawing editor
TEMPPREFIX	R	Path and name of directory for temporary files
TEXTEVAL		Identifies a (or a ! as initiating an AutoLISP command
TEXTSIZE		Current text height
TEXTSTYLE		Current text style
THICKNESS		Current 3D thickness
TILEMODE		Enable/disable Pspace
TRACEWID		Current trace width
UCSFOLLOW		Controls automatic execution of plan(UCS) command
UCSICON		Controls display and positioning of UCS icon
UCSNAME	R	Name of active UCS
UCSORG	R	Coordinates of active UCS origin relative to WCS
UCSXDIR	R	Positive X-direction of current UCS
UCSYDIR	R	Positive Y-direction of current UCS
UNITMODE		Display mode for surveyor's angles
USERI1-5		5 unused integer variables for package development
USERR1-5		5 unused real variables for package development
VIEWCTR	R	Coordinates of centre point of active viewport
VIEWDIR	R	Vector direction between camera and target (Dview)
VIEWMODE	R	Code number defining scene (clipped, perspective etc)
VIEWSIZE	R	Height of current viewport in drawing units
VIEWTWIST	R	Dynamic view twist angle
VSMAX	R	Coordinates of upper right of virtual screen
VSMIN	R	Coordinates of lower left of virtual screen
WORLDUCS	R	Indicates active UCS same as WCS
WORLDVIEW		Changes operation of Dview and Vports from active UCS to WCS

Note: In the case of ON/OFF variables, AutoCAD uses the convention that 0=OFF and 1=ON

A4.2 AME SYSTEM VARIABLES

NAME	*READ ONLY*	*FUNCTION*
SOLAMEVER	R	AME version
SOLAREAU		Units of area
SOLAXCOL		Motion Coordinate System icon colour
SOLDECOMP		Mass property decomposition axis
SOLDELENT		2D entity deletion
SOLDISPLAY		Wireframe or mesh display
SOLHANGLE		Hatch angle
SOLHPAT		Hatch pattern
SOLHSIZE		Hatch scale
SOLLENGTH		Units of measure - length
SOLMASS		Units of measure - mass
SOLMATCURR	R	Default material
SOLPAGELEN		Text page length
SOLRENDER		Rendering type
SOLSERVMSG		Solid server message display level
SOLSOLIDIFY		Control of 2D solidification
SOLSUBDIV		Accuracy of mass property calculation
SOLVOLUME		Units of measure - volume
SOLWDENS		Wireframe and mesh density

Appendix 5
Useful utilities in the bonus directory

AutoCAD supplies a number of bonus AutoLISP programs which are located under the BONUS screen option.

These programs if picked from the screen menu will be loaded automatically - once loaded then the programs may be run directly by typing the name from the keyboard.

A number of these programs are very useful; a brief description of each is given below.

ALIAS   This gives a list of the currently defined aliases in the ACAD.PGP file.

ASCTEXT   Allows the import of ASCII or DOS text files into an AutoCAD drawing.

> Command: ASCTEXT
> File to read (including extension):
> Start point or Center/Middle/Right/?:

The **?** gives a list of the text justification (alignment) modes.

> Height <default>:
> Rotation angle <0>:
> Change text options?<N>: Y
> Distance between lines/<Auto>:
> First line to read/<1>:
> Number of lines to read/<All>:
> Underscore each line? <N>:
> Overscore each line? <N>:
> Change text case? Upper/Lower/<N>:
> Set up columns? <N>:

ATTREDEF Allows the re-definition of a block with attributes.

> **Command: ATTREDEF**
> **Name of block you wish to redefine:**
> **Select entities for new block...**
> **Select objects:**

AXROT This very useful program is used to rotate selected entities about the X, Y or Z axis.

> **Command: AXROT**
> **Select objects:**
> **Axis of rotation X/Y/Z:**
> **Degrees of rotation:**

> The angle specified follows the AutoCAD right hand rule.

> **Base point:**

CALC Initiates a simple calculator.

> **Command: CALC**
> **First number:**
> **Calc:Clear/Exit/Mem/Sq-rt/Trig/Y^x or + - * /<Clear>: T**
> **ACosine ASine ATangent Cosine Sine Tangent <Exit>:**

CHBLOCK Edits blocks already inserted into a drawing.

> **Command: CHBLOCK**
> **Select objects:**
> **Insertion point/Rotation/Scale/<Exit>:**

CHFACE Allows the editing of 3DFACE entity vertices.

> **Command: CHFACE**
> **Select objects:**
> **1/2/3/4/Undo/Display/<Select vertex>:**

CHTEXT This is a more versatile version of the AutoCAD CHANGE command and allows the editing of text entities.

Command: CHTEXT
Select text to change.
Select objects:
Height/Justification/Rotation/Style/Text/Undo/Width:

CL   Places a centre mark on selected arcs and circles which can be orientated at any angle to the current UCS. The centre marks are placed on a new layer called CL.

Command: CL
Select arc or circle:
Length/<extension>:

If you respond with extension, then the distance specified will cause a centre mark to be produced of length equal to the circle or arc diameter plus the extension. The length option allows the input of the actual length of the centre mark.

DELLAYER Allows the deletion of a layer and its *contents*. This command should therefore be used with care.

Command: DELLAYER
Layer(s) to delete:

HEDGE   Used to change the visibility of 3DFACE edges.

Command: HEDGE
Fix/Redraw/Tolerance/<Select Edge>:

END   Almost identical to the standard AutoCAD END command.

Command: END
END the drawing session? Yes/<No>:

FACT   Responds with the factorial of a number.

Command: FACT
Enter an Integer:

LLISP   This program builds an AutoLISP library file including files of your choice. Once built the LISP routines which have been included in the file can be selected and run.

> **Command: LLISP**
> **Add/Remove an entry/<Number to load>: A**
> **Lisp routine name to load** <default>**:**

MFACE   Similar to the 3DFACE command but allows the construction of Pface entities. The command also has the ability to select the face colour and layer.

> **Command: MFACE**
> **Layer/Color/<Select vertex>:**

> **Select vertex** is prompting for a new vertex position *not* for an existing vertex. The layer and colour options must be set prior to constructing the PFACE elements.

MVSETUP   This is a useful program for setting out viewports in Paper Space. TILEMODE should be switched off.

> **Command: MVSETUP**
> **Align viewports/Create viewports/Scale viewports**
> **/Title block/Undo:**

> The most useful of these options is the **Create viewports** if this is selected you are prompted:

>> **Delete objects/undo/<Create viewports>: C**

>> **Available Mview viewport options:**

>> **0:**   **None**
>> **1:**   **Single**
>> **2:**   **Std. Engineering**
>> **3:**   **Array of viewports**

>> **Add/Delete/Redisplay/<Number of entry to load>:**

>> Of these options number 2 - **Std. Engineering** - needs some explanation. If selected, you will be prompted for a boundary area for the viewports to occupy. Once

specified, four viewports will be created each one containing a standard engineering view, i.e. a front elevation, a plan, a side elevation and an oblique view.

PROJECT   This program contains two options PROJECT1 and PROJECT2. PROJECT1 allows a flat projection of a 3D wireframe construction to be produced on the current UCS. PROJECT2 projects an entity onto a defined UCS.

> **Command: PROJECT1**
> **Layer name <0>:**
> **Select objects:**
> **Projecting . . .   please wait**
> **Project another entity? Y/N <N>:**
> **Make into a block? <N>:**
> **Write to disk as drawing file? <N>:**
>
> **Command: PROJECT2**
> **UCS name or <RETURN> to select 3 points:**
> **Layer name <0>:**
> **Select entity to project**
> **Project another entity? Y/N <N>:**

PTEXT   This is a paragraph text editor which is a little slow in operation.

> **Command: PTEXT**
> **Centre/Edit/Fit/Right/Slack/?/<Start point>:**

For more information about this command select **?** from the above menu.

RECTANG   Creates a user defined rectangle or square using a polyline.

> **Command: RECTANG**
> **Corner of rectangle or square:**
> **Length:**
> **Square/<Width>:**
> **Rotation angle:**

RPOLY   Draws a closed polyline figure and then generates a number of closed entities within this figure. Each line of the new entities starts and ends at the mid-points of previously constructed lines.

> **Command: RPOLY**
> **Number of cycles:**
> **Retain polygon at each cycle? <Y>/N:**

SPIRAL   Creates a user defined 2D spiral.

> **Command: SPIRAL**
> **Centre point:**
> **Number of rotations:**
> **Growth per rotation:**
> **Points per rotation <30>:**

TABLE   Lists certain current drawing settings such as layers, UCS's, linetypes, text fonts and viewports.

Appendix 6
Simple 2D construction tutorial

Figure A6.1 shows a simple drawing of a kitchen. To re-create this drawing you will need to employ virtually all of the commands outlined in Chapter 3. There are numerous ways in which the drawing may be constructed but the following suggestions are designed to minimise needless repetition and to familiarize you with basic CAD drawing concepts.

No dimensions are specified but you should aim to preserve the appearance of the original drawing.

A6.1 WALLS, DOOR, WINDOW AND WORK SURFACES

i)   Set the snap resolution to a suitable value and turn snap On. Use parallel lines to draw the walls of the kitchen, leaving spaces for the door and window. You may prefer to use ortho for this operation but with snap On it is not really necessary.

ii)   Draw one pillar of the door frame and COPY this to form the other pillar. To produce the door, draw a LINE between the two pillars, enter the ROTATE command, select the line and choose the left hand end of the line as the base point of rotation. ROTATE the line through a suitable angle. Using the ARC command in Center, Start, End mode select the previous base point of rotation as the centre point, the middle of the inner face of the right hand door pillar as the start point and finally a suitable end point.

iii) Construct the two window frame pillars. Draw in two more parallel lines to form the window.

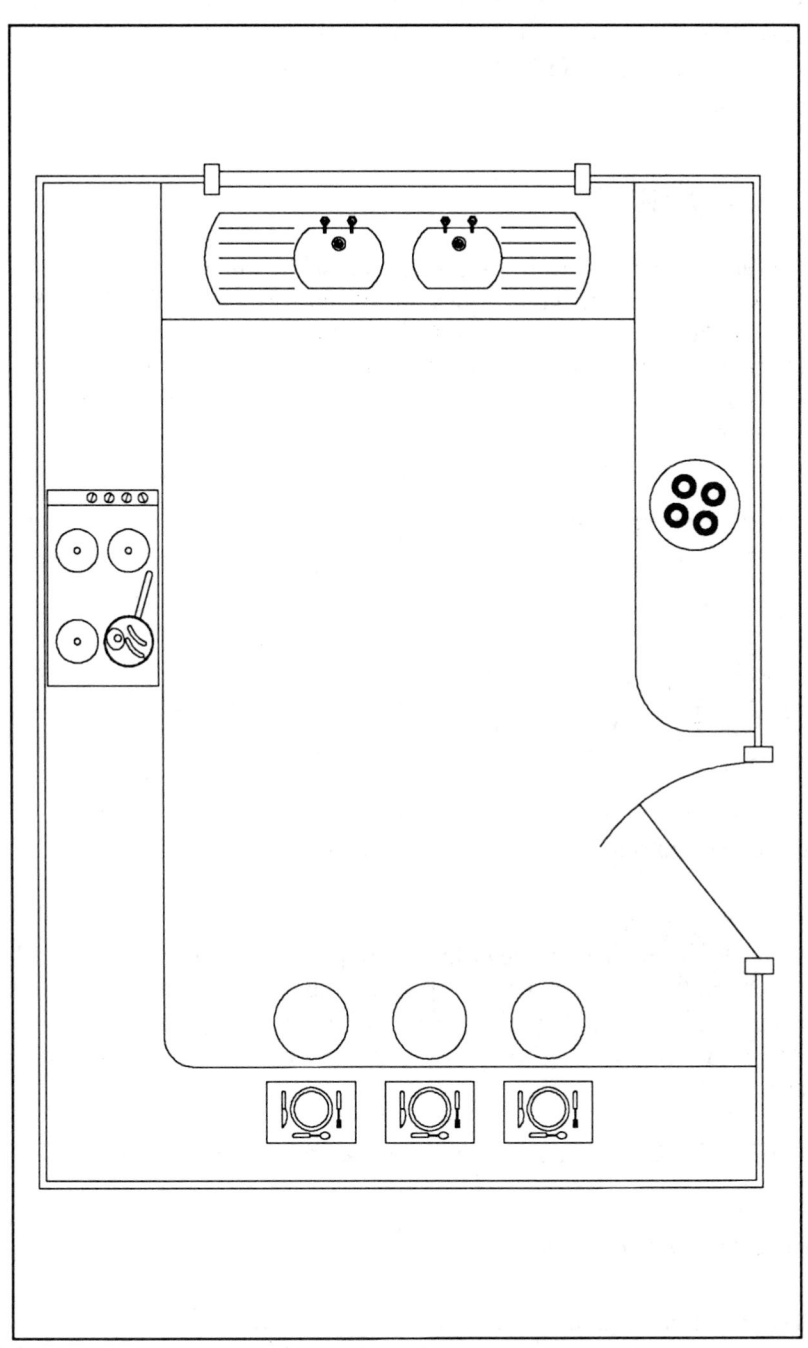

Figure A6.1 Kitchen plan

iv)   The work surfaces are constructed with LINES and ARCs. Draw in one of the work surface edges using LINE, enter the ARC command (Continue mode) and draw in an ARC of a suitable radius. Resume the LINE command and at the first prompt (**From point:**) respond with a return, complete the rest of the work surface.

A6.2 THE COOKER

i)   Construct the outline of the cooker shown in Figure A6.2 and use ZOOM Window to give a magnified view on screen. Draw two CIRCLEs to represent one of the hotplates. Use COPY (Multiple) to give the other two hotplates. Draw one of the control knobs and again use COPY (Multiple) to draw in the three other knobs. ROTATE one knob about its centre point to show that it is turned on.

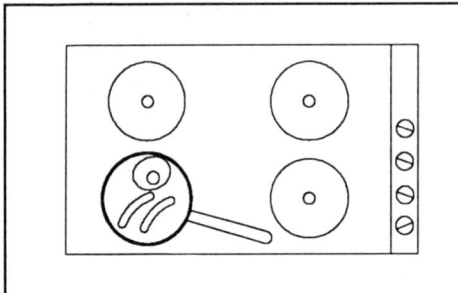

Figure A6.2   Detail of cooker   **Figure A6.3**   Detail of place setting

ii)   Draw in the circular outline of the frying pan and add a handle using LINE and ARC and again use ZOOM to give a convenient view on screen. The egg consists of a CIRCLE within an ELLIPSE. A sausage is constructed from 4 ARCs - it may take some practice to create a good sausage! Copy this sausage as required.

iii)   Use ZOOM Extents to return to an overall view of the kitchen.

A6.3 PLACE SETTINGS

i)   The detail of the place setting is shown in Figure A6.3. Draw the rectangular mat and use ZOOM Window to give a magnified view on screen. Add two concentric CIRCLEs for the plate.

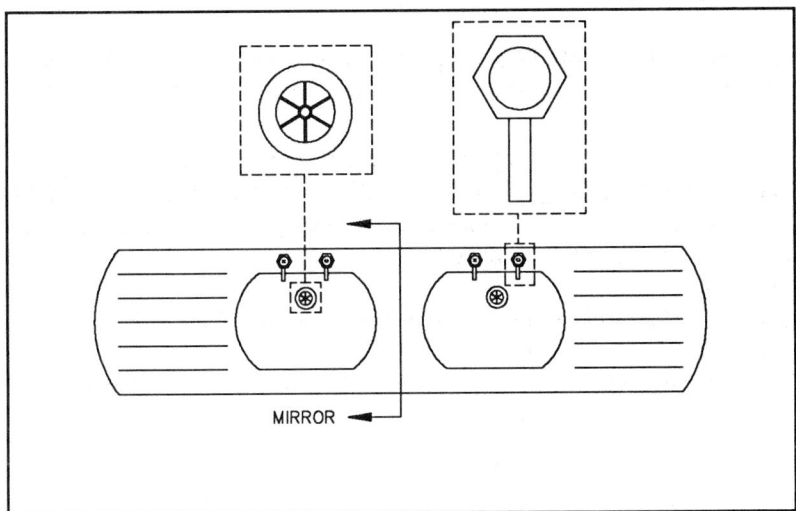

Figure A6.4   Detail of sink unit

ii)   The bowl of the spoon is an ELLIPSE. Use LINEs and an ARC to construct the body and handle of the spoon.

iii)   COPY the handle of the spoon and ROTATE it by -90° to create the handle of the fork. Add the body and prongs of the fork using LINE.

iv)   COPY the fork handle to create the handle of the knife. The blade is constructed using a LINE and an ARC. Use ZOOM Extents to return to an overall view of the kitchen.

v)   Add a circular seat and use COPY (Multiple) to produce the other place settings and seats.

A6.4 THE SINK UNIT

The double sink unit, (see Figure A6.4), has a line of symmetry through its centre. Therefore it is only necessary to construct one half of the unit, the other half being obtained using the MIRROR command.

i)   Using LINEs and ARC create the outline of one half of the sink unit. Use a suitable ZOOM command to give a working view.

ii) Similarly, use LINEs and ARCs to construct the sink bowl and add the five parallel LINEs.

iii) Draw concentric CIRCLEs to represent the drain hole. Use ZOOM to give a magnified view. Add a small CIRCLE and radial LINEs to form the grill.

iv) Using ZOOM Previous, return to the previous view and draw a hexagonal handle for the tap using the POLYGON command. ZOOM in on this, add a concentric CIRCLE and complete the tap using LINEs. ZOOM Previous and COPY the tap to make the pair.

v) Use the MIRROR command to complete the other half of the sink.

vi) Use ZOOM Extents to return to an overall view of the finished kitchen.

Appendix 7
Three dimensional drawing tutorials

A7.1 3D COORDINATES AND 3DFACES

i)   Use the LINE command to construct the outline of a house using the absolute
        coordinates given in Figure A7.1.

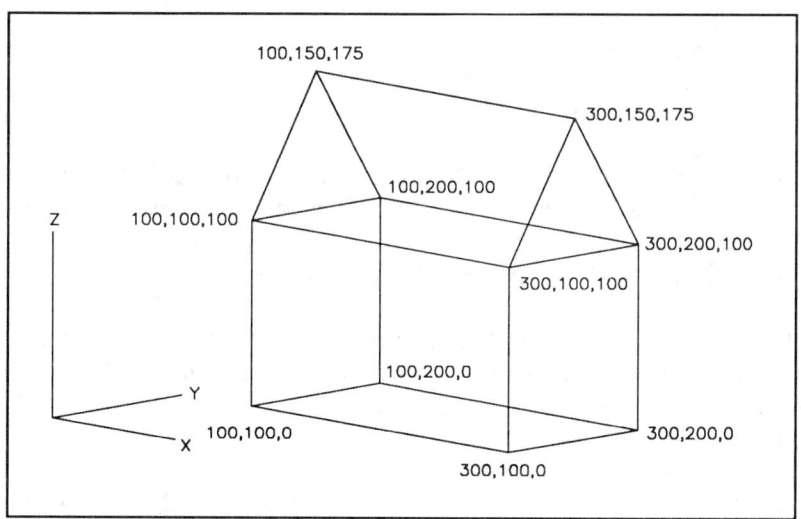

Figure A7.1   Outline of house

Command: LINE
From point: 100,100,0
To point: 300,100,0
To point: 300,200,0
To point: 100,200,0
To point: 100,100,0
To point: 100,100,100
To point: 300,100,100
To point: 300,200,100
To point: 100,200,100
To point: 100,100,100
To point: 100,150,175
To point: 100,200,100
Command: LINE
From point: 300,100,100
To point: 300,150,175
To point: 300,200,100
Command: LINE
From point: 100,200,0
To point: 100,200,100
Command: LINE
From point: 300,100,0
To point: 300,100,100
Command: LINE
From point: 300,200,0
To point: 300,200,100
Command: LINE
From point: 100,150,175
To point: 300,150,175

View the drawing from a suitable oblique angle (say -1.5,-1,1) using either the Vpoint 3D... icon display or the VPOINT command. This drawing will be in wireframe form and HIDE will therefore have no effect.

SAVE this outline drawing as HOUSE for future use.

ii)   While retaining the same oblique view, use Object Snap (Endpoint mode) to add 3DFACEs to all four sides and the roof. Check, using HIDE, that this now gives the effect of a solid model, (see Figure A7.2). SAVE as HOUSE1 and QUIT to the main menu.

iii)   Re-load HOUSE. Use the LINE command to construct a doorway 45 units high and 30 units wide in the centre of the front wall and subsequently add 3DFACEs to produce the drawing shown in Figure A7.3.

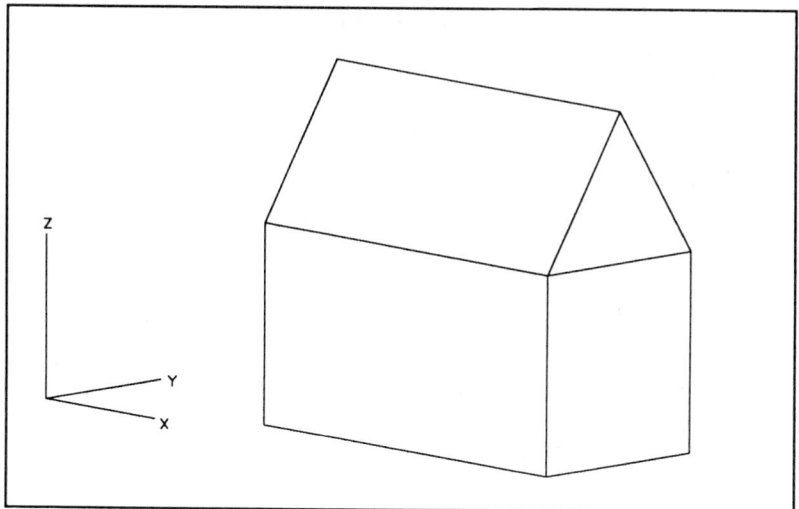

Figure A7.2   Solid house using 3DFACE

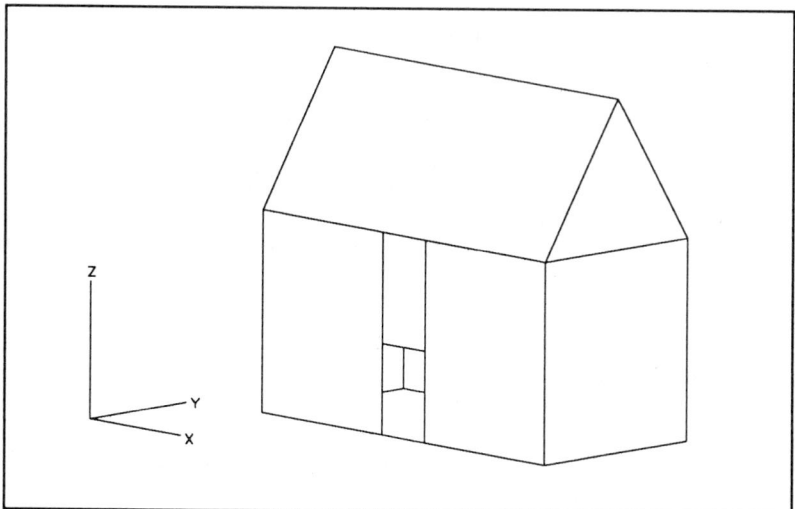

Figure A7.3   Doorway constructed using visible 3DFACEs

One possible way to achieve this is as follows:

Command: ID
Point: MID
of   Select base line of front wall
Command: LINE
From point: @15,0,0
To point: @0,0,45
To point: @-30,0,0
To point: @0,0,-45
Command: 3DFACE
First point: END
of   Select upper left corner of front wall
Second point: END
of   Select lower left corner of front wall
Third point: END
of   Select lower left corner of door
Fourth point: PERP
to   Select top line of front wall

Add the two remaining 3DFACEs to complete the front wall. The other walls and the roof sections may also have 3DFACEs added. Use the HIDE command to demonstrate that the door forms a true opening in the wall. SAVE as HOUSE2.

iv)   Repeat the previous exercise but using invisible 3DFACEs to give Figure A7.4.

        .

        .

        .

        .

Command: 3DFACE
First point: END
of   Select upper left corner of front wall
Second point: END
of   Select lower left corner of front wall
Third point: I
END
of   Select lower left corner of door
Fourth point: PERP
to   Select top line of front wall

Repeat for the remaining 3DFACEs and SAVE as HOUSE3.

v)   Using HOUSE3, delete the 3DFACE covering the front face of the roof. Add a skylight centred on this face which is 60 units wide by 50 units high.

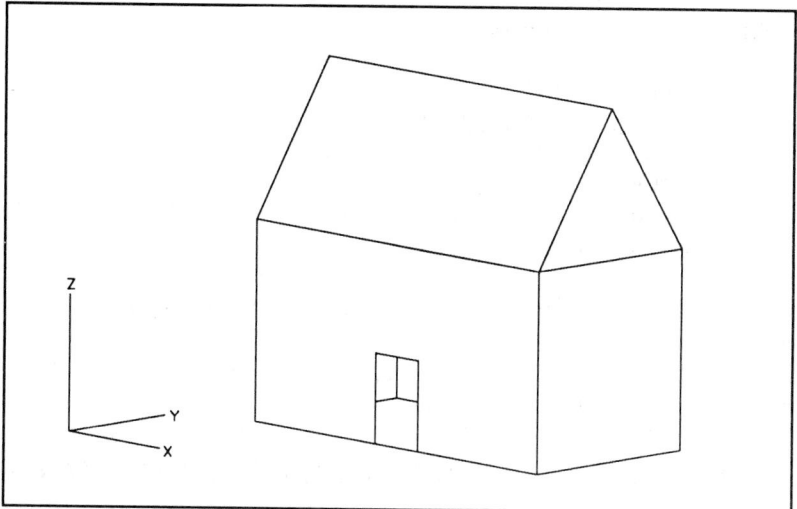

Figure A7.4   Doorway constructed using invisible 3DFACEs

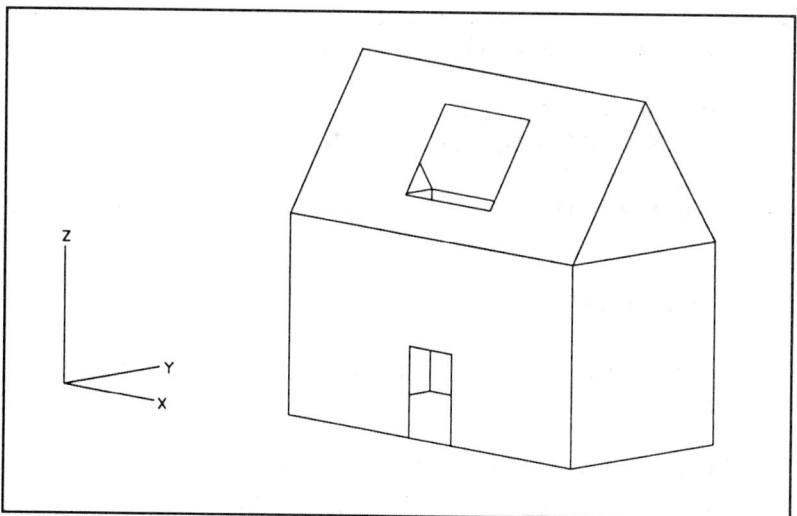

Figure A7.5   Doorway and skylight constructed using invisible 3DFACEs

This section is included to show the difficulties encountered in versions of AutoCAD prior to Release 10 when constructing objects lying in planes which are not in line with, or orthogonal to, the axes of the original drawing. In practice the easiest way is to calculate the coordinates of the corners of the skylight using trigonometry.

> **Command:** LINE
> **From point:** 170,138.87,158.30
> **To point:** 170,111.13,116.70
> **To point:** 230,111.13,116.70
> **To point:** 230,138.87,158.30
> **To point:** C

Invisible 3DFACEs may now be added to produce Figure A7.5. SAVE as HOUSE4.

A7.2 MASTERING THE USER COORDINATE SYSTEM (UCS)

This is a virtual repeat of of the previous example but uses the UCS facilities of the package. As a result it is possible to make quite complex additions to the basic drawing with ease.

i)   Using the drawing HOUSE, add a door and some windows to the front wall.

Use the UCSICON command to set the icon so that it is automatically located at the origin of each new UCS.

> **Command:** UCSICON
> **ON/OFF/All/Noorigin/ORigin <ON>:** OR

Create a new UCS with its origin at the lower left corner of the front wall and its plane in the plane of the wall, (see Figure A7.6).

> **Command:** DDUCS

Define new current UCS and name it FRONT using Origin, X axis, Plane

> **Origin point<0,0,0>:** END
> **of**   Point to lower left corner of front wall
> **Point on positive portion of X axis <1,0,0>:** END
> **of**   Point to lower right corner of front wall
> **Point on positive Y portion of the UCS X-Y plane <0,1,0>:** END

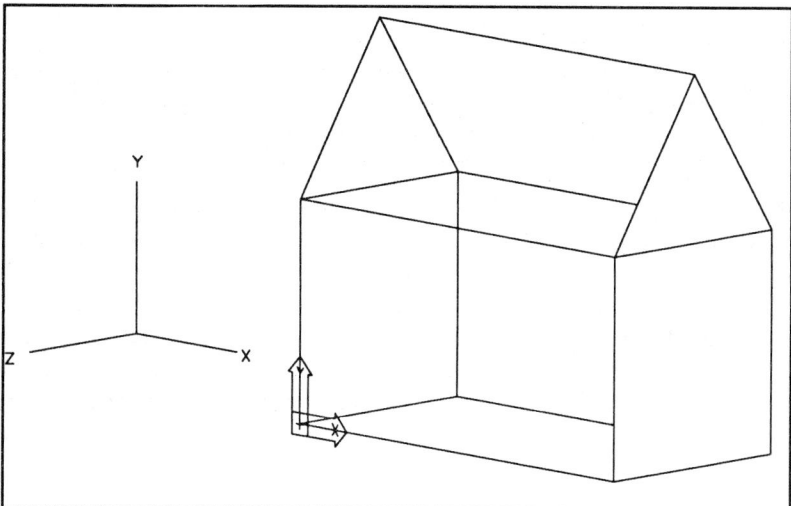

Figure A7.6   New UCS: FRONT

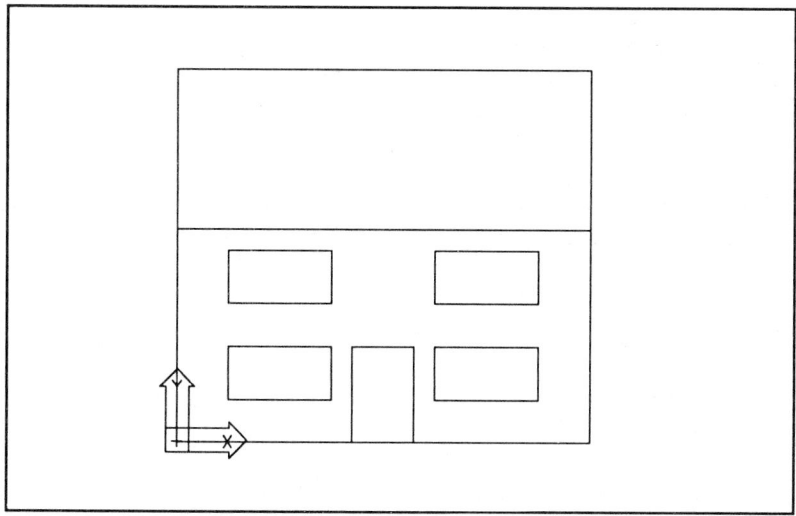

Figure A7.7   Doorway and windows constructed on UCS FRONT

of Point to upper right corner of front wall
Command: PLAN
<Current UCS>/UCS/World: C

Note: An alternative to using the PLAN command is to set the system variable UCSFOLLOW to 1. This in effect automatically issues the PLAN command after a new UCS has been defined.

A door and windows may now be drawn-in directly using standard 2D techniques, (see Figure A7.7). 3DFACEs may be added as required.

ii) Place a window in the right hand end wall.

Create the required new UCS in two stages. First create a temporary UCS with its origin at the lower right corner of the front wall and its plane in the plane of the wall and then rotate this UCS about the Y- axis, (see Figure A7.8).

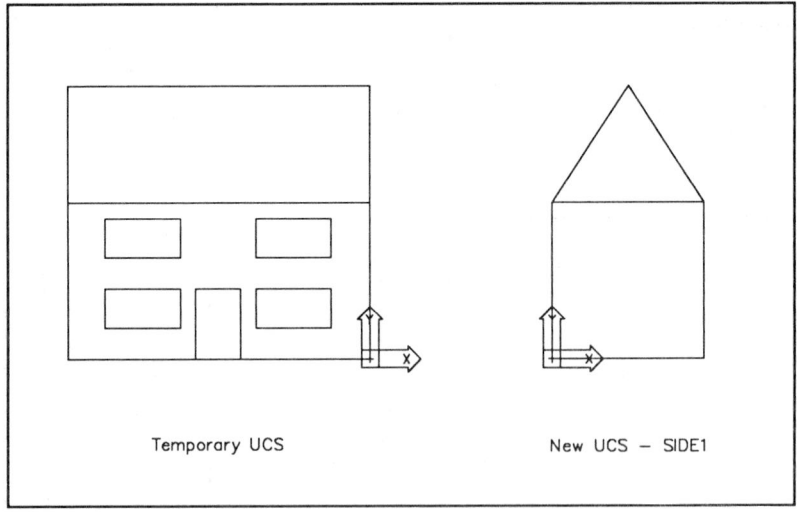

Temporary UCS   New UCS — SIDE1

Figure A7.8 New UCS SIDE1 created in two stages

Command: DDUCS

Define new current UCS using New origin

Origin point <0,0,0>: END
of Point to lower right corner of front wall

Command: DDUCS

Define new current UCS and name it SIDE1 using Rotate about Y axis

Rotation angle about Y axis <0.0>: 90
Command: PLAN
<Current UCS>/UCS/World: C

A window may now be added, (see Figure A7.9).
The above may repeated to place other windows etc., in other walls.

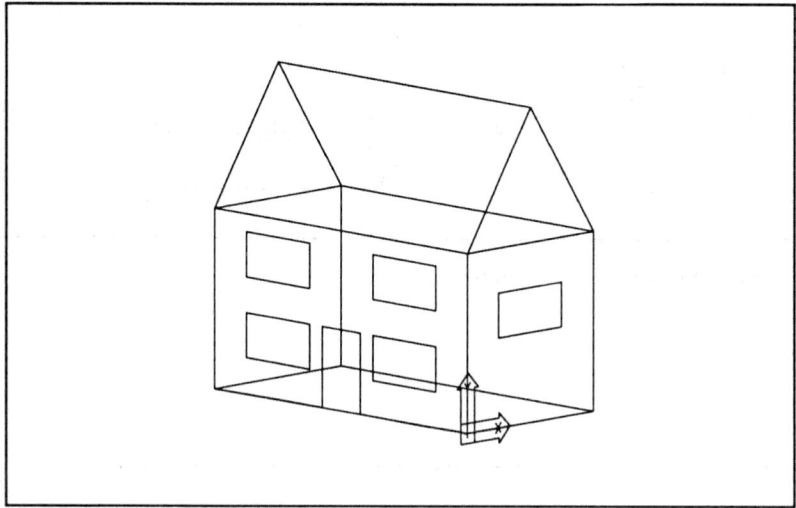

Figure A7.9   Window constructed on UCS SIDE1

Note: The reason that the SIDE1 UCS was defined in two steps was that only the plan view was available on screen and it would have been necessary to return to an oblique view to define SIDE1 in a single step (using Origin, X axis and Plane as in section (i)). To overcome this problem, multiple viewports may be used to provide alternative views of the drawing.

---

iii)   Place a skylight in the roof as A7.1(v).

Firstly, make two viewports - the left-hand one with an oblique view of the drawing (which will act as a reference view) and the right-hand one showing a plan view of the current UCS (UCSFOLLOW=1 in this viewport). See Figure A6-10.

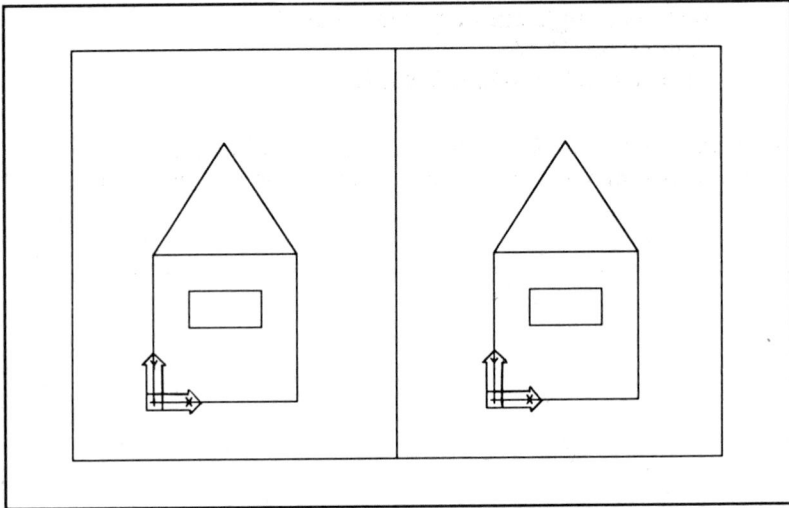

Figure A7.10 Creation of two viewports

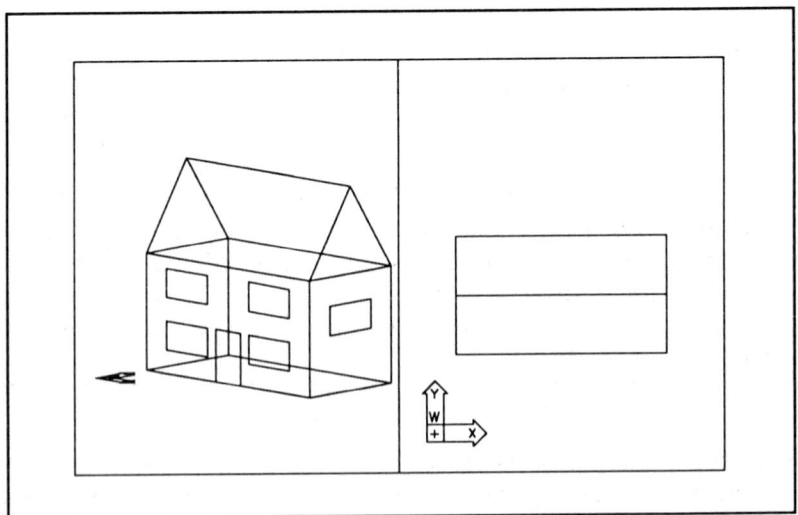

Figure A7.11 Oblique and plan world views

Command: VPORTS
Save/Restore/Delete/Join/SIngle/?/2/<3>/4: 2
Horizontal/<Vertical>: V

Take the cursor into the right-hand viewport, press the pick button to make it the active viewport and set UCSFOLLOW to be 1.

Make the left-hand viewport active, change the UCS to World and select a suitable oblique view of the drawing, (see Figure A7.11).

We now need to create a new UCS, called ROOF1, which has its origin at the bottom left-hand corner of the front face of the roof and which lies in the plane of this face. Using the oblique view in the left-hand viewport and with object snap set to Endpoint mode:

Command: DDUCS

Define new current UCS and name it ROOF1 using Origin, X axis, Plane

Origin point<0,0,0>: Point to lower left corner of roof
Point on positive portion of X axis <1,0,0>:

Point to lower right corner of roof

Point on positive Y portion of the UCS X-Y plane <0,1,0>:

Point to upper right corner of roof

Note that the right-hand viewport has automatically changed to the plan view of the new UCS, (see Figure A7.12). Make this active and draw in the specified skylight using standard 2D techniques.

iv)   Convert the skylight into a dormer window as shown in Figure A7.13.

Use the UCS dialogue box to set the previously-defined UCS, SIDE1, to be the current UCS. Then define a new UCS, called DORMER:

Command: DDUCS

Define new current UCS using New origin

Origin point <0,0,0>:

Point to the a bottom corner of the skylight

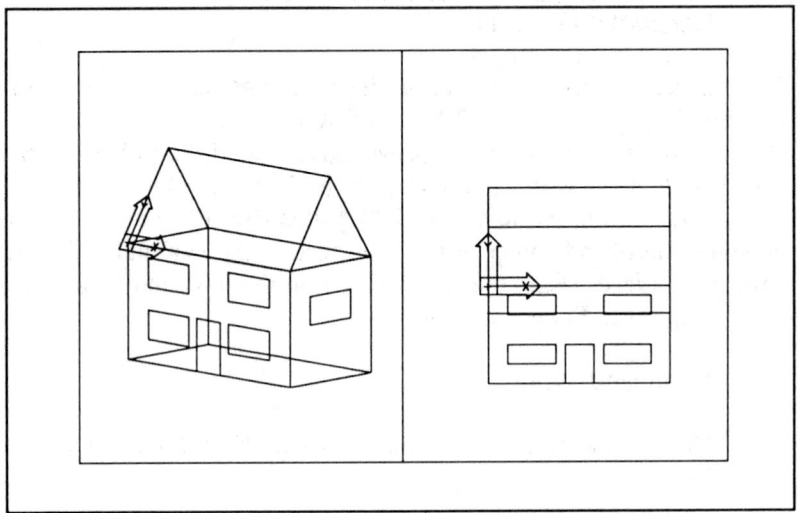

Figure A7.12   UCS ROOF: oblique and plan views

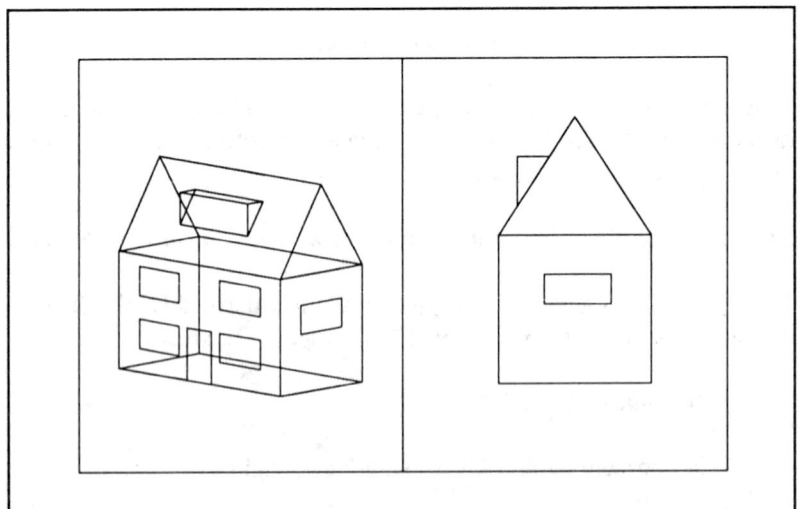

Figure A7.13   Making a dormer window

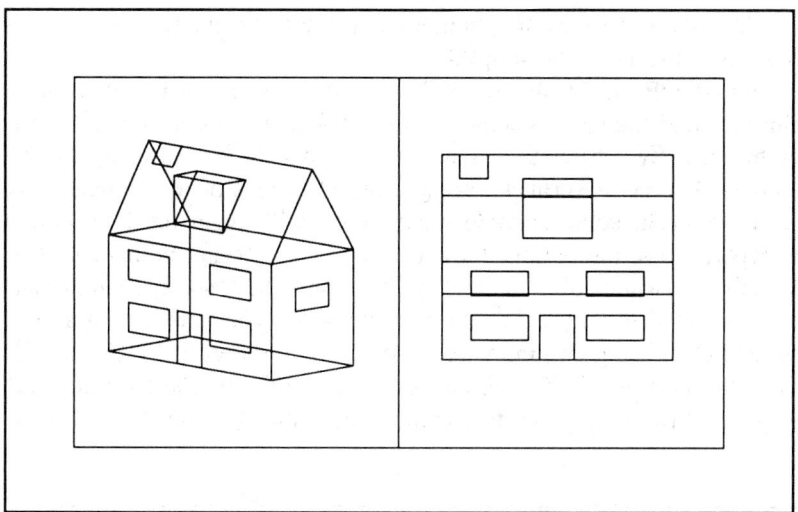

Figure A7.14   Chimney/roof interface

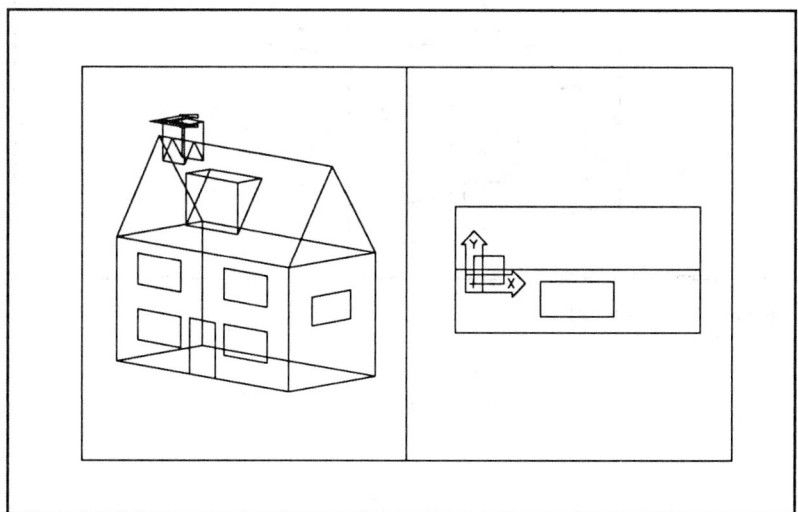

Figure A7.15   UCS POT

Use the LINE command and work in both viewports to construct one side of
the dormer window. Copy this to the opposite end of the skylight. Complete the
construction by adding the dormer roof.

v) Finally, add a chimney and chimney pot. There are many ways to achieve this
but this is probably the simplest:

Set ROOF1 to be the active UCS and draw in the interface between the
chimney and the roof as shown in Figure A7.14. Repeat this on the other face
of the roof by setting SIDE1 to be the active UCS and using the MIRROR
command. Erect 4 verticals representing the edges of the chimney stack from
each corner to some suitable height (you will again need to work in both
viewports - use the oblique view to locate these corner points and the view in
the other viewport to set the height). Complete the stack by joining together the
top ends of these lines. To add a chimney pot you must create a new UCS -
called POT - using Origin, X-axis and Plane, (see Figure A7.15). Set Thickness
to 20 and use the CIRCLE command to place the pot on the stack. 3DFACEs
may be added as required to complete the drawing as shown in Figure A7.16.

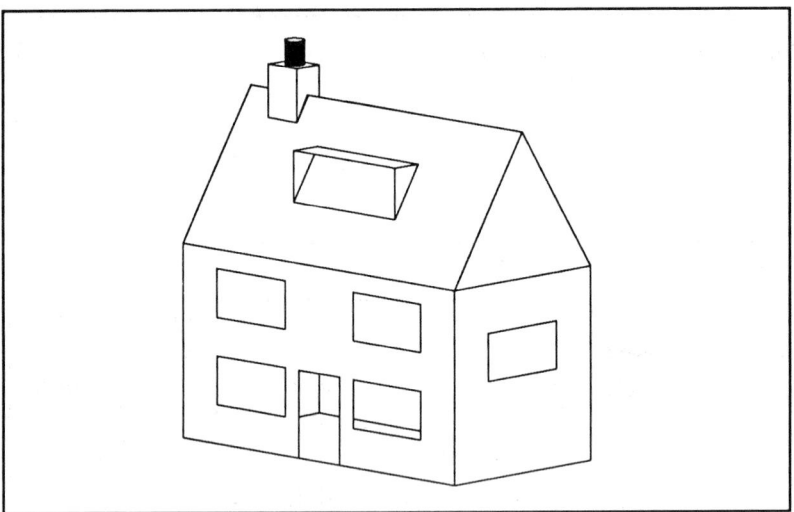

Figure A7.16 Completed house

A7.3 REVSURF AND RULESURF

The dart shown in Figure A7.17 may be constructed using both REVSURF and RULESURF.

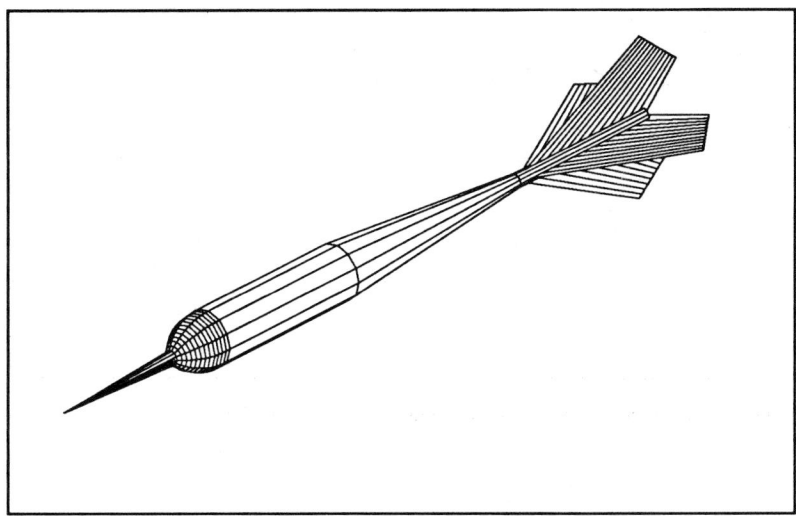

Figure A7.17   Dart

Set the UCSFOLLOW system variable to 1 - this will automatically generate the plan view on each change of UCS.

The first step is to use a 2D Polyline to draw the profile of the dart and the axis of revolution. The profile will be used as the path curve for the REVSURF command, (see Figure A7.18).

```
Command: REVSURF
Select path curve:
Select axis of revolution:
Start angle <0>: 0
Included angle ( +=CCW, -=CW) <Full circle>: 360
```

This will produce the body of the dart as shown in Figure A7.19. Now erase the axis of revolution which is no longer required.

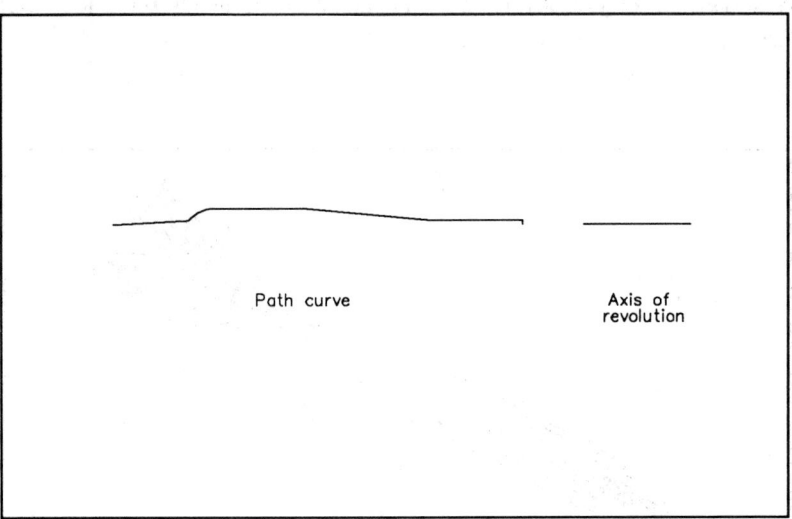

Figure A7.18 Profile and axis of revolution to be used by REVSURF

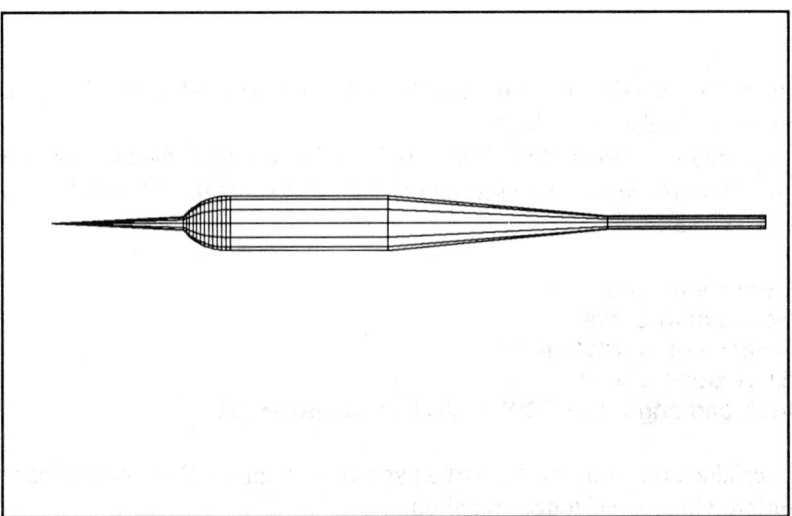

Figure A7.19 Body of dart produced by REVSURF

To construct the tail of the dart it is only necessary to draw one of the four fins. First use LINE to draw the two defining curves as shown in Figure A7.20.

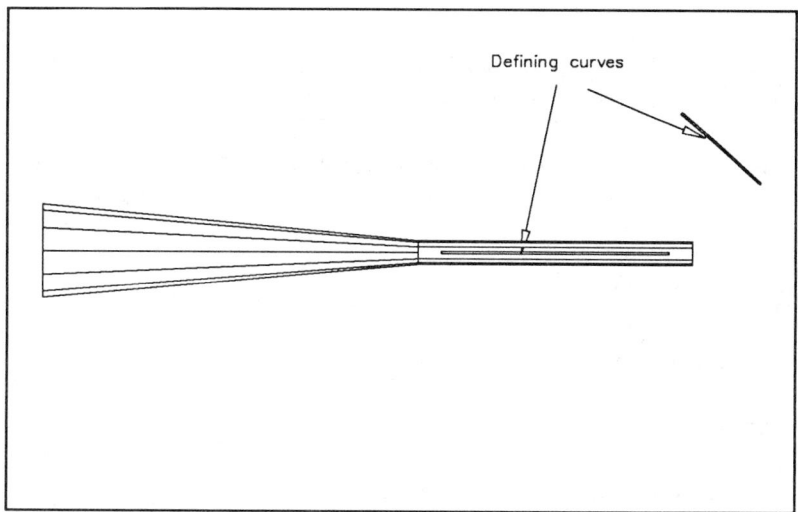

Figure A7.20   Two defining curves for use with RULESURF

Then use RULESURF. (See Figure A7.21.)

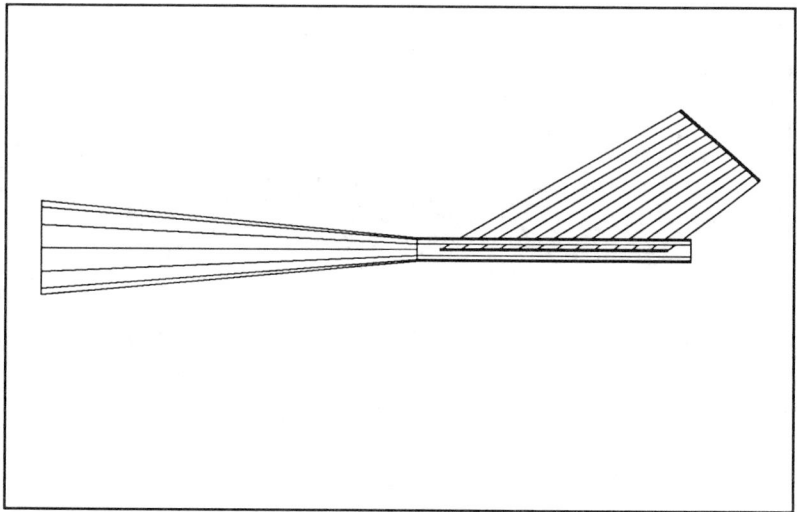

Figure A7.21   A single fin constructed using RULESURF

Command: RULESURF
Select first defining curve:
Select second defining curve:

> *Note:* When selecting the defining curve, the choice of selection point will affect the final shape of the ruled surface. (See Figure 16.41.)

The remaining three fins may be produced using ARRAY but it is essential first to change to a suitable UCS which is orthogonal to the axis of the dart, (see Figure A7.22).

Command: DDUCS

Define new current UCS using New origin

Origin point <0,0,0>:

Position new origin on the fin end of the dart

Command: DDUCS

Define new current UCS and name it END using Rotate about Y-axis

Rotation angle about Y axis <0.0>: 90

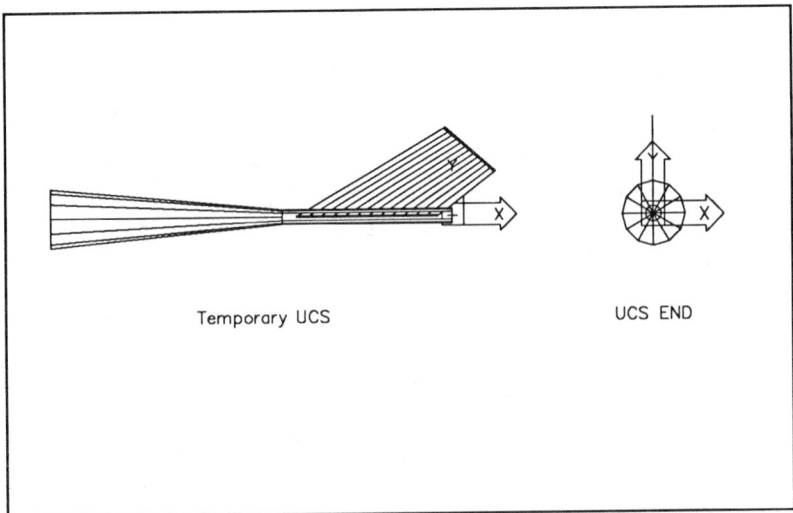

Temporary UCS   UCS END

Figure A7.22   Defining new UCS END

Now use a polar ARRAY, remembering to use a Crossing Window to select the components of the fin, to create the remaining fins and complete the drawing, (see Figure A7.23).

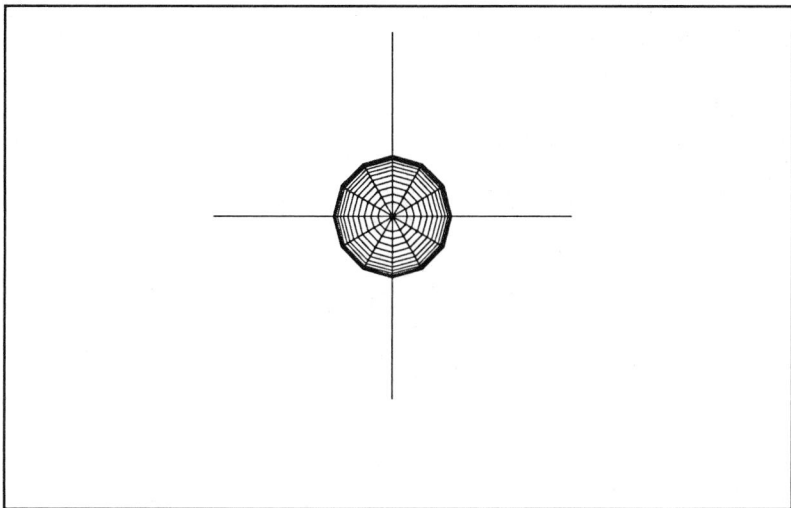

Figure A7.23   Rear view of completed dart

A7.4 REVSURF AND TABSURF

The links of the chain shown in Figure A7.24 are constructed using REVSURF and TABSURF. Each link is composed of 4 sections - 2 curved and 2 straight.

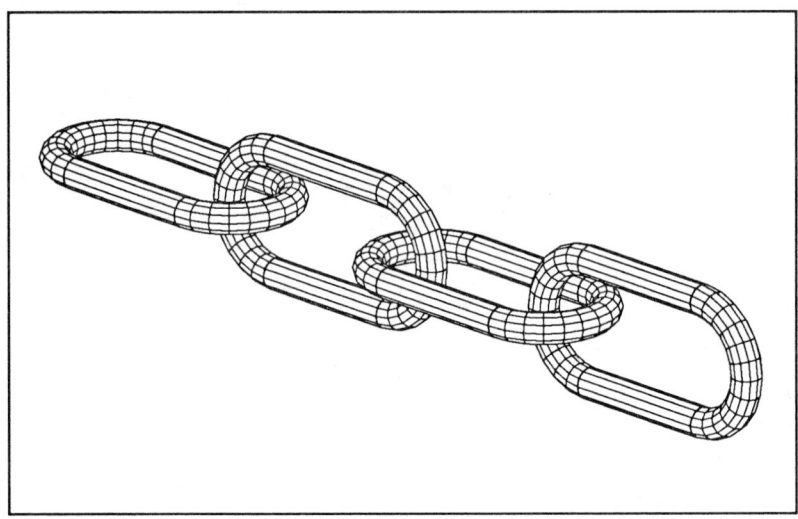

Figure A7.24   Chain

Set the UCSFOLLOW system variable to 1 - this will automatically generate the plan view on each change of UCS.

One of the curved sections may be constructed as follows:

Draw a CIRCLE representing the cross section through one arm of the link. Draw a LINE as the axis of revolution.

> **Command:** REVSURF
> **Select path curve:**   Select the circle
> **Select axis of revolution:**
> **Start angle <0>:** -90
> **Included angle (+=CCW, -=CW) <Full circle>:** 180

This is shown in Figure A7.25. Erase the axis of revolution to complete this section.

Use the MIRROR command to give a replica of this end section of the link. To complete the link the two straight sections need to be constructed using TABSURF which in turn requires a circular path curve and a direction vector.

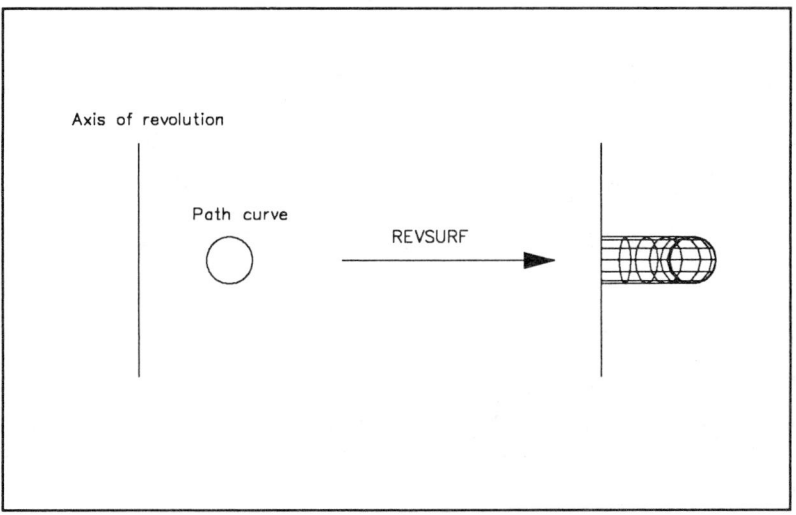

Figure A7.25 Construction of an end section of a single link

Note: Despite appearances, there are no circles at the ends of the previously drawn sections - the circular effect is due to an end-on view of the component 3D faces of the mesh.

To place a circle on one of the ends it is necessary to create a new UCS in the plane of this end face. (See Figure A6-26.)

Command: DDUCS

Define new current UCS using New origin

Origin point <0,0,0>: Position new origin on end of link

Command: DDUCS

Define new current UCS and name it END using Rotate about Y axis

Rotation angle about Y axis <0.0>: 90

Draw two CIRCLEs - one on each end face - to the same radius as that of the original REVSURF path curve, (see Figure A7.27). Reset the UCS to World. Create a new UCS:

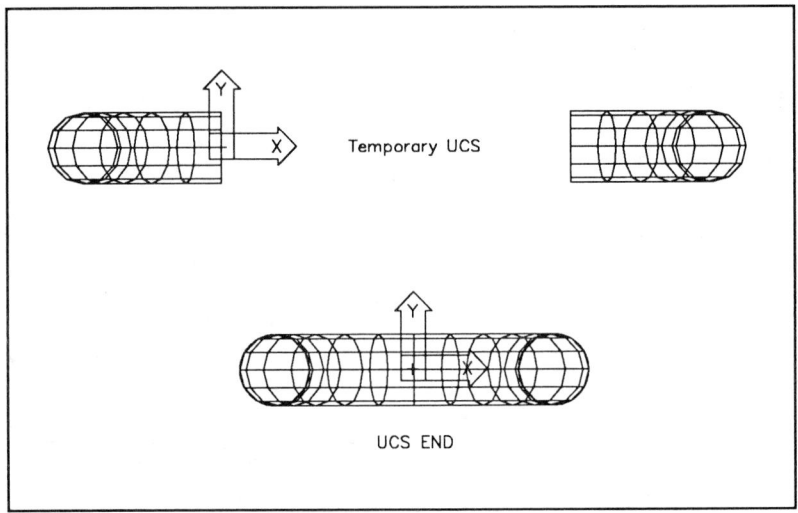

Figure A7.26 Defining new UCS END

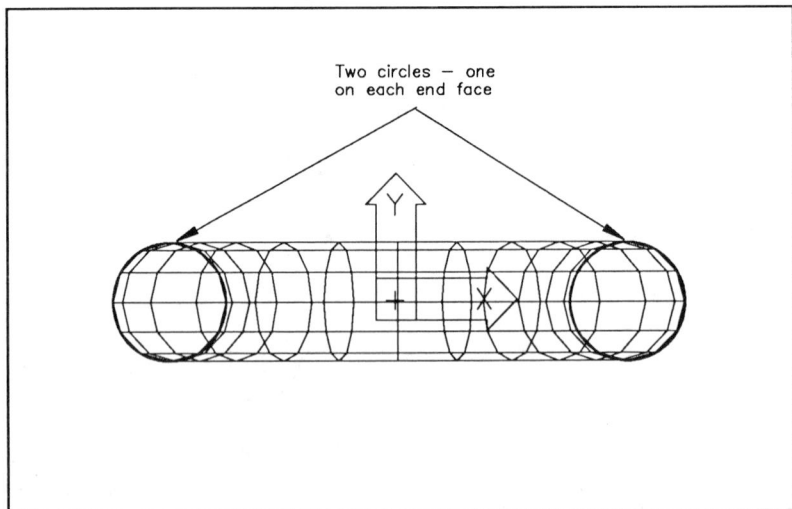

Figure A7.27 Creating end sections

Command: DDUCS

Define new current UCS and name it SIDE using Rotate about X axis

Rotation angle about X axis <0.0>: 90

Draw in the direction vector, the length of which is the distance between the two opposing faces of the end sections, (see Figure A7.28).

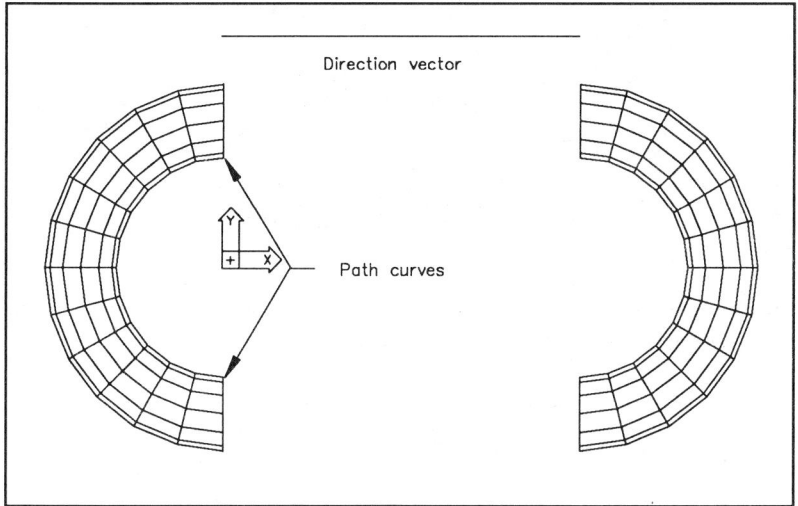

Figure A7-28   Two opposing end sections

Command: TABSURF
Select path curve: Select one of the circles
Select direction vector: Select the end nearest to the path curve

Repeat for the other straight section and erase the direction vector, (see Figure A7.29), to finish one complete link of the chain.

Subsequent links may now be derived. COPY the link and place the copy above the original. Change the UCS to END and ROTATE the copy through 90°. Change the UCS back to SIDE and MOVE the rotated link to couple with the original, (see Figure A7.30). Indefinite extension of the chain may be achieved by simple copying of this pair of links.

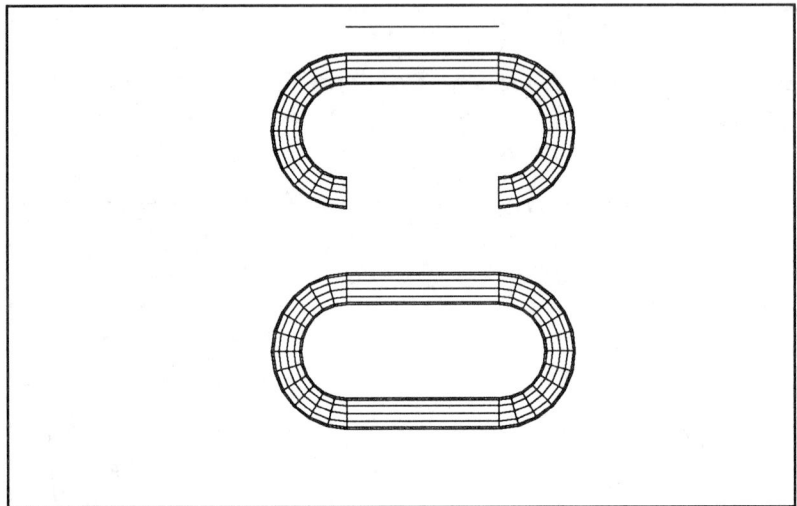

Figure A7.29 Using TABSURF to complete the link

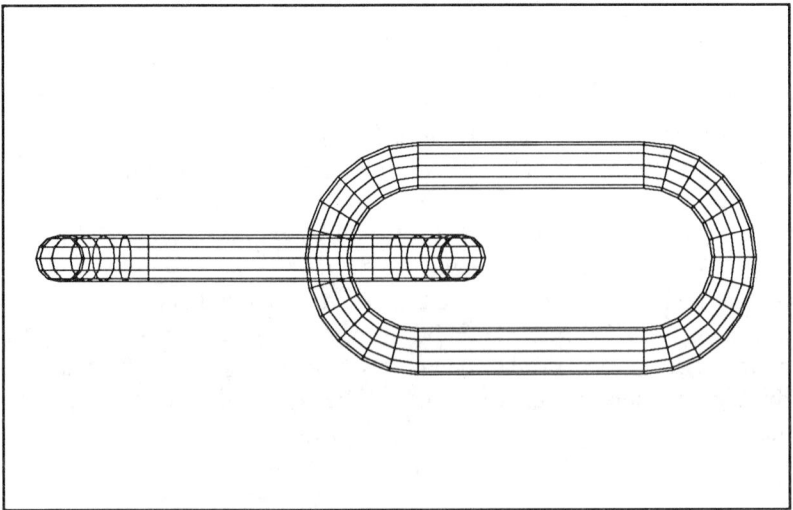

Figure A7.30 Second link formed by COPY, MOVE and ROTATE

Appendix 8
AME solid modelling tutorial

A8.1 SETTING OUT THE DRAWING ENVIRONMENT

The solid key, shown in Figure A8.1, may be constructed within AutoCAD's AME environment, using a selection of the most useful AME commands.

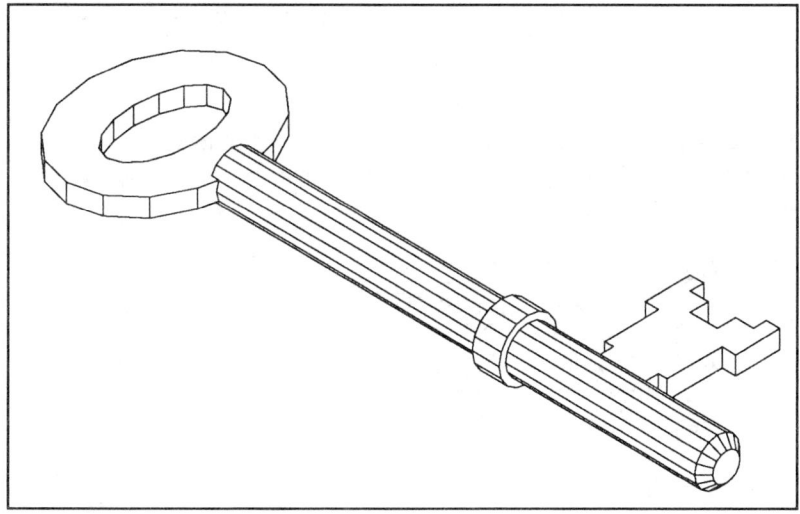

Figure A8.1   Solid key

Before any solid construction is possible it is first necessary to load the AME software into the AutoCAD environment. Pick Load AME from the **Solids** pull down menu or, alternately, load AME from the keyboard:

Command: (XLOAD"AME")

It takes a short time to load this software - be patient. If this is the first time that AME has been requested, you will be prompted for your AME authorization code, (see Section 17.3). When AME has been loaded, the full AME pull down menu structure will become active.

Now set the LIMITS to 0,0 and 80,50 to match the drawing dimensions (millimetres) and ZOOM All.

A8.2 CONSTRUCTING THE KEY

i)   To produce the basic bow entity pick Cylinder from the **Sol - Prim's** pull down menu, or enter SOLCYL from the keyboard, and select the **Elliptical** option:

> **Command:** SOLCYL
> **Elliptical/<Center point>:** E
> **Axis endpoint 1:** 10,25
> **Axis endpoint 2:** 10,47
> **Other axis distance:** @8.5<0
> **Height of cylinder:** 2

This will produce a solid elliptical cylinder of major axis length 22mm and minor axis length 17mm.

ii)   The cut-out in the bow is achieved by the subtraction of a second solid elliptical cylinder from the first. This must be placed accurately for the subtraction to be successful.

> **Command:** SOLCYL
> **Elliptical/<Center point>:** E
> **Axis endpoint 1:** 10,29.5
> **Axis endpoint 2:** 10,42.5
> **Other axis distance:** @3.5<0
> **Height of cylinder:** 2

(See Figure A8.2.)

To subtract this cylinder from the first, pick Subtract from the **Sol - Modify** pull down menu or enter SOLSUB from the keyboard:

> **Command:** SOLSUB
> **Source objects...**
> **Select objects:**   Select the large elliptical solid

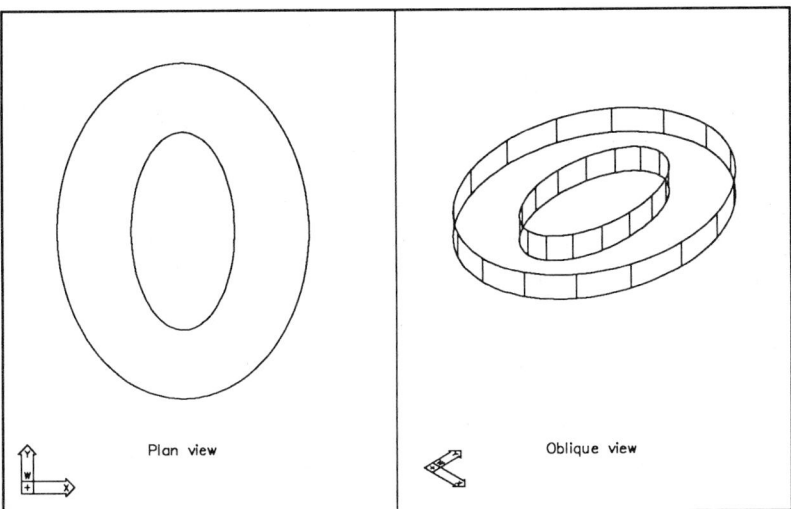

Figure A8.2 Bow construction using elliptical cylinders

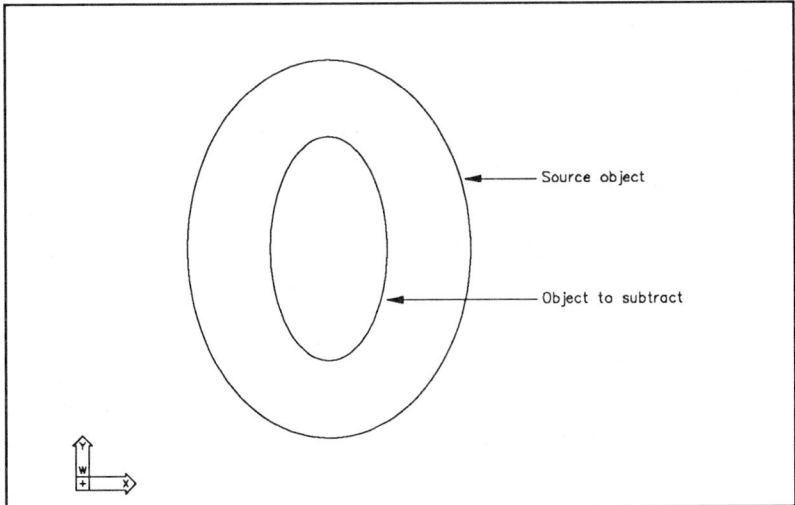

Figure A8.3 Solid selection for SOLSUB

1 solid selected.
Objects to subtract from them...
Select objects: Select the small elliptical solid
1 solid selected.

(See figure A8.3.)
 The result will be a single solid entity, but the screen display will not look any different at this stage.

iii) The stem of the key is formed from another solid cylinder, placed on a new UCS, at right angles to the previous UCS. First define and save a new UCS called BOW. (See Figure A8.4.)

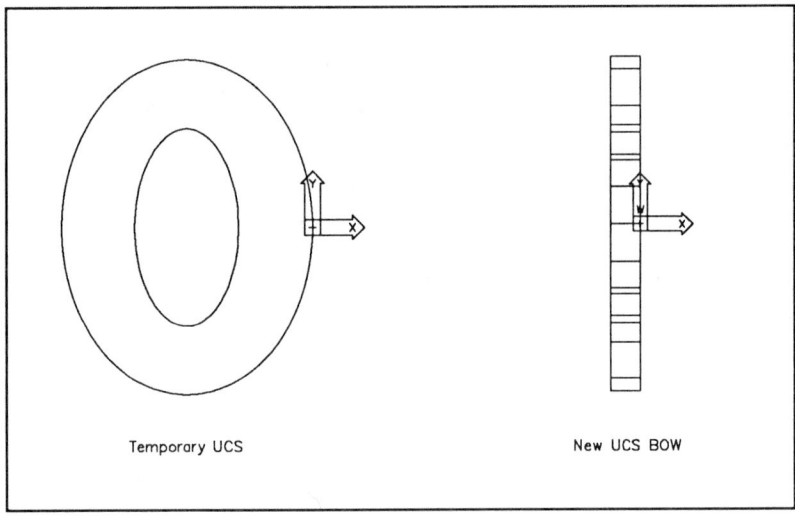

Temporary UCS   New UCS BOW

Figure A8.4 Defining new UCS BOW

Command: UCS
Origin/ZAxis/3point/Entity/View/X/Y/Z/Prev/Restore
  /Save/Del/?/<World>: O
Origin point <0,0,0>: Pick right hand minor axis point of large ellipse

Command: UCS
Origin/ZAxis/3point/Entity/View/X/Y/Z/Prev/Restore
   /Save/Del/?/<World>: Y
Rotation angle about the Y axis <0.0>: 90

Command: PLAN
<Current UCS>/Ucs/World: return

Command: UCS
Origin/ZAxis/3point/Entity/View/X/Y/Z/Prev/Restore /Save/Del/?/<World>: S
?/Desired UCS name: BOW

Now draw the stem using the SOLCYL command, (see Figure A8.5).

Command: SOLCYL
Elliptical/<Center point>: 0,0
Diameter/<Radius>: 2.5
Height of cylinder: 55

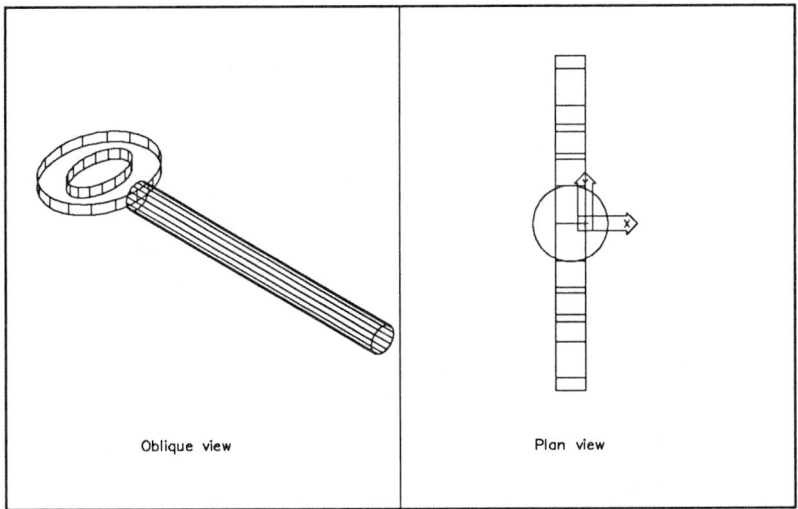

Oblique view   Plan view

Figure A8.5   Stem created using SOLCYL

iv)   It is useful at this stage to divide the screen into two equal vertical viewports using the VPORTS command. Set the UCS back to World. In the left hand viewport set an oblique view of the drawing using VPOINT (1,-1,1). In the right hand viewport set the UCSFOLLOW system variable to 1 (automatic plan view generation).

v)   The next set of operations will create the key collar. It is first necessary to change the UCS and align it with the end face of the stem. Use the special AME UCS command SOLUCS:

Command: SOLUCS
Edge/<Face>: F
Select a face:　Select the end face of the stem
<OK>/Next:　If the end face is not highlighted, then respond **Next**

Command: UCS
Origin/ZAxis/3point/Entity/View/X/Y/Z/Prev/Restore
　　　/Save/Del/?/<World>: S
?/Desired UCS name: END

The UCS icon will now move to the centre of the end face of the stem, (see Figure A8.6).

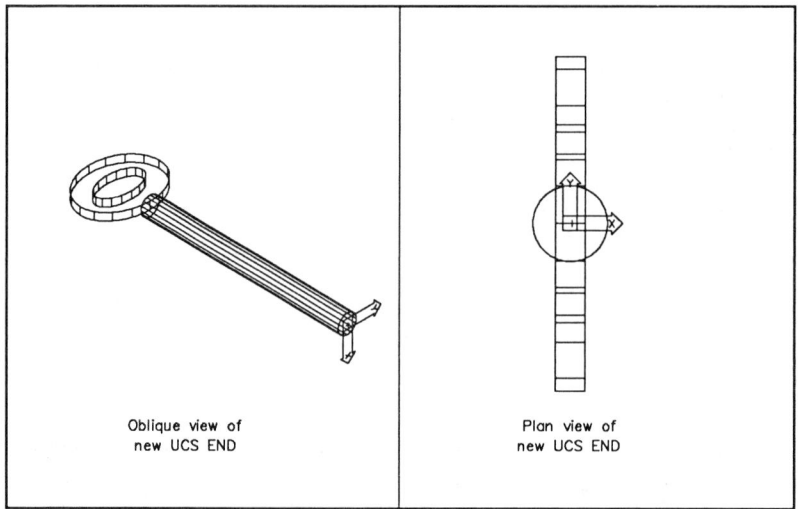

Oblique view of
new UCS END

Plan view of
new UCS END

Figure A8.6　Defining a new UCS END using SOLUCS

The collar is created by another subtraction process.

Command: SOLCYL
Elliptical/<Center point>: 0,0
Diameter/<Radius>: 3.25
Height of cylinder: 3

Command: SOLCYL
Elliptical/<Center point>: 0,0
Diameter/<Radius>: 2.5
Height of cylinder: 3

Command: SOLSUB
Source objects...
Select objects: Select the large cylinder
1 solid selected.
Objects to subtract from them...
Select objects: Select the small cylinder
1 solid selected.

(See Figure A8.7.)

To translate the collar along the stem by 25mm, select Solid Move from the **Sol -Modify** pull down menu or enter SOLMOVE from the keyboard:

Command: SOLMOVE
Select objects: Select the collar; the MCS icon will appear
<Motion description>/?: TZ-25
<Motion description>/?: Return to exit

(See Figure A8.8.)

vi) The stem and collar need to be placed to intersect with the bow. This is achieved using SOLMOVE:

Command: SOLMOVE
Select objects: Select the collar and stem; the MCS icon will appear
<Motion description>/?: TZ-1
<Motion description>/?: Return to exit

vii) The bit of the key is constructed by the solidification of a 2D polyline which has thickness. First change the UCS back to World and set the thickness to 2 by selecting Entity creation... from the **Options** pull down menu or by invoking the ELEV command:

Command: UCS
Origin/ZAxis/3point/Entity/View/X/Y/Z/Prev/Restore /Save/Del/?/<World>: W

Command: ELEV
New current elevation <0.0>: return
New current thickness <0.0>: 2

Construct the outline of the bit using the PLINE command:

Command: PLINE
From point: 56,40
To point: @2<90

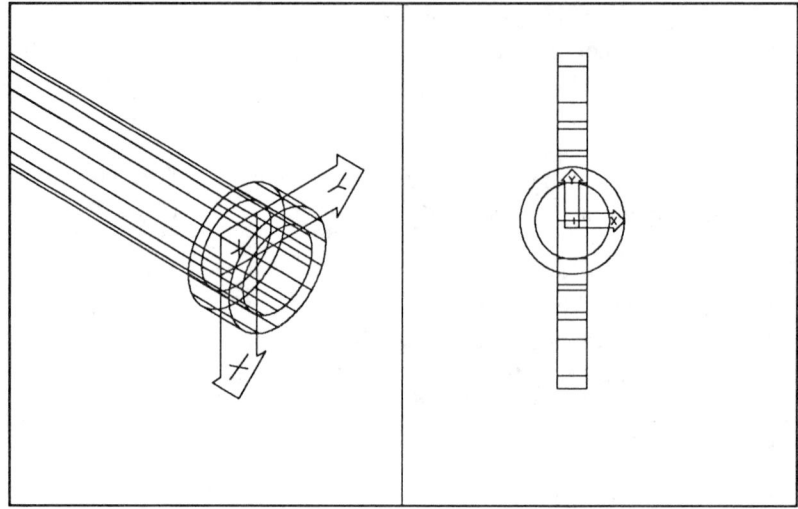

Figure A8.7 Construction of the collar

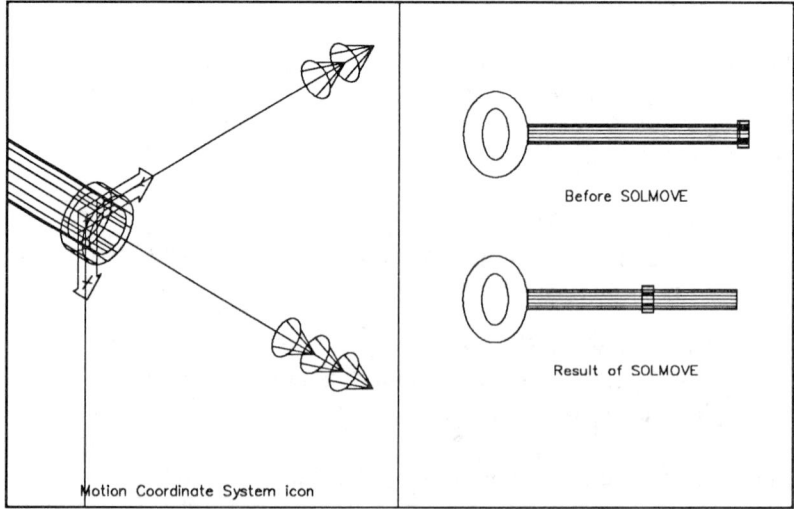

Figure A8.8 Placing the collar on the stem using SOLMOVE

To point: @1<180
To point: @6<90
To point: @1.5<180
To point: @5<90
To point: @1.5<0
To point: @1.5<-90
To point: @2<0
To point: @2<-90
To point: @3<0
To point: @2<90
To point: @2<0
To point: @1.5<90
To point: @1.5<0
To point: @5<-90
To point: @1.5<180
To point: @6<-90
To point: @1<180
To point: @2<-90
To point: C

This 2D polyline may be changed into a solid entity by selecting Solidify from the **Sol - prim's** pull down menu, or by entering SOLIDIFY from the keyboard:

Command: SOLIDIFY
Select objects: Select the 2D polyline

(See Figure A8.9.)

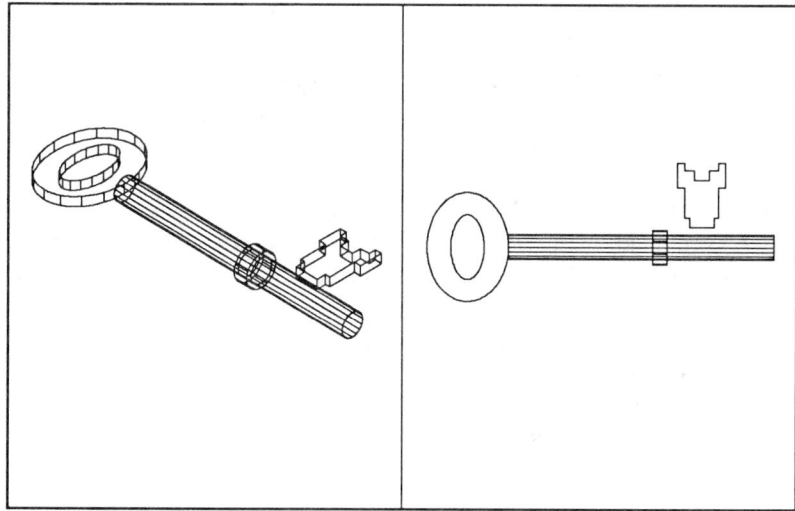

Figure A8.9   Solidified 2D polyline to form the bit

The bit must now be moved to intersect the stem. Use SOLMOVE:

Command: SOLMOVE
Select objects: Select the bit; the MCS icon will appear
<Motion description>/?: TY-2
<Motion description>/?: Return to exit

(See Figure A8.10.)

viii) To chamfer the end of the stem, select Chamfer from the **Sol - Modify** pull down or enter SOLCHAM from the keyboard:

Command: SOLCHAM
Select base surface: Select the end of the stem
<OK>/Next: If the end face is not highlighted, then respond **Next**
Select edges to be chamfered (Press ENTER when done):
1 edge selected:
Enter distance along first surface: 1
Enter distance along second surface: 1

(See Figure A8.11.)

ix) Finally, join together all four parts of the key, i.e. the bow, stem, collar and bit, to form a single complex solid entity. Select Union from the **Sol - Modify** pull down menu or enter SOLUNION from the keyboard:

Command: SOLUNION
Select objects: Select the four parts of the key
4 Objects selected:

x) The complex solid is still in wireframe form and therefore the SHADE and HIDE commands will have no visible effect. To mesh the solid, select Mesh from the **Sol - Display** pull down menu or enter SOLMESH at the keyboard:

Command: SOLMESH
Select objects:
1 solid selected.
Surface meshing of current solids is completed.

xi) Use the SHADE command to produce a shaded display of the finished key.

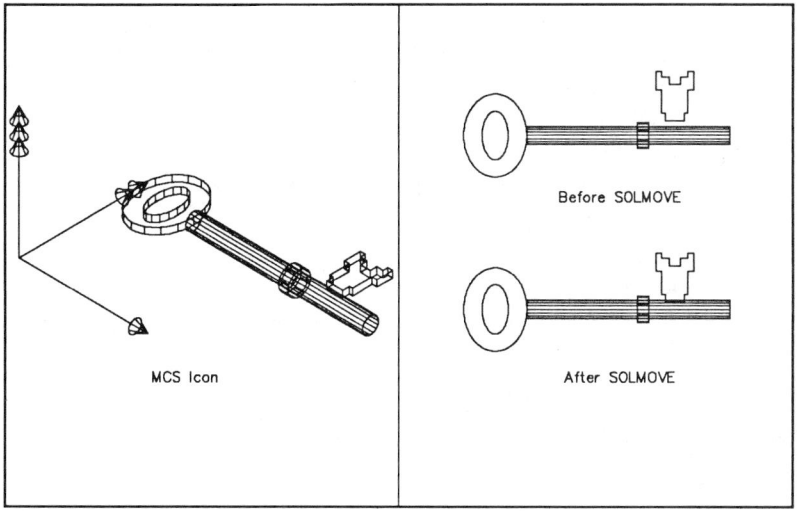

Figure A8.10   SOLMOVE of the key bit

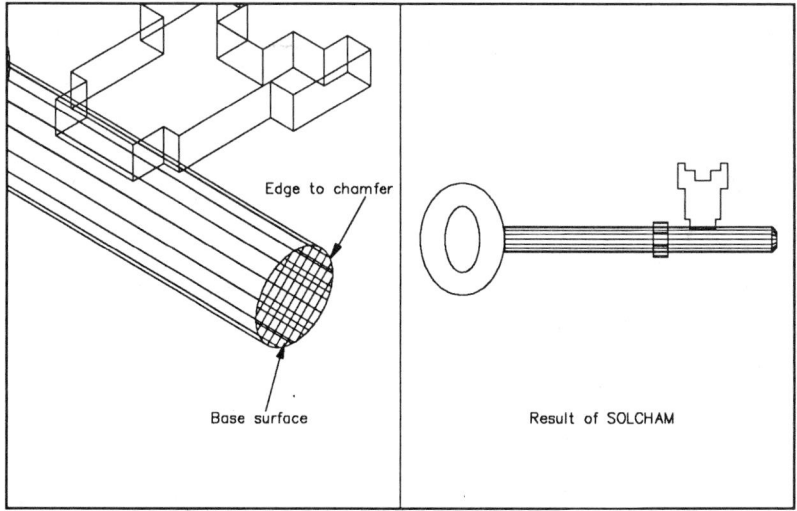

Figure A8.11   Chamfering the stem with SOLCHAM

xii) It is also possible to calculate the mass properties of the key by using the SOLMASSP command. It should be noted that the dimensions of the key are in millimetres whereas the SOLMASSP command uses units of either centimetres, metres or inches depending on the setting of the AME system variables SOLLENGTH, SOLAREAV and SOLVOLUME. This therefore requires that the reported mass properties should be scaled by the appropriate factor. For example if the units of measure are set to CGS and the material of construction is mild steel, then the reported mass of the key will be 13815g. This must be divided by a scaling factor of 1000 (because there are 1000mm^3 in 1cm^3) to give the correct mass value of 13.8g.

xiii) Enter the left hand viewport and use the VPORTS command to return to a single screen display. Save the drawing for use with the Paper Space tutorial in Appendix 9.

Appendix 9
Paper Space tutorial

The solid model of the key produced in Appendix 8 may be used as the basis for the A4 layout shown in Figure A9.1. Alternatively, any other drawing may be used. This layout does not conform to any specific engineering format but has been produced to show the flexibility of the Paper Space environment.

i)   Load the key drawing into the drawing editor.

ii)   Enter Paper Space by setting the TILEMODE system variable to 0:

> **Command:** TILEMODE
> **New value for TILEMODE <1>:** 0

The key will disappear from the screen and the Paper Space icon will appear at the bottom left hand corner of the screen.

iii) Set the LIMITS to that of a standard A4 sheet of paper and ZOOM All.

> **Command:** LIMITS
> **ON/OFF/<Lower left corner><0.00,0.00>:**   return
> **Upper right corner <400,300>:** 297,210

> **Command:** ZOOM
> **All/Center/Dynamic/Extents/Left/Previous/Vmax/Window**
> **/<Scale(X/XP)>:** A

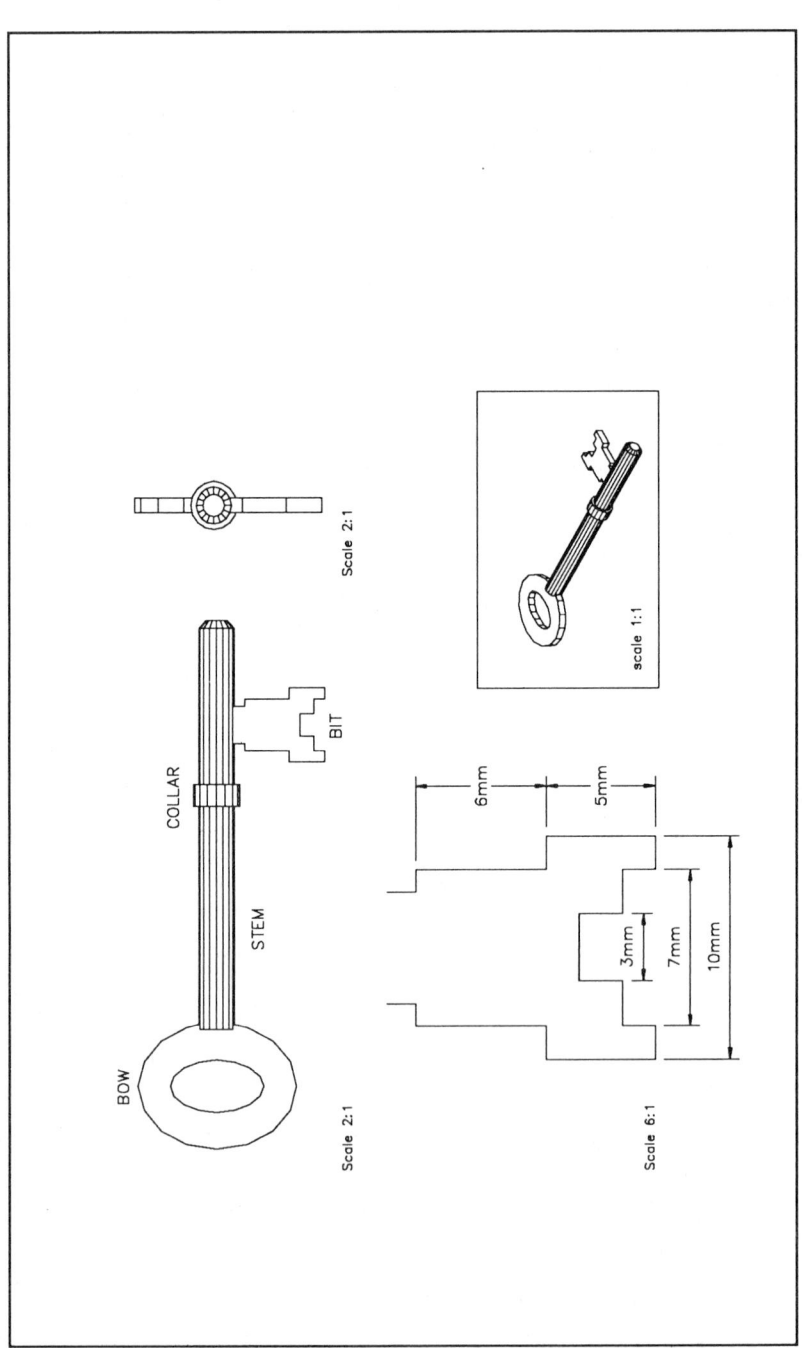

Figure A9.1 Paper Space layout

iv)   Create two new layers VP1 (red) and VP2 (green) for the viewports. Make VP1 current. Use either the Layer Control dialogue box found on the **Settings** pull down menu, or alternatively, enter LAYER from the keyboard.

> **Command:** LAYER
> **?/Make/Set/New/ON/OFF/Color/Ltype/Freeze/Thaw:** N
> **New layer name(s):** VP1,VP2
> **?/Make/Set/New/ON/OFF/Color/Ltype/Freeze/Thaw:** C
> **Color:** RED
> **Layer name(s) for color 1 (red) <0>:** VP1
> **?/Make/Set/New/ON/OFF/Color/Ltype/Freeze/Thaw:** C
> **Color:** GREEN
> **Layer name(s) for color 1 (red) <0>:** VP2
> **?/Make/Set/New/ON/OFF/Color/Ltype/Freeze/Thaw:** S
> **New current layer <0>:** VP1

v)   Open up the Viewport 1. Invoke the MVIEW command by picking Mview from the **Display** pull down or by entering MVIEW from the keyboard:

> **Command:** MVIEW
> **ON/OFF/Hideplot/Fit/2/3/4/Restore/<First Point>:** 160,40
> **Other corner:** 240,90

The viewport will be outlined in red and will contain the view of the key which was active in Model Space. (See Figure A9.2.)

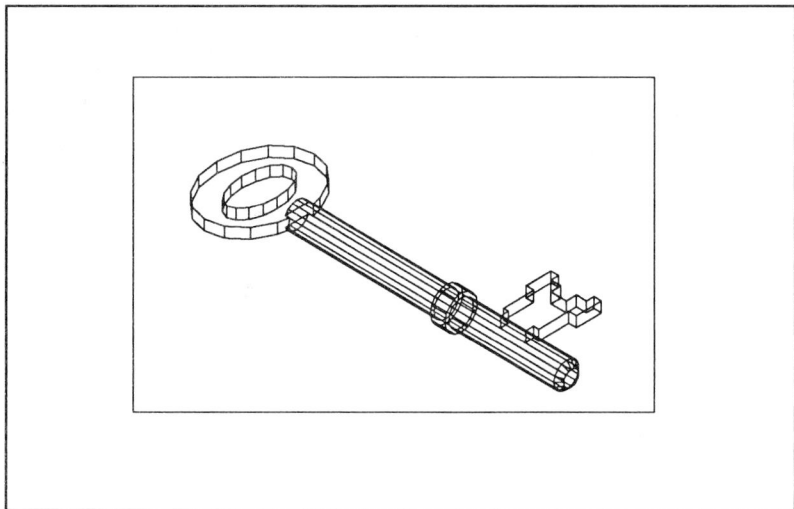

Figure A9.2   Viewport 1 - Oblique view of key

vi) Enter this viewport by using the MSPACE command and scale the key 1:1 by invoking ZOOM Scale(XP).

Command: MSPACE

Command: ZOOM
All/Center/Dynamic/Extents/Left/Previous/Vmax/Window
/<Scale(X/XP)>: 1XP

vii) Return to the Paper Space environment using the PSPACE command and make layer VP2 current. Create Viewport 2 using the MVIEW command.

Command: PSPACE

Command: LAYER
?/Make/Set/New/ON/OFF/Color/Ltype/Freeze/Thaw: N
New current layer <VP1>: VP2

Command: MVIEW
ON/OFF/Hideplot/Fit/2/3/4/Restore/<First Point>: 25,115
Other corner: 185,205

viii) To set up the correct view of the key, (see Figure A9.3), it is necessary to enter the new viewport and create a new UCS.

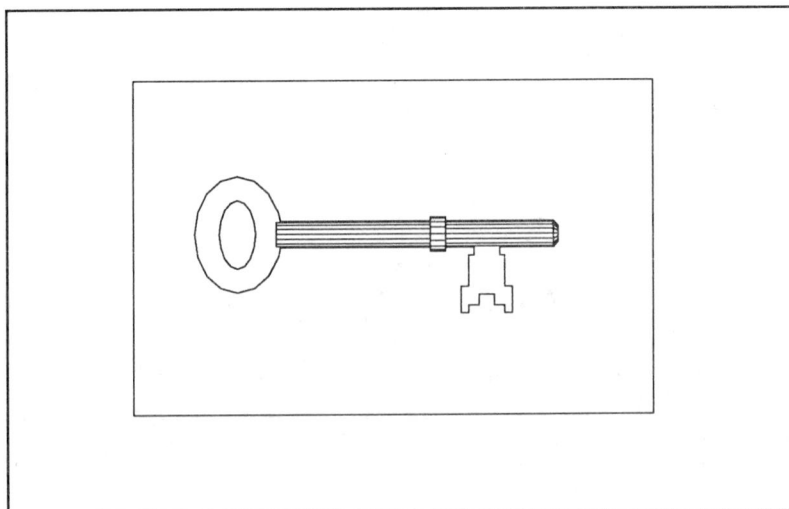

Figure A9.3   Viewport 2 - Plan view of key

The present UCS should be the World; if this is not the case, then change to World *before* issuing the following commands:

Command: MSPACE

Command: UCS
Origin/ZAxis/3point/Entity/View/X/Y/Z/Prev/Restore
  /Save/Del/?/<World>: X
Rotation angle about the X axis <0.0>: 180

Command: PLAN
<Current UCS>/Ucs/World: return

ix)   Scale the key 2:1 by invoking ZOOM Scale(XP) and PAN the key to the centre of the viewport:

Command: ZOOM
All/Center/Dynamic/Extents/Left/Previous/Vmax/Window
  /<Scale(X/XP)>: 2XP

Command: PAN
Displacement: Select the centre of the key
Second point: Move the selected point to the centre of the viewport

x)   Return to the Paper Space environment and create Viewport 3 using the MVIEW command:

Command: PSPACE

Command: MVIEW
ON/OFF/Hideplot/Fit/2/3/4/Restore/<First Point>: 42.5,15
Other corner: 152.5,115

xi)   Enter this new viewport using the MSPACE command and scale 6:1 by invoking ZOOM Scale(XP), PAN the resultant figure to the position shown in Figure A9.4:

Command: MSPACE

Command: ZOOM
All/Center/Dynamic/Extents/Left/Previous/Vmax/Window
  /<Scale(X/XP)>: 6XP

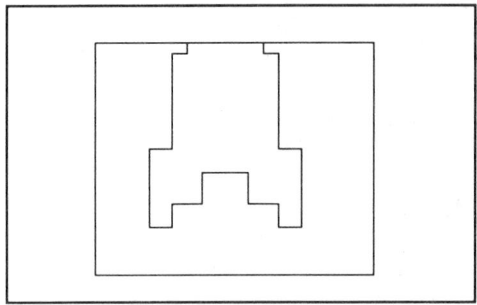

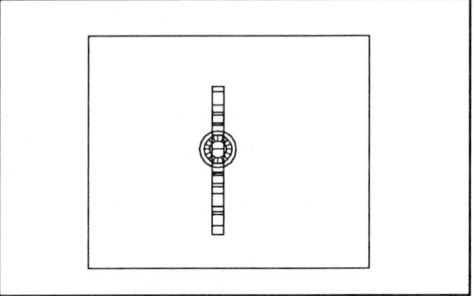

Figure A9.4 Viewport 3 - Detail of bit

Figure A9.5 Viewport 4 - End view of key

Command: PAN
Displacement:
Second point:

xii) Re-enter Paper Space and create Viewport 4:

Command: PSPACE

Command: MVIEW
ON/OFF/Hideplot/Fit/2/3/4/Restore/<First Point>: 115,117.5
Other corner: 165,207.5

xiii) Enter this new viewport using the MSPACE command and create a new UCS. PAN the resultant figure to the centre of the viewport and scale 2:1 by invoking ZOOM Scale(XP). (See Figure A9.5.)

Command: MSPACE

Command: UCS
Origin/ZAxis/3point/Entity/View/X/Y/Z/Prev/Restore
/Save/Del/?/<World>: Y
Rotation angle about the Y axis <0.0>: 90

Command: PLAN
<Current UCS>/Ucs/World: return

Command: PAN
Displacement:
Second point:

Command: ZOOM
All/Center/Dynamic/Extents/Left/Previous/Vmax/Window
/<Scale(X/XP)>: 2XP

xiv) Create two new layers called TEXT and DIMS. Using the VPLAYER command
      freeze both these layers in all the viewports:

Command: LAYER
?/Make/Set/New/ON/OFF/Color/Ltype/Freeze/Thaw: N
New layer name(s): TEXT,DIMS

Command: VPLAYER
?/Freeze/Thaw/Reset/Newfrz/Vpvisdflt: F
Layer(s) to Freeze: TEXT,DIMS
All/Select/<Current>: A

xv)   Enter Viewport 3 and thaw the DIMS layer using the VPLAYER command.
      Make this layer current:

Command: VPLAYER
?/Freeze/Thaw/Reset/Newfrz/Vpvisdflt: F
Layer(s) to Thaw: DIMS
All/Select/<Current>:   return

Command: LAYER
?/Make/Set/New/ON/OFF/Color/Ltype/Freeze/Thaw: S
New current layer <VP2>: DIMS

xvi) Set DIMSCALE to 0 and change the UCS to align with the view. Add the
      dimensions as indicated in Figure A9.6.

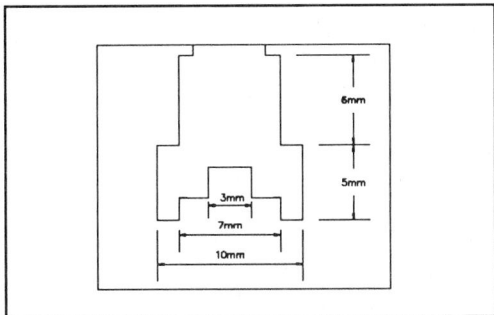

Figure A9.6   Dimensioned bit

Command: DIMSCALE
New value for **DIMSCALE <1.0000>:** 0

Command: UCS
Origin/ZAxis/3point/Entity/View/X/Y/Z/Prev/Restore
/Save/Del/?/<World>: V

Command: DIM
Dim: Add the required horizontal and vertical dimensions

xvii)   Enter Viewport 2 and thaw the TEXT layer using the VPLAYER command. Make this layer current. Add the text (height 2) as shown in Figure A9.7.

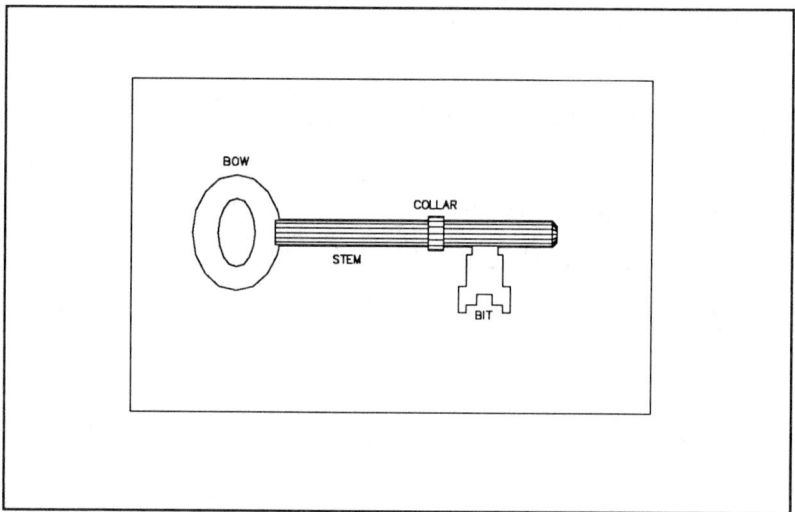

Figure A9.7   Plan view of key with legends

Command: VPLAYER
?/Freeze/Thaw/Reset/Newfrz/Vpvisdflt: F
Layer(s) to Thaw: TEXT
All/Select/<Current>:   return

Command: LAYER
?/Make/Set/New/ON/OFF/Color/Ltype/Freeze/Thaw: S
New current layer <VP2>: TEXT

Command: DTEXT
Justify/Style/<Start point>:
Height <3.00>: 2
Rotation angle <0.0>:
Text: Enter the required text

xviii) Return to Paper Space. Change the current layer to layer 0 and add the text
(height 2.5) describing the scale of each viewport:

Command: PSPACE

Command: LAYER
?/Make/Set/New/ON/OFF/Color/Ltype/Freeze/Thaw: S
New current layer <TEXT>: 0

Command: DTEXT
Justify/Style/<Start point>:
Height <3.00>: 2.5
Rotation angle <0.0>:
Text: Enter the required text

xix) Invoke the **Hideplot** option of the MVIEW command and switch Hideplot On
in viewports 1 and 4. Switch Off layer VP2 to remove the outlines of viewports
2,3 and 4, SAVE and print the finished layout:

Command: MVIEW
ON/OFF/Hideplot/Fit/2/3/4/Restore/<First Point>: H
ON/OFF: ON
Select objects: Select viewports 1 and 4

Command: LAYER
?/Make/Set/New/ON/OFF/Color/Ltype/Freeze/Thaw: OFF
Layer(s) to turn off <0>: VP1

Command: PRPLOT Plot to Limits at a scale of 1=1

This multi-viewport, Paper Space layout is associated with the original drawing and
will automatically be retained when the drawing is saved.

Appendix 10
An introduction to dBASE III+

A database is a collection of related information which is organised by the computer in such a way that comprehensive management operations can be performed. Such a system allows the user to store and selectively retrieve information when required. The data can be manipulated directly by typing instructions at the keyboard. However the dBASE package has a built-in programming language, which means that data manipulation can be customized and the system configured for easy operation by unskilled personnel.

A typical database structure is shown below:

	Field 1	Field 2	Field 3	Field 4
Field name	SURNAME	FIRSTNAME	ADDRESS	TOWN
Record 1	Adams	Andy	1 Green St	Bury
Record 2	Smith	Sandra	2 Grove St	Hull

A7.1 TERMINOLOGY

- A *database* is a group of records - the computer equivalent of a filing-cabinet.
- A *record* is a group of associated data such as **Adams,Andy,1 Green St,Bury** - the equivalent of a single card in the filing-cabinet.
- A *field* is an individual item of information such as a surname - **Adams** - or a place of residence - **Bury**.
- A *fieldname* is the name given to a field - eg. **SURNAME** - and is allocated by the user when the database is first created.
- The *dBASE prompt* (corresponding to the word **Command:** in AutoCAD) is simply a dot ".".

A7.2 THE ASSIST MENUS

dBASE III+ has a built-in assist facility with option menus which appear on the screen when the package is first loaded. To switch off the ASSIST menus press the Esc key : to switch back to assist type ASSIST from the dBASE prompt or press the F2 key. Considerable hands-on practice is required before the assist facility can be fully appreciated and some people prefer to work without it.

A7.3 CREATING A NEW DATABASE

The design of the database structure is crucial to the subsequent data management, and usually requires careful planning. The command used to create a new database structure is:

.CREATE

The new database file must first be named and you are then requested to define the structure of the database one field at a time. There are several types of field, including *Character, Numeric, Logical, Date* and *Memo*, and a choice has to be made when establishing each individual field.

- A *Character* field is used for any data which is never going to be used in calculation. The data may contain alphabet letters, numerals or symbols and are generally known as *alphanumeric* data. Names, addresses and telephone numbers are typical examples. Up to 128 different character fields are allowed in a single database and fields may be up to 256 characters wide.
- A *Numeric* field contains true numeric data which may be used for calculations. A numeric field may be up to 19 digits wide with up to a further 15 digits after the decimal point.
- *Logical* fields are used to tie a logical label on to a record. They are only one digit wide and may contain only T or Y representing a True condition and F or N representing a False condition.

> *Note:* Even when Y and N are used the data are always stored in the database as T and F

- The *Date* field is fixed at 8 characters wide and the date format can be set to British, American, Italian etc. The British format is dd/mm/yy.
- *Memo* fields, if used, can be up to 4000 characters wide. Memo fields are not commonly used and reference to the manual is recommended.

After the structure of the database has been defined data can be entered, using APPEND or BROWSE. The command DISPLAY STRUCTURE gives the field information for the currently open database. The command MODIFY STRUCTURE allows the basic structure to be changed, automatically appending the data after modifications have been completed.

The following is a simple example of a database called MYDBASE

Field	Field Name	Type	Width	Dec
1	Surname	Character	15	
2	Firstname	Character	15	
3	Age	Numeric	3	0
4	Sex	Character	1	
5	Occupation	Character	15	
6	British	Logical	1	

After the creation of the structure, a blank return shows that you have finished creating fields and a Y reply to the question

Input data records now (Y/N) Y

allows the immediate input of data. This process may be terminated with a blank return or an Esc.

A7.4 USING AN EXISTING DATABASE FILE

In order to use an existing database from the dBASE prompt:

.USE (database name)

You will now be able to check any existing records in the database (using LIST or DISPLAY), change data in existing records (using EDIT or BROWSE), add new records (using APPEND) and delete records (using DELETE and PACK).

A7.5 THE HELP FACILITY

At any stage you may check the full syntax of a command by using the built-in help facility. For example, if you type HELP LIST from the dBASE prompt, a full description of the LIST command with all allowed variations will be shown.

A7.6 THE FUNCTION KEYS AND ESC

A number of the more commonly used dBASE commands are available on the function keys F1 to F10. A list of the default functions can be obtained by typing LIST STATUS or by pressing key F6.

Programmable function keys:
F2	assist
F3	list
F4	dir
F5	display structure
F6	display status
F7	display memory
F8	display
F9	append
F10	edit

The Esc key can usually be used to abort to the dBASE prompt. If you are using ASSIST sub menus, an Esc will take you back to the previous level of menu.

A7.7 SHORTENED COMMANDS

All dBASE commands can be shortened to the first four letters. For example, BROWSE can be typed BROW.

A7.8 THE RECORD POINTER

The record pointer allows you to access any particular record in the database. It can be set manually from the dBASE prompt by simply typing the appropriate record number. This has several uses, one of which is to allow the user to insert a record at any particular point in the database using the INSERT command.

During listing the record pointer automatically increments to the last record listed. dBASE III+ gives the current value of the record pointer at the bottom of the screen.

A7.9 EXTRACTING SELECTED DATA FROM A DATABASE USING LIST

The LIST command can be used for more selective data extraction than simply listing the entire contents of the database.

The full LIST syntax is:

> LIST [OFF] [<scope>] [<fieldlist>] [FOR <condition>] [WHILE <condition>]
> [TO PRINT]

Upper case or lower case may be used when typing in an instruction unless a text condition has been specified in which case the exact text format is required.

The following example of the LIST syntax may be used with the MYDBASE database:

> LIST OFF surname,age,occupation FOR age>25 .AND. age<45 .AND. british

In this complex looking instruction, surname, age and occupation are three of the field names in the database. The > means greater than, < means less than, the .AND. (typed with both full stops) links the three conditions together.

The full instruction will list on the screen the contents of the three fields called surname, age and occupation only for those records where the age falls between the limits specified and where the logical field British is True. The OFF instruction in the command switches off the record numbers which otherwise would be included in the listing.

Alternatively:

> LIST NEXT 5 surname FOR .NOT. british

will LIST the NEXT five surnames in the database for which the logical field british is False.

In the above examples note the syntax used to establish the logical conditions for logical fields.

A7.10 OTHER WAYS TO EXTRACT DATA

- DISPLAY   This command is very similar to LIST - the standard format displays the contents of the current record. See the HELP facility to check the full syntax.
- ? <fieldname>   Translates as *What is ?* and can be used to display the contents of the designated field in the current record.
- LOCATE FOR   Searches for the record which satisfies the condition. For example:

> LOCATE FOR age>50

LOCATE will find the *first* record which satisfies the condition.
- CONTINUE   Continues the above search for further records.

- FIND <string>   Can be used like LOCATE if the file has been indexed.
- SKIP {+ or - number}   Moves forwards or backwards the specified number of records through the database.
- GOTO <number>, GO TOP, GO BOTTOM   Moves to a specific record or to the first/last record in the database
- COUNT [FOR expression] TO variable   Counts the number of records which meet the specified condition. It is possible to store the result of the count in a variable:

> COUNT FOR age<25 TO young
> ? young

- SUM <fieldname> [FOR expression list] TO variable   This is used numerically to add the contents of an indicated numeric field for specified records.

The above list covers most of the frequently used commands which are available for interrogation. You should consult HELP and the manual for further information.

A7.11 ADDING FURTHER RECORDS TO THE DATABASE

APPEND is a command which allows additional records to be added to the end of the database. The BROWSE command can also be used for this purpose but is less flexible than APPEND because it can not easily be incorporated in a dBASE program.

If a record needs to be inserted in an intermediate position in the database, then move the record pointer to the required position and use the INSERT command.

A7.12 CHANGING INFORMATION IN THE DATABASE

There are several different ways of changing information stored in a database. The database structure can itself also be modified if required.

- EDIT   The specified record will be displayed and information in the different fields may be changed. The screen editor is available for moving the cursor, deleting, inserting etc. After making the modifications press the Ctrl and End keys to save the new record (Ctrl W is an alternative way of recording the information). Pressing the return key at the very end of a record moves the cursor to the next record in the database, allowing it to be edited in turn. This also has the effect of making permanent any changes made in previous records.

> .USE <database filename>
> .EDIT <record number>

● BROWSE   In this mode of operation the records below the current position of the record pointer are displayed on screen. Information can be changed and a screen editor is available. If a record is wider than the screen width, a *panning* function may be used. Ctrl -> (right arrow key) pans to the right while Ctrl <- pans to the left.

> .USE <database file>
> .BROWSE

Additional records may added to the end of the database by pressing the return key. A screen assist table is normally displayed whilst in BROWSE mode.

The Esc key provides a convenient exit from BROWSE mode to the dBASE prompt but any changes made to the current record will not be saved. The commands Ctrl End and Ctrl W can be used to exit the BROWSE mode and make any editing changes permanent.

● DELETE, RECALL, PACK   Deleting records is a two-stage process, first the DELETE command is used to delete the chosen records, either single records controlled by the position of the record pointer or a range of records specified in the scope part of the command. Also records satisfying a specified condition can be deleted. (See the HELP file for the full syntax).

The DELETE command marks a record or range of records for deletion by inserting a * symbol in the first field.

After marking records for deletion it is possible to reverse the decision by using the RECALL command.

To complete the delete process it is necessary to use the PACK command.

EXAMPLE

> .USE MYDBASE
> .DELETE ALL FOR age>30
> .LIST   notice the marked records
> .RECALL ALL
> .LIST
> .DELETE ALL FOR age>25
> .LIST
> .PACK

● REPLACE   This command is used to scan through the database, changing entries as required.

EXAMPLE

.USE MYDBASE
.REPLACE age WITH age+20
.LIST   To check change

●   CHANGE   This command is very similar to EDIT. The fields to be changed may be specified but be careful to set the record pointer first.

EXAMPLE

.USE MYDBASE
.CHANGE FIELDS surname,occupation

Only the fields surname and occupation will be displayed for editing purposes.

A7.13 SORTING AND INDEXING

Data, which is very often entered in a random fashion, can be organized with the SORT and INDEX facilities.

●   SORT   This command creates a new database with information sorted in ascending (A) or descending (D) order for any field or fields which are specified. The syntax is:

SORT TO filename ON fieldname [A/D], fieldname [A/D]

The new database is specified by the filename and the field names are chosen as required. The command defaults to A if this parameter is not specified.

With a large database this operation can be time consuming and it is preferable to INDEX the database against a key field for faster retrieval of data.

●   INDEX   The syntax is:

INDEX ON fieldnames TO filename

If one or more index files have been created for a database, then the command

.SET INDEX TO <filename>

should be used in order to activate the index files.

Index files can be identified on the directory by the file name extension .NDX

A7.14 PRODUCING A REPORT

A simple print out of lists of records can be achieved by directing output to the printer with the command:

.SET PRINTER ON

If this command is given from the dBASE prompt, then any information displayed on the screen will also be printed.

If single sheets of paper are being used, then first type:

.SET EJECT OFF

This command stops the printer paging (automatically moving the print head to the top of the next page) at the end of each page.

More elaborate reports can be produced if required with the aid of the built-in REPORT facility.

● REPORT This is a command which initiates a series of questions relating to the data output and the format required. After establishing a report format a new file is created (with the file extension .RPT) This can be used at any time to produce printed output.

To print the report, include TO PRINT at the end of the REPORT command.

A7.15 CUSTOMIZED DATA ENTRY SCREENS - FORMAT FILES

A customized screen format file can be produced for displaying fields in any desired order and position on the screen. The specified format can then be used for entering and editing records. This is particularly useful when the field names do not adequately describe the data or when not all the fields in the database are required.

In order to achieve this it is necessary to construct a dBASE file called a FORMAT file, with file extension .FMT . This file contains information, descriptions for the required fields, and field names. The format file can either be created directly through the MODIFY COMMAND procedure or with the aid of the ASSIST facility.

Screen locations are established by row and column numbers. dBASE III+ defines screen positions starting from the top left-hand corner (0,0). Lines are numbered from 0 to 23 and columns from 0 to 79.

The command SAY is used to position text on the screen and the command GET is used to input information from the keyboard into the record structure. Each line of a format file must start with the symbol @ followed by a space and then the screen position e.g.

@ 2,0 say "THIS IS SOME TEXT"

A7.16 DBASE III+ PROGRAMMING

One of the major strengths of dBASE III+ is its built-in programming facility. This allows the user to *automate* all the standard dBASE commands thus customizing the package. People with no knowledge of the operation of a database can then use the package to perform specific functions such as costing, stock control etc.

A full treatment of this extensive subject is beyond the scope of this book but some sample programs are included. These may be typed in from within dBASE using the MODIFY COMMAND procedure or by using an external word processor and saving the file in DOS text format with a .PRG extension. They may be activated from the dBASE prompt by use of the DO command:

.DO (program name)

Appendix 11
Attribute extraction and dBASE III+ programming tutorial

A11.1 ATTRIBUTE EXTRACTION

The central heating drawing, shown in Figure A11.1, is constructed solely from lines and blocks. In this example the blocks have the following names:

    COLDTANK
    HOTTANK
    RADIATOR
    BOILER
    PUMP
    RADVALVE
    PIPEVALV
    ELBOW
    TEE

and each of the blocks has the following five attributes:

Attribute Tag		Attribute Type
ITEM	(descriptive name of block)	Constant
COSTWHSL	(wholesale cost)	Preset
COSTRTL	(retail cost)	Preset
CODENO	(a 4-digit identification code)	Constant
LOCATION	(stores location of the item)	Variable

Selected attributes of all the blocks in the drawing may be extracted using the ATTEXT command.

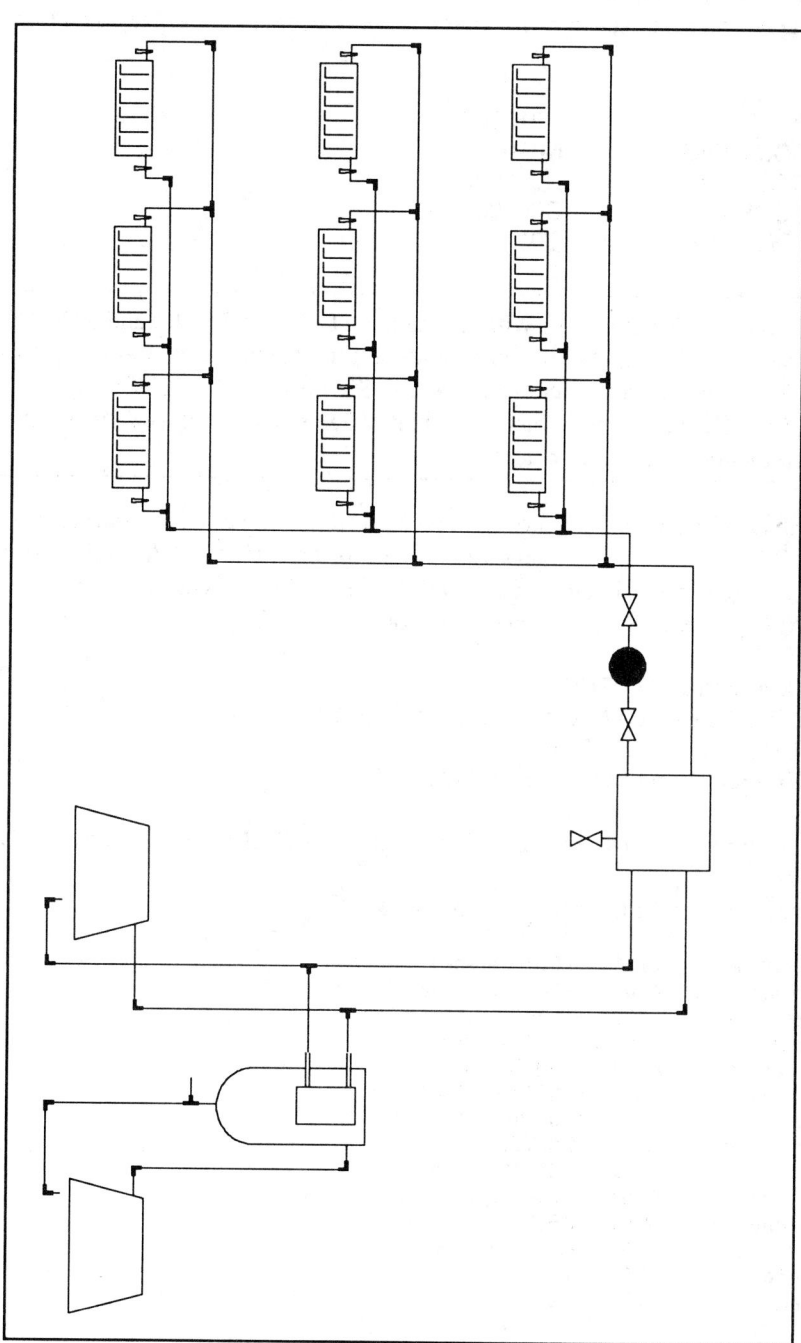

Figure A11.1   A domestic central heating system

A template file must first be created using a text editor or word processor.

The following template file, called MYTEMPL.TXT and saved into the current AutoCAD working directory will enable every attribute to be extracted from the drawing.

```
ITEM            C012000
COSTWHSL        N010002
COSTRTL         N010002
CODENO          C006000
LOCATION        C012000
```

> *Note:*   The attributes with tag names ITEM, CODENO and LOCATION are to be treated as character fields in the database with field lengths of 12, 6 and 12 characters respectively. Similarly, COSTWHSL and COSTRTL will be treated as numeric fields with a total of 10 digits, *including* 2 decimal places.

The attribute extraction may now be performed by creating an extract file called MYEXTRAC and using SDF (space delimited format). If the dBASE III+ software is resident in some other directory, called DBASE say, then it is convenient if the extract file is written directly into this directory from AutoCAD.

Command: ATTEXT
CDF, SDF or DXF Attribute extract (or Entities)? S
Template file: MYTEMPL
Extract file name: C:\DBASE\MYEXTRAC

This will write an SDF extract file called MYEXTRAC.TXT into the DBASE directory.

A fragment from a typical file would look like:

```
coldtank     15.00    20.008759  shed1
hottank      45.00    75.007699  shed2
coldtank     15.00    20.008759  shed1
boiler      150.00   225.003354  shed3
radiator     20.00    30.001020  shed1
pump         50.00    85.002298  shed1
pipevalve     8.00    10.009087  shed1
pipevalve     8.00    10.009087  shed1
radvalve      5.00     7.502341  shed1
radiator     20.00    30.001020  shed1
elbow         0.50     0.658897  shed4
tee           0.60     0.758899  shed4
elbow         0.50     0.658897  shed4
elbow         0.50     0.658897  shed4

<----------><----------><-------><-----><---------->
    12           10         10      6        12
```

> *Note:*   Because character fields are left justified and numeric fields are right justified, fields 3 and 4 appear to be run together. This will not cause any problems as long as the database is created with a structure to match the template file.

This database may now be created within the DBASE directory. The structure should be:

```
Structure for database: C:HEATING.DBF
Number of data records:
Date of last update:
```

Field	Fieldname	Type	Width	Dec
1	NAME	Character	12	
2	WHOLESALE	Numeric	10	2
3	RETAIL	Numeric	10	2
4	CODE	Character	6	
5	STORE	Character	12	
** Total **			51	

> *Note:*   It is only the *structure* which must match the template file - there is no need for the field names to match the tag names of the attributes.

Transfer of data held in the extract file to the empty database may now be achieved from the dBASE prompt as follows:

```
.APPEND FROM MYEXTRAC.TXT SDF
```

An excerpt from a typical dBASE III+ file derived from this drawing is shown below:

```
. LIST
Record#  NAME   WHOLESALE        RETAIL      CODE       LOCATION
     1   coldtank     15.00        20.00      8759       shed1
     2   hottank      45.00        75.00      7699       shed2
     3   coldtank     15.00        20.00      8759       shed1
     4   boiler      150.00       225.00      3354       shed3
     5   radiator     20.00        30.00      1020       shed1
     6   pump         50.00        85.00      2298       shed1
     7   pipevalve     8.00        10.00      9087       shed1
     8   pipevalve     8.00        10.00      9087       shed1
     9   radvalve      5.00         7.50      2341       shed1
    10   radiator     20.00        30.00      1020       shed1
    11   elbow         0.50         0.65      8897       shed4
    12   tee           0.60         0.75      8899       shed4
    13   elbow         0.50         0.65      8897       shed4
    14   elbow         0.50         0.65      8897       shed4
```

A11.2 DBASE PROGRAMS

The following suite of six programs may be typed in for use with the HEATING data base just created.

A second database called STOCK giving the supposed levels of stock for the various components of the central heating system should be created separately and manually filled with nominal stock levels. The structure of the STOCK database is shown below:

```
Structure for database: C:STOCK.DBF
Number of data records:
Date of last update:
Field   Fieldname        Type            Width        Dec
1       NAME             Character       12
2       NUMBER           Numeric         6
3       REORD            Numeric         6
4       BRITISH          Logical         1
** Total **                              26
```

A11.2.1 DBASE III+ PROGRAM LISTING - INVENT.PRG

This program provides the main menu for the suite and calls on the other programs - parts.prg, stock.prg, list.prg, totals.prg and reorder.prg as required. The whole suite may be run by calling this program with the command .DO INVENT.

```
set safety off
set talk off
store 0 to choice
do while choice<5
    clear
    @2,5 say "Inventory System"
    @4,5 say "Make a selection from the following menu items:"
    @6,0
    TEXT
    ===================================================
    1. COUNTING AND COSTING PARTS IN THE AUTOCAD DESIGN
    2. UPDATE MAIN STOCK INVENTORY
    3. LIST ITEMS BELOW THE REORDER LEVEL
    4. TOTAL WHOLESALE & RETAIL VALUES FOR PARTS
    5. EXIT THIS PROGRAM
    ===================================================
    endtext
    input "Enter a number:" to choice
        if choice > 5
        clear
```

```
      @2,2 say "Please type a number from 1 to 5."
      @3,2
      input "Enter a number now:" to choice
   endif
   do case
      case choice = 1
      do parts
      case choice = 2
      do stock
      case choice = 3
      do reorder
      case choice = 4
      do totals
      case choice = 5
      return
   endcase choice
enddo
```

A11.2.2 dBASE III+ Program Listing - PARTS.prg

```
use heating
set talk off
clear
text
   This demonstration dBASE III+ program is designed to be used
   with an AutoCAD design file called heating.dbf.
   The program evaluates the numbers and costs of items used in
   a typical central heating system layout.


endtext
wait to cont
accept "Do you wish to see the wholesale cost? (y/n) " to wcost
?
accept "Do you wish to print the results? (y/n) " to prin
store "y" to choice
store 0 to total
store 0 to total1
if prin = "y"
   set printer on
endif
do while choice = "y"
   clear
   ? "The items in the list are as follows:"
   ?
do list
   ?
```

```
accept "Type in the name of the item  " to item
count for name = item to no
?
? "The total number of these items in the design "
?? " is "
? no
?? " --------- "
?? item
if wcost = "y"
   sum wholesale for name = item to cost
   ?
   ? "The total wholesale cost of these items is "
   ? cost
   ?? "  pounds."
   ?
   ? "The cost of a single "
   ?? item
   ?? " is"
   ? cost/no
   ?? "  pounds"
   store cost + total to total
   ?
   ? "Wholesale cost to date:"
   ?? total
endif
if wcost = "y"
sum retail for name = item to sale
?
? "The total retail cost of these items is "
? sale
?? "  pounds."
?
? "The cost of a single "
?? item
?? " is"
?  sale/no
?? "  pounds"
store sale + total1 to total1
?
? "Retail cost to date:"
?? total1
endif
?
accept "Do you wish to have another count? (y/n)" to choice
enddo
close all
set printer off
return
```

A11.2.3 dBASE III+ Program Listing - STOCK.prg

```
clear
text
    Enter the name of the stock item you wish to update:
endtext
?
?"The stock items are as follows:"
?
do list
?
select 1
use heating
select 2
use stock
store "y" to cont
do while cont="y"
    accept "enter the item name  " to stock
    select 1
    count for name=stock to no
    clear
    ? "The number of "
    ?? stock
    ?? "s in the AutoCAD design is "
    ?? no
    select 2
    sum number for name=stock to s2
    ?
    ?"The original number of "
    ?? stock
    ?? "s in stock is"
    ?? s2
    repl number with number-no for name=stock
    sum number for name=stock to ns
    ?
    ?"The number remaining in stock is "
    ?? ns
    sum reord for name=stock to re
    if ns<re
        ?
        ? "The number of "
        ?? stock
        ?? "s in stock is LESS than the reorder level "
        ?
    endif
    if ns>=re
        ?
        ? "The number of "
```

```
            ?? stock
            ?? " in stock is above the reorder level "
            ?
        endif
        accept "Do you wish to do another stock item? (y/n) " to cont
        ?
    enddo
    close all
    return
```

A11.2.4 dBASE III+ Program Listing - LIST.prg

```
    close all
    use stock
    go top
    do while .not. EOF()
    ? name
    skip
    enddo
    use heating
    return
```

A11.2.5 dBASE III+ Program Listing - TOTALS.prg

```
    set exact on
    select 1
    use stock
    select 2
    use heating
    set talk off
    select 1
    store 0 to total
    store 0 to total1
    clear
    ? "NAME            WHOLESALE    RETAIL "
    go top
    ?
    do while .not. eof()
    store name to n1
    select 2
    sum wholesale for name = n1 to cost1
    sum retail for name = n1 to sale1
    ? n1
    ?? cost1
    ?? sale1
```

```
store cost1 + total to total
store sale1 + total1 to total1
select 1
skip
enddo
?
? "TOTALS:
?? total
?? total1
?
wait to cont
close all
return
```

A11.2.6 dBASE III+ Program Listing - REORDER.prg

```
use stock
set talk off
clear
go top
? "Please REORDER the following"
?
? "NAME        NUMBER  REORDER "
?
do while .not. eof()
if reord>number
? name, number, reord
endif
skip
enddo
?
wait
set talk on
close all
return
```

The above programs have been written to provide a simple introduction to dBASE programming and may of course be improved. It is hoped that they have given some insight into what may be achieved by combining the two powerful packages, AutoCAD and dBASE III+.

General Index

Index of Commands